Romans in Context

Romans in Context

A Theological Appreciation of Paul's Magnum Opus

DELANO VINCENT PALMER

RESOURCE *Publications* • Eugene, Oregon

ROMANS IN CONTEXT
A Theological Appreciation of Paul's *Magnum Opus*

Copyright © 2011 Delano Vincent Palmer. All rights reserved. Except for brief quotations in critical publications or reviews, no part of this book may be reproduced in any manner without prior written permission from the publisher. Write: Permissions, Wipf and Stock Publishers, 199 W. 8th Ave., Suite 3, Eugene, OR 97401.

Resource Publications
An Imprint of Wipf and Stock Publishers
199 W. 8th Ave., Suite 3
Eugene, OR 97401
www.wipfandstock.com

ISBN 13: 978-1-60899-754-1
Manufactured in the U.S.A.

Unless otherwise identified, Scripture quotations are from the HOLY BIBLE, NEW INTERNATIONAL VERSION; copyright © 1973, 1978, 1984, **2010** by the International Bible Society, and Biblica, Inc.™ Used by permission. All rights reserved worldwide.

Scripture quotations identified NRSV are from the New Revised Standard Version of the Bible, copyright 1989 by the Division of Christian Education of the National Council of Churches of Christ in the U.S.A. Used by permission. All rights reserved.

Scripture quotations identified NKJV are from the New King James Version of the Bible. Copyright © 1979, 1980, 1982, by Thomas Nelson, Inc., Publishers. Used by permission. All rights reserved.

Scripture quotations identified AV/KJV are from the King James Version of the Bible.

All quotations marked DV (Darby Version) are taken from John Nelson Darby, *Holy Bible: A New Translation*. London: Morrish, 1929.

All quotations marked NET are taken from the NET Bible® copyright ©1996-2006 by Biblical Studies Press, L.L.C. www.bible.org All rights reserved.

Scripture quotations identified REB are from The Revised English Bible published jointly by the Oxford University Press and Cambridge University Press, 1989. All rights reserved.

BWHEBB, BWHEBL, BWTRANSH [Hebrew]; BWGRKL, BWGRKN, and BWGRKI [Greek] Postscript® Type 1 and TrueTypeT fonts Copyright © 1994–2009 BibleWorks, LLC. All rights reserved. These Biblical Greek and Hebrew fonts are used with permission and are from BibleWorks, software for Biblical exegesis and research.

To the memory of Professor Keith Bradshaw (1940–2009), my first theology teacher, who ably taught us Romans from his Greek New Testament

Contents

List of Tables ix
Foreword xi
Preface xiii
Acknowledgments xv
Abbreviations xvii

Part One: Biographical and Cultural

1 Paul: Missionary Theologian 3

2 Theology, Culture, and the Book of Romans: A Canonical-historical Dialogue 21

Part Two: Exegetical and Theological

3 Romans 4:1–25: Paul on Justification 39

4 Romans 5, the *Imago Christi*, and a Former Archbishop of Canterbury 72

5 "I-n-I" in Romans 7 and the Rest of the Pauline Corpus 94

6 Romans 8 and the People of God in Messiah 129

Part Three: Missiological and Pastoral

7 Romans 10 in Biblical Context 145

8 Romans 12 and the Gifts of the Spirit within the Context of the Pauline Letters 165

9 Pronominal "I" in Romans 15 193

10 Romans 16 and "Archbishop Priscilla": Female Pastors in the Early Church? 210

Appendix A   *Contextualizing Theology in the Caribbean*   225
Appendix B   *All Things Work Together*   245
Appendix C   *Dialectic of Sanctification*   248
Appendix D   *Dei Voluntas*   249
Appendix E   *Sabbath, Sunday, and the Third-Millennium Saint*   250
Appendix F   *Should Christians Be Involved in Jamaican Politics?*   254
Appendix G   *Reflections on Theological Education*   272
Bibliography   275
Scripture Index   297
Subject Index   299

List of Tables

Table 1: Messianic Community in Tension and Transformation   129
Table 2: The Great Commission   161
Table 3: God's Will in Romans   166

Foreword

JAMAICAN PATOIS HAS BEEN used in these theological essays. When I first saw the Patois, I said "Patois in theology? How limiting!" But as I started to write, my thoughts began to change. Patois in theology? Why not? The world has heard our music; they have seen our stunning performances at the Olympics; they have tasted our food and they keep coming back for more. Given the global popularity of the Jamaican brand, they may want to hear our words, our Patois, not too much of it for fear of incomprehension, but just enough to whet the appetite; just enough to give insight into the culture that shapes the Jamaican theological framework.

D.V. Palmer has done just that. He has effectively included bits of the Jamaican Patios to educate and to inform the readers in these essays, and to help them make the cultural connection which is so vital to understanding any people group. For some scholars, culture, or local custom is to be divorced from "pure" theology. For such people, reggae music is never played in church because it is not pure; it is not holy; it is associated with dancehall; therefore, it should never be played in church. In the same thinking, Patois is not spoken in church because it is not proper for church. The real question for theologians is whether they understand the people they are trying to reach—the people who speak Patois and play Reggae music. Is the music an expression of rebellion? Is Patois a rejection of the ruling class and its proper speech requirement? Every theological student needs to address these questions. Only when we answer these burning questions can we become authentic evangelists and Bible teachers.

D.V. Palmer is a theologian who is versed in both Patois and the Queen's English. He can speak proper English at the House of Parliament, and he can wax eloquently in Patois in the inner-cities of Jamaica. That is a valuable linguistic asset for the purpose of communicating the gospel to all segments of society. Hence, Patois in theology is rather appropriate and timely.

Prof. Palmer is not an armchair theologian; he is an engaging theologian—immersed in the lives of the people, the culture of the community, and the struggle for the souls of Jamaica. To that end, he plays soccer in various venues so that he and his team may reach thousands for Christ. Palmer is the right man to write this kind of theological book; it is scholarly, cultural, and authentic. As a professor of theology at the Jamaica Theological Seminary, Palmer has demonstrated excellence and effectiveness which inform his life and work.

With my discussion of Patois in the first few paragraphs, readers may think that these essays are primarily about Patois. These essays are primarily about content which demands our urgent attention. Readers will find the content of the book to be rather interesting. One of the first essays (*Theology, Culture, and the Book of Romans*), for example, establishes the theme of all the rest—the idea that theology must be connected to the culture of a people; otherwise, theology becomes meaningless.

Readers will find these essays to be theologically sound, culturally sensitive, and profoundly relevant for today.

Dr. Joseph Wint
Founder and President: Global Education Services Corporation
New York

Preface

Romans in Context is a response, a Caribbean response to Paul's most influential piece of work. It is not a commentary. (Hopefully that will be written in 2099!) It is instead an appreciation of the theological content and contribution of the book of Romans in its First-Century context. This context is multifaceted, encompassing at least biblical, political, cultural, and linguistic dimensions that form the backdrop to the entire Pauline corpus.

With this in mind, the first two essays draw attention to Paul's world of ideas, and the third attempts to explore one of those ideas expressed in Romans 4. The rest of the book traces certain important themes found in Romans, such as the image of God, Paul's pronominal "I", the concept of spiritual gifts, and the controversial role of wives in the early church.

If I were asked to place this book in a particular modern genre, it would have to be New Testament (NT)Theology; more precisely, Pauline Theology. This may be more wishful thinking than anything else, but it does reflect one of my main interests over the last ten years. Because of this interest I have tried to relate the various themes treated in these pages to antecedent theological motifs as well as those more or less contemporaneous with the writer.

Biblical Theology (of which NT Theology is a subset), we are made to understand, is a relatively recent literary genre. In fact, according to Carson and Moo (*Introduction to the New Testament*, Grand Rapids: Zondervan, 47), the first tome with such a "title was *Teutsche biblische Theologie* ('German Biblical Theology')" by W.J. Christmann, published in the seventeenth century. The *Teutsche* (German) in the title points in a particular direction, that every theology, whether qualified or not, is contextual, that is, written from a certain perspective and reflective of the writer's place in history.

So, although *Romans in Context* is a collection of previously published essays and a few others, it nevertheless seeks to make a modest contribution to the field of NT Theology by reflecting on the inspired documents of the Pauline corpus from the context of the English-speaking Caribbean, particularly Kingston "Jahmeckyah," where the best language since sliced bread is spoken. (Where else in the world do people drop their aitches at Arbour Street and pick them up back at Heast Street; where a guy can order *two patti an wan drinks*?).

Theology in recent times has fallen flat on her face; even theological students have been shunning the woman who was once queen of the sciences. But increasingly a few are coming to realize that the discipline is of paramount importance for the vitality of the church, less she (the church) be tossed about by every hurricane of doctrinal departure. One of the suggested meanings of Theology proffered by the Little Oxford Dictionary is the "study of God," and why would anyone not want to do that? Of course, there are solid biblical reasons for this sad state of affairs and they are not confined to the twenty-first century.

In fact, one of the greatest theologians who ever lived prophesied that a day would come when people would not want to embrace sound (i.e., healthful) theology, and while prophecy is always tricky, I dare say that we can see fulfillment in our day.

If we further define the discipline as reflection on things divine, then everyone theologizes in this sense, and when the atheist does so s/he concludes that there is no god. Now atheists constitute a consistent breed of thinkers, since they say there is no god and live as if there is no god. The real problem lies with people like me who affirm strongly that there is indeed a God and then turn around and worry if Usain Bolt will successfully defend his 100 meters crown in the London Olympics. He may or may not, but there is no point worrying about it. Bob Marley is right: "*Don't worry 'bout a ting*." Theology, rightly understood, is intensely practical (see, e.g., Dr. Carlton Dennis's *Jonah*. Kingston: SRI, 2008).

One thinker puts it this way: Because we were made by God all our problems are theological. It is said that our worldview (the core of which is our theology) is like a football referee; nobody goes to a match to see her, but guess who controls the game? The more qualitative our worldview, the more we can appreciate what life is all about, and, all things being equal, the better will be our philanthropic engagement. The theological shape of Paul's letter to the Romans, fortunately for us, facilitates such formulation, as is hinted by Brevard Childs in his *New Testament Canon* (Philadelphia: Fortress, 1984, 262).

D. V. Palmer
JTS, Kingston, Jamekyah
October 10, 2010

Acknowledgments

I OWE A SPECIAL debt of gratitude to the following individuals: Sandy Goulbourne, who typed several pieces for me and who always enthusiastically volunteered to make a positive contribution; Jude Hector from the "Spice Island," who edited some of the material with the skill of a JTS don. Tanya Snape from the "Patti-Care Group" also helped at a critical stage of the project, as well as the Rev. Suzanne Sang of CGST. I am also quite grateful to my beloved life partner who from time to time inquired about my progress, and prayed with and for me daily for its completion.

To give the tome some respectability, I have included the contributions of my colleagues, E. Christine Campbell, David Pearson (JTS professors), David HoSang (former JTS lecturer), Gay Ward-Foster, and Rev. Anthony Chung (JTS grads) as excursuses and appendices. Thanks guys.

The president of the JTS is still encouraging his faculty to write. I owe him not only a note of thanks but an apology as well for simply collecting and editing previously published essays as a way of fulfilling the mandate. On account of his positive influence on my life and ministry, I am tempted to say at this juncture that if there is any flaw in this book he should share some of the responsibility; but I must not yield.

The penultimate round of thanks goes to the editorial boards of the following journals for permission to adapt: "Pauline Charismata and the Twenty-first Century," *Binah 1(1996):13–23;* "The Nature of the Christian" *CJET* 2 (1998):73–89; "Romans 5 and the Archbishop of Canterbury" *CJET* 5 (2001): 58–70; "Theology and Culture in Canonical-Historical Dialogue" *CJET* 7 (2003):78–96; and "Romans 4: Justification as Soteriological Orthodoxy *CJET* 10(2006); 121–143.

And finally, *Thanks be unto God for his indescribable gift*!

Abbreviations

AA Assembly Affairs

ABD Anchor Bible Dictionary

AJET African Journal of Evangelical Theology

ANE Ancient Near East

Ant. "Antiquities," in *The Works of Josephus*, edited by William Whiston, Peabody, MA: Hendrickson, 1987.

BAG Bauer, W., et al., eds. *A Greek-English Lexicon of the New Testament and Other Early Christian Literature.* Revised by F. W. Danker. Chicago: Chicago University Press, 1957.

BBC Bethel Baptist Church

BDAG Bauer, W., et al., eds. *A Greek-English Lexicon of the New Testament and Other Early Christian Literature.* Revised by F. W. Danker. Chicago: Chicago University Press, 2000.

BDF Blass, F., A. Debrunner, and R. Funk. *A Greek Grammar of the New Testament and Other Early Christian Literature.* Chicago: University Press, 1961.

BECNT Baker Exegetical Commentary of the New Testament

BETS *Bulletin of the Evangelical Theological Society*

BibSac Bibliotheca Sacra

BT Bible Translator

CAP Concordia Academic Press

CBR *Christian Brethren Review*

CEC *The Christian Evangelical Communicator*

CETA *Caribbean Evangelical Theological Association*

cf. *confer*, compare

CGST Caribbean Graduate School of Theology
CJET *Caribbean Journal of Evangelical Theology*
CJRS *Caribbean Journal of Religious Studies*
CLI Chose Life International
CT *Christianity Today*
CTJ *Calvin Theological Journal*
CUP Cambridge University Press
DBI *Dictionary of Biblical Interpretation*
DM Dana and Mantey
DPL *Dictionary of Paul and His Letters*
DV Darby Version
EB *Encyclopedia Britannica*
EBC The *Expositor's Bible Commentary*
EGT *The Expositor's Greek Testament*
EJ *Emmaus Journal*
et al. *et alii*, and others
EMQ *Evangelical Missions Quarterly*
ERT *Evangelical Review of Theology*
ET *The Expository Times*
EWC Elders and Workers Conference
GELS *Greek-English Lexicon of the Septuagint*
GTJ *Grace Theological Journal*
GK Greek
HE *Historia Ecclesiastica*
Ibid *ibidem*, in the same place
ICC International Critical Commentary
IRM *International Review of Missions*
IVP Intervarsity Press
JBL *Journal of Biblical Literature*
JBR *Jamaica Baptist Reporter*

JBU Jamaica Baptist Union

JEH *Journal of Ecclesiastical History*

JETS *Journal of the Evangelical Theological Society*

JMM *Journal for Ministry and Mission*

JPC *Journal of Psychology and Christianity*

JPP *Journal of Pastoral Practice*

JPS The Jewish Publication Society

JPT *Journal of Psychology and Theology*

JSNT *Journal for the Study of the New Testament*

JTS *Journal of Theological Studies*

JTS Jamaica Theological Seminary

KJV King James Version

κτλ και. τα. λοιπά, *and the rest*

LCL Loeb Classical Library

LN J. P. Louw, and Eugene A. Nida, eds. *Greek-English Lexicon of the New Testament Based on Semantic Domains*. New York: United Bible Societies, 1988.

LXX Septuagint

MM J. H Moulton and George Milligan. *The Vocabulary of the Greek Testament*. Grand Rapids: Eerdmans, 1930

n. d. No date

NET New English Translation (NET Bible)

NG *National Geographic*

NIB *New Interpreter's Bible*

NICNT New International Commentary on the New Testament

NIGTC New International Greek Testament Commentary

NIDOTTE *New International Dictionary of Old Testament Theology & Exegesis*

NIV New International Version

NLT New Living Translation

NRSV New Revised Standard Version

NT New Testament

NTC *New Testament Commentary*

NTS New Testament Studies

NovT Novum Testamentum

Op. cit. *opere citato*, work cited

OT Old Testament

OUP Oxford University Press

PBI Pontifical Biblical Institute

PIB Pontificii Instituti Biblici

PUP Princeton University Press

REB Revised English Bible

SAP Sheffield Academic Press

SCFSU Schools Christian Fellowship & Scripture Union

SJT Scottish Journal of Theology

TDNT *Theological Dictionary of New Testament Theology*

TNTC Tyndale New Testament Commentaries

TUP *Temple University Press*

UBS United Bible Societies

UBS4 Aland, Barbara, and Kurt Aland, Johannes Karavidopoulos, Carlo M. Martini, Bruce Metzger, K Elliger, W. Rudolph, eds. *Biblia Sacra Utriusque Testamenti Editio Hebraica et Graeca*. Stuttgart: Deutsche Bibelgesellshaft, 1994.

UMI University Microfilms Incorporated (*ProQuest*)

UPA University Press of America

VE Vox Evangelica

Vol. Volume

WBC World Biblical Commentary

WH Wescott and Hort

WTJ Westminster Theological Journal

YUP Yale University Press

PART ONE

Biographical and Cultural

1

Paul: Missionary Theologian[1]

A SKETCH OF PAUL'S LIFE

It was the late professor of counseling psychology at the Caribbean Christian University who once said that all our theology[2] is biography. Although the case may have been overstated, Dr. Dave Carlson was indeed correct, because theology is a human enterprise. It is one of the things humans do: they theologize. One of the best ways to study theology is to do so within the context of biographical genre, like, for example, what Elwell[3] and Marty[4] have done. Unlike Elwell and Marty, this chapter does not examine the life and thought of modern theologians but one from whom most if not all of them have learnt. We briefly then take a look at the thought of the apostle Paul as it is mirrored in the legacy of his language and theology.

In the minds of many the Apostle Paul is the greatest missionary theologian the world has ever seen.[5] Even if we disagree with this judgment, there can be no doubt regarding the tremendous impact he has made in advancing the cause of Christ in our world.

Yet, in the words of Tucker,[6] "Paul is a less awesome figure than some adulatory devotees would have him to be. In many ways, he was a

---

1. For a contribution of a twenty-first century missionary theologian, see Appendix A.
2. For some definitions of Theology, see Thomas, *Confronting Suicide*, 110–11.
3. Elwell, *Handbook*.
4. Marty, *Reinhold Niebuhr Revisited*.
5. "The view that Paul was the greatest missionary among Gentiles in the first century is a notion based on the fact that writings of Paul survive that allow us to describe his theological convictions..." (Schnabel, *Early Christian Mission*, 923). We will explore some of these convictions below.
6. Tucker, *From Jerusalem to Irian Jaya*, 7.

very ordinary man facing ordinary problems that have confronted missionaries ever since." This observation, paradoxically, serves to highlight the Apostle's greatness even more, for if he was so ordinary whence his greatness as a missionary? An examination of the Apostle Paul's role as an evangelist, teacher and writer may furnish the answer to the above query.

Paul was indeed an evangelist. But he was not always so, because he once sought to impede the progress of the Gospel of Jesus Christ. He relentlessly persecuted the people of God until he himself submitted to the Lord of Glory one bright and sunny day on the way to the city of Damascus. It was the Lord who announced to Ananias that this once proud Pharisee would be an evangelist. "Go! This man is my chosen instrument to carry my Name before the Gentiles and their kings before the people of Israel," was the heavenly injunction (Acts 9).

It was not very long before the now converted Saul began preaching the good news of Christ in Damascus, showing convincingly that Jesus who was crucified was indeed the awaited Messiah (Acts 9:19–22). He began, quite naturally, with his own people. However, his efforts were greeted with almost immediate opposition.

Sometime after this bitter experience the Apostle Paul began to have a more or less settled ministry in the thriving assembly at Antioch. It was from this church that he received further direction through the Spirit to be involved in a wider ministry. He was to embark on a missionary career that would take him as far as Rome, the capital of the then known world, and he was to henceforth serve not as a loner but as a laborer among many. His evangelistic partner from the home base was Barnabas, the man who was instrumental in gaining an entry for him among the believers at Jerusalem.

Having left the church at Antioch to fulfill their missionary vocation, Barnabas and Saul stopped in Salamis after passing through Seluecia on the mainland. Salamis was a city on the isle of Cyprus which boasted an apparently large community of Jews, so "they preached the Word of God in the synagogues..." (Acts 13:6). If evangelism is witnessing that confronts the uncommitted with the claims of Jesus Christ, then Paul was an evangelist *par excellence*. As a fisher of men he went where the fish were, and as a result he was constantly found in the synagogues where there was always a gathering of Jews with their proselytes, "For Moses of old times hath in every city them that preach him, being read in the synagogues every sabbath day" (Acts 15:21; see Appendix E on the Sabbath question).

But Paul in particular was not just acting out a principle. He was expressing a heartfelt concern for first century Jewry. He confessed: "I say the truth in Christ, I lie not, my conscience also bearing me witness in the Holy Ghost, that I have great heaviness and continual sorrow in my heart. For I could, that I myself were accursed from Christ for my brethren, my kinsmen according to the flesh who are Israelites" (Rom 9:1–4a). However, while the apostle Paul had the privilege of seeing a number of Jews coming to the Lord, his greater success was with the Gentiles. And as he moved along he evangelized, preached, argued, testified, and persuaded his non-Jewish audience (e.g., Acts 17:26).

The missionary activities of the Apostle Paul were not confined to evangelism alone but included a calculated effort to foster the spiritual development of new believers. Even before Paul went on his first missionary journey, the importance of nourishing babes of the faith was impressed on him when he first visited the church of Antioch. A revival had broken out in that city after certain itinerant evangelists powerfully proclaimed the gospel to both the Jewish and Gentile inhabitants. News of this activity reached Jerusalem, and the church there sent Barnabas to conduct follow-up work.

After being involved in some intensive counseling sessions with the new believers and seeing further numerical growth, Barnabas decided to instruct them more accurately in the things of the Lord. To help him accomplish this task he enlisted the help of Saul of Tarsus, a man in whom he had discerned the gift of teaching. "And when he had found him he brought him unto Antioch. And it came to pass that a whole year they assembled themselves with the church, and taught much people. And the disciples were called Christians first in Antioch" (Acts 11:26).

This must have been a memorable experience for Paul, because as a result of this concentrated teaching the disciples were dubbed "Christians." Their fellowmen had seen a difference in their lifestyle. There was no doubt in the young teacher's mind that there was a close connection between the nickname *Christian* and the creed he and Barnabas had so faithfully expounded. Later on in his writing to the church at Ephesus he had clearly a thought out philosophy of edification. The flow of Paul's thought expressed in chapter 4:11–15 is as follows: The risen and glorified Christ has given certain gifted persons to His church

(v. 11). The task of these persons is to equip the saints for service (v.12a). The involvement of the saints in the ministry is with a view "to the edifying of the body of Christ . . . till we all come . . . unto the measure of the statue of the fullness of Christ." (vv. 12b, 13).

Paul's plan to see the maturity of God's people was squarely based on the Word of God. Writing to Timothy just before his martyrdom, he reminds the young pastor of the authenticity and potency of Scripture (2 Tim 3:15–17) and proceeded thereafter to urge its proclamation. With a note of sadness the aged Apostle anticipated a time when even saints will resist any effort made to ensure genuine spiritual maturity (2 Tim 4:1–4).

Prior to writing this epistle to his young companion, he had met briefly with the Ephesian elders en route to Rome. In this solemn meeting the tent-making missionary who was instrumental in founding the church at Ephesus unburdened his heart to the elders of that church. His heart was for their survival. Committed as he was to spiritual development his concern went beyond this; he wanted to leave behind a vibrant, God-glorifying church that would make him proud at the judgment (cf. 1 Thess 2:19).

It is in this light that we must understand Paul's discourse at Miletus. "And from Miletus he sent to Ephesus, and called the elders of the church. And when they were come to him, he said unto them, Ye know, from the first day that I came into Asia, after what manner I have been with you at all seasons, serving the Lord with all humility of mind, and with many tears, and temptations, which befell me by the lying in wait of the Jews: and how I kept back nothing that was profitable to you, but have showed you, and have taught you publicly, and from house to house...Wherefore I take you to record this day, that I am pure from the blood of all men. For I have not shunned to declare unto you all the counsel of God" (Acts 20:17–20, 26–27). Two verses are worthy of comment: verses 20 and 27. The latter is an expansion of the former. As an instructor in righteous living Paul did not fail to teach such truths as election, predestination, and the perseverance of the saints, as well as the fact that God is to his people a consuming fire to those who shun their responsibility to live holy.

Yet another aspect of Paul's concern for the people of God is seen in his prayer life. If, as the epigram goes, "intercession is love on its knees," then there is no doubt that the Apostle to the Gentiles really loved his converts. It is worthy of note that in most of his epistles written from prison, prayers are mentioned at the beginning and end. (Eph 1:15–22;

6:18; Phil 1:3; 4:6; Col 1:9; 4:1). Paul's prayer for the Colossians is quite significant in the light of the fact that he did not start that assembly. He was so committed to helping people attain Christlikeness that he constantly cried out to God who alone can effect any lasting change in human nature.

Did the Apostle Paul have any plan to ensure that the church throughout her history would have a true "apostolic" succession, that is, an unbroken line of leaders who would genuinely care for God's heritage? And if so, what is it? I believe that the answer to the first question is in the affirmative. The balance of this chapter attempts to address the second.

Already in Paul's day there was a shortage of Christian leaders. He could say to Timothy his trusted co-laborer, "Do thy diligence to come shortly unto me: for Demas hath forsaken me, having loved this world, and is departed unto Thessalonica" (2 Tim 4:9–10). It must have been with tears in his eyes that he penned these words to the Philippian Christians, "But I trust in the Lord Jesus to send Timothy shortly unto you, that I also maybe of good comfort, when I know your state. For I have no man likeminded, who will naturally care for your state. For all seek their own, not the things which are Jesus Christ's."

But if this was indeed the case in the first-century church it was not Paul's fault, for it is evident from a study of his ministry that one of his priorities was the training of Christian leaders. This he sought to do by way of positive example. Once again we turn to Acts 20:17–35. What Paul did among the early converts at Ephesus was not accidental. He consciously stressed certain traits and habits, because he wanted his spiritual children to follow suit. If the Ephesian elders had missed this point the apostle is at pains here to put the issue beyond doubt. He wanted to underscore such virtues as humility, patience (v. 14), longsuffering, boldness (vv. 20, 21, 22, 23, 24), faithfulness (26, 27), and watchfulness (v. 28–31). He was particularly desirous of imparting to his converts in general and leaders in particular a meaningful work ethic: "I have coveted no man's silver, or gold, or apparel. Yea, ye yourselves know that these hands have ministered unto my necessities and to them that were with me. I have showed you all things, how that so laboring ye ought to support the weak, and to remember the words of the Lord Jesus, how he said, It is more blessed to give than to receive" (Acts 20:33–35). This is confirmed by his reference to this same kind of ethic in Ephesians 4:28 and his use of the word "labor" on both occasions.

If one does not understand the apostle, his anxiety to have people follow his pattern of life seems to border on egotism. Indeed, an enumeration of the number of personal references in Acts 20 would definitely convince some of his conceit. But statistics in this case does not give a true picture of the man. Living an exemplary life was at the root of his strategy to train leaders. Twice Paul urged the Philippians to take his life-style seriously (Phil 3:17–18; 4:9).

Evidently, from 2 Timothy 2:2 Paul had a class of specially handpicked men whom he trained to carry the burden of the ministry in the succeeding generation. Every believer should be concerned about telling the gospel to others. However, this passage is particularly applicable to leaders. Every such servant of God, while not neglecting the whole congregation, should endeavour to develop other leaders who will be qualified and competent to carry the gospel effectively to others. This is how the gospel reached the twenty-first century. It is our responsibility to prepare others to reach the next generation.

What was Paul's curriculum for potential Church leaders like? This we are not explicitly told, but from his various emphases here and there it may be possible to put together a fairly accurate picture of at least his "core disciplines." We can be fairly certain that such a curriculum was squarely based on the sacred writings. It is highly improbable that the young pastor at Ephesus was hearing the words of 2 Timothy 2:2 for the first time. The apostle must have imparted to his students sound Bible study principles, drawing both from his rabbinic and Christian traditions. In some places we find this missionary theologian stressing (rather than straining) certain points of grammar (e.g., the singular number in Gal 3:16). He wanted Timothy to give heed to "sound words" (2 Tim 1:13). Imprisonment and impending execution did not stop the apostle Paul from serious study of God's Word (2 Tim 4). This must have had a tremendous effect on his protégé Timothy.

As a missionary theologian the Apostle Paul was faithful both to his evangelistic call and his follow-up efforts. He also sought to reproduce himself in men and women ("men," generic in 2 Tim 2:2) who would carry the torch of leadership to yet another generation of believers. It is the apostle's work in these three areas that made him great in my judgment. It seems evident, then, that Paul was consciously carrying out in his ministry what is commonly known as the great commission (Matt 28:18–20; cf. John 14:15; 2 Cor 5:14). What the apostle Paul and others did for the first century is left for us to do in the twenty-first.

A SKETCH OF PAUL'S LANGUAGE

If the language of Jesus was Semitic, Paul's was definitely Greek. His letters have come down to us in this language, and that of the koine variety. At the time of the apostle it was the *lingua franca* of the Mediterranean world, legacy of the great Alexander of Macedonia; and while Jesus must have been fluent in Hebrew and especially Aramaic, Greek must have been known to him as well.[7] Once thought to be a combination of the Classical and Hebrew by some scholars, we have come to realize that the language of Paul was indeed the language of the common wo/man.[8] This knowledge has been vouchsafed through the discoveries of various papyrus material in Egypt.[9]

The Greek language in general has over 3000 years of history, from the sixteenth century BCE to the present. The Koine, the language of Paul, flourished between BCE 300–300 CE. In comparison to the forms which preceded it, the Koine was characterized by simplicity of syntax, form, and vocabulary amenable and useful for merchants, travelers, soldiers and statesmen alike. This is well attested by the thousands of Papyri found in North Africa, preserving "for us the actual life of the day and includ[ing] letters of all sorts . . . contracts, receipts, proclamations, anything, everything."[10]

Accepting the overall contribution of the masses of Greek papyri on our understanding of the NT, Nigel Turner[11] feels however that their value has been overstated to the neglect of other important features, such as the influence of the LXX and, what the REB calls, the Jewish languages. In other words, not all important terms in the Greek New Testament can be elucidated by invoking the papyri.

There are many words that are best understood against a Semitic background, and even where the papyri shed light on some terms, a

---

7. Horsley, *Archaeology*, 154–71.

8. Horrell, "*Familiar Friend or Alien Stranger?*," 403.

9. Moulton, *Grammar*, 5: "The conclusion is that "Biblical Greek, except where it is translation Greek [like the LXX], was simply the vernacular of daily life."

10. Robertson and Davis, *New Short Grammar*, 12–13.

11. Turner, *Christian Words*, vii–xiv.

more complete coloring can be seen from the perspective of the Aramaic or Hebrew.

So with this caveat[12] in mind, there is a wealth of knowledge to be gained by carefully weighing the vocabulary of Paul in the light emanating from the ancient Orient. Writing on "the more or less *popular*" appeal of the NT writers Deissmann remarks:

> St. Paul too can command the terse pithiness of the homely gospel speech, especially in his ethical exhortations as pastor. These take shape naturally in clear-cut *maxims* such as the people themselves use and treasure up. But even where St. Paul is arguing to himself and takes more to the language of the middle class, even where he is carried away by priestly fervor of the liturgist [cf. Rom 15] and the enthusiasm of the psalmist [e.g., Rom 3:10–18], his Greek never becomes literary. . . . thickly studded with the rugged, forceful words taken from the popular idiom [like that of Jamaican], it is perhaps the most brilliant example of the artless though not inartistic colloquial prose of a traveled city resident of the Roman Empire, its wonderful flexibility making it just the Greek for use in a mission to all the world.[13]

Since Deissmann wrote not a few studies have demonstrated that the apostle was a much better literary artist than was first imagined.[14] But what Deissmann and his followers have done is to put beyond doubt the character of Paul's writings as Holy Ghost language dressed in the garment of a Greco-Roman. But where the nominative "I" is concerned there does not seem to be any great deal of difference between the Koine usage and its classical counterpart. The only possible exceptions to this are the Gospels, where the influence of Hebraism appears substantial.[15] The few published examples from the papyri seem to support this.[16]

More recent studies of the language of Paul's letters have returned to an emphasis which was that of early Greek grammarians, that is, on the verb.[17] In fact the modern study is enriched by the study of linguis-

---

12. "It is important, therefore, to guard against two opposing errors: not everything which conforms to Semitic idiom is a Semitism, nor is everything which appears somewhere or sometime in Greek genuine Greek" (BDF, 4). Cf. Neil, *Interpretation*, 150.

13. Deissmann, *Light*, 63–64.

14. Spencer, *Paul's Literary Style*.

15. BDF, 4.

16. MM, 180.

17. Porter *Idioms of the Greek New Testament*, 20.

tics, particularly the investigation into the nature of the verbal system. Sometime ago two scholars, namely, Fanning[18] and Porter,[19] published revisions of their doctoral theses in the area of aspectual theory. The latter, for instance, defines verbal aspect as "*a semantic (meaning) category by which a speaker or writer grammaticalizes (i.e. represents a meaning by choice of a word-form) a perspective on action by selection of a particular tense-form in the verbal system.*"[20]

This understanding of aspect, then, links the form of the verb (morphology) with its function. Although the concept of aspect is closely tied to the tense forms, Porter feels strongly that the verbs *qua* verbs have nothing to do with temporal matters. These can only be inferred from the context. For Porter, there are three verbal aspects that were available in Paul's day. This therefore means that in the writing of Romans, for example, one may very well find 1) the aspect complete in which "*the action is conceived of . . . as complete and undifferentiated process*' (e.g., Rom 5:14), 2), the aspect continuous in which the language depicts an action on progress (Rom 6:8), or 3) the aspect as complex, in which '*the state of action is conceived of by the language user as reflecting a given . . . state of affairs*" (e.g., Rom 6:7).[21]

Certain verbs, however, particularly "I am" (εἰμι/*eimi*), found regularly on the lips of the Jesus of the Gospels, may not carry any aspectual feature whatever, and so as a consequence may have very little exegetical significance.[22] Of course, an affirmation like "I am the truth" (ἐγώ εἰμὶ ἡ ἀλήθεια/*egō eimi hē aletheia*; John 14:6) or "I am carnal" (ἐγὼ εἰμι σάρκινός/*egō eimi sarkinos;* Rom 7: 14) will have exegetical significance in their respective contexts that would be determined not by the aspectually challenged linking verb, but perhaps by the prominent nominative and the contextual force of the discourse.[23]

In essential agreement with Porter, at least at the level of definition, is Buist Fanning.[24] His conviction is that "verbal aspect is too dependent

18. Fanning, *Verbal Aspect*.
19. Porter, *Verbal Aspect*.
20. Porter, *Idioms*, 21; italics his.
21. Ibid., 22.
22. Ibid., 23. Future tense verbs are also aspectually vague.
23. This, however, is not the view of Campbell, *Verbal Aspect*, 27.
24. Later (p.1) he seems to cite approvingly those scholars who distinguish the tenses from aspect, which is "concerned rather with features like duration, progression,

on other features of the context for it *alone* [his emphasis] to be determinative in interpretation. However, [aspect] in combination with other features . . . is a significant linguistic element to be weighed in interpreting a number of texts in the NT."[25]

Porter would agree with Fanning's distinction between *aktionsart*, an early twentieth-century description of the fundamental function of the verb, and aspect. Whereas *aktionsart* is said to describe how an action actually occurs, aspect, on the other hand, "involves a way of viewing the action; [it] reflects the subjective conception or portrayal by the speaker; focuses the speaker's representation of the action."[26]

But despite their general agreement on the importance of the subject, Porter and Fanning, it has been observed, have some serious differences in the way they perceive how this promising approach to the study of the Greek verbal system apply to the Pauline and other NT corpora. For instance, Porter believes that the high incidence of present subjunctives in 1 Thessalonians may have been chosen by the writer to express urgency, while Fanning gives a similar emphasis to corresponding aorists.

Since aspectology is such a young and complex discipline, and since its serious application to the NT has barely begun, it is definitely too early to determine its full contribution to the understanding of Paul's usage of language, particularly in the book of Romans. Notwithstanding this reality, the work of Porter or Fanning in this regard should be consulted for any light it may shed on even familiar passages, along with that of Caragounis's[27] *which purportedly provides important checks and correctives.*[28]

The character of the Greek of Paul and the other NT writers may best be summarized in the words of a twentieth-century translator:

> I must, in common justice, confess here that for many years I had viewed the Greek of the New Testament with a rather snobbish disdain. I had read the best of Classical Greek both at school and

---

completion, repetition, inception, current relevance and their opposites."

25. Fanning *Verbal Aspect*, vi.
26. Ibid., 31.
27. Caragounis, *Development*, 317–336.
28. After commenting on a methodological problem that may be responsible for differences between Fanning and Porter, Silva, "Response," advises pastors and exegetes to say very little about aspect.

Cambridge for over ten years. To come down to the *Koine* of the first century A.D. seemed, I have sometimes remarked rather uncharitably, like reading Shakespeare for some years and turning to the Vicar's letter in the Parish Magazine! But I think now that I was wrong: I can see that the expression of the Word of God in ordinary workaday language is all a piece with God's incredible humility in becoming Man in Jesus Christ. And, further, the language itself is not as pedestrian as I had at first supposed.[29]

We turn now to one of the apostle's greatest contributions to the development of the Christian faith.

A SKETCH OF PAUL'S LEGACY

Our chief aim in this section is to map out a theology of Paul and his letter to the Romans with the aid of a creedal document[30] framed in the last century.

> To write a *theology* of Romans cannot mean to forget about our own place in the history of interpretation. Rather, we should widen our concept of *theology* so that it includes pastoral, social, political,[31] and emotional dimensions. If theology centers on God, the creator of all, then it stands to reason that it should be holistic. And, after all, encountering Paul means facing a man of *passion* both before and after the famous turning point of his life connected with the city of Damascus. The letter to the Romans makes no exception—although it turns out to be the most elaborate, sometimes sophisticated, and in a way most mature of his extant writings.[32]

Scripture

Many books on Systematic Theology are heavily indebted to the apostle for his statement to young Timothy on the trustworthiness of the Hebrew Bible (2 Tim 3:16). The statement outlines the usefulness of Scripture in terms of its doctrinal, practical, and spiritual benefits. The term "inspired" literally means to "breathe out." That is what we do when we speak, and this action provides a suitable image of how God's Word

---

29. Phillips, *Ring of Truth*, 18.
30. Anderson, *Statement of Faith*. The influence of Paul on this document is immense.
31. See especially Appendix F and Perkins, *Justice as Equality*.
32. Hacker, *Theology*, 2; his italics.

comes to us. Inspiration, then, is the result of God "breathing" out his word to his people. In Romans chapters 3–4 and 9–11, in particular, Paul demonstrates just how reliant he was on these Scriptures,[33] which were endorsed as well by the Jesus tradition (e.g., Matt 5:18).

God

In all of Paul's letters the unity, sovereignty,[34] sufficiency, and glory of the Supreme Being are all highlighted (1 Cor 8:6a; Rom 11:33–36). He also laid the groundwork for the understanding of God as a Triune Being (I Cor 8:6; Phil 2:5, 6; Col 2:9; cf. Matt 28:19). This is one of the most difficult doctrines to grasp. It is important for the Christian not to reject it because s/he cannot understand it. The doctrine states that there is only *one* Supreme Being whom we call God. This Being uniquely exists in three persons identified in the New Testament as Father, Son, and Holy Spirit (Matt 28:19).[35] Mysteriously, both the Spirit (Rom 8:26–27) and the Son (Rom 8:34) are praying for believers. It is the Father who answers the prayers.

"The relationship of all three members of the Godhead is harmonious and simultaneous in operations yet in the provision of man's salvation each makes a distinctive contribution. (Eph 2:18)"[36]

The thrust of this statement is to demonstrate the perfect co-operation among the Spirit, Son, and Father as they seek to accomplish especially the divine scheme of redemption. This is beautifully brought out in Eph 1, where the "distinctive contribution" of the Father (vv. 3–7), Son (vv. 7–12), and Spirit (vv.13–14) are itemised and celebrated (*Nota Bene*,

---

33. Bible students also speak of Christ as the living Word. The Bible today is God's written Word, consisting of 66 books, 39 in the OT and 27 in the New. According to one Jewish arrangement of the Old Testament, there are 22 books. This is because certain books were combined, (e.g., Judges and Ruth), to make the number of books correspond to the number of letters in the Hebrew alphabet and when this is added to the number of books in the NT, the new number is the perfect multiple of seven. The other important point is that the Bible is a closed canon. Evidence of this closure may be seen in the Apostle John's solemn warning in Rev 22:18–19.

34. Richards, *Godincidences*.

35. See also John 1:1; 20:28; Heb 1:8; Acts 1:3, 4; Heb 9:14; Is 48:16; I Cor 12: 4–6; 2 Cor 13:14; Prov 30:4; John 14:7, 17. Practically speaking, we must obey the voice of the Father (Matt 17:5); Son (John 14:15); and Holy Spirit (Rev 2:7).

36. Anderson, *Statement*, 14.

"To the praise of His glory;" vv. 6, 12, 14, connected to each Person). A similar passage is I Cor 12:4–6, where spiritual gifts are in focus.

It is worthy of note that the apostle Paul does not expressly speak of "first person," and the like. However, in the outworking of God's program there is a discernible structure of hierarchy in which the Son submits to the Father (I Cor11:3) and the Spirit to both (cf. Acts 2:33). This arrangement is purely functional and does in no way suggest the inferiority of the Spirit and the Son to the Father, in terms of their "supreme being-ness."

The unity of the Godhead is also seen in that the Son and the Spirit share in other divine activities well (e.g., Col 1:16–17; 2 Thess 2:6–7).

Jesus the Messiah

The apostle to the Gentiles evidently believed in the deity of Christ (Rom 9:5).[37] This is of paramount importance. Rejection of this truth means dishonouring the Father (cf. John 5:22–23; Heb1:5–8). He affirmed the full humanity and sinlessness of Christ, who is uniquely divine and human at the same time (Phil 2:5–8; cf. John 20:28). Scholars call this the theanthropic union. Here an interesting comparison can be made with the doctrine of the Trinity, which states that God is one *being* but three *persons*. In the theanthropic union we have one *person* but two *beings* (human and divine). Paul also affirmed the restorative work of the Messiah relative to Adam's loss. The fact is that His redemptive work (i.e., Messiah's death and bodily[38] resurrection) accomplished far more than what Adam lost (Eph 1:3–14; Rom 5:12–21; Rom 4:24, 25, 8:34).

The chief function of our Lord's priestly office right now appears to be that of advocacy (Rom 8:34; cf. Heb 4:14–16; 7:25; I John 2:1). Along with this vital ministry, he is preparing a place for the redeemed (John14:1–4), sanctifying believers (Eph 5:28–29), distributing spiritual gifts (Eph 4:7–11), and empowering his people to bear fruit (John 15:1–10).

---

37. Contra Eisenbaum, *Paul*, 172–95. For a Rastafari perspective, see Taylor, "Messianic Ideology," 390–411; see also Selassie, *"Building an Enduring Tower."*

38. The bodily nature of the resurrection (a body characterised by numerical identity, physical materiality, and celestial glory) is here emphasized. The Apostle Paul argues strongly for the importance of this tenet in I Cor 15. Without the resurrection: Christian faith and ministry are empty (vv. 14, 17); Christian servants are blasphemers (v 15); the Christian doctrine of forgiveness is meaningless (v 17); and Christian hope is futile (vv 18–19).

Holy Spirit

Perhaps the greatest activity in which the Spirit played a significant role was the founding of the Church, the body of Christ (I Cor 12:13; cf. Acts 2). The Spirit continues to minister to the members of the Messianic community in a number of ways including:

1. *Directing* He provides divine guidance through the Scriptures (Rom 8:13–14)

2. *Teaching* He provides divine instructions from the Scriptures (Rom 15:3–6)

3. *Filling* He empowers believers to obey the Scriptures (Eph 5:18)

4. *Praying* He provides divine intercession in our weakness (Rom 8:26–28)

5. *Assuring* He provides inner certitude of sonship (Rom 8:16)

6. *Equipping* He provides gifts for service (Rom 12:1–8; I Cor 12:7–8)

Angels

Our word "angel" comes from a similar sounding Greek word that means, "messenger." This meaning pretty much sums up the chief function of these creatures. In the writings of Paul, there are several references to these created beings (Col 1:16; Rom 8:38; 1 Cor 4:9; 6:3; 1 Tim 3:16; Eph 2:2).

Although angels are said to be of a "higher rank and possess greater power"[39] than humankind, it was never said that they bear the image of God (cf. the AV and NRSV renditions of Ps 8:5). In addition, only human beings benefit from God's plan of salvation, not angelic spirits. The spirits that have remained faithful to God are the elect angels of I Tim 5:21. In respect of the "already but not yet" doctrinal tension in the NT, Colossians 2:15 affirms the fact that the forces of darkness (evil spirits)[40] have already been defeated in the first century; but the promise of Romans 16:20 still awaits fulfilment in the twenty-first.

---

39. Anderson, *The Statement of Faith*.

40. These fallen angels are also called demons or unclean spirits. They are very active in the promotion of false teachings (I Tim 4:1).

Humanity

The apostle believed that humans were created by God as special beings composed of spirit/soul and body, uniquely bearing the image of God and in having moral responsibility and accountability (1 Cor 11:7; 15:49; cf. Gen 1:26; 1 Thess 5:23). This basically means that every human being resembles God in some sense. The image of God seems to exist in mankind's spiritual (John 4:24), moral (Rom 2:15), social (Gen 1:27), rational (Isa 1:18), aesthetic (Gen 1:31), creative (Gen 2:19; 3:7), linguistic (Gen 3:9, 10, 13), and governmental (Gen 1:28) endowments.

"Originally the creature man (male and female) was without sin, and lived in a perfect spiritual relationship with God, in a perfect physical environment . . . but in course of time the first human pair, Adam and Eve, fell prey to the wiles of the devil and by their disobedience to God, brought condemnation to the human race. (Rom 3:23; 5:12)."[41]

In the Genesis 3 account mankind's condemnation was brought about by (1) human experimentation/rebellion and (2) satanic deception. The enemy's intentions were to:

- Mislead God's crown-creation (v.1)
- Misrepresent God's counsel (vv. 2–4)
- Malign God's character (v. 5; cf. 2 Cor 11:2–3)

Although we still bear the divine image which gives us our fundamental *dignity*, as children of Adam we also bear the "scar" of his fall. This accounts for our *depravity*. This model of humanity (a creature of dignity and depravity) is vital to bear in mind as we evaluate its achievements in terms of technology and culture (dignity), as well as observe its genocidal and vandalising tendency (depravity). The former renders man saveable, while the latter points up the need for such.

Redemption

It was also Paul's conviction that: "Salvation is God's provision for the redemption of condemned man from the awful consequences of sin: past, present and future, through the exercise of personal faith in Christ and His finished work on the Cross. (Rom 4:7, 8; 8:1, 38, 39; Titus 2:11–15)."[42]

---

41. Anderson, *Statement*, 3.
42. Ibid.

"Condemnation" is just one of the "awful consequences of sin" (John 3:18). Others include man's ruin (he is not serving his purpose; 2 Cor 4:3), blindness (being unable to perceive his purpose; 2 Cor 4:4), depravity (he is unable to serve his purpose; Eph 2:1), and slavery (he serves the purpose of another; Eph 2:2). The salvation that God provides nullifies all the above and, as stated already, embraces the past (salvation from sin's penalty), present (salvation from sin's power), and future (salvation from sin's presence). One of the benefits of salvation is forgiveness, which may be defined as the removal of punitive action (Rom 8:1). Another is Sanctification, a separation unto God. Its goal is Christlikeness (Rom 8:29–30; I Cor 1:30). Cleansing from sin is a means to that end. Sanctification is also progressive, since in it the child of God progresses in holiness. The full co-operation of the believer in this regard is highlighted in 2 Pet 1:3–10 (see also Gal 5:16–24; Phil 2:12, 13).

This means every effort should be made to live a holy life as Rom 8:12–14 says. The other side of the coin is emphasized in terms of yieldedness and constant submission to the gracious ministry of the Holy Spirit. This is what the Spirit-filled life is all about (Eph 5:18). This is what it means to "walk in the Spirit" (Gal 5:16).

Church

The Church, according to Paul, is *Corpus Christi*, the body of Christ (I Cor 12:12–14; Eph 1:22, 23; 2:14–16, 19–22; 3:2–11). "Body" is one of several metaphors used of the Church in the New Testament. It underscores the vitality of God's community of believers with Christ as head. The church therefore is not just a worldwide organisation. It is an organism of global, even universal proportions. Other metaphors of the Church include "bride" (implied in 2 Cor 11:2; Eph 5:31–32) and "building" (1 Cor 3:9).

The local expression of the church, many people find, is difficult to define. For example, do we have a church where two or three are gathered in the Lord's name (e.g., Matt 18:20)? Is it possible to have a local church without leadership (Elders, Pastors, and Deacons/Deaconesses? Notice in Acts 14:23 that the various groups of believers were *churches* before the official appointment of elders (who must have served as interim leaders before their ordination.)

In light of the above, then, we would suggest that an assembly or local church is a group of believers who meet regularly to do God's will as it is set out in a passage like Acts 2:42. The New Testament suggests that the regularity of meetings should be at least once a week in a permanent location (1 Cor 1:1, 16:1–2), with a clear focus on the church's objectives in terms of exaltation (worship), edification (welfare), exhibition (works), and evangelisation (witness).

Paul also refers to the two ordinances of the church: baptism and the Lord's Supper. Some have made the distinction between *real* baptism (i.e., incorporation, I Cor 12:13; cf. Acts 2:38) and *ritual* baptism (immersion; 1 Cor 1:16–17; Acts 2:41). The former is an integral part of the salvation event, whilst the latter symbolically represents the former. A text which brings together both senses of the word is Acts 1:5, "John, as you know, baptized with water [ritual] but within the next few days you will be baptized with the Spirit [real baptism]."

With regard to the Lord's Supper, the early believers evidently broke bread every day (Acts 2:42, 46), but settled later into a pattern of commemorating it on the Lord's Day (1 Cor 11:20; cf. Rev 1:10). The focus, of course, was never on a day but on the Messiah who died and was vivified. Thus Paul can say: "God forbid that I should glory . . ." (Gal 6:14); cf. 1 Cor 5:8, "let us keep the festival . . ." (NIV).

Believers need to assess themselves spiritually to effectively and meaningfully partake of the Lord's Supper, Paul says (1 Cor 11:27–34). Paul also points to a final assessment or judgment at the end of the day. The three main passages which discuss this judgement of believers are Rom 14:10–12; 1 Cor 3:11–15, and 2 Cor 5:10. According to 1 Cor 3:15, some Christians will not be rewarded. However, even these same Christians, apparently, will receive some commendation (1 Cor 4:5).

Future Events

Paul has written a great deal concerning future events in passages like 1 Thess 4:13–17 and 1 Cor 15:51–56. First Corinthians 15, for example, emphasizes the marvellous transformation that the Lord will bring about in the believer's body (cf. Phil 3:20–21; 1 John 3:2–3). The fact that all believers will be raptured at this time and every Christian "shall have praise of God" (I Cor 4:5), underscores once again the amazing grace of our Lord Jesus Christ (2 Cor 5:10; 1 Cor 3:13–15, 4:5; Rom 14:10). Another event high on God's agenda, according to Paul, is the judgment of unbelievers. In Romans 2, for instance, the apostle outlines the principles of that judgment.

CONCLUSION

> A distinguished professor . . . was offering a special seminar entitled "Origins of Christianity" at the university I was attending on the East Coast. One day the class sidetracked the professor into discussing his understanding on the meaning of Romans 1–5. With unusual eloquence and masterful exegesis, he walked through these chapters with a precise deftness, affirming that everyone in the class had sinned and therefore had come short of the glory of God. But for those who would believe in God's sacrifice of His Son for their sins, they would not just be made righteous; no, they would be declared righteous by a God who justified sinners, much as a judge did who dismissed a case that had failed to prove its defendant guilty. Rarely have I ever heard such a bold and fair treatment of this text of Paul. After two hours, however, the spell was suddenly broken when one of the Jewish students in the class who, along with many others had sat uncomfortably through this long and, to them, seemingly parochial tirade, blurted out (amid all the nervous smoking that was going on in the seminar by now), "Do I get the impression that the professor of this class believes this stuff?" Immediately the professor responded in a scoffing tone, "Who said anything about believing it? I am just arguing that this is what Paul said. I'm sick and tired of hearing the younger neo-orthodox scholars say, 'This is what this or that text means to *me*.' I was trained under the old liberal theology; we learned what *Paul* said. We just don't happen to believe what Paul said!"[43]

Unlike this professor, my exegesis of Paul, regrettably, falls far short of mastery. Nevertheless, I have outlined above what I think the Apostle was convinced of, in so far as that can be traced from his writings. Because of the occasional nature of Paul's letters, one does not expect any systematic treatment of any of the main biblical teachings delineated above. However, it may be too much to claim that the apostle does not touch on all the major doctrines in his *magnum opus*. I think a more careful reading may prove otherwise. One thing is certain: we can only reflect on matters of which we have only a partial grasp (1 Cor 13:9–12).[44] However, by God's Spirit our display of Love—that eternal virtue (1 Cor 13:13; 1 John 4:7–8)—can be full and beneficial (1 Cor 8:1b; Gal 5:22–23). There is no better statement of faith (cf. John 13:35; Deut 6:5).

---

43. Cited by Walter C. Kaiser, *An Introduction to Biblical Hermeneutics*, 167–68.

44. For a useful synopsis of Paul's theology in Romans, see Fitzmyer, *Romans*, 103–72.

2

Theology, Culture, and the Book of Romans:
A Canonical-historical Dialogue

INTRODUCTION

I THINK IT IS a truism that both culture and theology are as old as humankind. If theology is defined as sustained reflection on things divine, and if culture is the way we shape our environment,[1] then our first parents were indeed theologians of a sort and environmentalists of a kind. Theologically speaking, humanity is primarily *Homo sapiens* (wise people?) and culturally *Homo faber* (working people)—creatively shaping and re-shaping the world around.[2] Looking at wo/man holistically, we can begin to see the integral (missing) link between culture and theology: right thinking about God cultivates rich manufacturing. It therefore follows that the more "atheological" we become the less culture will reflect our dignity. Whether we view the past from the perspective

---

1. Turnau, "Reflecting Theologically on Popular Culture," 272. Another of the 99 or so definitions is: "Culture refers to the network or system of shared meaning in a society, a conceptual collection of ideals, beliefs and values . . . attitudes and assumptions about life that is woven together over time and is widely shared among a people. It is a kind of invisible blueprint—a map of reality that people use to interpret their experience and guide their behavior." See also Vanhoozer, "The World Well Staged?"; Carson, *Christ and Culture Revisited*, and Gorringe, *Furthering Humanity*.

2. A few useful definitions of culture are conceptual, rendering the neat distinction between thinking man and tinkering man virtually useless. Both theology and culture are in a sense humanly generated. See Gangel "Christian Higher Education," 105, for the relationship of the "queen of sciences" and other disciplines. I submit that sin *and* Satan have corrupted the "queen," the only "person" who can guarantee high quality cultural sustainability (cf. Prov 9). Elsewhere Gangel, "Moral Entropy," 156, dubs the influence of evil on culture as "The law of *theo*-dynamics" (emphasis added).

of sacred history (*Heilsgeschichte*) or not, the baneful influence of bad theologising on culture is clear to see.[3]

This is richly illustrated in Scripture and other literatures (e.g., Rom 1:18–32)[4] and firmly substantiated by experience. In the light of the above, this essay seeks to survey some of the cultures of antiquity with a view to addressing once again the prevailing human condition. It examines these ancient (and not so ancient) civilisations to ascertain the dynamic interplay between their cultural advancement and their theology, and closes with a brief word concerning our cultural engagement.

> Over a decade ago New Testament scholar N. T. Wright published his first book of an ambitious five-volume project which will re-assess the full gamut of Christian origins. In the first volume, Wright carefully sets out his methodology, which sought to avoid radical post-modern approaches on the one hand, and naïve modernistic historical reconstructions on the other. Wright opts for what he calls a "critical realism" which investigates the theological posture of a group by way of its dominant story, praxis, symbols and questions that form its world-view.[5]

World-views, Wright says, "are like the foundations of a house: vital, but invisible. They are that *through* which a society or an individual normally looks; they form the grid according to which humans organise reality."[6]

Armed with this approach, Wright later turns his attention to Judaism and Christianity. Both groups, according him, share a common set of beliefs in terms of what he describes as creational, providential, and covenantal monotheism. Where Christianity differs from Judaism, Wright believes, is in its radical assertion that Jesus is the climax of this monotheistic covenant. I will now proceed to employ Wright's methodology and an appraisal of the Judeo-Christian nexus as the yardstick (especially the book of Romans) against which to measure the cultural progress of ancient peoples as well as our own.

THE ANCIENT NEAR EAST (ANE)

For though they knew God, they did not honor him as God or give thanks to him, but they became futile in their thinking, and their senseless minds were darkened (Rom 1:21. NRSV).

3. Williams, "*Death on the Nile*," 2–25.
4. Boring, *Hellenistic Commentary*, 339–342.
5. Palmer, *Pronominal 'I'*, 3–4.
6. *New Testament*, 125.

We begin our panoramic sketch of ancient cultures by looking at the Sumerian civilisation (southern Iraq) that flourished between the fourth and third millennia. The worldview of the Sumerians can be sketched by an examination of the rich archaeological and literary sources we have at our disposal. Unlike the Israelites, at no stage of their religious history could the Sumerians be classified as creational/covenantal monotheists.

On the contrary, a good percentage of the available records shows various kinds of polytheism. Because the Sumerians "were the first people to place inscriptions on the cornerstones or foundation stones of temples, palaces and other structures," it is relatively easy to trace some of their significant religious symbols and praxis. For example, inscriptions were found on sacrificial altars related to certain deities[7] and each of these deities was more or less in charge of a city-state. In the city-states were to be found great temple edifices around which all of life was organised. According to Harrison, "great importance was attached to religious activities, and a considerable amount of time was devoted to the formation of theological concepts and cultic traditions."[8] This is not surprising, because humankind is not just *homo faber* but *homo religious* as well.[9] In respect of the Sumerians and the other cultures influenced by them, there are abundant artefacts illustrating this point. The literary evidence in its broad outline is even clearer, and, from its sheer abundance, complex. Part of this clarity is in the stark contrast between, say the Judeo-Christian account(s) of creation (cosmogony) recorded in Genesis[10] and elsewhere in the Tanak-NT versus the account(s) of the *Enuma Elish*. It is true that in both the book of Genesis and the *Enuma Elish* we find matters like a watery chaos, but what stands out most of all is that in the former the supreme Deity is generating everything, while in the latter a successive "pantheon" of deities comes to birth.

---

7. Harrison, *Old Testament Times*, 8.

8. Ibid., 42.

9. Tillich *Theology of Culture*, 3–9.

10. Says Harris, *Letter*, 76: "God appears to have an even greater fondness for viruses. Biologists estimate that there are at least ten strains of virus for every species. . . . Many viruses are benign, of course . . . [but many] of them invade our cells only to destroy them, destroying us in the process—horribly, mercilessly, relentlessly. . . . Evolution both predicts and explains this phenomenon; the book of Genesis does not." Is that really so? Rightly understood, it is the book of Genesis which gives us the best explanation of what has gone horribly wrong with our world. It tells us also that it was not always like this (Gen 1–2), and it predicts the radical reversal that will usher in a time when not even a computer virus will survive (Gen 3:15; 12:1–3; 49:10).

According to E. A. Speiser "The struggle between cosmic order and chaos was to the ancient Mesopotamians a fateful drama that was renewed at the turn of every year. The epic that deals with these events was therefore the most significant expression of the religious literature of Mesopotamia."[11] This creation epic, *Enuma Elish*, was solemnly recited at the beginning of every year. The following excerpt, a tribute to Marduk, quite likely formed a part of the recitation:

> *Thou art the most honoured of the great gods,*
> *Thy decree is unrivalled . . .*
> *From this day unchangeable shall be thy pronouncement*
> *To raise or to bring low—these shall be (in) thy hand*
> *Thy utterance shall be true; thy command shall be impeachable,*
> *No one among the gods shall transgress thy bounds!*
> *O Marduk, thou art indeed our avenger.*
> *We have granted thee kingship over the universe entire.*[12]

The text later goes on to describe in graphic detail the battle between primordial Tiamat, from whom sprang all the other gods (except Apsu) and the younger and stronger Marduk:

> *They strove in single combat, locked in battle.*
> *The lord spread out his net to enfold her,*
> *The Evil Wind, which followed behind, he let loose in her face.*
> *When Tiamat opened her mouth to consume him,*
> *He drove in the Evil Wind that she close not her lips.*
> *As the fierce winds charged her belly,*
> *Her body was distended and her mouth was open wide open.*
> *He released the arrow, it tore her belly,*
> *It cut through her insides, splitting the heart.*
> *Having thus subdued her, he extinguished her life.*
> *He cast down her carcass to stand upon it.*[13]

The carcass of Tiamat became the basic raw material from which the world was manufactured:

> *The lord trod on the legs of Tiamat whom,*
> *With his unsparing mace he crushed her skull.*
> *When the arteries of her blood he had severed,*
> *The North Wind bore (it) to places undisclosed. . . .*

11. Speiser, *The Creation Epic*, 31.
12. Ibid.
13. Ibid.

> Then the lord paused to view her dead body,
> That he might divide the monster and do artful works.
> He split her like a shellfish into two parts:
> Half of her he set up and ceiled as sky. . . .

Later we read about the fashioning of a very familiar creature.

> When Marduk hears the words of the gods,
> His heart prompts (him) to fashion artful works.
> Opening his mouth, he addressed Ea
> To impart the plan he had conceived in his heart:
> "Blood I will mass and cause bones to be.
> I will establish a savage . . .
> Verily, savage man I will create.
> He shall be charged with the service of the gods
> That they might be at ease!"[14]

There is some similarity here with the Genesis[15] account with respect to (1) inter/intra-divine dialogue; (2) the purpose of man's creation for service; (3) the creator's "rest," and (4) the corresponding chiastic structures:

```
A  I will
   B  establish
      C  a savage
      C' savage man
   B' create
A' I will
A  God[16]
   B  created
      C  humankind
         D  in his image
      C' humankind[17]
   B' created
A' He
```

14. Ibid.
15. Gen 1:27.
16. Wenham, *Genesis 1–15*, 28, understands the plural *elohim* to somehow include angels, while Waltke, *Genesis*, 58, opts for the more traditional "majestic" or "honorific" view.
17. According to Wenham, *Genesis*, 32, "Whereas v. 26 used the anarthrous אָדָם, here in v. 27 the definite הָאָדָם is used, and clearly mankind in general, 'male and female,' not an individual is meant."

But there is no *ex nihilo* phase of Marduk's creative engagement, and, interestingly, Marduk's "man" is a savage from day one. Notice too that although there is no explicit doctrine of an *imago dei*, it is difficult to miss the savagery of Marduk in creating the sky from the "monster's remains," and his expressed desire, "I will establish a savage . . . savage man I will create."

Drawing on a work of Gerhard Hasel, Wenham[18] cites "five areas in which Gen 1 appears to be attacking rival cosmologies [Babylonian, Canaanite, Egyptian]."[19]

Genesis Account	ANE Account
Sea creatures	Sea monsters as divine rivals
Separation of waters by divine fiat	Separation of waters by divine fight (BCE)
Sun and moon created	Sun and Moon worshipped
God provides food for humankind	Mankind provides food for the gods (Babylonian)
Creation through mandatory fiat	Creation through magical formula (Egyptian)

Wenham further points out that the ANE creation stories are usually poetic but the Genesis account is by and large prosaic.[20] What emerges from an examination of these early civilisations, whether we are looking at their cosmogonies or later historical records, is what may be called a pattern of polytheistic idolatry which forms the core of their worldviews. There is nothing in them that closely approximates the creational/covenantal monotheism that Wright speaks about relative to Israel's system of belief—a system that can be traced right throughout the nation's history. This belief system is almost identical with and squarely based upon the Torah. Torah, then, becomes for us the fundamental frame of reference against which to analyse the various cultures of the ANE, including even that of Israel itself.

But why Torah? Why not the celebrated code of Hammurabi that preceded it? In fact there are those who argue that the Mosaic code borrowed heavily from this Mesopotamian code, and indeed a comparison

---

18. Wenham, *Genesis 1–15*, 10.
19. BCE.
20. Kitchen, *Reliability*, 424.

between the two shows many striking parallels, perhaps most important of which is that both lay claim to divine revelation. The larger than life difference between the two for me, though, has to do with their stance toward what I have called above the pattern of polytheistic idolatry (PPI). The Mesopotamian code assumes the reality and even propriety of the PPI, while its Mosaic equivalent inveighs against it. The latter also claims inspiration from the only Deity that knows the end from the beginning (Is 46:9–10), while the former is received from the sun god Shamash.

As was said above, even Israel herself stands under the judgment of her own Torah, especially when it comes to PPI. Consider the following piece from the sixth century:

1. The word of the LORD came to me, saying,

2. "Go and proclaim in the hearing of Jerusalem, Thus says the LORD, I remember the devotion of your youth, your love as a bride, how you followed me in the wilderness, in a land not sown.

3. Israel was holy to the LORD, the first fruits of his harvest. All who ate of it became guilty; evil came upon them, says the LORD."

4. Hear the word of the LORD, O house of Jacob, and all the families of the house of Israel.

5. Thus says the LORD: "What wrong did your fathers find in me that they went far from me, and went after worthlessness, and became worthless?

6. They did not say, 'Where is the LORD who brought us up from the land of Egypt, who led us in the wilderness, in a land of deserts and pits, in a land of drought and deep darkness, in a land that none passes through, where no man dwells?'

7. And I brought you into a plentiful land to enjoy its fruits and its good things. But when you came in you defiled my land, and made my heritage an abomination.

8. The priests did not say, 'Where is the LORD?' Those who handle the law did not know me; the rulers transgressed against me; the prophets prophesied by Baal, and went after things that do not profit.

9. "Therefore I still contend with you, says the LORD, and with your children's children I will contend.

10. For cross to the coasts of Cyprus and see, or send to Kedar and examine with care; see if there has been such a thing.

11. Has a nation changed its gods, even though they are no gods? But my people have changed their glory for that which does not profit.

12. Be appalled, O heavens, at this, be shocked, be utterly desolate, says the LORD,

13. for my people have committed two evils: they have forsaken me, the fountain of living waters, and hewed out cisterns for themselves, broken cisterns, that can hold no water. (Jer 2, RSV).

Verse 8 is particularly sad. Both the priests and the prophets, those constituting the highest form of spiritual leadership in the land, had forsaken Torah. What naturally follows is the appalling condition described in verses 10–13. Notice how the PPI of the surrounding nations (v. 10) is taken for granted in verse 11a (especially the contrast between the singular "nation" and "gods"). This has been the story of the human race as far back as recorded history takes us —a dogged determination to stick to its gods. And, ironically, this was the story of Israel in the Promised Land, although divine righteousness was always available to her.[21] Over a hundred years after the ten northern tribes had been taken captive by the Assyrians for their repeated breach of Torah, Judah and Benjamin suffered a similar fate at the hands of the Babylonians. Seventy years after, the Chronicler sums up the whole situation in these solemn words:

14. All the leading priests and the people also were exceedingly unfaithful, following all the abominations of the nations; and they polluted the house of the LORD that he had consecrated in Jerusalem.

15. The LORD, the God of their ancestors, sent persistently to them by his messengers, because he had compassion on his people and on his dwelling place;

16. but they kept mocking the messengers of God, despising his words, and scoffing at his prophets, until the wrath of the LORD against his people became so great that there was no remedy.

17. Therefore he brought up against them the king of the Chaldeans, who killed their youths with the sword in the house of their sanctuary, and had no compassion on young man or young woman, the aged or the feeble; he gave them all into his *hand*.

---

21. Oliver, "Righteousness of God and Man."

This I submit is an important key to understanding ancient cultures or any culture for that matter (see note 42 below), that is, to inquire after their theological system to see whether or not it is consistent with the ideals of Torah.

Is it not ironic that one of the greatest gifts given to us (the ability to think) is employed so often to construct a theology of which our Maker disapproves? In an insightful piece, Zemek[22] points out that the biblical record "is a persistent witness to the fact that behaviour flows from a noetic wellspring . . . necessitat [ing] a redirection of man's faculties." While "repentance establishes an initial reorientation . . . the Scriptures stress that the key to a godly life-style is a sustained spiritual mindset. This is the focal point of Biblical ethics," and, we might add, the foundation of cultural sustainability. In fact, the ante-Sumerian civilisation fell prey to the evil machinations of the mind to the extent that a new world order was necessitated. In examining one of the Hebrew equivalents for "mind," Zemek further points out that humanity is proud in heart, stubborn in heart, hard in heart, perverse in heart, and evil in heart. He asserts that there is one OT passage that adequately summarizes man's heart condition and intellectual bankruptcy. That passage is Genesis 6. Zemek [23] writes, "Of all the passages in which *lev* [heart] is associated with *hashav* [think] . . . in a negative sense Gen 6:5 is especially critical." *Then the Lord saw that the wickedness of man was great on the earth, and that every intent of the thoughts of his heart was only evil continually.* "Every word in the predicate," declares Zemek, "is crucial." To him one can hardly find a more emphatic statement of the wickedness of the human mind. A professor of homiletics at Cornerstone University used to put it this way: The heart of the human problem is the problem of the human heart. That is the core of cultural and theological inertia.

All the cultures mentioned so far were quite advanced as far as the technology of the day was concerned. The Sumerians had their ziggurats, the Egyptians had their pyramids, the neo-Babylonian empire its hanging gardens, and even Israel her magnificent temple built by the wisest man in the ANE. But there was something common to all these civilisations; all were sadly committed to the PPI, and this, in the final analysis, spelled the death of their cultures. They carried within them the idolatrous seeds of their own destruction. For example, in Mark 13 our Lord's theological stu-

22. *Aiming the Mind*, 207.
23. Ibid.

dents were quite impressed with the magnificent architecture of Herod's temple, "the product of human creativity and ingenuity." But their Master was thinking on another level. "He evaluates the patterns of evil in this world, the false religious pretensions... the judgement that will fall." Mark 13, Carson believes, is reminiscent of Acts 17:16–34 where Paul is found in Athens. The Apostle's reaction to the city is striking. He too was not impressed with its spectacular cultural expressions, "[its] Architecture... history of sheer learning... literature... produced or... glory of her heritage." Here neither the Master's estimate of the holy city nor his student's evaluation of Athens is superficial.

> In both cases the evaluation looked at things from God's perspective. Those who are impressed by mighty buildings and spectacular human accomplishments could profitably think through the account of the tower of Babel (Gen. 11). Doubtless there were some then who were impressed by the edifice. But God, looking at the human heart and the reasons for the building, saw it as one more evidence of insufferable hubris. In much the same way, we too are called to understand and evaluate our culture from God's perspective. Because human beings are made in the image of God, *there is much we can do that is worthy and admirable* [emphasis added].... But it is possible to be far too impressed by wealth, power, architecture, fame, learning, physical prowess, and technology, with the result that we do not think through the moral and spiritual dimensions of the world around us. We may see the glory, and overlook the shame; we may detect human accomplishments, and neglect the under girding idolatry.[24]

The ancient gods, then, may be viewed as the cultural termites that gnawed away at the very fabric of the societies over which they were given control. Put another way, the presence of the Egyptian Apis (the bull god of the Nile), Heqet (the frog-headed goddess), Set (the desert god), Re (the sun god), Hathor (the cow head god), Isis (healing goddess), Osiris (fertility god), Nut (sky goddess; quite a fitting name for a god/ess in English transliteration), and Min (god of reproduction) meant that the one known as El Elyon eventually had to judge the superpower of the day, Egypt (Ex 12:12). So effective was this judgment that the ex-slaves soon sang:

> *Who is like you, O LORD, among the gods?*
> *Who is like you, majestic in holiness,*
> *awesome in splendour, doing wonders?* (Ex 15:11NRSV)

24. Carson, *For the Love of God*, 2/10.

Later Baal of Canaan, Aserah of Syria, Chemosh of Moab, Molech of Ammon, and Dagon of Philistia all bit the dust, so to speak, before the eyes of the very peoples whose cultures they corrupted. And when the people of God once again flirted with exotic gods, men like Isaiah would then exert all their literary skills to demonstrate the futility, not to mention the stupidity, of such fatal attraction.[25]

THE GRECO-ROMAN WORLD

For I am a debtor both to Greeks and to barbarians, both to the wise and to the foolish, hence my eagerness to proclaim the gospel to you also who are in Rome. (Rom 1:14, 15; NRSV).

Coming to the NT era we meet the equally decadent Greco-Roman culture.[26] On their return from captivity the Jews had apparently learnt their lesson that idolatry was inimical to their spiritual health. When we open the pages of our NT, we see Jewish sects like the Sadducees and Pharisees but no adherents of Baal or any of the gods mentioned above. Instead, the Jewish culture was now centred on Torah, perhaps like never before in its history. Ironically, Torah, as they knew it, was being replaced by a new Torah as a result of a genuine replacement theology that was taking place quite unobtrusively.

In fact certain well known cultural features were paving the way for this: better arterial lines of communication as well as a *Pax Romana* (Roman peace) to go along with it, all courtesy of imperial sponsorship. There was a common language throughout the empire that facilitated meaningful cultural exchange. This was made possible through the Macedonian conquest of centuries before. But things were quite different in the Greco-Roman world theologically. Religious pluralism was the order of the day. Old deities were being exchanged for new ones,[27] making the PPI even more complex (Acts 17:22–23). However, the cultural enrichment that this dimension of life was supposed to have brought did not materialise. Conversely, large-scale impoverishment—social and cultural—was the order of the day, and the greatest testimony of this is to be found in the profile of Romans 1,[28] written against the background of a city which had

25. Merrill, "Isaiah 40–55," 3–18; cf. Childs, *Isaiah*, 294–97.
26. Roetzel, *The World*.
27. Gaebelein, *EBC*, 1:494.
28. Chisholm, "*The Church*," 8–9.

> Become the greatest and finest . . . in the world. Her population neared a million. Ships from all over the known world fed and clothed and beautified her. Her corn came from Africa, Egypt, Sicily, and Sardinia; her pepper from as far as India . . . her tin from Britain and Northern Spain. Silk came from China. . . . Latin was everywhere the official language of government, and this became the basis of [some] modern languages. . . . Roman law was enforced over the whole Empire and remains the basis of European law today.[29]

One, then, is not surprised to find the first three chapters of the book of Romans couched in the form of a first-century courtroom drama in which the Heathen (chapter 1) and the Hebrews (chapter 2) are prosecuted in turn, with a summary statement following in chapter 3. Chapter 1:18–32, in particular, "shows that the moral chaos that has entered human society is rooted in human idolatry." Consequently, "Human unrighteousness most fundamentally consists in a refusal to worship God and a desire to worship that which is in the created order."[30] The solution to the chaos is delineated in the following chapters in terms of justification (deliverance from the guilt and penalty of sin; 3–5, 9–11) and sanctification (deliverance from the power and grip of sin; 6–8; 12–15).

It is this imperial world that was significantly impacted by the Messianic community eliciting the response in a particular setting, "These men who have caused trouble all over the world have now come here" (Acts 17:6b; NIV). Yet even this new and subversive community was itself vulnerable to the PPI which was wreaking havoc within the very culture(s) it was seeking to change (I Cor 10:13–14; 1 John 5:21).

Again, all of this is not to deny that there was real cultural progress in the Greco-Roman culture. Custance, for instance, sought to demonstrate how the three streams of humanity flowing from Shem, Ham and Japheth made significant socio-cultural contributions to the world. The chief legacy of the descendants of Japheth is, according to him, philosophy; that of Ham, technology; and the major contribution of Shem, spirituality.

"Where Japheth [Greco-Roman et al.] has applied his philosophical genius to the technological genius of Ham, *science* has emerged. Where Japheth has applied his philosophical genius to the spiritual insights of

---

29. Stanvrianos, *Readings*, 78.
30. Schreiner, *Romans*, 83, 88.

Shem [Jewish in particular], *theology* has emerged. Thus human potential reaches its climax when all three brothers (in their descendants) jointly make their contribution."[31]

But despite these positives, no significant grouping of Noah's posterity has managed to escape the vortex of the PPI. The Sumerians (Hamites), Hebrews (Shemites), as well as the entire Hellenistic and Roman empires were all caught up in a "world-wide web" (will of man, work of Satan, and *wrath* of God!) of theological and spiritual catastrophe that marked and marred any cultural achievement about which they might have boasted.

Is it any wonder then that in three crucial chapters in the book of Acts we see the divine initiative to salvage and purify the three streams of humanity through the Gospel: a representative Hamite in chapter 8, Shemite in chapter 9, and Japhetite in chapter 10? What this suggests is that cultural revitalisation is best preceded by new theological reflection, and all lasting solutions have theological roots as well. This is borne out clearly by even a panoramic sketch of history between the first and twenty-first centuries. Against the sordid background of a global PPI, history testifies to the fact of a divine intervention after divine intervention to stem the tide of cultural decay on all the continents and among those living in smaller territories.[32]

Generally speaking, "The rich theological tradition of Christianity has taken root in virtually every part of global culture, and given rise to some of the most creative and important reflection in the history of human thought. . . . Christianity has taken root in cultures, and set in motion a rich and dynamic process of interaction between ideas and values of the gospel, and those already present in the culture."[33]

Today countries like Uganda and Argentina[34] are experiencing a genuine work of God, although other indices of cultural progress are in reverse. We must never forget that concurrent with the brimful "iniquity of the Amorites" (Genesis 15) was a "land flowing with milk and honey" (Numbers 13, 14)—a land that was soon to experience judgment (Joshua).

31. Custance, *Three Sons of Noah*.

32. For example, after a revival in the British Isles one observer remarked, "The haulers are some of the very lowest. They have driven their horses by obscenity and kicks. Now they can hardly persuade the horses to start working, because there is no obscenity and no kicks."(Davies, *I Will Pour out My Sprit*, 191).

33. McGrath, *Christian Theology*, xvi.

34. Johnstone, *Operation World*, 96, 549.

THE MODERN WEST

Claiming to be wise, they became fools . . . they use their tongues to deceive.

> *Their feet are swift to shed blood; ruin and misery are in their paths, and the way of peace they have not known. There is no fear of God before their eyes* (Rom 1:22; 3:13–18 NRSV)

Now its time we take a broad look at our global village.[35] So far we have seen that the Torah stood in judgment on all expressions of ANE religion included that of Israelites. Can we use the same criterion to assess our own culture(s)? We have also insisted that a fundamental malady of all ancient cultures was their PPI. What about our modern world? Taking the last question, I think we will have to agree that the Western hemisphere of which we are a part is also grossly idolatrous. The former Archbishop of Canterbury[36] has identified three deities of the modern pantheon in wealth, therapy and education. In his Amsterdam 2000 homily he was careful to point out that all three of these preoccupations have their own legitimate place in life but have been elevated to a status in our lives where they cease to become our servants. For Newbigin,[37] the central deity of Western civilisation is science, for Ramachandra,[38] "Idols of Reason and Unreason." For Colson,[39] it is nature; and the list goes on. For instance, who can doubt that in the Caribbean[40] "Pleasure" (from carnival in the East to dancehall in West, with Hedonism in between) is the patron goddess of many? How can we gainsay the fact that she is attractive (Remember, "Men shall be lovers of pleasure more than lovers of God"; 2 Tim 3:1–4)? Like certain members of the Messianic community in the first century *we* need to hear the voice of the apostle on this matter (1 John 5:21), if we are to become a part of the solution; we are told that we are to help to preserve the culture of which we are

---

35. Klesius, "The State of the Planet," 103–115.
36. See chapter 5 below and Palmer, "Romans 5," 84–85.
37. Newbigin, *Foolishnesss*.
38. Says Ramachandra, *Gods that Fail*, 107, (citing Emile Brunner): "'For every civilization, for every period of history, it is true to say: show me what kinds of gods you have, and I will tell you what kind of humanity you possess.'"
39. Colson, *How Now Shall We Live?*
40. For the religious influence of African religion(s) on the region, see Warner-Lewis, *Central Africa in the Caribbean*, 138–198.

a part (Matt 5:13).⁴¹ This in one sense is en*light*ened self-interest (Matt 5:14). If our culture goes down, we go down with it.

But the perennial question still remains as to how best to be salt and light in a global village whose culture is characterised by neon lights and longevity, on the one hand, and on the other, darkness and decay. Since the middle of the previous century we have been encouraged to think through our own response to the challenges of culture using the typology of Nieburhr.⁴² Turning some of Nieburhr's indicatives into interrogatives, we ask ourselves: Should the Messianic community be opposed to culture? Must it accommodate culture? Or should it see itself as an intra-cultural agent of change?

Our answers to these questions must indeed be shaped by a holistic understanding of the church's mandate (Luke 24; Acts 1), filtered through the prism of the Sermon on the Mount (Mt 5–7),⁴³ and the Great Commandment (Mark 12).⁴⁴

CONCLUSION

Only clear theological thinking[45] squarely based on special revelation can best inform our action, because "Christian faith is a ferment of transformation. What it seeks first and foremost is the transformation of reality in accordance with God's ideal for life. Its aim is the removal of what is [cultural impoverishment] and its replacement by what ought to be [cultural enrichment]."[46]

41. Edmonds, "Ecological Crisis," 63–76.

42. Nieburhr, *Christianity and Culture*.

43. See, for example, Roper's ("Signs *of the Times*") creative application of the Lord's Prayer to the post-modern and North-Atlantic hegemonic challenge. The pluralism of the twenty-first century amply cultivates and encourages the modern PPI.

44. Contra Armstrong, *History of God*; Harris, *Letter to a Christian Nation*.

45. "So how should Christians press the battle for the mind? What practical solutions are there in combating the . . . plague of sin in heart, home, and humanity? [These] suggestions are offered. *Declare war on theological ignorance*. That is what Paul did in Athens when he proclaimed a real God in place of an unknown one (Acts 17:22–23). Nothing is to be gained by ignoring the theological dimensions of the creation conflict. In the final analysis the issue is theological, not scientific. Either God said what He meant and meant what He said, or the entire message of redemption is unreliable . . . *Declare war on theological indifference* [*indifference* is what's wrong with the world, but who care!"]. Too many believers are careless about the accuracy of their theology" (Gangel, "*Moral Entropy,* "168)—as well as the efficacy of their engagement (cf. Noelliste, "The Church and Human Emancipation;" Dick, *The Cross and the Machette*.).

46. Noelliste, "*Faith Transforming Context*," 97.

Part Two

Exegetical and Theological

3

Romans 4:1–25: Paul on Justification[1]

The greatest happiness of the thinking man is to have fathomed what can be fathomed, and quietly to reverence what is unfathomable

—JOHANN GOETHE

INTRODUCTION

THE DETAILS OF THE founding of the Roman Church are shrouded in mystery. Because the congregation seems to have been predominately Gentile in composition, the apostle Paul maintained a healthy pastoral interest in it.[2] So in A.D. 56 the apostle dispatches his epistle to the Christians in Rome, probably the most important letter he has ever penned, judging from its impact throughout the history of the Christian era.[3]

Paul had wanted on a number of occasions to visit Rome both for purposes of evangelization (1:13) and edification (1:11). But his precise purpose of writing is still debated today. The traditional view maintains that the apostle used the occasion, after over twenty years of ministry, to set forth a treatise of his theological position. Both Guthrie and Harrison find this view unsatisfactory for the following reasons: (1) there are at least two doctrines that are conspicuous by their absence, *ecclesiology* and *eschatology*.[4] Guthrie adds the doctrine of cosmic reconciliation, and rightly observes that chapters 9–11 are inexplicable if Paul were

---

1. See Excursus below for James' perspective. For a sophisticated re-reading of the chapter, see Campbell, *The Deliverance of God*, 746–65, who strongly believes that the "standard 'Lutheran' reading of Paul's justification texts is the interpretive equivalent of a computer virus" (6).

2. Guthrie, *New Testament Introduction*, 393–96.

3. Robinson, *Wrestling with Romans*, viii.

4. Harrison, *Introduction*, 305.

merely stating his understanding of Christian doctrines.[5] Kümmel gives a summary critique of the traditional proposal when he writes, "The old view that Romans is a systematic doctrinal presentation of Christian beliefs . . . is untenable, for important elements of Paul's teaching, such as Christology and eschatology do not receive full attention. . . ."[6] The other purposes listed by Guthrie[7] are the following: (1) Paul wrote to conciliate Jewish and Gentile factions, (2) the apostle wrote to provide a fitting summary of his missionary experience up to that point, and (3) he wrote to meet the immediate needs of the Christians at Rome. While all of these proposals seem to have some element of truth, none has commanded the respect of New Testament exegetes today.

In an article on the Purpose of Romans, Russell[8] evaluates the proposals of four prominent exegetes, namely, Barrett, Cranfield, Käsemann, and Murray. Russell points out that all four commentators reject the traditional proposal, while demonstrating a logical consistency in the way they correlate chapters 9–11 with the rest of the book. Although Russell feels that Western scholarship represented by the four scholars mentioned above is coherent in its purpose statement of Romans, he nevertheless questions its accuracy on contextual grounds. The reason for this is "that a purpose statement built solely on 'justification by faith' may be suspect because of western cultural biases. The epistle [then] should be evaluated from a perspective more resembling Paul's viewpoint." Russell writes that in a "letter confronting their Jewish/Gentile relationships, Paul challenged the Roman churches to participate fully in God's present harvest of all peoples by showing that their ethnocentrism opposed God's plan of justifying people by faith, of giving them new life in the Spirit, and of mercifully placing them in His redemptive plan."

Two of the strengths of Russell's proposal are (1) it includes the important theme of justification by faith, without awkwardly subsuming chapters 9–11 under the same rubric; and (2) it provides a more coherent framework that does justice to the Jew/Gentile tension intimated in the book in general and chapters 1–3, 9–11, 14–15 in particular. It also, of course, seeks to explicate the opening and closing chapters (note their missionary flavor) with the rest of the epistle.

5. Guthrie, *New Testament Introduction*, 398.
6. Kümmel, *Introduction*, 221.
7. Guthrie, *New Testament*, 398–400.
8. Russell, "Alternative," 174–184.

After greeting the Christians at Rome, the Apostle Paul announces his intention to carry out his missionary mandate in the imperial capital (1:1–15). He then declares the central motif of his message in verses 16 and 17. From 1:18 to 3:20 the apostle demonstrates the need and relevance of God's righteousness among Heathen and Hebrews alike, with a summary statement in 3:23 which "embraces all humanity."[9]

Paul will later seek to impress upon the minds of his readers the need to be involved in helping to spread the Gospel of righteousness beyond their borders.[10] But for the time being the writer invokes a powerful illustration from the Scriptures which, rightly understood, serves to establish the continuity between the Old and the New covenants and underscores his orthodox position in regard to justification.[11] This justification is part and parcel of the believer's liberation from evil powers that is effected "by the twofold work of Christ . . . his life of faithful perfection, which is imputed to the Christian, and his death and resurrection, which remove the penalty of eternal separation from God."[12] The overall structure of Romans may be set out as follows:[13]

A 1–5 *Gospel for Unbelievers: Liberation from Sins' Penalty*
       (Global Dimension)

    B 6–8 *Gospel for Saints: Liberation from Sin's Power & Presence*
           (Doctrinal Section)

A 9–11 *Gospel for Sinners: Liberation from Sins' Penalty*
        (National Dimension)

    B 12–16 *Gospel for Believers: Liberation from Sin's Power &*
            Presence (Practical Section)

---

9. Carson, "Cross," 346; cf. Gathercole, "Justified," 147–84.

10. Chae, *Paul the Apostle*.

11. Williams, "Justification", 649–667; cf. Donaldson, "Jewish Christianity," 27–54, contra Gaston, "Paul," 48–71.

12. Gruenler, "Theology," 691.

13. Adapted from Palmer, *Messianic 'I'*, 134. Some close patterns on the micro-level to the one we are proposing appear in Pss 27:14; 118:15–16 (ABA); Prov 17:25; Isa 30:31; Amos 1:3; Nahum 3:17; Ps 86:12; Cant 1:11–all ABÁ (Watson, *Hebrew Poetry*, 204). A similar (macro) pattern is to be found in 1 Cor (Palmer, *Gifts*, 32–33). For cautions on neat summaries like the above, see Caird, *Theology*, 119–26, and especially McGrath, *Justification*, 376–378. Broadly speaking, the 'A' and 'B' sections deal with Justification (righteousness by *decree*) and Sanctification (righteousness by *degree*) respectively; so Jong, *Righteousness*, 17–18, is incorrect in asserting that "Christianity today has degraded itself into a worldly religion due to the Doctrine of Justification and Doctrine of Sanctification."

DISCOVERY OF ABRAHAM WITH REGARD TO RIGHTEOUSNESS (4:1-5)

The passage begins with two text-critical problems; the first centers around the infinitive (ὑρηκέναι, *hurēkenai*; v. 1a) variously translated as "gained" (NRSV), "discovered" (NIV) and "found" (AV), and its position in the sentence. The influential Vaticanus manuscript (B) does not have this term and its different locations in several other manuscripts may seem to some to be a case of interpolation. As Metzger[14] points out, it is easy to argue that the shorter reading of Vaticanus be accepted since scribes tended to add to the text at times. However, the witnesses to ὑρηκέναι are impressive with respect to their age and geographical spread. It is also intrinsically probable to have been present in the original, because its absence would make an awkward ellipsis at this point.

The second problem has to do with whether the reading "forefather" (NIV) is superior to "father" (AV).[15] Although Greenlee[16] seems to question Westcott and Hort[17] for having included "forefather" in their critical text, I agree with Cranfield[18] that it should be retained on the grounds that it is the more difficult reading.

The next challenge is syntactical in nature. It concerns whether the prepositional phrase, "according to the flesh" (NRSV; κατὰ σάρκα, *kata sarka*) should be construed adjectivally or adverbially. In other words, does the phrase govern "ancestor" (NRSV) or the infinitive ὑρηκέναι? It does seem that the former construction is more in keeping with Pauline usage, (cf. Rom 1:3; 9:3, 5; 1 Cor 10:18; Eph 6:5 and Col 3:22).[19] The opening verse, then, inquires of the discovery of Abraham with reference to the issue of righteousness. The question is to be understood against the background of Jewish opinion which believed that the merits of this forefather commended him entirely before God.[20]

---

14. Metzger, *Commentary*, 450.

15. I.e., προπάτορα (a NT hapax) or πατέρα Black, *Romans*, 75, feels that perhaps the text at this point (v.1) is hopelessly corrupt. Kasemann, *Romans*, 106, however, expresses confidence that the "dominant reading is the only possible one...." What needs to be borne in mind is that "It is Abraham, not the issue of being a forefather, that is pursued in the following verses" (Porter, *Aspect*, 278).

16. Greenlee, *Introduction*, 81.

17. WH, *Greek New Testament*, in loc.

18. Cranfield, *Romans*, 226; also *GNT*.

19. However, Hays, *Echoes*, 54, rejects this construal, and is followed by Wright, *Romans*, 489; see also Wright's *Justification*, 177-248.

20. *Pace* Lieber, *Etz Hayim*, 83. "The Rabbis . . . maintained that long before the law was promulgated from Sinai, Abraham already had a thorough knowledge of it

The apostle follows up the argument in verse 2 by reasoning something like this: "Let us for argument sake assume that Abraham was justified by works, wouldn't he have had grounds on which to glory? Yes, but certainly not before God!"[21] A keyword in this verse is the term "boast" (καύχημα, *kauchēma*).[22] It is not only important in the development of Paul's argument, it also "exemplifies both literary and emotional 'color.'"[23] Paul already uses a cognate term (καύχησις, *kauchēsis*) to demonstrate that the principle of faith precludes human boasting (Rom 3:27). Here he links the word to probably the greatest religious role model before the Christian era. "But," a Jew might ask, "can you prove that Abraham was not indeed justified by works?' "Well, let us turn to the Scriptures," says the apostle.[24]

To support his claims, Paul invokes Genesis 15:6, which declares that it was Abraham's faith that brought him a right standing before God. At this point "Paul's versatility as a writer is seen.... He can move with agility from the employment of Hellenistic debating style . . . to a careful piece of exegesis based on the Old Testament. His exegesis follows the rabbinic principle of *gezerah sawah* . . . . The principle . . . states that when the same word or phrase is found in two passages of the Old Testament, one can be used to illumine the other. This is Paul's key to the Christian use of Genesis 15:6 adopted in Romans 4."[25]

---

and obeyed it in all its details" (Hendrickson, *Romans*, 154). He definitely had what we might call the 'Mesographic' variety (e.g., Rom 2:14–15; cf. Carson, *Love of God*, 4/14: "Much of the law of God is written on human conscience [?], so that societies without Scripture erect moral structures which, however different from the values of Scripture, overlap with Scripture in important and revealing ways."); but to say that Abraham had the Mosaic law is anachronistic.

21. The first class condition (v. 2a) assumes the case for sake of argument (Burton, *Syntax*, 262). In this connection, Young *New Testament Greek*, 29–49, feels that the traditional classification of conditional clauses short changes the exegetical process by narrowing the focus on surface features. Therefore, recourse must be taken to the speaker's/writer intent, morphology, as well as the situational and linguistic context in order to get a better grasp of the meaning. It is this consideration that has guided my paraphrase.

22. The apostle Paul almost has a monopoly on the use of this word-group (Bultmann, "καύχημα," 645–654).

23. Liefeld , *Exposition*, 87.

24. At this juncture (v. 3) the Old Testament scripture is personified. "Indeed, so habitual was the identification of the Divine Author with the words of Scripture that occasionally personality is attributed to the passage itself" (Metzger, "Formulas," 306).

25. Martin, *Approaches*, 247.

It would seem that the apostle not only attempts to substantiate his point from Genesis 15:6 but also to correct a misunderstanding of the verse based in part on the following: "Was not Abraham found faithful when tested, and it was reckoned to him as righteousness?" (1 Macc 2:52; NRSV).[26]

Having turned to Old Testament revelation for support of his claims that faith, not works, is the basis on which a person is justified, the apostle Paul now draws on the experience of daily life (v. 4). The analogy states that which was common knowledge in the first century: remuneration is commensurate with output ("Now when a man works, his wages are not credited to him as a gift, but as an obligation"—NIV). There is nothing gratuitous here.

Two word-pairs are set in stark contrast; each pair marking out a fundamental approach to God. Taking verses 3 and 4 together, the couplets are summed up as follows:[27]

ἐργαζομένῳ (works)   ἐπίστευσεν (had faith)

ὀφείλημα (obligation)   χάριν (grace-gift)

"The contrast between ['grace-gift'] and as ['obligation'] is instructive. 'Works' and ['obligation'] belong together as correlatives; 'faith' and 'grace' similarly correspond, and, and it is to this pair that ['credited'] belongs."[28]

In contrast, then, to the natural affairs of verse 4,[29] verse 5 declares the heart of the gospel proclamation. In order to grasp fully the import of this declaration, four key terms need to be looked at.

The first key word to be examined is the verb "believe." In its active form Paul used it twice before: in chapters 1:16 and 3:22. Like these occurrences, it is also employed in a soteriological sense and setting in chapter 4. Its meaning in 4:3, 5 is wholehearted trust and confidence.[30] It is the only kind of faith that brings justification.[31] This happens when

---

26. Αβρααμ οὐχὶ ἐν πειρασμῷ εὑρέθη πιστός καὶ ἐλογίσθη αὐτῷ εἰς δικαιοσύνην; (Rahlfs).

27. Verse 3 reads in the NIV: "What does the Scripture say?" Abraham believed God, and it as credited to him as righteousness."

28. Barrett, *Romans*, 88.

29. *DBI*, 738.

30. BAG, 666–667.

31. Sproul, "Works or Faith?" 187, sets out the Roman and Reformation positions

the believer (πιστεύοντι, *pisteuonti*) comes face to face with the Justifier (τὸν Δικαιοῦντα, *ton dikaiounta*: most likely a New Testament metonym for God).[32]

This brings us to another key term of verse 5: righteousness (δικαιοσύνη, *dikaiosunē*). Δικαιοῦντα (*dikaiounta*, Justifier) and δικαιοσύνη are cognate terms and both relate to the concept of justification (*"righteoustification"*?). It is the verb form ("was justified," ἐδικαιώθη, *edikaiōthē*) that occurs in verse 2 and elsewhere, which Bible students find problematic. The difficulty does not seem to be merely with the lexical idea which has to do with righteousness but with the theological import of the term. The question is, Should we view justification as forensic (i.e., imputed righteousness) or intrinsic (imparted righteousness)?[33]

While exegetes like Sandy and Headlam[34] have serious reservations about the concept of forensic righteousness in Romans, the idea seems to fit Paul's intention better than any other. First, because the suffix of the verb (δικαιόω/*dikaioo*) appears to carry the declarative/causative idea,[35] and second, the Septuagint, which Paul had already quoted, seems to have influenced the Apostle along forensic lines.[36] So to be justified is to be "pronounced and treated as righteous."[37]

The meaning of "counted" (KJV) or "credited" (NET) in verse 5 also bears out the forensic view of justification. Bauer cites Psalm 105:31 and 1 Macc 5:52 to support the meaning "credited" here.[38] Faith is credited or put to the "account" of the believing sinner.

This brings us to the other key-term in the verse: "ungodly" (ἀσεβῆ/*asebē*). As an adjective it is found one other time in Romans where we

---

respectively: Faith + Works = Justification; Faith = Justification + Works.

32. Others include "The Name . . . The Glory" (McCasland, "Metonyms," 99–114).

33. Karl Barth, according to Klooster, "Soteriology," 13, thought of justification in a universalistic and objective sense (cf. Turner, *Christian Words*, 240). All men, therefore, are automatically righteous because of predestination and redemption. With regard to the forensic/intrinsic question, Longenecker, "Faith," 203–212, feels that the disjunction is a false one. LN, *Lexicon*, 1:452, reject the forensic construct.

34. *Romans*, 36.

35. Black, *Romans*, 60, 69.

36. Abbott-Smith, *Greek Lexicon*, 116.

37. BAG, 196; ". . . it must be clearly recognized," says Bultmann, *Theology*, 273, "that there is complete agreement between . . . [the Jewish and Pauline conception] as to the formal meaning of DIKAIOSYNE: *It is a forensic-eschatological term.* The forensic meaning of 'righteous' . . . is already a clear implication of Rom. 2:13 . . . ." (italics original).

38. BAG, 477.

are informed that Christ died for the "ungodly" (5:6).[39] The term is a strong one denoting gross impiety; it is a deep-seated lack of reverence for God. The ungodly person is "not merely irreligious, but acting in contravention of God's demands."[40] Although God's wrath is unleashed against every form of impiety (1:18), in the eschaton God is going to remove it altogether (11:26). It is by sheer grace that God justifies such a person, based, of course, on the loving release of his Son (5:6). The context demands that even the Patriarch Abraham falls under the category of the "ungodly;"[41] after all, how else could he have been an example of justification, *sola fide*?

DELIGHT OF DAVID IN RESPECT OF REMISSION 4:6–8

A new witness to the orthodox teaching of justification is now called to the stand.[42] The apostle will now show that the testimony of David is in harmony with that of the patriarch Abraham, thus proving his case from the Law and the Prophets (cf. 3:21). The phrase "Even as David" (KJV; καθάπερ καὶ Δαυὶδ, *kathaper kai david*) shows the closest possible connection between verses 5 and 6, and is followed by the key referents discussed above. The parallel is as follows:

Verse 5	Verse 6
λογίζεται (*logizetai*, credited)	λογίζεται
τὸν Δικαιοῦντα (*ton dikaiounta*, the Justifier)	ὁ θεός (*ho theos*, God)
πιστεύοντι (*pisteuonti*, believing)	χωρὶς ἔργων (*chōris ergōn*, without works)
δικαιοσύνην (*dikaiosunē*)	δικαιοσύνην (righteousness)
ἀσεβῆ (*asebēe*, ungodly)	ἀνθρώπου (*anthrōpou*, human)

---

39. cf. Thompson, *Roots*, 16.

40. Vine, *Romans*, 63.

41. Cranfield, *Romans*, 232; "'The ungodly' is so called after he is justified. The epithet is still used by way of *Amplificatio*" (Bullinger, *Figures*, 690; cf. Jewett, *Romans*, 1015).

42. Denney, *Romans*, 616.

43. Cf. Martin Luther's "We are not Christian because we do good works; we do good works because we are Christian" (cited in Metzger, *Reminiscences*, 230).

The correspondence seems to underscore Paul's point of righteousness being credited to a person who believes in God (especially by the strong contrast in the third column above). The stem for "trusts/faith" (NIV) is used twice in verse 5 (πίστις/πιστεύοντι/*pistis, pisteuonti*) and the idea it conveys is further defined by "without works" (χωρὶς ἔργων). A quotation now follows in which we have an exact reproduction of the Psalm 32:1–2 (LXX).

Psalm 32 is traditionally understood to be one of seven penitential poems. However, it should be observed that there are strong elements of thanksgiving and wisdom expression found in the song. It has also been suggested that the life-setting "is to be found in the Temple worship ... during which the Psalmist offered his song of thanks in the presence of his fellow-worshippers."[44] The stanza which pertains to our discussion describes the happy estate of the person forgiven. But what has forgiveness to do with justification, and how do these verses from Psalm 32 serve Paul's purpose at this point?

In connection with the quotation from Genesis 15:6, it has already been pointed out that the Apostle is in all likelihood employing a Rabbinic form of exegesis to substantiate his claim (see verse 3 above). The catchword of the two passages is λογίζεται (*logizetai*).[45] On the one hand righteousness is credited (v. 3=Gen 15:6), and on the other sin is not taken into account (v. 8=Ps 31:2 LXX). Since Paul's use of the two Old Testament passages is not just formal but substantial, as Cranfield[46] observes, may be the Apostle is highlighting two dimensions of justification: (1) the receiving of righteousness (positive side) and (2) the removal of retribution (negative side).[47]

---

44. Anderson, *Psalms*, 254.

45. Writes Jeremias (cited in Longenecker and Tenney, *New Dmensions*, 259): "In Romans 4:1–12 we find, indeed, a twofold analogical deduction achieved with the help of λογίζεται. Next, at Ro. 4:3 the Scripture Gn. 15:6 is cited. The conclusion drawn from ἐλογίσθη finds its confirmation from Scripture through Ps. 32:2f."

46. Cranfield, *Romans*, 233.

47. Verse 8 seems to summarize the concept of this removal (i.e., forgiveness), while gathering up the parallel lines of the previous couplets. The plural terms for evil within the couplets may serve to emphasize both the gravity of sin and the graciousness of the pardon that removes it. For a comparison of the LXX and Massoretic texts at this point, see Archer and Chirichigno, *Quotations*, 66–67; cf. Seifrid, "Romans" in Beale and Carson, *Commentary*, 607–9). An emphasis in verse 8 is the double negative οὐ μὴ.

DEPENDENCE OF ABRAHAM WITH REFERENCE TO THE RITE (CIRCUMCISION) 4:9-12

Having demonstrated his case from Scripture that justification is by faith alone, Paul now inquires about the scope of this particular blessing (μακάριος, *makarios*). Is it for Jews exclusively or Gentiles as well? According to Alford, the particles underlying "or also" (NIV; GK η‡ καί) are already designed to prejudice the reader in favor of the latter group.[48] It is therefore surprising that Barrett seeks to limit μακάριος to "the blessing of forgiveness of which David speaks."[49] If there is a positive and negative side to the "blessing" (i.e., justification), then the limitation, though contextually and linguistically appealing, is unnecessary. In support of this contention is the resumption of the Abraham motif in the latter half of verse 9, and to a lesser extent, the generic sense of "man" (ἀνήρ/*anēr*, "one" in NSRV) in verse 8.[50] The blessing is both for Jews and Gentiles, whether male or female.

Again the patriarch Abraham is called upon to confirm another case just slightly different from the first. "Think back for a moment," urges the Apostle, "was he credited with the blessing while in a state of circumcision or otherwise?[51] Let me hasten to tell you: most assuredly, while still uncircumcised." (v. 10). When Abraham did receive the rite, Paul continues to argue, it became a sign or outward confirmation of the righteousness he already "possessed."[52] The purpose or result (telic/ecbatic) clause in verse 11 serves to underscore God's providential undertaking in the matter: God not only confirmed his earlier blessing on the patriarch through circumcision, but also made him the spiritual progenitor of both reliant heathens and repentant Hebrews (vv. 11, 12, 15). The phrase "who . . . walk in the footsteps" (στοιχοῦσιν τοῖς ἴχνεσιν, *stoichousin tois ichnesin*)18 which rounds out the description of Gentiles (v. 12), seems to be used by Paul in an emphatic sense both here and elsewhere (Gal 5:25; 6:16; Phil 3:16).[53]

---

48. Alford, *Greek New Testament*, 349.

49. Barrett, *Romans*, 96.

50. Beekman and Callow, *Translating the Word*, 110.

51. The participial phrase (ἐν περιτομῇ ὄντι η‡ ἐν ἀκροβυστίᾳ;) is temporal (*DM*, 226-227).

52. Moule, *Idiom*, 38.

53. This interpretation follows Chae, *Paul*, 192-5, in seeing two different racial groupings in v. 12. A number of exegetes see only one: Jews. Admittedly, the verse is quite difficult.

DESCRIPTION OF ABRAHAM IN REFERENCE TO THE REGULATION (CANON) 4:13–17

Abraham's right standing before God was not obtained by good works. Neither was it acquired through the rite of circumcision. Surely then the law does not enter the picture (v. 15). But why does Paul introduce the law at this point?

> For Judaism—or at least for a vociferous and growing legalistic element within late Judaism and Tannaitic rabbinic Judaism— trust in God and obedience to the law went hand in hand in the attainment of righteousness. And although Abraham lived before the actual giving of the Mosaic Law, he anticipated the keeping of that fuller expression of God's Torah. . . . Lev. Rab. 2:10 (on Lev 1:12), therefore, argues that "Abraham fulfilled . . . the whole Torah."[54]

Paul refutes this kind of thinking by pointing out that the promise to the patriarch was not associated with Law (νόμος, *nomos*).[55] The same thing also applies to Abraham's descendants (presumably his believing 'seed"; v. 13). What is the "promise" mentioned in verse 13? In Genesis Abraham is promised: posterity (12:2), prosperity (12:3) and property (15:7).

Bruce points out that when the promise is delimited in geographical terms, Egypt and the Euphrates form the southern and northern extremities, respectively.[56] However, in the New Testament this aspect of the promise should only be understood in a spiritual sense. In his attempt to explain the clause bearing the term "world," Hendrickson essentially makes the same point: "[T]he conclusion drawn by many, namely, that today . . . the entire land of Canaan, in its widest dimensions really belong to Jews, is unwarranted."[57] But why is such a view unwarranted? Is it not better to maintain the literal understanding of the promise without in any way diminishing its spiritual dimensions?20 And if this is done, how is the expanded territorial element of the promise[58] to be understood? The key seems to lie in the awkward phrase "or in

54. Longenecker, "Faith of Abraham," 205.
55. νόμος is a definite reference to the Mosaic code.
56. Bruce, *Romans*, 111.
57. Hendrickson, *Romans*, 154–55.
58. "The theme of ἐπαγγελία [promise] has central theological significance for Paul and the New Testament writings" (Käsemann, *Romans*, 118). Kaiser (*Old Testament Theology*, 255 and passim; cf. his *Promise-Plan*), draws out this significance for OT the-

his seed." It is possible that what we have here—quite apart from its more patent meaning, "descendants"—is a reference to the Messiah by way of corporate solidarity.[59] It is through Abraham's seed, the Messiah, that the promise takes on cosmic dimensions.[60]

Earlier in the chapter the indispensability of faith was established. Now in verse 1 the Apostle declares that God's redemptive scheme would prove self-contradictory if the "Torah-ites" (so Black) were the exclusive beneficiaries of God's gifts. In such a case, faith becomes void of its spiritual significance and the promise is nullified.[61] Verse 15 gives a rationale for the impossibility of the law being a medium of God's blessing in this connection. The law simply is not a promoter of the divine promises but instead produces divine punishment.

Paul now reveals the reason why faith is so important in God's redemptive scheme (v.16):[62] Faith is the only dynamic on humanity's part which highlights the grace of God. It also "guarantees" the fulfillment of the promise to both the Jewish and Gentile elements of Abraham's seed, for "Abraham had two seeds: one 'of the law' and the other 'of the faith'. The promise . . . is valid for both."[63] The fact that Abraham is the spiritual progenitor of Hebrew and Heathen alike is fully supported by the Old Testament, as the Apostle demonstrates by his citation of Genesis 17:5 (LXX) in verse 17.

If verses 3–8 highlight faith without works; 9–12, faith apart from circumcision; 13–16; faith apart from Law,[64] then verses 17–21 focus attention on the true character of the faith which establishes and maintains a right relationship with God. The syntax of verse 17 is difficult;[65] the

---

ology, as well as points out the literal and spiritual aspects of the promise. The articular infinitive (v. 13) helps to define the promise (Burton, *Syntax*, 156). "The promise . . . that he should be heir" should be taken epexegetically (BDF, 206). Notice that even within intertestamental Judaism the global scope of the promise seems to have been recognized: ἀπὸ θαλάσσης ἕως θαλάσσης καὶ ἀπὸ ποταμοῦ ἕως ἄκρου τῆς γῆς/from sea to sea, even from the River [?] to the end of the earth (Sir 44:21).

59. The concept of corporate personality is explained by Ellis, "How the New Uses the Old," 212–14; cf. Seifrid, "Romans," 625.

60. Cf. Black, *Romans*, 78.

61. BAG, 418.

62. Cf. Thomas, *Case*, 296–314.

63. Earle, *Word Meanings*, 157.

64. Moo, *Epistle*, 273; Osborne, *Romans*, 113.

65. For the nature of the difficulty and possible solutions, see e.g., Schreiner,

sense is perhaps clarified by the following rendition: "As it is written, 'I have made you the father of many nations'—in the presence of the God in whom he believed, who gives life to the dead and calls into existence the things that do not exist" (NRSV). The latter part of the verse brings into sharp focus the object of the patriarch's faith—the wonder working character of the God of the universe whose role in creation and re-creation is a source of encouragement to people of faith like Abraham.

Verse 18–22 turn the spotlight once again on father Abraham by defining more closely the nature of this faith and the creative/redemptive genius of the One who makes the dead come alive and creates something out of nothing. Verse 18a is memorable: "Against all hope, Abraham[66] in hope believed" (NIV; "Ὃς παρ' ἐλπίδα ἐπ' ἐλπίδι ἐπίστευσεν, *hos par elpida ep elpidi episteusin*). The result[67] of Abraham's confidence in God (v. 18b) is far-reaching: many now call him faithful father, and a great promise is fulfilled. The main verb of verse 18 ("believed") is given further explanation in verses 19–21, one of Paul's long sentences in Greek. The clause may be graphically displayed in translation thus:

> *without waning in his confidence*
> *He contemplated the reality that his body was as good as dead*
> *since he was approximately a century old and that*
> *Sarah's womb was barren*[68]
>
> *Yet he did not succumb to unbelief regarding God's promise,*
> *but [he] was strengthened in his conviction*
>   *giving glory to God*[69]
>
> *being fully convinced that God has ability*
> *to carry out his promise.*[70]

Romans, 239.

66. A surrogate for the relative pronoun; the NIV 'all' appears to be an over translation.

67. Moo, *Epistle*, 288, mentions a couple of other options for the infinitival clause: 1) it denotes the content of Abraham's faith, and 2) it specifies purpose.

68. Translation of νέκρωσιν as "barren" appears to be a word-play along with νενεκρωμένον, rendered "impotent" by Zerwick, *Philologica*, 343.

69. The phrase "is highly reminiscent of 1:20, and may form its positive counterpart—Abraham . . . the 'Gentile,' perceived God's eternal power and deity, and gave thanks!'" (Harrisville, *Romans*, 71).

70. My rendition; *"giving"* and *"being fully convinced"* help to define the main verb *"was strengthened"* (Robertson, *Grammer*, 86; cf. Porter, *Aspect*, 380). ἐνεδυναμώθη (*was strengthened*) gives us the positive side of the patriarch's faith, whereas the phrases καὶ

According to the above schema, "since he was approximately a century old" (ἑκατονταέτης που ὑπάρχων, *hekatontaetēs pou huparchōn*) modifies the implied subject-pronoun "he" of the verb "contemplated" (κατενόησεν, *katenoēsen*). Abraham, then, sized up the situation by confidently fixing attention ("was strengthened in his conviction"/ ἐνεδυναμώθη τῇ πίστει, *enedunamōthē tē pistei*) on the divine promise (εἰς δὲ τὴν ἐπαγγελίαν τοῦ θεοῦ, *eis de tēn epaggelian tou theou*/ in respect of the promise of God), and promise Maker (δοὺς δόξαν τῷ θεῷ/ *dous doxan tō theō*, giving glory to God). This is the qualitative faith that is associated with quality righteousness (v. 22).[71]

Paul is now ready to apply these pivotal moments from the Abraham cycle to the progeny of the patriarch: "The words 'it was credited to him' were written not for him alone, but also for us, to whom God will credit righteousness" (vv. 23–224a: NIV). The citation of Genesis 15:6,[72] the main text highlighted (cf. vv. 3, 9), is an example of both intratextual (the context of Romans) as well as intertextual (the biblical context) literary artistry[73] on the part of the apostle. In fact, the intertextuality[74] of the chapter is rich, and is both overt and covert.[75]

The other Genesis text cited by Paul (v. 17) is from the Septuagint's version of 17:5. Here the writer's application is in embryonic form and skillfully chosen, since he "passes over the fact that Abraham was convulsed in laughter at the thought that he might beget a son."[76] In commenting on verse 18, Cranfield quotes a stanza from one of Charles Wesley's pieces:

μὴ ἀσθενήσας τῇ πίστει (*Without waning in his confidence* (v. 19) and οὐ διεκρίθη τῇ ἀπιστία (*Yet he did not succumb to unbelief* v. 20) point to the other side of the coin, as well as bring into sharper focus the nature of the faith that pleases God (cf. Heb 11:6).

71. Verse 22 (NET): "So indeed [Διὸ καὶ] it was credited to Abraham as righteousness." On the significance of the items in square bracket, see BDAG, 250.

72. For a listing and classification of the major OT citations in Romans, see Longenecker, *Exegesis*, 92–93.

73. The creative treatment of Scripture here seems to be missed by Dodd, *Epistle*, 70.

74. This may be defined "as the study of all features that bring a given text into an open or hidden relationship to other texts" (Heim, *Perfect King*, 231).

75. Hays, *Echoes*, 34, 166.

76. Fitzmyer, *Romans*, 387.

In hope, against all human hope,
Self-desperate, I believe . . .
Faith, mighty faith, the promise sees,
And looks to that alone;
Laughs at impossibilities,
And cries: It shall be done.[77]

The lines, Cranfield believes, summarize well the faith of the patriarch at the high point of his sojourn, except in one area: the laughter. In fact, both Abraham (Gen 17:17 and Sarah (Gen 18:12) appear to have gained some measure of comic relief[78] from the promise, and not at their own expense. So both incidents are, to use Fitzmyer's language, "passed over" in what may be called paschal silence. This literary phenomenon is not limited to Paul. We see it, for example, in 2 Chronicles where another man (David) to whom righteousness is credited eulogized, not because he was perfect but because he was justified (cf. Rom 4: 6–8).[79]

---

77. Cranfield, *Romans*, 93–94.

78. Walton, *Genesis*, 451, speaks of the patriarchs "bemused incredulity about Sarah's bearing a son . . ." Is it then providentially significant that 'syllables of laughter' were added to their name (*ha* [Gen 17:5], *ah* Gen 17:15])? The 'syllables' are a transliteration of the MT; the spoken consonantal text would very likely give corresponding sounds, which may or may not carry the same overtone in the occidental world. There is, however, no doubt about the meaning of 'Isaac' (cf. Gen 21:1–6). For explorations into this general area, see Ellington, *Wit and Humour* and the following note.

79. Here we see "that historical memory is highly selective and interpretive. The popular tradition of Israel, conveniently forgetting the barbarity and disreputable incidents of David's reign, focused upon those elements which appealed to the political and religious aspirations of each succeeding age" (Caird, *NT Theology*, 307). According to Watty, "Significance," 211, the NT "writer [who identified Jesus as playing the paschal role; John 1:29] makes use of anonymity as response to a pastoral situation which seems to have necessitated a corrective to a developing Petrine tradition. 'Peter' stands for a negative strain in the gospel. The name focuses and highlights precisely what the evangelist wishes to correct. He goes out of his way to present a 'Peter of history' with warts and all, because, presumably, the name bestowed by Jesus was assuming an inordinate importance. Between the 'Peters' and the 'not Peters' an invidious distinction was being encouraged which augured ill. Names given by Jesus were becoming a stumbling-block, for 'Peter' identified not merely a person but a category of discipleship, a tradition and a generation. Included in that name were the first disciples who were the companions of Jesus and saw the Word made flesh. Their 'names' therefore created an unhealthy distinction between them and the 'others' (438) who laboured but who were never disciples and therefore could never be 'named'. To correct this unhealthy situation which the mere fact of proximity to Jesus precipitated, names are withheld, even the disciple whom Jesus loved is unnamed and 'Peter' gradually but steadily peters out."

Later, John's Gospel (cf. 1:29 with 13:10-11; 17:6) as well as Priscilla's homily (Heb 11:3-40), will employ the same literary strategy. All this seems to be another way of saying, "Therefore, there is now no condemnation for those who are in Christ Jesus" (Rom 8:1), that is, "for us who believe in him who raised Jesus our Lord from the dead" (Rom 4:24b; NIV). This literary strategy of paschal silence stands out in bold relief against the following backdrop:

> The holy books of no other religion depict their followers so negatively as the Bible does the Jews and the Christians. Scripture describes very graphically the doctrine that Jews and Christians are also sinners and capable of the most dreadful sins, and denounces not only the atrocities carried out by the Gentiles, but also those of the supposed (or true) people of God. This pitiless self-criticism is integral to Judaism and Christianity, in contrast to other religions. No other faith criticizes itself so severely as Old Testament Judaism or New Testament Christianity. Scripture exposes the errors of the leaders very clearly, and God often employs outsiders to recall His people to obedience.[80]

The paschal basis for this Passover blessing is once again set out (cf. 3:24-25):[81] "He was delivered over to death[82] for our sins and was raised to life for our justification" (v.25; NIV). Over seven centuries later a Jewish poet penned the following lines based on the Fourth Servant Song:

> *Messiah our Righteousness has departed from us;*
> *We are horror-stricken, and there is none to justify us.*
> *Our iniquities and the yoke of our transgressions*
> *He carries, and he is wounded for our transgression*
> *He bears on his shoulders our sins,*
> *To find pardon for our iniquities;*
> *We are healed by his stripes.*[83]

---

80. Schirrmacker, *Towards a Theology of Martyrdom*, 43.

81. Only this time the intertextual echo is Isaiah 53; cf. v. 12c (LXX): καὶ ἐν τοῖς ἀνόμοις ἐλογίσθη καὶ αὐτὸς ἁμαρτίας πολλῶν ἀνήνεγκεν καὶ διὰ τὰς ἁμαρτίας αὐτῶν παρεδόθη—and Rom 4:25a: ὃς παρεδόθη διὰ τὰ παραπτώματα ἡμῶν καὶ ἠγέρθη διὰ τὴν δικαίωσιν ἡμῶν.

82. "to death" is added by the translator(s). On the parallelism of the verse, see Winer, *Grammar*, 611, 639, and Lowe, "Oh διά".

83. Cited in Bruce, *Acts*, 193.

The antecedent of "He" in the Pauline text (Rom 4:25a) is the "Lord" of the previous verse, the One through whom the blessing is mediated on the basis of crucifixion and resurrection (cf. 1 Cor 15:1–10). Through these momentous events, then, justification is received and its chief benefit is *shalom* (Rom 5:1).

CONCLUSION

As the Apostle Paul elaborates on his claim in 3:21 that there is an available righteousness apart from the law covenant, he also appears to address a case of (incipient?) ethnocentrism in the Roman Church. In the first four chapters of the epistle, Paul demonstrates that human beings viewed both ethically and ethnically have no ground of boasting before God, because they are sinners (3:23; 29). However, through God's gracious hand, sinners may be justified.[84]

The case against ethnocentrism is advanced and strengthened by invoking two prominent Old Testament witnesses, Abraham (an 'Iraqi') and David (an 'Israeli'). Through the literary device of paschal silence both men are presented as paragons of virtue, particularly Abraham, whose walk with God "went from 'faith to faith.'"[85]

EXCURSUS 1: JUSTIFICATION BY CLICK (BY PROF. DAVID PEARSON, HOD THEOLOGY AND BIBLICAL STUDIES, JAMAICA THEOLOGICAL SEMINARY)

The personal computer has brought with it a certain ease of doing things previously unknown. Take for instance the field of publishing: setting text-type has traditionally been among the most painstaking processes of printing a story. In the old days the printer would have to manually create an entire story by placing each letter of every word on a kind of holding frame before inking it for printing. If he desired to have the text of the story aligned on both sides (called "justified") he would have to count and space letters in such a way as to gain his desired outcome. The process was painstaking, difficult and often inaccurate. It was much

---

84. Even those who believe that the God of Abraham and David is "jealous and proud of it; a petty, unjust, unforgiving control-freak; a vindictive, bloodthirsty ethnic cleanser; a misogynistic, homophobic, racist, infanticidal, genocidal, filicidal, pestilential, megalomaniacal, sadomasochistic, capriciously malevolent bully" (Dawkins, *God Delusion*, 31).

85. Conner, *Epistle*, 152.

easier to have the text aligned on one side, usually on the left (called "flush left") though the less popular "flush right" was not much more difficult. By counting letters and spaces, texts aligned in the center ("centered") were also popular.

I recall in the early 1980's working in Jamaica's leading advertising agency at the time as a graphic artist. The typesetter in our art department, the beautiful Pearl, used an advanced machine akin to something like an electronic typewriter. Justifying text was the most difficult duty for Pearl, as she had to first type out the entire story, use some formula to work out a code, which she then typed into the machine, hit enter, and watch as the gismo produced perfectly aligned stories on both sides. However, if one of Pearl's painstaking calculations went wrong, the text would come out in a mess, aligned in anyway the machine felt. Today we thank God for the personal computer, and software like Office Word and Word Perfect! With the click of the mouse on a little icon of five perfectly even lines at the top of the page, your story attains perfect justification. All you need to do is to ensure that the story is first highlighted in its entirety before you click. Three easy steps: type, highlight and click. Today, no one in his/her right mind attempts to justify text in the old way.

But how does one speak of "justification" without thinking about Christianity? Justification is the Christian doctrine which suggests that for man to be perfectly aligned with God he can do only one thing: place his trust in Jesus who gained his (man's) reprieve from damnation through his sacrificial death. When man yields his life to the control of Jesus it is as if his life becomes the perfect copy of God's, at least in the way God sees things. Then, as God reads man's script, all things are perfectly aligned with the standard that He sets. Man is then deemed to have been acquitted of the guilty charges leveled against him, and God's life is transferred to him. Christians call this "justification by faith" (Rom 3:24, 28; 4:1; 5:1, 9; 8:30). But not all are happy with it, because some see the teaching as suggesting that man can do as he likes, having been justified by faith. In their understanding, justification by faith grants man an initial reprieve from damnation; after that he has to work hard to maintain that salvation, lest he will lose it in the end. Thus the teaching of these fearful folk could be classified as "justification by faith, salvation by works."

The New Testament is replete, however, with teachings that show us that our efforts to properly align our lives on all sides to the standards of God are really much more about God than anything we can do. Apart from the Romans passages mentioned earlier, Philippians 1:6 reminds us that it is God who starts the new life in us, sustains it throughout our everyday toils, and completes it on that final day. And then there is that fantastic passage in Hebrews 10, especially verse 14:

[11]*Day after day every priest stands and performs his religious duties; again and again he offers the same sacrifices, which can never take away sins.* [12]*But when this priest had offered for all time one sacrifice for sins, he sat down at the right hand of God.* [13]*Since that time he waits for his enemies to be made his footstool,* [14]*because by one sacrifice he has made perfect forever those who are being made holy.*

Perhaps many people have misunderstood the message of the Gospel, as some in Paul's day did. The message of salvation is so stupendous that some actually believed that because God showed his love to them when they were vile sinners then they could go on sinning. If indeed "where sin abounds, grace much more abounds (Romans 5:20)" then it is ok, even mandatory, for us to go on sinning. The logic seems spot on, doesn't it? But such logic misses one important fact: Jesus died to deliver us from the dominion of sin and its effects. "Shall we therefore sin that grace may abound? God forbid! (Rom 6:1). The following verses explain man's deliverance from sin. So, justification by faith does not teach irresponsible Christian living. Both ideas are totally incompatible. But scripturally speaking, so are the ideas of being justified by faith and being saved by works. Whereas the former finds its base and meaning in scripture, the latter has no place there.

So here is my advice to my friends who are still attempting to justify the text of their lives through the hard work of deciphering codes, counting spaces and hoping for no mistakes—highlight your entire life's story and click on Jesus the Justifier. It is only then that you will walk in the life that Christ has prepared for you. And because you are now controlled by Him, make sure that everything you do mirrors his clear direction as seen in His Word and confirmed by His Spirit. After all, the scripture is clear that having justified us God now expects us to do the work He has prepared for us (Eph 2:10). Anything else would do a disservice to why He saved us in the first place. Click on Jesus, be justified and then walk in the way that God desires.

EXCURSUS 2: JAMES ON JUSTIFICATION (2:14–26)

I heard somebody telling somebody that the purpose of education was to improve the lot of mankind, and I was reminded of another definition, which was given several centuries ago by the most materialistic and down-to-earth philosopher, Francis Bacon. He said that education was to glorify God and to improve the lot of mankind. If, while I'm improving the lot of mankind, we forget to glorify God, then we are lost and our children are lost (Claude Levi-Strauss).

Introduction

Undoubtedly, James (and Paul for that matter) would have agreed wholeheartedly with the above. But who was this first-century philanthropist, Christian educator, and servant-writer of the Most High? Was he the son of Zebedee (Mark 1:19); the son of Alphaeus (Mark 3:18); the brother of Jude (v.1) and the offspring of the craftsman mentioned in Mark 6:3?[86] This last individual has been traditionally accepted as the writer of the epistle.[87] If this is correct, then Joseph *bar* Jacob (Matt 1:16) is the father of Jacob[88] *ben* Joseph (Matt 13:55), yielding "what we could call a chiasmus *in distance*:"[89]

A (Joseph)
    B (Jacob)
        B' (Jacob)
A' (Joseph)

The date of the epistle has also seen its fair share of debate among New Testament scholars, with suggestions ranging from AD 45 to AD 62 and

---

86. Schmoller, *Handkonkordanz*, 241; cf. Ehrman, *Introduction*, 331–32.

87. Laws, "James," 621–622; cf. Van Unnik "Origin," 195.

88. *Iakobos* in James 1:1. Of course, there are better Matthean links than that suggested above in terms of James' Christological echoes in passages like 1: 22, 25 (Matt 7:26); 3:12 (Matt 7:16); 4:13 (Matt 6:34); 1:2 (Matt 5:10–12); 1:5; 4:2 (Matt 7:7–8); 1:17 (Matt 7:9–11); 2:10 (Matt 5: 19); 2:13 (Matt 5: 7; 18:33–35); 3:12 (Matt 7:15–20); 3:18 (Matt 5:9); and 4:4, 13–15 (Matt 6:24). Yet "To be assigned . . . James in a book on Christology is a bit like the task several Catholic friends undertook, after Vatican II, to honor a colleague on his appointment to a traditional office. They presented him with a monograph on 'The Scriptural Origins of the Office of Domestic Prelate'—an elegant title page and ninety-eight blank sheets!" (Reumann "Christology," 128). Reumann did however find Jesus in James in places like 1:1; 2:7, etc. Marshall, *NT Theology*, 633 n. 9, sees six clear references to Jesus as "Lord" in 1:1; 2:15; 5:7, 8, 14, 15.

89. DiMarco, "Rhetoric," 484; his italics.

even beyond.⁹⁰ One interesting question here is whether or not James wrote after the epistle to the Romans circulated.⁹¹ This will no doubt influence one's understanding of the purpose of the Jacobean letter. But since there is no certainty in regards to the question to date, perhaps it is best to outline the purpose of James quite apart from looking at its bearing on the epistle to the Romans.

The purpose of the epistle is to urge Jewish Christians living outside of Palestine to make certain adjustments in their lives.⁹² The changes desired can be seen from an analysis of the book. This introduces yet another problem in James.

Gundry feels that the difficulty in outlining the book of James is severe, because it "shares the rambling and moralistic style of Proverbs and other wisdom literature . . . [and] the precepts are delivered in fashion of a fiery prophetic sermon."⁹³ In reading the epistle one cannot doubt this forcefulness of style and moral thrust. However, it is not at all convincing that the book lacks logical structure.

One who has attempted to show that James arranged his work around a single motif is Hiebert.⁹⁴ James, according to him, wrote to remind his audience that saving faith is a living faith, demonstrating itself by active service. In keeping with this basic purpose, the epistle is to be seen as a practical document presenting "a series of tests whereby his readers can determine the genuineness of their faith." This, says Hiebert, is the unifying theme of the epistle.⁹⁵ A survey of James, then, reveals the following literary structure.

---

90. Robinson, *Redating*, 118–138; These and other questions make "James" a disputed book in more ways than one (Eusebius, *Hist. eccl.*, 256–257).

91. Martin, *Foundations*, 1978, 362.

92. Morris, "Commentary," 163.

93. Gundry, *New Testament Survey*, 345; cf. Moo, *James*, 7; Ropes, *James*, 14.

94. Hiebert, "Unifying Theme." In his *Epistle*, there is an expanded analysis.

95. Westermann, *Handbook*, 148, describes the genre as "a hortatory composition (parenesis)." Watson, "James 2," 100, classifies chapter 2 as "deliberative rhetoric . . . intended to dissuade the audience from a particular course of action" and also to persuade said audience to demonstrate love through good deeds.

The Word (1:19–27)[96]

The experience of the new birth has its foundation in the Word of God (1:18). Therefore, James urges a threefold initial response to divine revelation: 1) Eagerness; 2) restraint; and 3) control of emotions (1:19–21). Believers must also complete their response to God's word by persistent obedience in areas such as a social engagement and personal piety (1:22–27).

Worship (2:1–13)

Here James comes out quite strongly against favouritism shown in the worship experience of his readers. The inspired writer points out that such partiality is not in keeping with Christian vocation, because it is contradictory to the command of love, a fundamental Christian tenet (2:1–13).

Works (2:14–26)

This section underscores the inter-relationship between faith and works, which will be explored below.

Words (3:1–12)

In this pericope the writer argues that faithfulness in the use of the tongue constitutes a means whereby the genuineness of one's confidence in God may be evaluated. The impropriety of an uncontrolled tongue is richly illustrated from the natural realm.

Wisdom (3:13–18)

These verses discuss the two basic types of wisdom available to mankind, divine wisdom and demonic wisdom. Both have their own spheres of influence as well as their distinctive consequences. What is instructive is that the believing community is not immune to the destructive effects of the "wisdom from below."

World (4:1–5–5:12)

In this extended section, James warns of the allurements of the present age. The fundamental threat of worldliness, he seems to point out, is that it clouds the believer's vision of the only proper object of faith, causing

---

96. The headings and expansions are adapted from Hiebert, "Unifying Theme."

her or him to look to another god. According to Hiebert, the threat of worldliness finds expression in at least four areas: 1) strife and faction (4:1–12); 2) presumptuous planning (4:13–17); 3) a wrong reaction to injustice (5:1–11); and 4) self-serving oaths (5:12).

Waiting (5:13–18)

"James brings his tests of a living faith to a logical conclusion by insisting the Christian faith finds its center and power in a vital relationship with God in prayer in all the experiences of life" (5:13). Waiting on God in prayer "constitutes the very heart of a vital Christian faith."[97] It is the "Works" section of the epistle that will be the focus of our attention.

A more recent proposal[98] regarding the structure of James posits a chiastic arrangement for the entire letter as follows:

A   Responding to troubles 1:2–18
   B   The need for patience 1:19–27
      C   The dangers of wealth 2:1–26[99]
         D   The misuse of the tongue 3:1–12
            E   True and false wisdom 3:13–4:10
         D'   The misuse of the tongue 4:11–12
      C'   The dangers of wealth 4: 13–5:6
   B'   The need for patience 5: 7–12
A'   Responding to troubles 5: 7–12

The two proposals (Campbell's and Hiebert's) are by no means mutually exclusive. They complement each other. For example, Hiebert draws attention to an *inclusio* embracing the prologue and epilogue, which is the 'A' sections in Campbell's scheme. And both have James' discussion of wisdom at the center of their respective "pentateuchal" frameworks.[100] There may be, however, a difficulty in integrating Campbell's 'C' section with the pericope on "Works."

97. Ibid, 230.

98. Campbell, *Story*, 234; Davids, *James*, 24, recognized that "The major blocks of material in the book take up the themes in reverse order, giving a chiastic effect" but made no effort to set this out.

99. Following Davids, Marshall, *NT Theology*, 630 n. 4, entitles this section "Poverty and riches; faith and deeds;" an improvement on Campbell's since it better reflects the concerns of 2:14–26. Campbell's 'C' section tacitly identifies James' interlocutor as a plutocrat.

100. Was James consciously echoing the five-fold structure of the Torah here, and did Matthew later follow him? Cf. Allison and Davies, *Matthew*, 59–60; 429–30?

FAITH DISCREDITED BY SOMEONE IN THE CONVERSATION: THE PLUTOCRAT? (14–19)

No church for me/Preacher standin on his pulpit/Pulping out your mind/ perverting, crucifying u . . . Raping your soul telling you to die again. Money for the preacher . . . Selling your soul to who?[101]

As is indicated by the broad structure outlined above, the test of faith that is treated in this pericope is that of the production of good deeds. For this vital discussion on faith, we need to recognise three participants, namely: James (the writer), the original readers of the epistle and an "objector" (a recalcitrant rich?) to James' orthodox position on the matter.[102] The problem could be framed this way: Is there a necessary connection between faith on the one hand and fruitfulness on the other? Having previously pointed out in verses 12–13 that deeds of mercy will be taken into account at the judgment, the question takes on added significance.

The opening verse[103] in our pericope contains two rhetorical questions and at least three key terms. These are "faith"(πίστις, *pistis*), "works"(ἔργα, *erga*) and "save"(σῴζω, *sōzō*). Since the verse establishes the theme of this portion, it is important to look at the meanings of these three words. However, it is to be borne in mind that their meanings here are not informed by mere lexical data, important though they are, but by the entire context of the periscope, and also one's theological understanding of the issues at hand.

"Faith" in these verses, at least as James argues, is genuine confidence in God which manifests itself in faithful acts. It is, from the point of view of the writer, the kind of faith that receives God's approbation (cf. Heb 11:6). The term (πίστις and its cognates) occurs approximately fourteen times in our paragraph and about four of these occurrences bear the pregnant sense that James intends. The other occurrences, which are

---

101. Mutabaruka, *First Poems*, 44.

102. Davids, *James*, 120.

103. The articular πίστις in v. 14 is in all likelihood emphatic ("that faith"; BDF, 131, and Cranfield, "Message", 338, though Moule, *Idiom*, 11, doubts this. " Why should 'faith' be translated the same in Romans 1:17 and James 2: [14], 26, when almost all interpreters are of the opinion that 'faith' as Paul uses it is quite different from the way James understands it?" (Archea, "Translation Task", 241. Cf. Luther, *Romans*, 65–71, and Haacker, *Theology*, 142). Of course, "faith" (142 times in the NT) is the vital link between God" (548x), and "Christ" (379x) on the one hand, and "humanity" (*anthropos* 126x), on the other (Yorke, *Church*, 24).

sometimes found on the lips of James' "antagonist," are that of a spurious species, a mere mental assent. The issue then is that of a serious faith on the one hand and a spurious kind on the other. However, it is to be noted that whenever the "antagonist" uses "faith" he has in mind the serious type. But James is about to prove "him" wrong.

According to Adamson, "works," the next key term in our verse, is better rendered "duty" in this context.[104] It is the visible manifestation of invisible faith.[105] The term "save," on the other hand, generally carries the idea of "deliverance," but the precise nature of the deliverance is not immediately evident from the context. In arriving at a decision it is helpful to bear in mind that salvation "is conceived by New Testament writers in three distinct stages of accomplishments. . . . 1. A past experience of release . . . 2 . . . A present and prolonged experience, which can be called sanctification . . . [and] 3. A future experience of salvation."[106]

So is James talking about salvation from the penalty of sin in the past, power of sin in the present, or presence of sin in the eschaton? Adamson says "the aorist signifies 'achieve salvation for him' not merely 'promote it.'"[107] If Adamson has an unbeliever in mind, the entire context and tenor of the passage seem to argue that James is not just talking about how that unbeliever may obtain salvation but how a believer may maintain and promote it in a practical way.

As the verse is summarised attention can now be given to the two rhetorical questions and their import. James certainly does not expect his first question to be answered in the affirmative. Using a substantive which occurs only in this chapter and once elsewhere (1 Cor 15:32), James asks, "What benefit (ὄφελος/*ophelos*; also v.16) it is for someone to claim the possession of faith without a corresponding faithful lifestyle?" The second question is even more emphatic in its negation, judging from its construction: "Can this kind of faith effect salvation?"

James continues his provocative discussion in verse 15, which, according to Motyer[108], also begins a chiastic arrangement embracing the rest of the chapter. With slight adaptation, the structure is reproduced below:

104. Adamson, *James*, 36.
105. BAG, 307–8.
106. Turner, *Christian Words*, 391–392; cf. Caird, *NT Theology*, 118–135.
107. Adamson, *James*, 121.
108. Motyer, *Message*, 108.

A (vv. 15–17)

    (a) Spurious faith examined horizontally (15–16)

    (b) Summary statement: This faith is dead (17)

B (vv. 18–20)

    (a) Spurious faith examined vertically (18–19)

    (b) Summary statement: This faith is fruitless (20)

B' (vv. 21–24)

    (a) Serious faith explored vertically (21–23)

    (b) Summary statement: This faith is fruitful (24)

A' (vv. 25–26)

    (a) Serious faith explored horizontally (25)

    (b) Summary statement: This faith is dynamic (26)

The chiasm provides a four-step definition of genuine faith both by way of affirmation and negation. Here Motyer's insightful comment is in order: "The two B-sections lie at the centre of a circle; they are the heart of the matter—what we are in relation to God. The two A-sections are the circumference of the circle, the interface where our life with God meets with the watching world and interacts with it."[109]

So faith and works, according to James, are to be viewed in the closest possible relation.

In verses 15 and 16 James begins to demonstrate the uselessness of faith without works by citing a hypothetical situation: a member of the believing community is in need of basic necessities of life[110] (cf. 1 Tim 6:8), and s/he is dismissed with pious words, even a benediction: "go in peace, and may you be warmed and receive your fill." A scenario like this, insists James, benefits no one and betrays the true character of the faith in question ("For out of the exuberance of the heart one brings forth evil things").[111] Moving from illustration to conclusion, James summarizes

---

109. Op. cit., 109.

110. The phrase in the original is an NT hapax (*BAGD*, 827), but it does not appear to have any affinity to Matt 6:11.

111. *Gos Thom* 45:1–4, in Robinson, *Sayings*, 89.

his point by stating categorically that faith by itself, that is, faith without works, is as useless as a corpse (νεκρά/*nekra*).[112]

The case for genuine faith is advanced in verse 18 as James confronts an objection. Now while the gist of the verse is plain, there is a difficulty that is not easily resolved. The problem has to do with the identity of the objector at this point. Hodges and Farstad give a punctuation to the verse which suggests that it is the faith of the writer that is called into question.[113] Another plausible suggestion is that of Adamson, who posits that the objector may be "a supporter of James'" view, at least on this point. . . ."[114] Motyer, on the other hand, sees the "someone" as an imaginary interlocutor who is not necessarily on James' side but just one in need of clarification.[115] However, Davids questions the very need of trying to find another person in the dialogue.[116] The fact that no one solution has proven satisfactory to date is one of the main reasons Davids has come to that conclusion. But, as was noted above, the main contention of the objector is clear. It is this: there is no necessary connection between works and faith. Viewed in this way we have the response of the writer in the second half of verse 18, beginning with the verb "show." In reality James here issues a stern challenge, which of course he knows cannot be met successfully. If we imagine James to be Moses in the courts of Pharaoh and the objector to be an Egyptian magician, then the rod of former, cast down, would become a living serpent, while the latter at best could only produce a dead snake, or worst, just the lifeless rod with which he begun. Such is power of James' argument.

In verse 19, James continues to press home his case against his "antagonist." First he commends him ("you do well") for his basic orthodoxy, his adherence to the Jewish monotheistic confession found in Deuteronomy 6:4. But even in this there is a subtle exposure of the inadequate faith against which our author inveighs, because verses 14–26 are "a natural sequel to the theme of religious self-deception that James began to develop in 1: 22, 25–26."[117]

112. BAGD, 534–35.

113. Hodges and Farstad, *Greek New Testament*, 681.

114. Adamson, *James*, 125.

115. Motyer, *James*, 112; cf. "A merely sophistic objection which (James) contrives in order to develop his own argument" (Dibelius, *James,* 156, n.36).

116. Davids, *James*, 120.

117. Fanning, "Theology," 426.

This is seen in the construction "you believe that" (v.19a), which differs from the phrase generally used to indicate an obedient faith.[118] In other words, a confession of Deuteronomy 6:4 is, to say the least, quite shallow if there is not a corresponding commitment to the following verse (Deut 6:5; and one might add Leviticus 19:18, which James has already cited in verse 8). Such utterance, says our writer, is demonic in its confession (cf. the kind of wisdom which is demonic in its expression; 3:15).

FAITH DEMONSTRATED BY SOMEONE WITHIN THE COVENANT: THE PATRIARCH (20–23)

Doubted, believed, and worshipped/Held in awe by all

—LEE 2005, 46

After pointing out in no uncertain terms that faith without works is dead and that there is a necessary connection between the former and the latter, James now launches into his final lines of evidence drawn from the Old Testament Scripture before resting his case. With a skilful blend of politeness,[119] firmness,[120] and no little passion,[121] James volunteers to offer more proof in support of his point (v. 20). He wants to show that faith apart from works is useless (ἀργή/*nekra*).[122]

Verse 21 introduces us to James' primary example from the Old Testament Scripture. The illustration involves the great patriarch, Abraham, and the incident in his life that best exemplifies the author's point is carefully chosen. With a powerful rhetorical device, James asks about the "justification" of Abraham. The construction of the

---

118. Davids, *James*, 125.
119. Robertson, *Grammar*, 878, on "Do you wish to know?"
120. Davids, *James*, 126, on "foolish man."
121. BDF, 81.
122. Zerwick, *Grammatical Analysis*, 695. Hodges and Farstad, *Greek New Testament*, 681, have *nekra* instead of *arge* (Aland, *GNT*); *nekra* is deemed to be a secondary reading by Metzger,*TC*, 610. Either reading makes sense in the context but the strong possibility of the use of paronomasia here makes the reading of *arge* ("Lit., 'without work,' *a + erga* [Johnson 1998, 198]) more attractive than the rhetorically "lifeless" *nekra* at this juncture.

question anticipates a definite affirmative, "so one should read it as a statement."[123]

The theologically problematic part of the question has to do with the justification of the Patriarch *by works*. We (and possibly the original readers) naturally expect "faith" as the object of the preposition. But is it not more natural for James to have laid emphasis on "works," since that has been his contention in this pericope all along? So what meaning, then, should be given to the crucial term "justified"? What does James mean when he says that works justified the patriarch? Is this not contradicting the assertion of Romans that Abraham was justified by faith alone? But before the key term is examined, we take a look at the "works" which "justified" Abraham who became the friend of God.

According to Davids, the term "works" in verse 21 refers to deeds of mercy in James. Therefore one is not to confuse James' use of this term with that of Paul's, which sometimes focuses attention on legalistic acts.[124] However, Moo has since questioned the validity of this conclusion. For Moo, "both Paul and James are operating with an understanding of works that is basically similar. . . . The difference between Paul and James consists in the *sequence* of works [his emphasis] and conversion: Paul denied any efficacy to pre-conversion works, but James is pleading for the *absolute necessity of post-conversion works* [my italics]."[125]

But despite his sound judgement on "works," Moo seems to miss the mark with respect to the meaning of "justified" in verse 21. Instead of giving the term a demonstrative sense,[126] he opts for a declarative signification.[127] The way James brings together Genesis 15:6 and 22:9,12 seems to favour the demonstrative idea. All this appears to militate against Moo's "final declaration."[128] In any case one cannot successfully posit a contradiction between the two biblical writers, since "One can say that 'James, like Paul, is repeating what Jesus said. Paul repeats Mt. 5:3, James

---

123. Davids, *James*, 127.

124. Davids, *James*, 127. Of course, the apostle also employs "works" quite positively as that which evidences genuine faith (McGrath, *Justification*, 380). For a competent treatment of the importance of "works" in Romans, see Rapa, *Meaning of "Works of the Law."*

125. Moo, *James*, 101–2.

126. Thayer, *Lexicon*, 150; Lust, *Greek-English Lexicon*, 115; cf. Oliver, "Righteousness," 31–44.

127. Moo, *James*, 109.

128. Moo, *The Letter*, 140.

repeats Matt 7:21–7. Paul representing the beginning, whereas James is representing the end of the Sermon on the Mount."[129] Whatever may be said of the writer's use of Genesis 22 here, it has to be conceded that he thought that the offering of Isaac best substantiated his claim at this point. This is confirmed by verse 22 as the writer attempts to show the nexus between faith and works in the story. Like the overall framework,

The verse is structured as a chiasm which functions to amplify by repetition:

(a) ἡ πίστις συνήργει   (b) τοῖς ἔργοις αὐτοῦ

(b) καὶ ἐκ τῶν ἔργων   (a) ἡ πίστις ἐτελειώθη

(a) Faith co-operates   (b) with his works

(b) and out of works   (a) this faith is completed.[130]

Like a husband and wife team, the author appears to be saying, faith and works are joined together, the former co-operates (συνήργει/ sunergei)[131] with the latter, and the latter completes the former (ἐτελειώθη/ eteleiothe).[132] To take some familiar words out of context, "Therefore, what God has joined together let no man separate" (Matt 19:6; NKJV).

James now applies Genesis 15:6 to his case that faith and works go together hand in glove. What took place in Genesis 22, says, our writer, is a fulfilment (ἐπληρώθη/eplērothē) of Genesis 15:6.[133] How are we to understand this "fulfilment"? Oesterley is certain that James is playing fast and loose with the Scripture at this point. Says he, "there is no connection between the quotation from Gen. xv. 6 and the offering-up of Isaac. This manipulation of Scripture is strongly characteristic of Jewish methods of exegesis."[134] But a study of a crucial term in verse 23 ren-

---

129. Riesner, "James," 1260; see also Balla, *Challenges*, 196; Jenkins, "Faith and Works," 62–78.

130. Watson 1993, "James 2," 115; translation mine.

131. BAGD, 787. Says McCartney, *James*, 169, "James is speaking... about a person's faith operating in synergy with his or her works as an unfolding of the righteous life."

132. Ibid 809.

133. Cf. 1 Macc 2:52 (at least a century before James): "Was not Abraham in his ordeal found faithful and it was credited to him for righteousness?" The Hebrew text of Gen 15:6, according to Chisholm, *Exegesis*, 129, is emphatic: "'*And he believed* the LORD, and he reckoned it to him as righteousness.'" (His emphasis); but James does not underscore this.

134. Oesterley, "James", 448.

ders this judgement premature. The verb for "fulfil" seems to be the key here. The standard lexica[135] list a number of senses the word can bear in various contexts, and only two of them, in my judgement, could possibly convey the sense that James intended: (1) to bring something to completion, finish something already begun, and (2) to bring to full expression, showing forth its true meaning. Some favour the former definition, but I think the latter is marginally preferable. Either way, the patriarch is seen as the "friend of God."[136]

The patriarch's contribution to James' argument is now summarized and given a wider application in verse 24 (notice the plural form[137] "you see" and the generic *anthropos* [person]). The main thrust of the argument is that a person is justified not by a naked faith but by a faith clothed in works. An orthodox claim to faith without works is never enough. Genuine faith must be evidenced by good works, for "Faith alone saves, but the faith that saves is not alone."[138]

FAITH DISPLAYED BY SOMEONE WITHOUT THE COVENANT: THE PROSTITUTE (25-26)

To serve, sustain, enrich/ this is our covenant;[139]

I know how to labour for good[140]

On a few occasions James' Lord would use a Gentile and/or a woman to underscore and illustrate the kind of faith that gains God's approval (e.g., Matt 15:21-25). In verse 25 James appears to follow that tradition by calling upon Rahab as his final witness.[141] His point here is that the matriarch was vindicated in the same way as the patriarch ("Likewise, was not Rahab the prostitute also justified by works . . . ?").

Considering James' background and his audience, this is a particularly strong claim. Although "The example of Rehab takes only one verse (2:25) . . . it is noteworthy first of all because it provides a straightforward

---

135. BAGD, 672; LN, 1: 199; cf. Liddell and Scott, Lexicon, 202.
136. An allusion to Is 41: 8, according to Aland , *GNT*, 907).
137. V. 22 has the singular; on this see Bratcher, *Translator's Handbook*, 31.
138. Wallace, *Grammar*, 219.
139. Earle, *Seasons*, 19.
140. *Vermes, Dead Sea Scrolls,* 398.
141. D' Angelo, "Rahab," 142.

female exemplar from Torah—a woman who is to be imitated for her own behaviour and not because of her relationship to a patriarch."[142]

Johnson also attempts to defend James' "unelaborated" mention of the paradigmatic matriarch by linking the writer's "odd" use of the plural "works" with the patriarch's singular deed (vv. 21–22). Since from a midrashic perspective "both figures were renowned above all for their hospitality,"[143] James may have intended his Jewish-Christian audience to make not only the historical connection, but also the intra-textual linkage with the marginalized poor of verses 1–4, as well as with the brother/sister motif established earlier in verses 14–16. And it is significant that whereas James portrays the "wicked judges" (vv. 2–4) as speaking, the callous believers (vv. 15–16) as speaking, and the dense interlocutor as speaking, Rehab and Abraham do not. Their faith is shown in *action*.[144]

The closing verses of the chapter are the summary of the entire pericope (2:14–25). A comparison is drawn between a corpse and a claim: the former is useless without its vital life principle and the latter, without works, is equally invalid.

CONCLUSION

How long shall they kill our prophets/While we stand aside and look?
Some say it's just a part of it /We've got to fulfil the Book[145]

Beginning with reason (14–19), James argues strongly that a faith that does not manifest itself in the performance of good deeds is a spurious one. James' chief support, however, comes from revelation (20–24).[146] Using the examples of Abraham and Rahab, James is able to show the cogency of his argument.

It is to be observed that while the argument of James becomes progressively shorter, the claim he makes increases in strength. There are at least two reasons for this: 1) the substantiation from Scripture for James and his original readers carried greater weight, and 2) his choice of ex-

---

142. Johnson, "James," 199.

143. Cf. 1 Clement XII. 1, 26 (rendition mine): "Rahab, the prostitute, was saved on account of fidelity and hospitality."

144. Johnson, "James," 1999.

145. Marley, *Songs of Freedom*, 156.

146. On the general nature of the application in v. 24, see Fanning, *Verbal Aspect*, 82.

amples and the order in which he discussed them (first the patriarch, then the prostitute) become at once a powerful way in which to clinch his case. James ends the pericope with a somewhat negative note ("faith apart from works is dead") that is certainly meant to supplement the three positive assertions made earlier.

Chapter 2:14–26, then, expresses James' *orthopraxy*—"the ongoing relationship between action . . . and reflection . . . between theological constructs and practical social experience."[147] The pericope demonstrates "concern for integrity [and] consistency, between theory and practice."[148] Once this concern[149] is properly grasped, then people of means, in particular, within the Messianic community will not yield to the temptation of mouthing an orthodox creed without a corresponding social engagement (vv.1–19). Neither will the poor within the community give deference to the rich and despise those who are "rich in faith" (cf. 2:5; Prov 14: 20).[150]

Instead, they and everyone else will adopt a posture of charity[151] that manifests itself "only in concrete action."[152] This alone is true religion (1:19–26)—a religion which interprets faith as philanthropic engagement with the poor.

---

147. Kritzinger, *Exploring Theology*, 140.

148. Tamez, *Message*, 54.

149. For inspiring accounts of two of those whose lives were an outworking of solid Jacobean theology, see Coke, *Eternal Father*, and Linton, *Gene Denham*.

150. Standing in the sapiential tradition (Schweizer, *Theological Introduction*, 109; Aune, *Dictionary*, 41), a verse like this may very well have been at the back of James' mind. The echo is most certainly in his text.

151. Cf. 1 Cor 13: 4–7 (AV). "Once again it is clear that the deeds approved are not technical observances, but *acts of love*" (Reicke, *James*, 32; italics added). The offering of Isaac (Gen 22) and the rescue of Lot (Gen 14) both demonstrate "how great was the love of Abraham our father" (Mishnah: *pirke Aboth* 5:3)—for God and man respectively. Cf. John 14:15. For another eulogy of this 21st century BC 'Iraqi,' see Philo, *Works*, 1661–1662.

152. Gutierrez, *Liberation*, 199; cf. Rose, "Social Problems," 29–45; Ama, "Rastafari," 97–102.

4

Romans 5, the *Imago Christi*, and a Former Archbishop of Canterbury

INTRODUCTION

Taking a backward glance it would appear that British scholarship has a particular love affair with Paul's letter to the Romans. A number of the better commentaries on that book, considered by some to be the apostle's *magnum opus*, have come from the pens of people like Dodd,[1] Barclay,[2] Bruce,[3] Barrett,[4] Cranfield,[5] and Dunn.[6] An interesting observation is that the last three mentioned scholars were all associated with the same university. Given the impact of Romans on various individuals and movements throughout history, one should not be surprised at its enormous attraction for lovers of the New Testament and its theology. F. F. Bruce[7] best sums up the influence of the letter:

> In the summer of AD 386 Aurelius Augustinus . . . sat weeping in the garden of his friend. . . . Almost persuaded to begin a new life, yet lacking the final resolution to break with the old. As he sat,

1. Dodd (*Romans*), the same gentleman who inspired the following limerick:
   *I think it extremely odd
   that a little professor named Dodd
   should spell, if you please,
   his name with three D's
   when one is sufficient for God* (Hagner, "C. H. Dodd," *DMI*).
2. Barclay, *Letters to Romans*.
3. Bruce, *Romans*.
4. Barrett, *Commentary on the Epistle to the Romans*.
5. Cranfield, *Critical and Exegetical Commentary*.
6. Dunn, *Romans*.
7. Bruce, op. cit., 58–60.

he heard a child singing . . . *Tolle, lege! Tolle, lege!* ('Take up and read!'). Taking up the scroll which lay at his friend's side [he read] . . . Rom. Xiii. 13b–14 . . .' instantly, at the end of this . . . [reading] a clear light flooded my heart and all darkness and doubt vanished away.' What the Church and the world owe to this influx of light . . . is something beyond our power to compute.

In November 1515, Martin Luther, Augustinian monk and professor of Sacred Theology in the University of Wittenberg, began to expound Paul's Epistle to the Romans to his students . . .

As he prepared his lectures, he came more and more to appreciate the centrality of the Pauline doctrine of justification by faith. . . . 'Thereupon I felt myself to be reborn and to have gone through open doors into paradise. . . . This passage of Paul became to me a gateway to heaven' . . . . In the evening of 24 May 1738, John Wesley went very unwillingly to a society in Aldersgate Street, where one was reading Luther's Preface to the Epistle to the Romans. 'About a quarter before nine . . . while he was describing the change which God works in the heart through faith in Christ, I felt my heart strangely warmed. I felt I did trust in Christ, Christ alone, for my salvation. . . .' That critical moment in John Wesley's life was the event above all others which launched the Evangelical Revival of the eighteenth century.

In August 1918, Karl Barth . . . published an exposition of the Epistle to the Romans.

'The reader . . . will detect for himself that it has been written with a joyful sense of discovery. The mighty voice of Paul was new to me. . . . And yet, now that my work is finished, I perceive that much remains which I have not yet heard. . . .' But what he had heard he wrote down—and that first edition of his *Romerbreif* fell 'like a bombshell on the theologians' playground.' The repercussions are with us still.

There is no telling what may happen when people begin to study the Epistle to the Romans. What happened [to the above individuals] . . . have happened much more frequently to very ordinary people as the words of this Epistle came home to them with power.

Facts like these predispose one to approach the book of Romans with a sense of excitement and anticipation, and that is how I began listening to Dr. George Carey, former head of the Anglican community worldwide. His message, "Preaching Christ in a Broken World," was delivered in one of the fourteen plenary sessions at Amsterdam 2000.

PROLOGUE

The Archbishop began by telling the story of a postcard he received in 1998 addressed to "Jesus Christ, C/O the Holy Trinity, Father, Son and Holy Spirit, The Heavenly Kingdom." A postal worker had redirected it with the words "Try Lambert Palace" (Dr. Carey's residence at the time). "I like to believe," he remarks, "that wherever I am, the Lord Jesus Christ in there." He then went on to thank Dr. Billy Graham for making himself available to God to be used in leading many thousands to Christ, including his (Dr. Carey's) wife in 1954.

As he proceeded with his introduction, he confessed that he found it ironic and deeply relevant to his theme that he was preaching in Amsterdam—the scene of Albert Camus' disturbing novel *La Chute* that so much underlines the hopelessness of the human condition, a motif in which its author passionately believed. But although Camus' grasp of man's dilemma was so realistic, he himself had no real solution to the weight of guilt and the burden of despair that characterized Europeans at that time, since in his brand of philosophy there is no redeemer and no saviour. The archbishop then went on to expound the second part of his bipolar topic.

DIALOGUE

Our World

The Archbishop first of all laid stress on the positive elements of our world: its beauty as well as its relation to and reflection of divinity. No true Christian, he said, ever despises the world. On the contrary, the true believer cherishes it and recognizes that its chief inhabitants are stamped with the *imago Dei*. They are immensely loved by their almighty Creator and must be loved by us as well. But along with this fact, we know the world is broken. Even the most skeptical and irreligious among us know this. But neither Camus nor any other person provides the analytical depth of our brokennesss as the apostle does in Romans 5.

Here the apostle describes sin in two graphic pictures: 1) sin kills and 2) sin reigns. In fact, the verb "reigns" (ἐβασίλευσεν/*ebasileusen*) occurs five times in the passage and three times it is used of sin as a tyrant holding mankind subject. In the next occurrence, it is used of God's people reigning in life through the victory of Christ on the cross. But for the most part the kingdom language that Paul uses depicts a world in which evil is triumphant. Sin reigns as a tyrant in every place, except where Christ's victory is received. So as we look at the world around us, we are in no doubt about the destructive power of sin. It is enslaving, and destroying human lives to an alarming degree. Citing the Catholic writer G.K. Chesterton, Dr. Carey reminded the audience that of all Biblical doctrines, the doctrine of Original Sin is the only one that is directly observable. We can see it all around. It is evident in our literature, and songs, and our films. For example, in Woody Allen's film, "Hannah and her Sisters," the protagonist commits adultery. Under the weight of his own guilt he confesses, "in spite of all my learning and capabilities, I do not know my own heart." "That is the reality of all of us," remarked the archbishop.

Human nature, however, tries to run away from that analysis. But the very tendency to shift the center of attention somewhere else is evidence of the triumph and reign of sin. "So while the predicament of human nature is so clearly shown in our powerlessness over wrongdoing, we seek solutions elsewhere, we try to shift the blame. But in all this there are no substitutes for Christ. There is no false god."

The Archbishop then went on to delineate three alternative saviors which dominate Western culture: 1) therapy; 2) education; and 3) wealth. People, he said, are obsessed with these "gods," although none of them can provide any lasting solution to our broken world.

Therapy

Western culture is facinated with the healing of the body and the mind. The unspoken assumption is that if we can but keep in tune with the wellbeing of our inner selves, all will be well. "Yet there is nothing virtually wrong with many therapeutic practices. Jesus himself is the supreme example of a whole person, at one with himself. However, therapy easily fails to face up to the reality of sin in our lives." Furthermore, therapy and its techniques become idolatrous and a surrogate to the gospel, when they replace faith, and are seen as the total answer to humanity's needs. This is seen in many sermons today where Christ the Savior is replaced by Christ the counselor, and almost invariably a therapeutic approach is favoured over theological one. Missing is what Romans 5 highlights as that true holiness of God, and our need for salvation.

Education

This is the second god preferred by the world. "Again, there is a proper focus on education in all our societies. In fact the Church, for example, began to invest in education long before the state woke up to it, and throughout the world today the Christian community continues to provide resources in this area." But when education is seen as *the* answer to the problems of the human race, then there is serious trouble. "Why is it?" queried the Archbishop, "that in spite of universal education in many, many countries today, there is still such crime, such vandalism, such a break down of family life? Why is it that so many terrible atrocities have occurred in advanced societies? Why is it that education does not meet the loneliness of the human heart and the feelings of guilt?"

Like therapy, when education is introduced as an alternative to the Gospel, it promotes a different kind of saviour. Jesus is seen merely as an enlightened teacher who leads us from ignorance to education. But such a posture is not new. The early Christians encountered the same thing under the guise of Gnosticism. But whether in our century or theirs, this "knowledge" has failed to address the true condition of the human heart.

Wealth

The other pseudo-savior is money. Although the American dollar bears the laudable adage, "In God We Trust," the archbishop heard an American businessman retort "but in City Bank we invest." As with the other two gods money has a proper place, because without wealth creation societies cannot prosper and the endeavor to help the poorer countries would founder. But the power of money to corrupt, along with its insidious temptation, should never be underestimated. When wealth and riches becomes the ultimate aim of life, an idol is erected. In church circles "think of the number of tele-evangelists for whom the lure of money has become for them an inescapable part of the Gospel. Think of the rise of prosperity gospels which have lured poor people to a false faith based on the promise of riches!" This is called the "cargo" gospel in some parts of the world. "If you believe in Jesus you too will be prosperous and will succeed." In contrast, the good news we preach, declared the archbishop, is one in which a cross is central. So despite the attraction of riches, it cannot solve the problem of humanity and the impoverishment of the human heart.

These three gods—therapy, education and wealth—are but three of the powerful defenses that human nature sets up to avoid the reality of brokenness which the Bible identifies as sin, that which enslaves, that which kills, that which now reigns. What is really sad is that even in the church we shy away from that analysis. "If we consider our world at the beginning of the twenty-first century, particularly the Western world, it seems out of tune with the Christian analysis of the human condition, though it will agree with you that no one is perfect and that we all fall short of our ideals." Yet the world is not prepared to accept the radical diagnosis that the apostle offers much less the wonderful solution he, through Jesus Christ, proffers. "Man has put his trust in man, and, seemly, has not been disappointed. Trusting in health and wealth and universal education, he believes that all our problems will be eradicated." However, that is a road that leads to nowhere but despair.

The task then of the Christian community is to address this world with the true analysis of its condition, and to enable our fellow human beings to discover the true solution to be found in Jesus Christ. But if we are to do so effectively we need to ask two pertinent questions: 1) "What kind of Savior does this world need?" And 2) "What kind of church can bring this Saviour to our world?"

"As we think about this first question, it could be so easily deduced that the only saviour that Christians can bring to our multicultural and religiously pluralistic world is our contribution to the market place of religions—an understandable Christ, a tolerant Christ, a cheerful chappy of a Christ, who doesn't make too many demands on people, a Christ who simply came to make a contribution to the religious storehouse of mankind." That is not the kind of Christ described in Romans 5. Using some strong terms, the apostle Paul describes Christ as the universal Saviour from sin, as God's gift to mankind, and the one through whom a new reign has begun. So the relevance of the Christian Gospel,

> lies not simply in the experience of renewal (because you know many other philosophies offer that) but in the incomparable person of Jesus Christ and there must be no apology for preaching what the theologian Hans Frei refers to as the unique identify of Jesus Christ. And churches fail and preachers fail when they cease speaking of what the theologians call the singularity of Christ or the scandal of particularity, that in this man Jesus Christ, God has appeared for all mankind. When Christians and churches depart from a committed faith in Christ, who was not

> only an incomparable teacher [and] visionary leader, but the one whom God raised from the dead, the only Lord and only Saviour—when we depart from that we depart from the throbbing heartbeat of authentic Christian faith [that is] grounded in the New Testament and anchored in the creeds of the church. This is the Saviour that came to our world some 2000 years ago and this is the Saviour that our world needs to hear afresh today. But this begs the question: Does it work? It certainly does.

Every evangelist, every dedicated pastor, and teacher, declared the archbishop, can testify of the very many lives that have been touched by the amazing grace of God revealed in the proclamation of the Gospel of Jesus Christ. "I come as a person born and bred in the working class district of East London; my parents had nothing to do with the Christian faith, but God broke into our family in a most remarkable way," he testified. "And as Archbishop, I am privileged to see God at work in so many different parts of the world as well as in my own country, and a week scarcely fails to go by without someone writing to me to tell me of how God has come in their lives."

One therefore is humbled at such testimonies of God's love that points to the Saviour our world so desperately needs. "But it would be wrong to conclude from this that this emphasis on the particularity of Jesus and the Gospel leads to a fundamentalist, bigoted, narrow, and dogmatic message that we thrust down people's throat. Of course not! The Christ we follow, I follow, you follow, is one who allows people to think, argue, dispute and doubt." In line with this, authentic Christianity is not afraid of scholarship, including the critical study of the Bible. Therefore, the true evangelist/pastor has everything to gain by helping people explore the haunting questions thrown up by the human condition. In so doing people will be helped to embrace a strong faith with deep foundation. So the pastor or evangelist, who follows in the footsteps of the compassionate and tolerant Master will approach his/her task with equal compassion, tolerance and humility, because we all stand under the cross. "In the words of Max Warren: 'If the cross stands at the center of history as Christians believe, if it is the central key in understanding the nature of God, the dilemma of man, the mystery of life and death, then we have to expound its meaning as the way in which all men are meant to live and die.'"

Romans 5, the Imago Christi, and a Former Archbishop of Canterbury   79

Dr. Carey continues: "And so what kind of Saviour does our world need? The same kind of Saviour yesterday and forever. The one that the apostles wondered about, the one the church has taught down the centuries, the Christ who saves us, liberates us, and reigns in us. If the church today does not preach this kind of Saviour, it has no good news to share with our broken world."

This leads to a second question: What kind of Church can bring such a Saviour to our world? First of all, a truly ecumenical church, a church that is willing to work together like it did just after World War II with a meeting in Amsterdam. "Perhaps one of the most distinctive things about this conference is not only have we brought together representatives from over 200 countries and over 10, 000 delegates, but I would guess that this is a very unusual conference in that most of us here tonight are prepared to recognize Christ in one another and to affirm that all Trinitarian churches are authentic expressions of Christ' body here on earth."

What kind of a church can bring such a Saviour to our world? Second, a truly energetic church. "How we long to see our churches transformed into authentic bodies reaching out to our needy and broken world in love and service," opined the Archbishop. "There is a very sad truth in the doggerel attributed to an English bishop, who on his deathbed muttered:

> *Tell my priest when I'm gone o'er me*
> *To shed no tears*
> *For I shall be no deader then*
> *Than they have been for years.*

"We may think of congregations that appear to be stuck as well, and for whom at best the routine of church life appears to be the only object of the game and at worst, survival is the name of the game." In a situation like this, it is no surprise that the communication of the gospel becomes ineffective. But what a difference it makes when churches like this work in unison with the Holy Spirit to revitalize themselves. When they do, declared Dr. Carey, at least four changes are effected. (1) Based on a common faith, new ecumenical partnerships will emerge; (2) rooted in the culture of those to whom they minister, an effective evangelistic strategy will be forged; (3) with a focus on human needs, the gospel will be related to the whole of life, and (4) genuine worship will be practiced; a worship which is vibrant, enthusiastic, joyful.

"Those of us like me who come from a tradition where liturgy has a central place, we must pay particular attention that liturgy doesn't become a straightjacket that confines our worship or a framework that stops the Holy Spirit from working in his people. Let me add another health warning: nonliturgical churches have their problems in a different kind of repetition that may lead to a different kind of deadness."

EPILOGUE

The Archbishop then concluded by saying that through passionate preaching, powerful testimony and wonderful singing, we will be enabled to win others in our broken world. Though we live in uncertain times, he believes that they are also thrilling times for any Christian to serve, for the Christian message is as relevant as it has ever been, and the need for a Saviour is more urgent than ever.

Although this message did not get the kind of response that was given to an Anne Graham-Lotz or a Dr. Gerry Gallimore, there can be little doubt about its effectiveness in terms of addressing the assigned theme. Neither can it be doubted that it was based upon a faithful exposition of the mind of the apostle expressed in Romans 5. If it is correct that "an exposition without application is an abortion," then Dr. Carey has also done well from that perspective, and in this regard one wishes that the full transcript of his sermon would be made available to a wider audience.

OUR HUMANITY: IMAGO DEI, IMAGO CHRISTI

There are at least two points that are worth highlighting. The first has to do with the archbishop's diagnosis of the human condition. He is to be commended first of all for underscoring the fact that man was originally created in the image of God and still bears that resemblance. More often than not in our anxiety to zero in on man's spiritual bankruptcy we neglect to point out his value in the sight of his Maker. In a recent publication Dr. Faith Linton also makes this positive affirmation.[8] This is what former University of Technology sociology professor Rev Martin Schade calls "original grace." But it appears that the trend nowadays is toward

---

8. Linton, *What the Preacher Forgot*; see also Middleton, *Liberating Image*.

a denial of the other side of the coin: man's brokenness. Thus Gleaner columnist Peter Espeut can write, "Man is good by nature (When God made man he looked and saw that he was very good!). His good nature, however, has a flaw, which causes man not to perceive the whole good. And so when man sins he does not reach for evil *per se* but for an imperfect good."[9] The archbishop skillfully avoided this imbalance.

All this once again raises the important query ("What is man?") that still remains one of the most difficult questions amongst social scientists today. In our attempt to formulate an answer we will also address the issue of the fundamental character of the believer. With an ever increasing post-modern outlook, even Biblical scholars are beginning to doubt whether the foregoing questions can be answered in any meaningful way.[10] Notwithstanding such uneasiness, our purpose below is to attempt working definitions of humanity in Adam as well as the humanity in Christ in light of Romans 5:12–18, with a little help from the discipline of psychology.

The need to constantly strive for a better understanding of human beings is underscored by Cosgrove when he writes: "Surprisingly, the accumulated wealth of knowledge from the past several thousand years has advanced only slightly our understanding of human nature. Even with the aid of scientific technology in fields like psychology and biology, the critical study of man has lagged far behind."[11] He goes on to point out that part of the problem is the difficulty of the subject matter.

---

9. "The Value of Humanity," *The Daily Gleaner*, December 20, 2000. This was followed by another article ("Capital Punishment and the Intrinsic Goodness of Man," *The Daily Gleaner*, January 10, 2001, A4). Responses in the same medium contradicting Espeut's position include the following: Dennis McKoy, "Man's Depravity and Capital Punishment"; Martin Henry, "Is Humanity Intrinsically Good?" both on January 16, 2001. Coming out in support of Roman Catholic deacon, Peter Espeut, was Anglican Rector Rev Ernle Gordon, "Humakind is Intrinsically Good," January 27, 2001. In his rejoinder, Espeut writes, "The idea that humanity is intrinsically evil is fundamentally anti-Christian, for how then could the Word have become flesh and dwelt amongst us?" *The Daily Gleaner*, January 31, 2001. The most balanced approach was from Dr. Linton. She counsels, "We need a theology which embraces both the strength and the weakness, the dignity and the depravity of humans; a theology that gives priority to what the Bible puts first" in "The Dignity and Depravity of Humanity," *The Daily Gleaner*, February 19, 2001.

10. For a useful survey, though somewhat dated, see Stevenson, *Seven Theories*; for the post-modern challenge in this regard, see Draney, "Christian Responses," and Geisler, *Creating God*. The second question has been boldly addressed by Needham, *Birthwright*.

11. Cosgrove, *Essence*, 7.

If humanity in general is complex, it can be argued that the problem is compounded when the subject is that which is described in positive terms in the latter part of Romans 5. In answering the forgoing and following questions (of those concerning the first Adam and last Adam), we take our queue from the apostle's discussion in Romans 5 by keeping the two sets of investigation together.

Creature of Dignity?

The constitutional nature of humanity in Christ can only be understood by seriously reflecting on the Biblical concept of the *imago Dei*, because the Creator gave special attention to Adam and Eve in contrast to the lower life forms. In this context, humanity's unique nature and life must be considered along with the other complexities involved such as personhood. Carter and Narramore point out that the persons who advocate that psychology and Christianity are to be integrated maintain that personhood "is rooted in the fact that the human being is created in the image of God. All thinking about the human being is colored by the view we take of human origin and *destiny*."[12] Elsewhere the significance of man being the image of God is highlighted by Narramore: "The Biblical view of man raises human worth to its highest level."[13] But what exactly is this image?

Does man today really bear this divine likeness? In an attempt to explore the issue, Grudem[14] delineates four or five aspects of the question: the mental, moral, spiritual, relational, and the physical. We may review these in reverse order. Here Grudem is careful to point out that God's spiritual nature precludes any notion of physicality (John 4:24). However, it should not be forgotten that it is *man himself*, according to Grudem, that is created in the divine image, so both the substantial and spiritual aspects of man's existence simultaneously, though in different ways bear out that fact.[15] In regard to the relational aspect, it is now a truism that man is an intensely gregarious being.

> Although animals no doubt have some sense of community with each other, the depth of interpersonal harmony experienced in

---

12. Carter and Narramore, *The Integration*, 107 (italics mine).
13. Narramore *Parent Leadership Styles*, 352.
14. Grudem, Systematic *Theology*, 445–49.
15. Silva, *God, Language and Scripture*, 23.

human marriage, in a human family when it functions according to God's principles, and in a church when a community of believers is walking in fellowship with the Lord and with each other, is much greater than the harmony by any animals. In our family relationships and in the church, we are also superior to angels, who do not marry or bear children or live in the company of God's redeemed sons and daughters.[16]

The above quotation also alludes to man's spiritual nature, which was made to function "according to God's principles." This presupposes that generic man is made "a little lower than God" (Ps 8).[17] We are therefore enabled to worship our Maker and enjoy him forever. Closely connected to this is our capacity to relate to God and to one another in moral and ethical ways. Here our accountability becomes crucial and our conscience necessary. Interestingly, the universal recognition of conscience is a phenomenon that some evolutionists find inexplicable.[18] Finally, our ability to use our minds to communicate both rationally and logically, in the opinion of many, definitely points to the fact that we are in the image of God.[19]

Other areas such as sexuality and immortality are also explored by theologians. For example, Mary Hayter, building on Barth's affirmation that the basis of the doctrine of the *imago Dei* is to be found in the relationship between the sexes, seeks to understand the limits of such a thesis by the examination of crucial terms like *elohim* in the creation narrative. Rejecting the position of those who would say that human sexuality reflects that of deity, Hayter concludes that "the term . . . as applied to Yahweh can denote that the God of Israel incorporates and transcends masculinity and femininity."[20]

---

16. Grudem *Systematic Theology*, 447.

17. NRSV, v.5. The LXX renders *elohim* as "angels" in this Psalm; modern scholars seem to favor "God;" e.g., Craigie, *Psalms*, 105–10. Whereas the NIV appears to reflect the LXX, the REB has the intriguing "You have made him a little less than a *god*," (italics mine).

18. Tinkle, "Evolution," 18:995, confesses: "The most important difference between man and animals is his moral sense, and this presents difficult evolutionary problems. . . . This leads to the paradox that, despite his claimed moral sense, man is the only species in the animal kingdom that will perform wholesale massacres of its own members." It does seem that an acceptance of the Biblical doctrine of Creation (Gen 1–2) and rebellion (Gen 3) resolves Tinkle's "paradox."

19. Silva, *God, language and Scripture*, 20–22.

20. Hayter, "Human Sexuality," 198: "Although God does use a comparison to

It is in the New Testament that the image of God in humanity in general and in the Christian in particular comes into sharp focus. Both the fact of the incarnation specifically and many features of the teaching ministry of Christ indicate the dignity of humankind. It is the Christ himself in the Gospel records who is portrayed as the only human being fully reflecting the *imago Dei*. It should come as no surprise, then, that Christians are the very ones who are being renewed after the *imago Christi* (2 Cor 3:18; Eph 4:22–24; Col 3:9–10).[21] But how perfectly does the believer in Christ bear this divine image? Put another way: To what extent does adamic corruption still affect the Christian, if any at all?

Creature of Depravity?

Some theologians and not a few psychologists take exception to the description of the Christian as a sinner saved by grace. The question that therefore confronts us at this point has to do with the relation of evil and the believer in Christ. Decades ago psychologist Bruce Narramore shared with his CGST students some of the lively discussions on this topic he used to have with his father-in-law, whom he described as a dedicated Christian gentleman. Whereas Narramore believed in the possibility of sin in the Christian life, this was strenuously denied by his beloved father-in-law. Recently New Testament scholar Douglas Moo recounts an experience he had involving someone who holds a similar view to Narramore's father-in-law:

> About ten years ago I was invited to speak in a church that was becoming divided over a certain view of the Christian life propagated by one of its members. This individual made a great deal of Peter's claim that Christians have a "divine nature." He insisted that this meant that a Christian was given an entirely new nature, basically incapable of sinning. After all, he reasoned, God's "nature" is obviously a sinless one; if we had this nature, then it stood to reason we could not sin! The whole matter "hit the fan" in this church when he counselled a Christian woman to "submit" to her non-Christian husband's demands that she have sex with him

---

a woman in childbirth (Is 42:14), nonetheless there is a strong scholarly consensus that God is regarded as non-sexual. . . . This consensus finds explicit support in Deut 4:15–16, 'you saw no form of any kind the day YHWH spoke to you at Horeb . . . so that you do not make for yourself an idol or an image in any shape, whether formed like a man or woman.'"

21. Adamo, "Christ," 23–35.

and another man at the same time—after all, she had a "divine nature" that could not be touched by such sin!²²

I think both stories illustrate the dire need for us to have a proper understanding of the character of the Christian living in a fallen world. Certainly, those theologians who say that the essential nature of the Christian is that of a saint are correct. However, that statement does not go far enough in addressing the question of the possibility of sin in the Christian life. If the believer is not just a sinner saved by grace, does this mean that s/he is not in some sense depraved? Whether used of Christians or non-Christians the term "depravity" is problematic.²³ If the term is used in the general sense to mean that sin affects every facet of a person's being, then we can begin to explore to what extent this is true in the Christian life.

In this regard, one passage that almost invariably enters the discussion is Romans 7:14–25. Here the apostle's language is sometimes jarring to the ears of theologian and therapist, especially the latter who is anxious to have God's people maintain a proper self-esteem. What, for example, does Paul mean by the statement, "I know that nothing good lives in me, that is in my sinful nature" (v. 25, NIV)? Is the apostle describing his own struggle with indwelling sin in this passage or is he giving a vivid testimony of his existential encounter with the law prior to his conversion? Cranfield has no doubt that the former is correct. Commenting on the chapter on a whole and verse 14 in particular, he writes:

> With regard to the objection that it is incredible that Paul could speak of a Christian as "a slave under sin's power," we ought to ask ourselves whether our inability to accept this expression as descriptive of a Christian is not perhaps the result of failure on our part to realise the full seriousness of the ethical demands of God's law (or Gospel). . . . Is it not true that the more the Christian is set free from legalistic ways of thinking about God's law and so sees more clearly the full splendour of the perfection towards which he is being summoned, the more conscious he becomes

---

22. Moo, *2 Peter*, 54.

23. "The Bible clearly states that all aspects of man's being are corrupt. Every facet is affected by original sin . . . intellect . . . affections and will." (Owens, "*Evangelism*," 17). For the lingering effects of these on the believer, see Wenham, "Christian Life," 80–94, and Lawrence, "Traitor," 115–131.

of his own continuing sinfulness [depravity?], his stubborn all-pervasive egotism?"[24]

In substantial agreement with the above is Cranfield's former colleague at Durham, James Dunn,[25] as well as J. I. Packer,[26] who seems to locate the moral weakness of the believer within the unredeemed body.[27] But this reading of Romans 7 has not gone unchallenged and recent commentators on Romans have sought to demonstrate how wrong-headed this understanding of the Christian really is. One such is Moo.[28] We have seen above that he does not believe that the Christian is sinlessly perfect. But neither does he subscribe to the idea that the Christian ought to be described as *depraved* or merely a sinner saved by grace. So how then does he understand Paul's "testimony" in Romans 7:14–25? His latest summary of the controversial passage is as follows:

> Verses 14–25 describe the situation of an unregenerate person. Specifically, I think that Paul is looking back, from his Christian understanding, to the situation of himself, and other Jews like him, living under the Law of Moses. Of course, Paul is not giving us a full picture of the situation; he is concentrating on the negatives because this is what he must do to prove how useless the law was to deliver Jews from their bondage to sin. We might say, then, that Romans 7:14–25 describes from a personal viewpoint the stage in salvation history that Paul delineates objectively in Gal 3:19–4:3. . . . Paul in Romans 7 uses *ego* to represent himself, but himself in solidarity with the Jewish people.[29]

Pentecostal scholar Gordon Fee[30] is also a supporter of this position, which seems to be the dominant one among scholars in the last century. Romans 7 aside, it does seem that whatever label we may choose to use of the Christian, the NT presents the believer as one who is sometimes dangerous to himself/herself and to the community of God's people. How else can we read passages like 1 Corinthians 5, Galatians 5 (especially vv. 16–21), and the host of other strong passages which warn the believer against living a life of depravity?

---

24. Cranfield. *Romans*, 158.
25. Dunn, *Romans*, 387–412.
26. Packer *Keep in Step with the Spirit*, 268.
27. Gundry, *Soma*, 204–16.
28. Moo, "Israel and Paul," 122–123, 453–54.
29. Moo, *Romans*, 447–78.
30. Fee, *Gods Empowering Presence*, 509–15.

The probe concerning the fundamental nature of the Christian may even be carried on from the perspective of psychology, with special reference to what is called the mechanisms of defence. These are "indirect and typically unconscious manners of gratifying a repressed desire."[31] They are ways and attempts to deal with conflicts with a view to protecting and enhancing a person's self-concept.[32] According to certain other authorities in the field, all people employ psychological defences and "the only human who never used . . . defence mechanisms is Jesus Christ,[33] whose self-esteem was valid and who had no sinful motives to be aware of."[34] Defence mechanisms may also be viewed as forms of dishonesty. If these assumptions are granted—that psychological defences are both unrighteous and universal—does it mean, then, that even Christians are engaged in this subtle form of deception?

An affirmative answer is given by Melvin Nelson[35] in his study of James chapter 1 and forms of psychological maladjustment. He sees James describing various kinds of self-deception resulting from double-mindedness. These acts of self-deception in turn distort spiritual formation and are similar to some defence mechanisms often found following prolonged inner struggle associated with anxiety and guilt. What are the "defences" seen in the book of James? Nelson is careful to point out that it is not the author's objective to delineate these defences *per se* but to expose the distorted thinking[36] of his first-century audience. Nelson sees five defences in James 1.

Rationalisation

In rationalisation, a "person gives well thought out and socially acceptable reasons for certain behaviour, but these reasons do not happen to be the real ones."[37] Nelson sees such a kind of disguise in vv. 6–8, and warns that rationalisation of this nature can seriously distort one's prayer life.

---

31. Narramore, *Psychology*, 288.
32. Ibid.
33. Instead, Christ is the healer of all kinds of human pathology; his salvation "impacts and revolutionizes the whole person (Luke 19:10), including the psychological domain." (Beck, *Healing Words*, 13); cf. Allen, *Caring*.
34. Meier, *Introduction*, 231.
35. Nelson, *Psychology*, 37–43.
36. On deception in the passage, see Martin, *James*, 57.
37. Sue, *Understanding Abnormal Behaviour*, 47.

Projection

In vv. 13–17 may be present yet another distorted way of thinking stemming from spiritual conflict. This entails the shifting of threatening desires outside oneself by perceiving others as experiencing the difficulties that are actually one's own.[38] Projection in the life of the believer, according to Nelson, not only gives a false sense of relief, but, as is the case in vv. 13–17, also twists the truth of God's character.

Repression

Nelson sees this defence in vv. 22–25. It may be defined as "a protective device by means of which forbidden impulses or painful memories are banished from consciousness." Two more defences are to be seen in vv. 17–21 and 24–27. These are intellectualisation and reaction formation respectively. While the former keeps the believer from receiving the engrafted word, the latter leads him or her into ceremonialism.[39]

But this kind of integrative approach valid? Can psychological analysis shed light upon the Biblical text? If so, what method should the interpreter employ to yield the best results? These are just some of the questions raised by Nelson's article.

Well over a decade after Nelson's publication, Biblical scholar Jerry Gladson and professional counsellor Charles Plott tackle some of these very queries in an interdisciplinary study. The study presupposes that the universal principles in a text may be compared to more general conclusions in the field of psychology. They ask, for example, about the "conflicted self" as a psychological category vis-à-vis a similar experience Biblically or theologically described. Would the stark "admissions" of, for instance, Romans 7:22–23 qualify?[40] In this context, are therapists and theologians bound to give mutually exclusive explanations?[41]

Much caution needs to be exercised whatever answer one gives to these questions, particularly on account of the fact that several genres are represented throughout the Bible, all needing to be handled with sensitivity.[42] In addition, the question of which psychological theory or

---

38. Ibid.
39. Nelson, *Psychology*, 39–40.
40. Gladson and Plott, Unholy *Wedlock*? 56.
41. Clarke, "Interpreting Biblical Words," 309–17; Carter, "Psychology," 277–85.
42. Johnson, "A Place for the Bible," 346–55.

theories to be applied in various cases is also critical. When the matter of historical distancing is added to the equation, one wonders how feasible the whole enterprise becomes. Notwithstanding the above, Gladson and Plott are still optimistic that some progress, however incremental, can be made: "Despite limited data available to assess a character in Scripture, it is nonetheless possible to gain some insight into the behaviour—or even attitudes—by using what information is available. When psychologists analyze someone's journal, without immediate access to the writer, they use a similar approach."[43] Is not this what Biblical scholars do, especially redaction critics, when they attempt to probe the motives and authorial disposition of the writers of Scripture?[44]

What is surely to be avoided, though, is the kind of extreme analysis reported by Muilenburg:

> Psychologically Ezekiel presents problems of great difficulty. His ecstatic transports and symbolic prophecies are very strange. They have been accounted for in various ways—catalepsy, schizophrenia, Freudian presupposition, etc. But most of these diagnoses fail to point out that this 'abnormality' is consistent with his theology. . . . Ezekiel was one of the greatest spiritual figures of all time, in spite of his tendency to psychic abnormality—a tendency which he shares with many other spiritual leaders of mankind. A certain 'abnormality' is required to divert a man's thoughts and his emotional experiences from the common treadmill of human thinking and feeling.[45]

But what these one might say crude assessments do suggest is what Gladson and Plott call a "common humanity" which demonstrates itself for example in the process of grieving observed both cross-culturally and diachronically. Gladson and Plott also add the further caveat that any psychological theories about the Biblical material must remain inferential, since the kind of empirical rigor that is needed is certainly beyond our competence.[46]

In light of the foregoing, are we now in a better position to evaluate Nelson's suggestions based upon his "scientific" analysis of James 1? Can his conclusions be validated given the above strictures? If the common-humanity criterion is invoked and strictly applied, one could say that Nelson's attempt to apply the relevant Freudian theory to the text is at

43. Gladson and Plott, Unholy *Wedlock*? 61.
44. Ibid.
45. Muilenburg, "Ezekiel," 369.
46. Gladson and Plott, op. cit., 61.

least plausible but not necessarily compelling. Certainly, the careful observation of experts on people's maladaptive behaviour appears to be capable of some sort of comparison with the prophet's commentary on the "psycho-pneumatic" condition of his own countrymen (Jer 17:9). Here then it may be said that Nelson's study is more intuitively correct than empirically sound. All this, though, has still left unanswered the absorbing question of Christian depravity, or whether or not the believer can still be described in these terms. Hopefully some light will be shed on this question in the following section.

Creature of Destiny?

Some time ago Robert Saucy addressed the question of the true identity of the Christian. One of the first things he pointed out is that what emerges from the scriptural material in this regard is a curious "mixture" of purity and impurity. This of course partially accounts for the difficulty in gaining a consensus among theologians, especially concerning whether or not believers should be labelled as (to use the title of Saucy's article) "Sinners" who are forgiven or "Saints" who sin. While Saucy is quick to admit the presence of evil in believers' lives, he is equally eager to stress that the Biblical portrait of the woman or man in right relation to God is usually very positive. This is true in regard to both Testaments, particularly the New which frequently refers to Christians as "saints" (Acts 9:32; Eph 1:1), "sons" (Rom 8:14), "sons of light" (1 Thess 5:5) and "new creation" (2 Cor 5:17), all terms by which their new status and nature are highlighted.

The weight of this kind of evidence, Saucy feels, is overwhelmingly in favour of not seeing the believer as merely a sinner saved by grace but a *saint* who is being delivered from the grip of Satan and sin.[47] Since the term saint in the original bears the idea of holiness,[48] the people of God can properly be designated as "holy ones." Is not this how the writer to the Hebrews addresses his/her audience (Heb 3:1)?[49] It is difficult to doubt that Saucy is on the right track. Where I think his thesis could have been strengthened is in the fertile area of the New Testament's eschatological vision of the believer. Here, I believe, is where lies the most

---

47. Saucy "'Sinners," 402–4.

48. LN, 1:745.

49. Interestingly, the term used in two Hebrew versions of the NT is *kedoshim,* an OT appellation for God (Prov 9:10).

Romans 5, the Imago Christi, and a Former Archbishop of Canterbury 91

promising locus for anyone who wishes to understand the character of the Christian.

Because we are destined for glory and at the same time already glorified (Rom 8:30b),[50] it is not an easy task to fully grasp the essential character of the Christian life. Given this fact, it is no surprise that some writers only stress the present dimension of the new life. Narramore,[51] for example, writes, "God already considers us to be new persons" (2 Cor 5:17).[52] The moment we place our faith in Jesus Christ we are different. We are alive to spiritual principles, open to the voice of God, and actively involved in a process of total restoration." No one can gainsay this. A revolutionary change has taken place in a person's life when s/he enters God's kingdom.

However, what some NT exegetes are concerned about at this very point is that the change in question should be explicated within its proper eschatological context, in order for its character to be fully appreciated. Here it is pointed out that the concept of newness found in the NT is a reality, the expectation of which is rooted in the OT. This makes the new creation "the glorious end of the revelation of God's salvation . . . the supreme goal of the entire Biblical *heilsgeschichte* ('history of salvation')."[53] Seen in this light the continuum of newness that the NT envisages embraces the entire period between the incarnation and the eschaton, the consummation of which holds out the strong hope of total universal transformation (Rom 8:21). The significance of this for defining the NT concept of the Kingdom and for identifying its true citizens should not be missed. Although the Kingdom has broken into the old aeon with radical effects, this present aeon still continues. What this means for those related to the King/Kingdom is nothing less than liberation from the present aeon that is evil to the core (Gal 1:4), as well as a radically new "Suzerainty-vassal pact" in effect (Matt 26:26–29). Additionally, a new "metamorphosis" is not only possible but imperative for Kingdom citizens, with the corresponding refusal to be shaped by a rapidly ageing dispensation (Rom 12:1–2; 1 John 2:15–17). As these

---

50. Glorification is among the "five undeniable affirmations" of vv. 29–30 (Stott, *Romans*, 248–49).

51. "Parent Leadership," 19.

52. For an excellent study on personhood, see Demarest and Beck, *The Human Person*, 27–304.

53. Ladd, *Theology*, 522.

last two pieces of Scripture indicate, an ethical response is nonetheless demanded (Gal 5:16), and the responsibility to reflect the glorious light of the Kingdom in terms of good works is no less diminished (Matt 5:16; Eph 2:10). In the words of Ladd, "The underlying idea [here] is that while believers live in the old age, because they are in Christ they belong to the new age with its new creation (indicative) and they are to live a life that is expressive of the new existence (imperative)."[54]

But to return to the question with which we were occupied in the previous section, Why is it that sin often creeps into the believer's life when s/he is supposed to "live a life that is expressive of the new existence"? Ladd again provides a plausible answer: "In a sense, even believers are still in Adam, for they die; they are still in the old aeon for they live in a sinful world and share the falleness of creation. But redemptively . . . they have entered into a new existence in Christ—the life of the new aeon."[55]

The struggle, then, in the life of the believer is rooted in the fact that s/he is a "Wo/man in transition and tension."[56] While Christians experience the inner transformation wrought by the divine Spirit (2 Cor 3:18), they at the same time "work out" their salvation in tension—always with the possibility of overwhelming success (Rom 8:37) or miserable failure (Rom 7:24?).

SUMMARY

Bearing the *imago Dei* with the hope of fully reflecting the *imago Christi* (1 John 3:2), the Christian stands as a creation of dignity and destiny. Though s/he still, in a sense, struggles with human "depravity,"[57] s/he should not be viewed as such. "A believer conscious of his or her shortcomings does not need to say, Because I am still a sinner, I cannot consider

---

54. Ibid., 522–23.
55. Ibid., 525.
56. Palmer, *Messianic 'I,'* 198.

57. Although this thought seems somewhat contradictory, it is certainly in line with Carter and Narramore's "tolerance of ambiguity" (*Integration*, 118). Someone once "commended" the Corinthian congregation for its "consistency" in not only believing in total depravity but practicing it. Among the many fine works on consistent Christian living, see Hamilton ("Imperative," 24), Wenham, "The Christian Life," 80–94, and Taylor, *The Church*.

myself a new person. Rather, he or she should say, *I am a new person*, but I still have a lot of growing to do."[58]

The implications of all this, I believe, have no little moment for psychology[59] and Theology,[60] for therapy[61] on the one hand and preaching on the other. The perspective shared above is deemed to be advantageous since it is squarely based on the Judeo-Christian tradition and some of the more established results of the discipline of psychology.

Using the former, I have attempted to offer a definition of the very nature[62] of what it means to be a Christian in terms of bearing the divine likeness, the residual adamic image (cf. Gen 5:3), as well as the *imago Christi* in both its present and future manifestation. From the point of view of psychology, a measure of support was sought particularly in the area of the human tendency toward self-deception.

Much more could be done. For example, how does the indwelling Spirit contribute to a better understanding of what it means to be Christian? What does it really mean to be "in Christ"? And, is it possible to appreciate the nature of the Christian apart from the context of the Messianic community? These are just some of the questions that would need to be addressed, if a better understanding of the essential character of the person in Christ is to be had. I do believe that what would emerge from such study can be placed within the parameters of a Genesis (1–2; dignity); Romans (1–5; depravity); Revelation (20–22; destiny) model.

---

58. The following is also apt: "The new self in the New Testament . . . is not equivalent to sinless perfection . . . it is . . . not static but dynamic . . . [therefore] we live a life of victory, but it is qualified victory, we are not yet what we shall be. We are not yet totally like Christ (1John 3:2). We live in the tension between the 'already and the not.' We are *genuinely* new persons but not yet *totally* new" (Hoekema, *Sanctification*, 82, 190; emphasis mine).

59. Carlson, *Counselling*.

60. Noelliste, *Faith Transforming Context*.

61. In this regard, see Gregory's ("En Route," 3–39) and Bergeron's (Conceptualization," 1–9) thought provoking essays on contextual counseling.

62. By 'nature' is meant the essential quality of a thing. Much confusion surrounds the term in Christian circles; for instance, if we say that Christ has two natures in terms of his divinity and humanity, what do we mean when we say that the Christian has two natures? Of course, the semantic range of the term may include both concepts. What is being pleaded for here is less equivocation.

5

"I-n-I" in Romans 7 and the Rest of the Pauline Corpus[1]

INTRODUCTION

SERIOUS STUDENTS OF THE Bible have always realized the significance of Romans 7:14–25 to a proper understanding of the nature of the Christian, and there is probably no passage of the New Testament upon which so much labor and ingenuity have been expended. This has led Robinson, as he wrestles with it, to say, "More ink, I suppose, has been spilled over this passage of Romans than any other."[2]

Nygren complains of its difficulty when he writes "[The passage] presents us with one of the greatest problems in the New Testament. It was already recognized in the first century; and since that time it has never come to rest."[3]

---

1. *Egō / eimî* (literally, "I [even] I"). Apart from the Fourth Gospel, this corpus has the highest percentage of "I" predications in the NT. Not until the twentieth-century Rasta movement have we had such a phenomenon in any professedly Christian discourse. Says Clark, "New Religious Movements," 494: "A movement that perhaps makes more use of the Bible than any other . . . is the Rastafarian movement . . . [which] is now to be found in Africa, Europe, and North and South America. . . . [T]he Bible is used by Rastafarians as a vehicle for the restoration of their dignity and identity as individuals and as a race which was ravaged by slavery." Weiss, "Die Rastafari-Bewegung auf Jamaika," also observes that *"Die römische Zahl I, wie etwa hinter dem Namen von Haile Selassie [formely Ras Tafari], wird wie das Pronomen 'I' gesprochen, ebenso das 'i' am Ende von Rastafari (=RastafarI). . . ."*/ The roman numeral I at the end of the name Haile Selassie is treated like pronominal "I" in "Rastafari." On this, see Palmer, *Messianic 'I' and Rastafari*, 17–39, and for the letter in general, Hoyt, "Romans," 249–75. Theologians such as McGrath ("A Particularist View," 171) and Moltmann (*A Broad Place*, 226; *Weiter Raum*, 218) have shown some interest in the Rastafari movement.

2. *Wrestling with Romans*, 82.

3. *Romans*, 284.

Two crucial questions seem to stand in the way of a proper understanding: Does the use of the first person singular indicate genuine self reference? And does the passage refer to Paul's Christian or pre-Christian state? This chapter will attempt to answer these two queries, and more.

CONTEXT

It seems to me that one factor brings together Romans 7:14–25 and the preceding context (going back to Paul's argument in chapters three through six), It is the sin (ἁμαρτία/*hamartia*) to which the Christian is no longer subservient. This sin is identified with that from which Christians are justified (3:30–26; 4:7). The apostle places the origin of this sin with the sinful act of Adam (Rom 5:12). This sin became a reigning power in each member of the human race until replaced in the believer by grace reigning through righteousness (5:12).

In Romans 6:1–14, Paul answers a key question: "Shall we go on sinning so that grace may increase?" (NIV).[4] His answer, first emotional then rational, is that it is a categorical impossibility. The qualitative relative pronoun[5] helps to bring this out. Sanday and Headlam express this idea thus: "Naturally the relative of quality: 'we, being what we are, men who died to sin.'"[6] The believer's relation to sin then is that s/he died to it in Christ's death (6:2–3, 10). The chapter as a whole (as well as the first section of the next chapter) makes the point that the Old Me died (1–11), the Old Monarch is dethroned (12–14), the Old Master is deposed (15–23), and the Old Marriage is dissolved (7:1–6).[7]

The apostle then deals with another objection in 6:15 that takes us into chapter 7, into the "autobiographical" section of 7:14–25. The passage, from verse 7, may be outlined thus.

---

4. "In chapters 6 and 7, Paul answers the criticism that salvation by grace encourages sin (6:1–14), allows sin (6:15–7:6), and makes the law a sinful thing" (Adewuya, *Transformed*, 17).

5. Οἵτινες, *oitines*, who.

6. Sanday and Headlam, *Romans*, 156.

7. Adapted from Philips, *Exploring Romans*, 99. "Old Me" does not refer to sin but to all that believers were in Adam (the KJV has "old man" (6:6), prompting some to believe that this "man" was Paul's father (Luke 23:42). Paul's "mother" is also mentioned in Rom 16:13!). Verses 12–23 will refer to indwelling sin which is the husband who has become a widower in 7:1–6. Interestingly, the resurrected ex-wife still lives under the same roof with him until the return of her new husband (Rom 7:4; cf. John 14:1–3).

A. The Involvement of the Law		7:7–13
	1. In revealing sin	7
	2. In arousing sin	8–9
	3. In activating sin	10–11
	4. Summary: the true nature of the law	12
B. The Ineffectiveness of the Law		7:14–25
	1. To effect change in the believer	14–17
	2. To enable the believer to do good	18–20
	3. To emancipate the believer	21–24
	4. Summary: tension within the believer	25

Within this framework we first examine verses 14–17.

> We know that the law is spiritual; but I am unspiritual, sold as a slave to sin. I do not understand what I do. For what I want to do I do not do, but what I hate I do. And if I do what I do not want to do, I agree that the law is good. As it is, it is no longer I myself who do it, but it is sin living in me (NIV).

In the previous verses, it would seem that the apostle is speaking of himself, because there is a generous use of the pronoun (ἐγώ/*egō*). In fact, in verses 7–25 one can count about 47 personal references in the English text (NIV).

Kümmel does not believe that Paul is speaking autobiographically here,[8] but the natural way to understand the passage, it seems to me, is to see the apostle referring to himself.[9] Granted, the clause (ἐγὼ δὲ σάρκινός εἰμι πεπραμένος ὑπὸ τὴν ἁμαρτίαν/*egō de sarkinos eimi pepremenos hupo ten harmatian*/ But I am unspiritual, sold as a slave to sin) seems incongruous with what has been said previously in chapter 6, but how else does one account for the emphatic personal references, and the change of tense in verse 14? While Kümmel may be correct in seeing

---

8. "According to Kümmel, *Röm 7*, 89, Paul 'employed the first person for portrayal of general human experiences' . . . *er benutze die erste Person zur Schilderrung allegemein menschlicher Erlebnisse* . . . [and] that it is 'impossible' ('*Umoglichkeit*') for these verses to be describing Paul as a Christian or any other Christian." (Middendorf, *'I' in the Storm*, 24 n. 43, 37 n. 116.)

9. E.g., Shulum, *Romans*, 250–51.

the "I" in a generalized sense, it seems preferable to side with Nygren in positing an autobiographical reference.[10]

But what of the statement *"But I am unspiritual, sold as a slave to sin?"* After a brief discussion of various views of the passage, Cranfield strongly asserts is agreement with Nygren.[11]

While Cranfield does not seem to grasp the believer's radical cleavage from the Mosaic law (cf. 7:6), he nevertheless is worth hearing on this particular point of the believer's struggle with sin.

The apostle then elaborates (verse 15–17) on his shocking statement of verse 14 as he begins to lay bare the tension that is taking place in his life. Following this he takes up another "weakness" of the law, its incapacity to enable the believer to do good (vv. 18–20): *"I know that nothing good lives in me, that is, in my sinful nature. For I have the desire to do what is good, but I cannot carry it out. For what I do is not the good I want to do; no, the evil I do not want to do, this I keep on doing. Now if I do what I do not want to do, it is no longer I who do it, but it is sin living in me that does it."*

While the term "flesh" (KJV, translating σάρξ/*sarx*) in verse 18 is certainly to be understood in an ethical sense, I wonder whether or not the translation above is not perpetuating a possible confusion by translating it "sinful nature." The point is that in discussing the uniqueness of Christ, theologians talk about his two natures, human and divine. But when we say that the believer has two natures, we seem to change the meaning a bit. Therefore, the literal rendering of the NIV margin is to be preferred.

That the apostle in the above paragraph is speaking autobiographically is our view. But Ridderbos embraces a contrary position.[12] Longenecker, on the other hand, believes the passage should not be restricted to just believers. The experience of 7:7–24 is indeed a universal one, he contends, and finds its most intense expression in the spiritually sensitive.[13]

So verses 18–20 inform us of the spiritually sensitive apostle desiring to do the right, but only managing to do the evil he loathes. The reason? Indwelling sin (v. 20; ἡ οἰκοῦσα ἐν ἐμοὶ ἁμαρτία/*hē oikousa en*

---

10. Nygren, *Romans*, 286; he believes, however, that the 'I' is pre-conversion in orientation.

11. Cranfield, *Romans*, 346–47.

12. Ridderbos, *Paul*, 126–30.

13. Longenecker, *Paul*, 116; cf. Packer, *Keep in Step*, 263–70.

emoi hamartia). Cranfield's comment is pertinent here: "This verse is not intended as an excuse, but is rather an acknowledgement of the extent to which sin dwelling in the Christian, usurps control over his life. But . . . the fact that there is real conflict and tension is a sign of hope."[14]

The law is also powerless to emancipate the believer from the grip of sin (21–24). *"So I find this law at work: When I want to do good, evil is right there with me. For in my inner being I delight in God's law; but I see another law at work in the members of my body, waging war against the law of my mind and making me a prisoner of the law of sin at work within my members. What a wretched man I am! Who will rescue me from this body of death?"*

Now what is the nature of the "law" mentioned in this portion? The answer to this question seems to be a key in understanding this paragraph, because the term appears five times (and twice in verse 25). Denney maintains that Paul means nothing more than the Mosaic code. Thus he says "I agree with those who make *ton nomon* as the Mosaic Law . . . since the subject of the whole paragraph is the relation of 'the law' to sin."[15] This view may have much to commend it. However, other possibilities must be explored.

Sanday and Headlam picked up an interpretation that was rejected by Denney, that *nomos* bears the sense of "principle," at least in verse 21.[16] Since this is almost certainly the apostles meaning in 3:27, this understanding is not a kind of anachronism as Denney suggested.[17] But is the law of God of verse 22 identical with the *nomon* (law) of the previous verse? Cranfield,[18] also sees the phrase as a clear reference to the Mosaic code, and he may be correct.

But I want to suggest that the phrase parallels "the law of Christ" of Galatians 6:2. This understanding is based upon the assumption that the apostle viewed the Mosaic code (in its entirety) as having been abrogated by the work of Christ, both as a means of justification and sanctification (Rom 10:4).33 It is this Messianic law that the apostles delights in; it is this law which provides a bond between Paul and his Lord (1 Cor 9:21); and it is this law to which the 'sinful mind' (NIV) cannot submit (8:7).

---

14. Cranfield, *Romans*, 360–61.
15. Denney, *Romans*, 642.
16. Sanday and Headlam, *Romans*, 182.
17. Denney, op. cit., 642–43.
18. Cranfield, *Romans*, 362.

But the apostle's delight in God's law seems to be the ground on which war is declared against him in verse 23. This other law, then, this "foreign principle," makes him at times a prisoner of war. So Paul, it would appear, did taste defeat occasionally.

As a consequence, the spiritually sensitive apostle dreads these losses and so cries out: Ταλαίπωρος ἐγὼ ἄνθρωπος· τίς με ῥύσεται ἐκ τοῦ σώματος τοῦ θανάτου τούτου; (*Talaipōros egō anthrōpos; tis me rusetai ek tou sōmatos tou thanatou toutou*/Wretched person *I* am! who will liberate me from this decaying corpse?[19] But are we not assuming too much by applying these words to the esteemed apostle? When one considers that the cry appears to reflect the struggle of any wo/man who strives to be consistently good,[20] one may be surprised as well at the opposite assumption of Denney that "Ταλαίπωρος κτλ is not the cry of the Christian Paul."[21] Perhaps it is better to conclude with Longenecker that here we have "Paul uttering mankind's great cry of its own inability. It is Paul's and humanity's realization that in our history and experience we have become so bound up by sin that there can be deliverance and victory only through God."[22] It is to that victory that the apostle turns in verse 25.

"*I thank God through Jesus Christ our Lord. So then with the mind I myself serve the law of God; but with the flesh the law of sin.*"

Summary Statement concerning the Spiritual Tension within the Believer

The first part of this verse speaks of a victory that is "already but not yet," so it is not necessary in my opinion to posit, like Cranfield,[23] a resurrection deliverance only. The struggle continues, but it is one based upon solid hope (cf. Rom 8:23).

In sum, I see the passage as a call to humility. One can hardly read this passage aright without having a sense of "smallness" in the face of its difficulty. While many have taken a dogmatic approach towards Romans 7, it is difficult to see how such expositors can remain that way after

---

19. My paraphrase; "*Ich elenber Mensch . . .*" (Nestle, *NovT*, 405); "*Las moy home mise,rable! . . .*" (Calvin, *Épître aux Romains*, 171); "*I-man jus rahtid! . . .*" (Jamaican).
20. Theissen, *Psychological Aspects*, 177–201.
21. Denny, "Romans," 653.
22. Longenecker, *Paul*, 116
23. Cranfield, *Romans*, 368–71.

wrestling with it. The passage is also a call to integrity. When this portion is read existentially and not just exegetically, all without exception can identify with its tension. Honesty in interpretation would then give way to a life of integrity.

Finally, it would seem to me that Romans 7:14–25 invites us to live responsibly, even when defeat may be a part of our history.[24] The "wretched man" of 7:24 is (or should be) the "watchful man" of I Corinthians 9:27. The passage, then, is a call to spiritual responsibility.

We now turn to Paul's[25] other I-style lexicon to see how he employs "the usually emphatic" pronoun[26] in the letters dispatched to churches that he himself founded.[27]

FIRST THESSALONIANS

The earliest section of this epistle is full of reminiscences of Paul's visit to the city of Thessalonica. A church was well established in that vicinity around AD 50 on the second missionary journey. According to the book of Acts 17:1–10, after Paul had ministered for nearly a month he had to leave because of the outbreak of persecution against the fledgling church. Of course the apostle's shepherd instincts could not allow him to abandon this church so he apparently attempted another visit (1 Thess 2:18) after his co-workers had left Berea.[28] He eventually sent his young missionary colleague Timothy, to inquire of their welfare.

On returning to Paul, Timothy gave him quite a positive report of the Thessalonians' growth and outreach, despite continued hostility from outsiders and certain undesirable tendencies among the insiders. As was pointed above, Pauline recollections are quite prominent in this letter.

Thus in chapter 2 we are not surprised to find autobiographical elements related to his visit, such as verses 1,5,7 and 9–14; verses which describe the strong bonding which took place between a father and his children. It is no wonder that in verses 17 and18 Paul expresses his yearning to return. Verse 18, which provides a brief explanation for the thought expressed in the previous verse, reads: "Wherefore we have

---

24. See especially, Adewuya, *Transformed by Grace*, 84–100; also Appendix C.

25. "The most self-conscious of all writers of the New Testament," (Lofthouse, "'I' and 'We'" 241).

26. Abbott-Smith, *Greek lexicon*, 128.

27. With the exception of Colossians.

28. Hogg and Vine, *Thessalonians*, 82.

desired to come to you, even *I Paul*, [italics added] both once and twice [ἅπαξ καὶ δίς²⁹], and Satan has hindered us"(DV).³⁰

Wanamaker³¹ views "I Paul" as proof that the apostle is the real author of the letter. But its function seems to underscore Paul's deep and personal eagerness to revisit his children. The phrase surrounding "I Paul" also manifests a few emphatic features that seem to support my point. First, the particle *men* (μέν) without the corresponding *de* (δέ), may be rendered "indeed" in this context, bringing out the emotional state of the apostle.³² Second, *I* (in tandem with "Paul" undoubtedly heightens the emphasis of the phrase, and, finally, "more significant than his use of [I], is that Paul refers to himself by name in the body of the letter. . . . [Compare] 2 Cor. 10:1 and Philemon 22 . . . in both of which his name heightens the emotion."³³

In sum, Paul, particularly in 2:17–20, demonstrates his goodwill toward his readers by sharing his desire to rejoin them "and [by] his sending of Timothy as his *alter ego.*"³⁴

There are only two occurrences of the emphatic singular pronoun in the Thessalonian correspondence, and a note of interest is that both are used in connection with some mention of the Satan. In 2:18 Paul gives the reason for his failed attempts to revisit the new converts as the work of Satan, and at 3:5 the same adversary is called *the tempter*.³⁵ It

29. ἅπαξ καὶ δίς, according to Williams, *Thessalonians*, 54, is to be construed with evgw. Pau/loj and not with ἠθελήσαμεν ἐλθεῖν πρὸς ὑμᾶς. Cf. NRSV.

30. The significance of the "we-I" collocation "is raised in an acute form" in this verse (Moule, *Idiom*, 119). The 'we' is taken to be "editorial or epistolary" by Malherbe, *Thessalonians*, 184. Lofthouse, "'I' and 'We' in The Pauline Letters,"

245, concludes, "It would thus appear that in Paul's use of the singular and plural there is neither caprice nor carelessness. When he says 'I,' he means 'I'—there can be no doubt about that. But the barrier of singular and plural is constantly breaking down."

31. Wanamaker, *Thessalonians*, 121.

32. Here Malherbe, *Thessalonians*, 183, cites Rom 10:1 as a parallel, as well as BAGD, 503. 2a.

33. Malherbe, *Thessalonians,* 184.

34. Krentz, *Thessalonian Debate,* 309.

35. Other names for this malevolent force within the Pauline corpus include, evil one (2 Thess 3:3), devil (Eph 4:27; 6:11), the god of this age (2 Cor 4:4), and the ruler of the authority of the air (Eph 2:2; Williams, *Thessalonians*, 60). Williams, *Thessalonians*, 54, is correct in pointing out that Satan is always subject to God, but, I think wrong in stating that "in the NT, Satan's activities are spoken of only in relation to Christians and his attempts to hinder them in one way or the other." 2 Cor 4:4 and Matt 13 seem to say otherwise.

is in relation to the Satan's role as tempter that Paul reveals his unease concerning the Thessalonians: "For this reason *I* also, no longer able to refrain myself, sent to know your faith, lest perhaps the tempter had tempted you and our labour should be come to nothing" (DV).[36]

The sentence expresses Paul's parental response in an effort to try to mitigate the baneful effect of the enemy. Verses 6–8 inform us that Paul's effort was not unsuccessful. "In Corinthians, Galatians, and Philippians there is a convergence of two factors that strongly indicate Paul's designed usage of personal example as a literary strategy: literary markers exhorting the auditors to imitation (1 Cor. 4:6, 16; 7:8; 11:1; 12:31; Gal 4:12 Phil 3:17; 4:9) and a corresponding self-portrayal that serves to model behaviour and attitudes appropriate to those who are 'in Christ.'"[37]

But in the Thessalonian correspondence, according to Dodd, no such pattern is to be found. "There is however, a surrogate literary feature for emulation . . . found in the predominant use of the 'recall motif,' where Paul repeatedly appeals to the Thessalonians' recollection of his past presence with them,"[38] as we have mentioned above. "This utilization of reminiscence," Dodd continues, "draws attention to the past nature of Paul's example which he exemplified when he was present with them but in each case this past example is related to the present expository topic."[39]

Paul, however, may be doing more. In the two instances of ἐγώ found in the first Thessalonian correspondence, the writer appears to be laying stress on the need to be vigilant in face of satanic opposition. Paul's 'I' in these contexts, then, functions as literary strategy within "the present expository topic."[40]

GALATIANS

The letter to the Galatians is one of Paul's earliest. According to Longenecker,[41] it is possibly Paul's first, with a kind of "programmatic

---

36. The crasis [κἀγώ] is thought to be emphatic by Malherbe (*Thessalonians*, 195), along with the singular "I sent."

37. Dodd, *Paul's Paradigmatic 'I'*, 196.

38. Ibid., 213.

39. Ibid., 214.

40. Ibid., 214. Interestingly, in this early epistle the enemy is Satan (see note 35 above), whereas in the later and less occasional letter to the Romans, the enemy is primarily sin: "I know that nothing good lives in me, that is, in my sinful nature" (Rom. 7:18; NIV). In both letters the 'I' has the responsibility to resist evil, whatever form it takes.

41. Longenecker, *Galatians*, xli.

primacy for 1) understanding Paul's teaching, 2) establishing a Pauline chronology, 3) tracing early apostolic history, and 4) determining many NT critical and canonical issues."

In Galatians, if we are to follow Betz,[42] we have a full-scale *apologia* or defence of the apostle and his gospel. After the introduction (*exordium* 1:6–11), and a statement of the issues at hand (*narratio* 1:6–2:14), Paul outlines his central thesis (*propositio*) in 2:15–21. These verses contain capsule statements of some of the most significant truths of Christianity, "[in] particular ... the doctrine of justification by grace through faith.... The words 'justify' and 'justification' occur in these verses for the first time ... the verb, three times in v. 16, once v. 17; [and] the noun in v.21."[43]

The point of these verses is that justification came through faith in Christ and not by law. This being the case Paul argues: "But if in our endeavour to be justified in Christ, we ourselves were found to be sinners, is Christ then an agent of sin? Certainly not. But if I build up again those things which I tore down, then I prove myself a transgressor. For through the law, I [ἐγώ/*egō*] died, that I might live to God" (vv 17–19).

Here we have the essence of Paul's theology "in encapsulated form ... vis-à-vis Jewish nomism (vv 19–20),"[44] and here "The 'I' of verse 17 ... has changed to the 'I' of v. 18, which in turn gives way to the emphatic 'I' of verse 19."[45] In fact one may discern a tripartite structure encompassing the verb "to live."

A I (through the law) died (to the law) that *I might live* to God [v. 19]

B I have been crucified with Christ; it is *no longer I who live* but *Christ who lives* in me [v. 20a]

A The life *I now live* in the flesh, *I live* by faith in ... the Son of God, who loved me and gave himself for me [20b].[46]

Paul's theology is intensely personal. Verse 20 in particular supports this point, and unveils as well the emphatically Christological character of Paul's life and ministry. But what does it mean? First of all, it is im-

42. Betz, *Galatians*, 16–22; for an assessment of Betz's structure, see Boers, *Justification*, 43–76.
43. Boice, "Galatians," 448.
44. Longenecker, *Galatians*, 91.
45. According to Boice, this 'I' (v. 19) is in sharp contrast to the "in Christ" in v. 20.
46. Barclay, "Paul's Story," 142–143.

portant to recognise that though Paul's 'I' in this pericope is intensely personal, its use does not necessarily preclude anyone else. In fact, it has been suggested that here we have a case of generic usage.[47] In other words, what is expressed in the verse is true of the Galatian Christians as well. Second, though the thought of the second half of the verse is emphatically stated, there is no eclipse of the believer's personality.[48] Christ *lives* in and through Paul and he lives also as a new creation (cf. 2 Cor 5:17). "The repetition [therefore] of 'I' (ἐγώ) is not accidental. But so completely is self dethroned in the new order that in this context Paul will not only say ἐγὼ ζω (*egō zō*, I live) but "it is no longer *I* who lives; it is Christ who lives in me."[49] More to the point, we believe, is Fung's reflection:[50] "To have Christ living in Paul . . . does not mean some kind of mystical depersonalization, as though the human 'I' of Paul were absorbed into the pneumatic 'I' of Christ; on the contrary, Paul fully retains his identity as an 'I' who sustains an 'I-Thou' relationship with Christ."[51]

In chapters 3–4, the apostle continues to make the point that the gospel he preached among the Galatians is non-negotiable and all sufficient to meet human needs. Therefore, the insistence of some on circumcision, and the like, is way off the mark. Added to this is his argument based upon their own experience with the Spirit (3:2–5; 4:8–10), and the experience of Abraham himself (3:6–4:7).

Paul's further self-exemplification and personal appeal in 4:12–20 are to follow. Thus in 4:12 "we read a familiar Pauline appeal for imitation, though the word itself (μίμησις) is lacking."[52] This appeal, according to Dodd,[53] is well in keeping with the "self-presentation that has already occurred in the letter."[54]

In continuing his strong reaffirmation of the liberty found only in the gospel, Paul once again exposes the futility of obtaining a righteous

---

47. Beekman and Callow, *Translating the Word of God*, 108.
48. Harrison, "Galatians," 1290.
49. Bruce, *Galatians*, 144, (italics his).
50. Fung, *Galatians*, 124.
51. Rapa (*Meaning of Works of the Law*, 145) takes the 'I' of v.20 to be universal or gnomic and as representative of all Christians. He believes that the pericope in which it is located is the most theological of the epistle (127).
52. Dodd, *Paul's Paradigmatic 'I'*, 162.
53. Ibid.
54. Cf. Lyons, *Pauline Autobiography*, 165.

standing before God by keeping the law (5:2–12). Accordingly, circumcision is authoritatively (v. 2) and summarily dismissed, and Spirit related matters like grace, faith, love, and hope are all promoted in its stead. He evidently speaks in this manner because "others had . . . undertaken to say what Paul believed or practised in the matter of circumcision (cf. v.11); here is Paul's own account,"[55] which begins with the solemn statement of verse 2. Equally emphatic is the expression of confidence on the part of Paul that his Galatian converts will adopt the proper posture on the matter, that the offenders in question will be brought to book (v.10), and that his cruciform focus of ministry is not misplaced (v.11). As the apostle draws the letter to a close he strongly expresses the hope that his converts "will avow with him a belief in christocentric and cross-centered theology that eliminates the necessity for circumcision,"[56] so that they may reaffirm their creation status in Christ (v.15; cf. 5:2 2:6). In the apostle's own closing words: "But far be it from me to boast save in the cross of our Lord Jesus Christ, through whom the world is crucified to me, and I to the world . . . For the rest let no one trouble me, for I bear in my body the brands of the Lord Jesus" (DV).[57]

The passage in which these words are found is not an ordinary first-century epilogue. In it Paul fitly summarises the crucial elements he has already discussed in the body of the letter,[58] and that by way of "self-exemplification and self-portrayal . . . [he] drive[s] a wedge between the Galatians and the Judaizers by convincing them to side with Paul against his opponents."[59]

FIRST CORINTHIANS

As founder of the Corinthian congregations, Paul, according to Horsley,[60] was anxious to articulate "ways in which the assembly of saints is to constitute a community of a new society alternative to the dominant imperial society." This dominant society was controlled in turn by a "pre-

---

55. Bruce, *Galatians*, 229.
56. Longenecker, *Galatians*, 234.
57. Ἐμοὶ δὲ μὴ γένοιτο καυχᾶσθαι εἰ μὴ ἐν τῷ σταυρῷ τοῦ κυρίου ἡμῶν Ἰησοῦ Χριστοῦ, δι' οὗ ἐμοὶ κόσμος ἐσταύρωται *kavgw.* κόσμῳ . . . Τοῦ λοιποῦ κόπους μοι μηδεὶς παρεχέτω· *evgw.* γὰρ τὰ στίγματα τοῦ Ἰησοῦ ἐν τῷ σώματί μου βαστάζω (vv. 14, 17).
58. Bruce, *Galatians*, 268.
59. Dodd, *Paul's Paradigmatic 'I,'* 169.
60. Horsley, "1 Corinthians," 230.

tentious aristocratic Hellenistic culture" whose elite benefited greatly from Rome's reign of terror, which included the brutal subjugation of all the intransigent. "But," Horsley continues, "it is through the despicably crucified Christ and now his lowborn, weak and despised followers, the Corinthian believe themselves, that God has shamed the pretentious elite questing after power, wealth, wisdom, noble birth, and honorific public office (1. 21–23, 26–29; 4. 8, 10)."

Paul, obviously, wanted his alternative society to be different. Hence, one can understand his chagrin when he first learnt that the church he founded—a church that "took the form of a number of small 'assemblies' based on households"[61]—was exhibiting one of the worst traits of the dominant society: pride. One way in which this pride came to the fore was in their employment of the first person pronoun cited in what has come down to us as Paul's first piece of correspondence to the Corinthians (1:10). Paul's use of the said pronoun (below) will then be both corrective and paradigmatic to a group of "protognostics" who believed themselves to have occupied the place of "special religious status, as 'wise' or 'righteous' or "perfect.""[62]

The apostle's first use of 'I' (ἐγώ) in this epistle draws attention to his own frailty that was exhibited while ministering in the city of Corinth (2:1, 3).[63] Earlier in chapter 1:12, he quotes members of the Corinthian factions,[64] possibly in an exaggerated manner (I am Paul's, I am of Apollos, I am of Cephas, and I'm of Christ).[65]

Now Paul denigrates himself[66] to make the point that he is not deserving of such accolades, even from a small segment of the church he himself founded: "And *I*, when I came to you, brethren, came not in excellency of word, or wisdom, announcing to you the testimony of

---

61. Ibid., 231.

62. Ibid., 122.

63. Garland, *First Corinthians*, 85–87. Conzelmann, *First Corinthians*, 54, sees verse 3 as a variant of the opening verse, with its use of κἀγώ. For the possible nature of Paul's weakness as well as the rhetorical character of the pericope, note Witherington, *Conflict & Community*, 122–125.

64. Theissen, *The Social Setting of Pauline Christianity*, 168.

65. ἐγὼ μέν εἰμι Παύλου, ἐγὼ δὲ 'Απολλῶ, ἐγὼ δὲ Κηφᾶ, ἐγὼ δὲ Χριστου.

66. "At a much deeper level, the Pauline lifestyle witnesses to identification with the crucified Christ and *a theology of the cross*" and "By rejecting the cry 'I am for Paul' (1:12), Paul personally adopts a cruciform posture in relation to 'power'" (Thiselton, *First Corinthians*, 128, 157; italics his).

God. For I did not judge *it well* to know anything among you save Jesus Christ, and him crucified. And *I* was with you in weakness and in fear and in much trembling."[67] His humble service is something that they themselves could recall (2:4–5).

The next occurrence of Paul's emphatic 'I' is located in 3:1. In chiding the Corinthians for their factiousness, the apostle confesses, "And *I,* brethren, have not been able to speak to you as to spiritual, but as to fleshly; as to babes in Christ." "And I" (Κἀγώ/*kagō*), in this context, is a part of Paul's emphatic broadside against a group that thought it was indeed so special that corporeality is at best something to be endured until the coming of Christ. To be told that they were not spiritual (πνευματικοι,/*pneumatikoi*) but fleshly (σαρκίκοι/*sarkikoi*),[68] was a big blow on two counts, since the latter points to the fact that they were in denial, and the former was what is emphatically affirmed in their own circles. Paul then proceeds to set the records straight concerning the true status of Christian workers by a couple of rhetorical questions designed to demonstrate their equality (3:4–5), despite the obvious division of labor (v.6).

The stress on his own foundational ministry ("I planted," ἐγὼ ἐφύτευσα/*egō ephuteusa*)[69] is not to be equated with the Corinthian boasting, but it is to be seen as a firm reminder of the role God allowed him to play in their own Christian experience at the very beginning. This thought is repeated under a different image in the following chapter (4:15), when Paul declares that he is their sole spiritual father (*a mi faada unnu*[70]/ἐγὼ ὑμᾶς ἐγέννησα/ *egō humas egennēsa*), despite the fact they had many "foster-parents." Similar Pauline images (cf. 1 Thess 2:11) include "parent (2 Cor 12:14) . . . mother (Gal 4:19; cf. . . . 1 Thess 2:7) and brother implicitly . . . e.g., Rom 1:13; 7:1; *passim*."[71]

Chapter 5 begins to highlight another of the many problems of the Corinthian congregation. If favoritism lies at the root of their divisions in the first four chapters, another set of fleshly desires can be seen to underlie the difficulties outlined in the next three. The first two verses of chapter 5 inform us that a member of the church is in an il-

---

67. DV; ἐγώ, *egō*, 'I'.

68. Verse 3; verse 1 has the synonym σαρκίνοι.

69. With the strong ἀλλά following, the greater emphasis is on o` qeo.j hu]xanen (BDF, 233: "but . . . not Apollos or I, but God.").

70. Jamaican for: "I brought you into the family of God."

71. Lyons, *Pauline Autobiography*, 10.

licit sexual union with a woman that was somehow related to his father. The Apostle's judgment on the matter is that the immoral man must be excommunicated. This judgment is expressed by another pronominal antithesis:[72] "And ye are puffed up, and ye have not rather mourned, in order that he that has done this deed might be taken away out of the midst of you.3 For *I* . . . in spirit, have already judged . . ." (DV).[73] It is now the congregation's responsibility to do likewise.

The next Pauline "I" in this piece of correspondence is part of Paul's effort to counter the kind of theology that was popularly expressed in a Corinthian slogan, "All things are permissible" (6:12).[74] The point is somewhat granted by the apostle, but he hastens to add, "but *I* will not be brought under the power of any" (DV; ἀλλ' οὐκ ἐγὼ ἐξουσιασθήσομαι ὑπό τινος/*Alla ouk egō exousiasthēsomai hupo tinos*).[75] In so doing Paul sets the stage "for his discussion of the horrors of sexual immorality and in contrast the holy use of the body,"[76] and ἐγώ ('I') is part of his transitional summation as well as paradigmatic injunctive (e.g., 5:12; 8:13; 10:28–11:1; 12:31–13:3; 13:11-12; 14:11,14,18).[77]

In chapter 7 the apostle addresses yet another Corinthian problem. There is a sense in which it is related to the problem of sexual immorality dealt with in the previous chapters. This is seen in verse 2 where marriage is recommended to avoid sexual immorality. The accent is on other challenging matters related to marriage: singleness, separation, service, and some thoughts on mate selection.

With reference to the issue of singleness and marriage, Paul reveals is strong bias for celibacy, though he acknowledges that he cannot impose such a lifestyle on others (7:7). Nevertheless, the advantage of the single state cannot be overstated ("But I say to the unmarried and to the widows, it is good for them that they remain even as I"; v. 8).[78]

---

72. Robertson and Plummer, *Commentary*, 97.

73. καὶ ὑμεῖς πεφυσιωμένοι ἐστὲ (5:2); ἐγὼ μὲν γάρ . . . τῷ πνεύματι, ἤδη κέκρικα (5:3; *UBS*⁴).

74. "This is confirmed by the way Paul cites it again in 10:23; in both cases he qualifies it so sharply as to negate it" (Fee, *First Corinthians*, 251).

75. Meeks, *Writings*, 32, sees a pun (?) in *"exestin / exousiasthesomai."*

76. Mare, "Corinthians," 224.

77. Dodd, *Paradigmatic 'I,'* 46–49; Garland, *Corinthians*, 228.

78. Λέγω δὲ τοῖς ἀγάμοις καὶ ταῖς χήραις, καλὸν αὐτοῖς ἐὰν μείνωσιν ὡς κἀγώ.

Even more emphatically ("But to the married I enjoin, not *I*, but the Lord, Let not a wife be separated from husband"; DV), divorce is discouraged (v. 10).[79] In the matter of a mixed marriage (v. 12), divorce is also discouraged if the unbelieving partner wishes to remain in such a union.[80]

The language of verse 12 differs markedly from verse 10, despite the presence of the emphatic pronoun. On the matter discussed in verse 10, dominical support (whether by way of tradition or revelation) is cited. No such substantiation is invoked in verse 12. Yet despite the seemingly less authoritative language in the latter case, one should not reduce the apostle's counsel as mere personal opinion.[81]

Later in the chapter Paul offers realistic counsel concerning marriage, almost as though he were speaking from experience.[82] Whether or not Paul was ever married, his caveat is forceful.

The final 'I' employment in the chapter comes in the last verse, in which Paul summarises his marriage counsel with the somewhat enigmatic: "but I think that *I* also have God's Spirit" (δοκῶ δὲ κἀγὼ πνεῦμα θεοῦ ἔχειν/*Dokō de kagō pneuma theou echein*). The clause properly rounds off his advice to "the widow" (v. 39); but what does it really mean? Is the mention of the πνεῦμα (*pneuma*, spirit) with κἀγω (*kagō*) "a subtle thrust at the pneumatics in Corinth"?[83] Or does he express here his acute awareness of divine enablement? Maybe a little of both, with the accent on the latter, for "what [Paul] says is more than the opinion merely of a private individual."[84]

In chapter 9 the discussion moves to the rights and privileges of apostles, among other things. A series of rhetorical questions (vv 4–8) forcefully makes the point of apostolic prerogatives that appear to have been questioned by Paul's antagonists in the Corinthian congregations.

79. Τοῖς δὲ γεγαμηκόσιν παραγγέλλω, οὐκ ἐγὼ ἀλλὰ ὁ κύριος, γυναῖκα ἀπὸ ἀνδρὸς μὴ χωρισθῆναι.

80. Ruef, *First Letter*, 56.

81. Says Barrett, *Commentary*, 163, "Jesus, whose ministry was cast almost exclusively within Judaism . . . did not have occasion to deal with mixed marriages between the people of God and others."

82. *Yu si if yu get married, Gaad naah sin yu; same ting wid di virgin. But dat a whole eep a baddaraashan, an mi a write fi spare unnu*/ ἐὰν δὲ καὶ γαμήσῃς, οὐχ ἥμαρτες, καὶ ἐὰν γήμῃ ἡ παρθένος, οὐχ ἥμαρτεν· θλῖψιν δὲ τῇ σαρκὶ ἕξουσιν οἱ τοιοῦτοι, ἐγὼ δὲ ὑμῶν φείδομαι- v. 28). Murphy-O'Connor (*Paul*, 62–65) believes Paul was indeed married.

83. Conzelmann, *Corinthians*, 136.

84. Morris, *Corinthians*, 123.

One of these rhetorical questions (v.6) contains the emphatic pronoun ἐγώ, which aids in developing Paul's theme along the lines of the latter part of chapter 8. Beginning there, the believers are urged to be considerate of others in living out the gospel. It is in this context that we read: "Are *I* and Barnabas alone supposed to work for a living?"[85]

"Nevertheless," the apostle continues, "we have not made use of this right, but we endure anything rather than put an obstacle in the way of the Gospel of Christ . . . [so although] the Lord commanded that those who proclaim the Gospel should get their living by the Gospel . . . I [ἐγώ] made no use of any of these rights, nor am I writing this to secure any such provision" (vv 12–15. NKJV).[86]

To drive home the point of his independence-for-the-sake-of-the Gospel, and the discipline it takes to maintain it, Paul employs one more interrogative in verse 24 ("Do you not know that in a race all the runners compete, but only one receives the prize?"). With another 'I' assertion[87] (*A so mi run*/ἐγὼ τοίνυν οὕτως τρέχω/ *egō toinun houtōs trechō*), Paul gives eloquent testimony to his serious and exemplary participation (v.26) in the "supra-Isthmian games."

The passage 10:23–11:1 returns the reader to the question raised in 8:13 in respect of one's liberty being limited by one's love for the community. Conzelmann[88] takes this pericope to be a self-contained unit, with no connection to the previous section. Preferable is Fee's[89] suggestion (which I have modified slightly) that the chapters in question bear the following structural relation:

A (8:1–13)   Discussion (in general)

B (9:1–27)   Digression

A (10:1–11:1) Discussion (in particular)

---

85. The REB, NLT and NRSV, except NIV, all place "Barnabas" before 'I,' possibly to conform to English convention. My rendition has retained the Greek order and thus the Pauline emphasis.

86. For possible reasons for such drastic apostolic action, see Thrall (*First and Second*, 68). On ἐγώ in v. 15, see Fee (*Corinthians*, 416, n. 10). Yet one should not miss the sensitivity with which Paul writes concerning financial matters in this chapter (Dunn, *Theology*, 709–711).

87. "Therefore I run in such a way . . ." (NIV; 1 Cor 9:26).

88. Conzelmann, *Corinthians*, 175.

89. *First Corinthians*, 16.

There is also a return to the rhetoric of previous sections. Accordingly, we read, "for why should my liberty be determined by another man's scruples? If I [ἐγώ] partake with thankfulness, why am I denounced because of that for which I [ἐγώ] give thanks?" (10:29b–30; NKJV). Here both the character of the question as well as the nature of the personal pronoun serve to hammer home the point that charity must give way to liberty, both for the good of others and the glory of God. The point is further grounded in the apostle's personal example ("Even as *I* also please all in all things; not seeking my own profit, but that of the many, that they may be saved." DV),[90] and forms the basis for the exhortation in 11:1.

Turning to another Corinthian problem, this time their abuse of the Eucharistic meal, the apostle solemnly repeats the tradition upon which it is based to remind them of its seriousness (*I received from the Lord that which I passed on to you all*-11:23).[91] Here ἐγώ seems to undergird his own apostolic authority and the solemnity of the feast that it seeks to promote.

The final emphatic 'I' in First Corinthians appears in the conclusion (16:10) of the letter, where the apostle pleads with the quarrelsome and disorderly congregations to be hospitable to his emissary Timothy, because "he does the work of the lord just as I" (τὸ γὰρ *e;rgon* κυρίου *evrga,zetai* ὡς κἀγώ/ *To gar ergon kuriou ergazetai ōs kagō*).[92] Given the rift between the church and himself, it was perhaps unwise of the apostle to express such an "egoistic" note at the end of a very sensitive letter.

Dodd,[93] for example, surmises that Paul toned down his I-statements and his personal examples as an explicit literary strategy in 2 Corinthians "perhaps partly [because of] . . . an unfavourable assessment of his extensive use of this technique in 1 Corinthians (cf. 2 Cor. 4:5)." Why then the phrase "as I also," ὡς κἀγώ/ *hōs kagō*)? Possibly to lend weight to and defend[94] the ministry of his young and bashful companion. So, although Paul's 'I' at this point (as well as elsewhere in this and other epistles) "may have sounded boastful to the Corinthians, drawing upon [himself]

---

90. καθὼς κἀγὼ πάντα πᾶσιν ἀρέσκω.
91. Ἐγὼ γὰρ παρέλαβον ἀπὸ τοῦ κυρίου, ὃ καὶ παρέδωκα ὑμῖν.
92. The cognate verb and noun appear to be a Pauline pun. see DV.
93. Dodd, *Paul*, 30.
94. Barrett, *Commentary*, 391.

the odium attached to *periautologia*, (self-discussion) in antiquity,"[95] the risk was well calculated.[96]

SECOND CORINTHIANS

As we have seen above, B. Dodd has argued that Paul has refrained from using personal statements in this epistle the way he did in the first piece of correspondence. So how does Dodd account for the 'I' statements below? Says he: "The few 'I' statements that may be thought to function paradigmatically are clearly related to criticisms or suspicions raised about Paul."[97] An examination of the data may reveal that Dodd has overstated his claims. Admittedly, it is difficult to fit almost any Pauline concept into a neat framework, and Dodd has ably defended his position in the other letter. But I believe he failed to effectively incorporate the I-statements of this epistle into his overall thesis.

The statement[98] in 2 Cor 1:23 definitely qualifies under Dodd's overarching category related to criticism or suspicions raised concerning the apostle. After the opening greeting (vv.1–2) and his equally customary thanksgiving section (3–11), Paul launches out into a spirited *apologia* (12–23) regarding his interrupted travel plans, and other matters. He partially concludes with "And God is my witness that I did not turn up at Corinth in order to spare you"[99] (v.23), which begins a new section of the epistle. Robertson and Plummer see the 'I' as "a great emphasis," and its occurrence here is to be contrasted with the plural pronouns above (e.g., vv.12, 21, 22). "Paul then returns to his own individual case in which Silvanus and Timothy are not included."[100]

The next 'I' statement in this concluding section is in 2:1–2, where Paul expands on the thought of verse 23. For Thrall,[101] "The stress [of v.2] is on what he sees as the mutuality of the relationship between himself and his readers." This is underlined by his use of 'I'/ἐγώ before the verb,

---

95. Dodd, *Paul*, 103.

96. Witherington, *Conflict*, 316.

97. Dodd, *Paul*, 30.

98. The ἐγώ δε, with which it begins "marks Paul's return to his specific personal circumstances" (Thrall, *Second Epistle*, 159; cf. Harris, *Second Epistle*, 212).

99. Ἐγὼ δὲ μάρτυρα τὸν θεὸν ἐπικαλοῦμαι ἐπὶ τὴν ἐμὴν ψυχήν, ὅτι φειδόμενος ὑμῶν οὐκέτι ἦλθον εἰς Κόρινθον.

100. Robertson and Plummer, *Corinthians*, 42.

101. Thrall, *The Second Epistle to the Corinthians 1–7*, 165.

which in turn throws emphasis on the "you."¹⁰² Paul had purposed in his heart not to make another painful visit (v 1). As we have seen in 1 Corinthians, Paul uses another interrogative to good effect: "For if I make you sorrowful, who is going to make me joyful except s/he whom I have made sorrowful?" (2:2). The point of the question (and in fact the entire *apologia* within the pericope, 1:12–2:17) is to explain that the adjustments to his itinerary were "not due to vacillation but to love."¹⁰³ For, he confesses, "I wrote you out of much affliction and anguish of heart and with many tears, not to cause you pain but to let you know the abundant love that I have for you" (v.4). For Alford¹⁰⁴ 'I'/ ἐγώ in this verse is used in a peculiarly emphatic sense, strongly implying that the Corinthians had already come to grief, possibly through their other instructors. But indeed it was one of their own numbers, it would appear, that brought grief to them.

The identity of this offender is not known. But what seems certain is that the Corinthian congregants had taken strong disciplinary measures against him. It was now time for restoration to take place, and the one who had just reaffirmed his love for them is now asking that they express their love to the ex-communicated brother (vv 5–9). Further encouragement to pursue this path is seen in verse 10: "If you forgive anyone for anything, I also [κἀγώ] forgive him–for indeed what I [ἐγώ⊠] have forgiven (if I have forgiven anything) I did so for you in the presence of Christ (NET)." This, in my view, has to qualify as a paradigmatic 'I', if ever there was one (*pace* Dodd), since it is part of the parenetic statement concerning forgiveness. We therefore agree with the ancient exegete Ambrosiaster that "Paul is practising what he preaches. He has the right to give orders; he cannot refuse to do himself what he is asking others to do."¹⁰⁵ Whatever the full meaning of this difficult verse, one thing is certain: the apostle did not want his children to be exploited by the evil one (v. 11).

---

102. *unnu*/ὑμᾶς (Jamaican and Greek 2nd person pl).

103. Spencer, *Paul's Literary Style*, 50.

104. *The Greek Testament*, 636. For Harris, *Second Epistle*, 217, the "emphatic evgw, points to Paul as the one who cooperates with the Corinthians in securing and maintaining their joy (1:24)."

105. In Bray, *Ancient Christian Texts*, 207. Bruce (*Corinthians*, 185) conjectures that Paul was personally hurt by the offending brother. If he is correct, then this would definitely rule out the person mentioned in 1 Cor 5.

In the second half of this epistle the apostle goes into full gear with his personal defence, so one is not surprised to find an apologetic 'I' at the very beginning of the section. Although the emphatic "I myslf"(αὐτός ἐγώ/*autos egō*, 10:1) here serves to underline apostolic authority (implicitly rather than overtly, according to Hughes), the note of affection established in 2:10 is not lost.[106] The firmness is aimed at the strong influence of false teachers rather than the Corinthians themselves.

Turning to chapter 11, one notices a number of occurrences of the apologetic 'I' (vv. 1, 2, 3, 5, 6, 7, 8, 9). Yet, as we observed above, Paul is not writing out of personal peeve or simply a desire to put himself in a good light. At the heart of everything is his compassion for the Corinthians as verses 1–3 clearly show. The posture he has taken in these chapters, though a bit distasteful to himself, is one which finds him baring his soul even at the risk of misunderstanding. The apostle, therefore, seeks permission to indulge in a little boasting himself,[107] to set the records straight in regard to those who in fact are emissaries of the devil, as well as to help his hapless friends to properly discriminate at this crucial and personal level. Thus we find the following bold ("*I* also am daring"/ τολμῶ κἀγώ, *tolmō kagō* -v.21) and balanced speech (vv. 22–23):

- Are they Hebrews? *I* also.

- Are they Israelites? *I* also.

- Are they seed of Abraham? *I* also.

- Are they ministers of Christ? (I speak as being beside myself) *I* above measure so.[108]

- Ἑβραῖοί εἰσιν; κἀγώ (*hebraioi eisin kagō*)

- Ἰσραηλῖταί εἰσιν; κἀγώ (*israēlitai eisin kagō*)

- σπέρμα Ἀβραάμ εἰσιν; κἀγώ (*sperma Abraam eisin kagō*)

- διάκονοι Χριστοῦ εἰσιν; παραφρονῶν λαλῶ, ὑπὲρ ἐγώ.[109] (*diakonoi Christou eisin paraphronōn lalō huper agō*)

106. Hughes, *Second Epistle*, 344.

107. As in 2 Cor 11:16–17: Πάλιν λέγω, μή τίς με δόξῃ ἄφρονα εἶναι· εἰ δὲ μήγε, κἂν ὡς ἄφρονα δέξασθέ με, ἵνα κἀγώ μικρόν τι καυχήσωμαι. ὃ λαλῶ, οὐ κατὰ κύριον λαλῶ ἀλλ' ὡς ἐν ἀφροσύνῃ, ἐν ταύτῃ τῇ ὑποστάσει τῆς καυχήσεως.

108. DV.

109. For the translational difficulties of ὑπὲρ ἐγώ, see *Caragounis, Development*, 216–218.

"I-n-I" in Romans 7 and the Rest of the Pauline Corpus 115

These lines seem to tell us something about the motive of the challengers of Pauline apostolicity, with the first three laying stress on Jewishness and the climactic one on the claim of the antagonists (Nomists?) to be servants of the Anointed.

Witherington's comments at this point are revealing: "Paul is at odds with his opponents not so much because they are offering 'another gospel' (11:4) but because they do not accept his vision of ministry, that is, its cruciform, Christ-like, and servant shape."[110] But although Witherington's analysis is accurate in terms of identifying the Pauline focus of ministry, it seems to set up a false disjunction between the false teachers' understanding of and practice of the gospel. Both their gospel and ministry were heterodox. The apostle then goes on to demonstrate his "superiority" over those pseudo-servants (11:23–33).

If Witherington[111] is on target that "self-admiration and self-praise were *de rigeur* in Greco-Roman society, especially for those who wanted to raise their social status and social evaluation in the eyes of others . . . [and that] self-praise was a priority characteristic of popular teachers of the day," then Paul, with some measure of sophistry, is using his own "ego" to counter that of the false teachers in the interest of the Corinthians. In fact they are the ones he is directly addressing, not the false teachers.

But is this strategy legitimate? Well, according to Dodd,[112] this kind of talk is made palatable if the speaker:

1. responds to a situation of slander
2. offers a defence against charges (ἀπολογία/*apologia*)
3. does so because of compulsion (ἀνάγκη/*anagkē*)
4. describes triumph over adversity or peril
5. includes personal shortcomings
6. credits God or luck for success; or
7. demonstrates that the goal of the self-discussion is the good of others . . .

Categories 1, 2, 3 and 7 seem to match the Pauline agenda in the examples we have examined so far, especially in 2 Corinthians.

---

110. Witherington's. *Conflict & Community*, 442.
111. Ibid.
112. Dodd , *The Epistle of Paul to the Romans*, 103; citing Plutarch.

The last verse of the chapter again provides us a glimpse into the heart of the apostle: "who is weak and I am not weak? Who is made to fall, and I (ἐγώ) am not indignant?" (11:29).[113] Here is the heart of a pastor. Here is one who does not burn so much on account of his own weakness but because of the weakness of another.

Chapter 12, like chapter 11, has its fair share of I-statements. As in the previous chapter, they could be classified as apologetic pronouns because they are located in the final section of Paul's boasting. After showcasing his fantastic spiritual experience (2–10), Paul bemoans the lack of support he receives from his own children, a failure which has forced him ("ye have compelled me"[114]/ἠναγκάσατε/*ēnagkasate*; v.11; this fits category 3 above) to vindicate himself. This leaves Paul no choice but to play the "fool," a role he would rather not be cast in. If only the Corinthians had rallied to his support ("I [ἐγώ] ought to have been commended by you"; v. 11 NRSV).

An even more emphatic statement is found in verse 13, where Paul reminds the Corinthians of his apostolic credentials and fulsome ministry in their midst. With sarcasm[115] he exclaims, "For in what were you less favoured than the rest of the churches, except that I myself [αὐτὸς ἐγώ/*autos egō*] did not burden you? Forgive me this wrong." It would appear that the Corinthians and/or the opponents of Paul grossly misunderstood (or twisted) Paul's stance in not receiving financial support from those in Achaia, thus his strident response. Nevertheless, it is the apostle's resolve to visit his children, and it is still his resolve not to become a financial burden to them (v.15). More importantly, he affirms his parental posture: "I [ἐγώ] will most gladly spend and be spent for your souls" (v. 15b). Verses 16 (with another emphatic 'I') returns to the quarrelsome tone expressed earlier in the section, and the final 'I' in the chapter strengthens the expression of Paul's fear that his next visit may prove too uncomfortable for them—and him (v.20).

---

113. Winer, *Grammar*, 153 para. 145.

114. DV.

115. Harris, "2 Corinthians", 398; *pace* Harris, *Second Epistle*, 879. Cf. v.16 and Witherington's, *Conflict and Community*, 442, recognition of Paul's repertoire of rhetorical skills, which according to him, not only includes irony but invective! Crafton, *The Agony of the Apostle*, 116–117, provides a helpful overview of the apostle's "self-disparaging irony" in this epistle. He sees Paul as ridiculing the super-apostles by making fun of himself. The "fool," which he plays is "a disarming character."

All in all in this epistle, the writer employs a variety of emotive terms in connection with his I-statements to maximize his communicative intent. In so doing he avoids the "narcotic blandness of plain speech that does not penetrate the reader's sense of self. . . . Forceful and imaginative language . . . , however, engages its readers profoundly in their personal orientation."[116] Unfortunately for us, we do not know how much influence our 2 Corinthians had upon its original readers. However, I think we are richer for reading their mail.

PHILIPPIANS

If we accept the principle that in the Greco-Roman world a well written letter could function as surrogate for personal presence,[117] then several of Paul's letters qualify, perhaps none more than the Philippian correspondence. Although this letter is highly personal, the writer himself was anxious to see his friends face to face and was somewhat confident that that would happen eventually (1:19–20; 2:24–26).[118]

In the mean time he will carry out his pastoral function through the vicarious ministry of his companion: "But I hope in *the* Lord Jesus to send Timotheus to you shortly, that *I* also may be refreshed, knowing how ye get on." (2:19; DV).[119] "I also" (Κἀγώ/*kagō*), according to O'Brien, is emphatic both by its presence and position, and serves to highlight Paul's anxiety over the Messianic community at Philippi.[120] Timothy is sent *inter alia* to relieve this anxiety. Chapter 4 points to the mutual relief surrounding the letter.

The next occurrence of κἀγώ (2:28) is in a verse that seems like a natural sequel to 2:19, only that it has its own context. The context of 2:19 concerns the mission of Timothy, and the context of 2:28 features Epaphroditus, originally the Philippians' missioner to Paul. The return of Epaphroditus, interestingly, is, according to Paul, of some therapeutic value reciprocally (v. 28: "I have sent him therefore the more diligently,

---

116. Plank, *Paul*, 72–73.

117. Dodd, *Paul's Paradigmatic 'I'*, 172.

118. For a useful commentary on the letter, see Cousar, *Philippians and Philemon*, 1–91.

119. Ἐλπίζω δὲ ἐν κυρίῳ Ἰησοῦ Τιμόθεον ταχέως πέμψαι ὑμῖν, ἵνα κἀγὼ εὐψυχῶ γνοὺς τὰ περὶ ὑμῶν.

120. *The Epistle to the Philippians*, 317; Silva, *Philippians*, 136–137.

that seeing him ye might again rejoice, and that *I* might be the less sorrowful"; DV).

The Philippians had heard about the illness of their emissary, and so Paul was the more eager to have them see again a healthy Epaphroditus (vv.25–30). An interesting parallel is seen between the two missionaries that are honored (cf.v.29) by Paul in this chapter. It would appear that both were willing to go anywhere, do anything and serve anyone in order to bring *shalom*, and both were a reflection, however imperfect, of the ἀπόστολος (*apostolos*, missionary/apostle) *par excellence* (Heb. 3:1), whose mission brings peace in its fullest salvific sense, whose honor, as a result, is unprecedented and unparalleled,[121] and whose praise is the focus of verses 5–11.

It is against this background that we should read the following chapter. In light of Christ's humiliation and exaltation, how can anyone boast in his/her own achievements? The nomists, against whom Paul inveighs in 3:2–3, may parade their religious accomplishments, but for the apostle to the Gentiles there is only one ground for religious boasting: what God has wrought on humanity's behalf through Christ Jesus (vv.7–10). However, as we see in the Corinthian correspondence, Paul can play the game of boasting himself, and this is exactly what he does in 3:4–6.

His polemic begins with a positive note concerning the nature of circumcision, with reference to the true people of God as well as an affirmation and negation of what it really means to "boast" liturgically (v. 3). This is followed by a concession clause[122] in which we have an exposé of the life and experience of one who did at one time have confidence in the flesh, "[allowing] the Philippians to see what his past religious life was like so that they may be able to understand why he has warned them so plainly."[123]

But Paul was more interested in re-presenting himself as a model of a maturing believer through the primary method of *ethos*. This, ac-

---

121. O'Brien, *Philippians*, accepts the suggestion of BAGD that the hapax avlupo,teroj may be rendered something like "free from anxiety," but this is stoutly resisted by Fee, *Philippians* , 281, n. 40, who writes (perhaps too dogmatically in my view) that this meaning "seems to be an invented [one] with no lexical basis whatever."

122. Fee, *Philippians*, 302.

123. Martin, *Phillipians*, 140.

cording to Marshall,[124] is accomplished in two ways: first, by identifying himself with his readers and, second, by underscoring his apostolic authority through an "identification" of himself with God and Christ. Paul's employment of persuasive ethos also sees him "functioning" as:

1. Slave/Envoy   1:1–2
2. Partner   1:3
3. Prisoner   1:1–4
4. Mediator   1:1–18
5. Guardian/Pedagogue   1:25
6. Commander   2:12
7. Athlete   3:14 (cf. 2:16)
8. Father   2:22
9. Super-Jew   3:3–6
10. Superlative Jew   3:7–11
11. Priest   3:17[125]
12. Victorious Athlete/Gospel Worker   4:1, 3.[126]

In the next occurrence of Paul's self-reference ("I myself"/ἐγώ ἐμαυτόν/egō emauton; 3:13a),[127] which appears between items 6 and 7, one senses a deliberate strategy of self-depreciation, possibly as a polemic against the nomistic intruders whose corresponding boast was evidently exaggerated. Although Paul could more than match their fleshly exhibition (as roles 1–7 imply), he would rather others see him as one who is persevering toward the end,[128] not as one who has arrived; thus the disclaimer in the first part of 3:13.

---

124. Marshall, "Paul's Ethical Appeal," 363.

125. All of these roles lend authority to the literary strategy of "persuasive ethos" (Marshall, op. cit., 366).

126. Ibid.

127. Both terms "are emphatic, expressing strongly Paul's own estimate of himself." (Vincent, *Epistles*, 109).

128. Notice the antithetic parallelism in v 13b (Fee, *Philippians*, 347). If Paul is picturing himself as a runner here, as Fee suggests, then his competitors are (possibly) the enthusiastic nomists, who have not 'divested' themselves of the weight of the flesh. Whether or not, it is his example that Paul expects the Philippians to follow and not that of their antagonists.

Recognizing the number of 'I' statements in the letter as well as their paradigmatic and parenetic value, Dodd[129] lists half a dozen components of these literary characterizations:

1. Affirmation of confidence "in Christ"   (3:3; cf.1:21)
2. Self-renunciation of confidence "in the flesh"   (3:4)[130]
3. Eschatological reserve   (3:11)
4. Eschatological encouragement   (3:12–14)
5. Ethical obedience   (3:17–18) and
6. Prayerful contentment   (4:6–13)

Chapter 4:11, part of Dodd's sixth category, is the final 'I' statement in the letter. The pericope in which it appears continues the writer's attempt to persuade his auditors through *ethos*, *logos* and *pathos*,[131] while at the same time acknowledging the kindness of the Philippians in sending a gift (vv. 17–18) to the incarcerated apostle, who in turn promises a rich reward for their effort (v. 19). But in 4:11 Paul is at pains to point out that his personal acknowledgement of their fellowship was exactly that, and not a kind of veiled way of soliciting further benefits. Thus he writes: "*Not that I speak as regards privation, for as to me *I* have learnt in those circumstances in which I am, to be satisfied in myself*" (DV).[132]

Fee sees the pericope (vv. 4:10–20) as outlining the first reason for the letter, that is, to thank the Philippians for their expression of friendship in their fellowship (cf. 1:5). This may explain the elaborate structure, which involves the following pattern:[133]

A. 1st Acknowledgement   v.10a

   B. Philippians qualifier   v.10b

      C. Personal qualifier   vv.11–13

---

129. Dodd, *Paul's Paradigmatic 'I,'* 182–193.

130. "The shift from 'we' to 'I' and the frequent use of 'I' show that what Paul has here is personal" (Loh and Nida, *Philippians*, 94). Paul's line of argument in 3:4–10 elicited the following comment from Engberg-Pedersen, *Paul and the Stoics*, 93: "[T]he merely subjective 'I' . . . no longer exists. It has been put out of action, and the person (*another* 'I') now finds himself or herself, as it were, *outside* (or 'above') him-or herself." Cf. Gal 2:20.

131. Snyman, "Persuasion," 330–335.

132. οὐχ ὅτι καθ' ὑστέρησιν λέγω, ἐγὼ γὰρ ἔμαθον ἐν οἷς εἰμι αὐτάρκης εἶναι (Nestle).

133. Adapted from Fee, *Philippians*, 425.

"I-n-I" in Romans 7 and the Rest of the Pauline Corpus   121

   A. 2nd Acknowledgement   v.14

      B. Philippians qualifier   vv. 15–16

         C Personal qualifier   v. 17

   A. 3rd Acknowledgement   v. 18

      B. Personal and Philippians qualifiers   v. 19

         C. Patristic[134] doxology   v. 20

The verse (4:11), then, constitutes the first of the apostle's qualifiers, and the most emphatic, to judge from the presence of ἐγώ. What Paul stresses here is his own resourcefulness (αὐτάρκης/*autarkēs*) that enables him to be satisfied with his lot in life, without surrendering optimism, ambition, hope.

Finally, in her study of three of Paul's letters (2 Cor; Rom; Phil) Spencer observes that "Philippians seems to have proportionately the most occurrences of the first-person singular." She also notes that after the salutation, which mentions Paul and Timothy, "the letter shifts to an almost continual use of the first-person ending, with the *I* personally entreating the Philippians (e.g., 4:2) and speaking of Paul's history."[135]

Interestingly, in the other three letters that are traditionally grouped with Philippians there is another eight occurrences of the emphatic 'I'— three each in Ephesians and Philemon, and the balance in Colossians. We will look at these letters in reverse order.

COLOSSIANS

After the hymn of Christ (vv. 15–20), Paul directly addresses his auditors in verses 21, 22 by way of a reminder of their former alienation and their present status as friends of God, a status that is all the more surprising bearing in mind that "One would expect that alienation from God would [normally?] result in judgment, not reconciliation [!]"[136] Verse 23 then underlines the auditors' responsibility to maintain their commitment to the faith—i.e., the universally proclaimed gospel (of which "*I* Paul became a servant"/ ἐγενόμην ἐγὼ Παῦλος διάκονος/*egenomēn Paulos egō diakonos*). What appears to be emphasized here is the marvel-

---

134. Πατρί (Father) is the object of Paul's praise in this verse.
135. Spencer, *Paul's Literary Style*, 88.
136. Young, *New Testament Greek*, 261.

ous privilege that was Paul's to be involved in the dissemination of such important information.[137]

The pivotal character of verses 21-23 is also noted by Dunn, who points out that the unit echoes earlier emphases and adumbrates "themes to be subsequently developed."[138] This, we believe, should remove the doubt concerning the emphatic function of ἐγώ in the concluding verse.[139] Two verses later we have the almost identical construction (Παῦλος ἐγὼ διάκονος [*Paulos egō diakonos*]) located at verse 23), only this time it affirms Paul's relationship to the messianic community and the struggle that he experiences in his ministry to and on behalf of this community.

PHILEMON

In this letter "Paul's hortatory use of personal example is worked out with substantial theoretical sophistication."[140] In fact, if we are to accept Lund's proposal, the rhetorical crafting extends to a number of verses to form a parallelism of the inverted variety:

A. Salutation vv. 1-3
  B. Philemon's conduct vv. 4-6
    C. Paul's joy v.7
      D. Appeal to Philemon ('Paul'; v.9) vv.8-11
        E. Paul & Onesimus vv. 12-15
        E'. Paul & Onesimus vv. 16-17
      D'. Offer to Philemon vv. 18-19
    C'. Paul's expectant joy v. 20
  B'. Philemon's conduct vv. 21-22
A'. Salutation vv. 23-25

Quite appropriately, taking Lund's proposal at face value, the first emphatic 'I' appears in the central section (E; i.e., in the *pathos*, vv. 13-14) in which the ambassadorial[141] apostle begins in earnest to plead the ex-slave's case.

---

137. Dunn, *Colossians and to Philemon*, 112.

138. Ibid, 105.

139. O' Brien, *Colossians and Philemon*, 71; Harris, *Colossians and Philemon*, 62.

140. Dodd, *Paul's Paradigmatic 'I'*, 196; See Lund, *Chiasmus*, 197-228, for the above structural proposal. Another proposal, based on classical rhetoric ("*exordium* [4-7] . . . *peroratio* [20-22]"), is shared by Young, *New Testament Greek*, 250. For a Caribbean theological reflection, see Thomas, *Biblical Resistance Hermeneutics*, 107-143. See also Felder, "Philemon."

141. Whether we construe πρεσβύτης (v. 8) as "elder" or "ambassador," one sees

In verse 10 Paul informs Philemon of Onesimus' new spiritual status, before alerting him of his renewed usefulness.¹⁴² Based on this, Paul declares his willingness to retain the services of the young man: *"whom *I* [ἐγώ] was desirous of keeping with myself, that for thee he might minister to me in the bonds of the glad tidings"* (v.13; DV).

According to Dunn, the "ἐγώ . . . indicates that it was (Onesimus) who remained undecided for so long."¹⁴³ With this, one senses that Paul is mustering up all his techniques of persuasion to shield as well as to commend his "child" (v.10). I say "shield," for if indeed Onesimus was a runaway slave, there was bound to be tension between him and his former master. But scholars question this notion today. In any case Paul is sending back Onesimus, because, despite his "usefulness," he must not be detained without Philemon's permission (vv.14–17).

In fact, the magnanimous apostle is doing more than simply sending back Onesimus: he is also offering to make some kind of reparation (v. 18) on his son's behalf, which is then sealed with his personal signature: "**I* Paul have written it with mine own hand; *I* will repay it.*" (DV).¹⁴⁴ The double emphatic 'I'/ ἐγώ as well as the explicit "Paul" serve to legitimize the IOU.

Paul will use the emphatic nominative one more time before bringing to a close this short epistle; this time to add a new twist to his appeal (v. 20). Wright¹⁴⁵ believes that Paul is here seeking "dividend on his investment in Philemon."

While the thought expressed in the verse seems unusual, Wright's proposal is unlikely to be true, because it seems to run against the grain of the letter. What appears certain is the verbal pun (*onaimen*/ὀναίμην) on Onesimus' name, adding to the adjectival one in verse 11. Added to this is Wright's observation of the "extraordinary" and "almost shocking" feature "that Paul is reconciling master and slave by taking on himself the role of Christ,"¹⁴⁶ resulting in the slave's debts being "put in the ledger under Paul's name: and there they find that they are more than cancelled out. They disappear as totally as the sins placed to Christ's account on the cross."¹⁴⁷

Paul's diplomatic skills at work here.

142. A Pauline pun on "Onesimus," according to Barclay, *Letters*, 311.

143. Dunn, *Epistles*, 330.

144. ἐγὼ Παῦλος ἔγραψα τῇ ἐμῇ χειρί, ἐγὼ ἀποτίσω· (v.19; UBS4).

145. Wright, *Colossians and Philemon*, 188.

146. Ibid, 187.

147. Ibid. 188.

EPHESIANS

Before we examine the I-statements of Ephesians, we first take a look at a recent proposal concerning the structure of the letter put forward by Heil.[148] He sees the letter as a macro-chiastic literary device with the central purpose of helping the believers to live a life of love and unity. The macro-structure also embraces smaller chiastic designs:

  A. 1:1–2: Grace and peace as gifts from God and Christ

    B. 1:3–14: "that we might be holy and blameless before him in love" (1:4) and "he graced us in the Beloved" (1:6)

    C. 1:15–23: "your love for all the holy ones" (1:15)

    D. 2:1–10: "because of his great love . . . with which he loved . . . us" (2:4)

    E. 2:11–22: Christ's gift of peace (2:14, 15, 17) is a gift of love

    F. 3:1–13: the references to God's "grace" and "giving" (3:2, 7, 8) refer to God's love

    G. 3:14–21: "in love . . . rooted and grounded" (3:17) and "to know the love . . . of Christ that surpasses knowledge" (3:19)

    H. 4:1–16: "forbearing one another in love" (4:2); "being fruitful in love" (4:15); "the building up of itself in love" (4:16)

    G' 4:17–32: The references to "give grace" (4:29) and "being gracious . . . as also God in Christ was gracious to us" (4:32) refer to God's love

    F' 5: 1–6: "beloved . . . children" (5:1) and "walk in love . . . just as also Christ Loved . . . us" (5:2)

    E' 5:7–14: that you are "light" (5:8) is a gift of God's love and the reference to "approving what is pleasing to the Lord" (5:10) is part of the love theme

    D' 5:15–6:9: "love . . . your wives as also the Christ loved . . . the church" (5:25); "so ought also husbands to love . . . their own wives . . . he who loves . . . his own wife loves . . . himself" (5:28); "each one of you should thus love . . . his own wife as himself" (5:33)

---

148. *Ephesians*, 1–357; cf. Lund, *Chiasmus*, 197–206.

C' 6: 10–13: the references to "be empowered" (6:10) and "have the power" (6:11, 13) are gifts of God's love

B' 6:14–22: "Tychicus the beloved . . . brother" (6:21)

A' 6:23–24: "Peace to the brothers and love" (6:23) and "grace be with all who love . . . the Lord Jesus Christ in immortality" (6:24).

The first occurrence of 'I' in this controversial[149] letter is at 3:1 (F above), not too far from the concentric centre (G). The construction in which it is found bears such striking resemblance to Colossians 1:23c that Lincoln[150] takes it as part of the evidence that the Ephesian correspondence is pseudonymous. In terms of wording, Lincoln notes the following parallel:[151]

Colossians	Ephesians
(1: 23) I Paul a servant	(3:1) I Paul the prisoner
(1:25) of which I became a servant	(1:25) of which I was made a servant
(1: 23) ἐγὼ Παῦλος διάκονος (egō Paulos diakonos)	(3:1) ἐγὼ Παῦλος ὁ δέσμιος (egō Paulos ho demios)
(1:25) ἧς ἐγενόμην ἐγὼ διάκονος (hēs egenomēn egō diakonos)	(3:7) οὗ ἐγενήθην διάκονος (hou egenēthēn diakonos)

We have already surveyed the ἐγὼ παῦλος (egō Paulos) phrase as it appears in the Colossian epistle. So now we give attention to its Ephesian counterpart. But before that is done, a brief comment about Lincoln's hypothesis of pseudonymity is perhaps in order. There can be no doubt that the resemblance of the two epistles is stark. What it boils down to is how best to interpret the evidence.

I think that an analogy could be drawn from the controversy between evolutionists and creationists. Both see the strong resemblance between monkey and man. The former theorists interpret the evidence along the lines of the following model: *monkey > man*, whereas the latter believe that a *Maker: monkey + man* model is better. To build on

---

149. A major part of the controversy surrounds the authorship of the letter. Lincoln, *Ephesians*, lix–lxxxvi, carefully argues for pseudonymity, while Hoehner, *Ephesians*, 2–61, and to a lesser extent, Yorke, *The Church*, 99–100, stoutly defends Pauline authorship.

150. Lincoln, *Ephesians*, 169.

151. The one cited below is just one of nine. Lincoln also cites thematic parallels as well.

this analogy, the traditional view of Pauline authorship of both epistles corresponds to the creationist perspective, and (rather loosely, I must say) Lincoln's proposal, the evolutionist. In both cases (i.e., the creationist/evolutionist debate and the traditionalist/revisionist discussion in respect of authorship) the evidence remains inconclusive—even for this family below:

> *A little girl asked her mother: How did the human race appear? The mother answered: God made Adam and Eve and they had children and so was all mankind made. Two days later she asks her father the same question. The father answered: Many years ago there were monkeys from which the human race was developed. The confused girl returns to her mother and says: Mom', how is it possible that you told me that the human race was created by God and Papa says they were developed from monkeys. The mother answers: Well dear, it is very simple. I told you about the origin of my side of the family while your father told you about his side.*[152]

With the aside aside, the emphatic phrase in Ephesians 3:1 will be treated on its own merit. Lincoln[153] feels that a couple of features in this verse may support his theory of pseudonymity: the opening two words, which do not appear in the major Pauline epistles, and the collocation of the phrases "I Paul" and "the prisoner of Christ." "I Paul" (ἐγὼ Παῦλος, *egō Paulos*) appears in 1 Thessalonians 2:18; Galatians 5:2; 2 Corinthians 10:1; Colossians 1:23; and Philemon 19, but what raises Lincoln's suspicion is the unique appositional construction at Ephesians 3:1. For Hoehner,[154] the same construction is strong evidence of Pauline authorship. Hoehner also points out the ἐγὼ Παῦλος (*egō Paulos*) phrase in the passages cited above, all indicating a friendly tone. "As he personally (κἀγώ, 1:15) had heard of their faith, now he was personally suffering for their acceptance of his message."[155]

The next 'I' statement in Ephesians begins the parenetic section of the letter. There the writer makes his appeal by once again referring to his incarceration (I Paul the prisoner/ἐγὼ Παῦλος ὁ δέσμιος, *egō Paulos ho desmios*). At 3:1 the writer is the prisoner *of* the Messiah; here he is a prisoner in the Lord. Here one ought not to think that the writer is

---

152. Author unknown.
153. Lincoln, *Ephesians*, 172.
154. Hoehner, *Ephesians*, 419.
155. Ibid, 419.

soliciting some kind of sympathy from his auditors. On the contrary, he appears to be reminding them that his condition is very much in keeping with the will of his Master. This may be brought out by the periphrastic rendering of verse 4:1, "I urge you, then—I who am a prisoner because I serve the Lord: live a life that measures up to the standard God set when he called you."[156]

The final 'I' in Ephesians is part of an interesting construction; interesting on account of the fact that it is the seventh in a series in the NT canon, the first six of which are found in Matthew's Gospel (5:22, 28, 32, 34, 39, 44).[157] From a chronological standpoint the writer of Ephesians, especially if he is Paul, in all probability wrote before Matthew.

Whether this is true or not, it begs the question of literary in/dependence. There is also the question of the writer of Ephesians being influenced by the Jesus tradition recorded by Matthew. Of course, the whole matter may just be coincidental. Matters of literary dependence and the like are all too complex to detain us here. What I am prepared to say in respect of the "and I say" (ἐγὼ δὲ λέγω, *egō de legō*) in Ephesians 5:32 vis-à-vis Matthew 5:21–48 is that we have an echo, but one along the lines of John 3:8—we hear "the sound thereof, but canst not tell whence it cometh and whither goeth."

The function of the phrase in question is perhaps as equally mysterious as its relation to Matthew's use of its quintuplet. In Ephesians 5:32 it comes immediately after the writer's interpretive signal, "this is a profound revelation," which in turn introduces his *double entendre* (i.e., husband and wife/Christ and the church) on the quotation from Gen 2:24. For Lincoln, "and I say" (ἐγὼ δὲ λέγω, *egō de legō*), then, is stressing the writer's own interpretation that has a strong typological element. Like the antitheses of Matthew 5, it also serves to "introduce an interpretation contrary to the generally accepted interpretation of the Scripture passage in view ... which limits the meaning of Gen 2:24 to the physical union between a man and a woman...."[158] I believe that Lincoln's treatment here is essentially correct. However, the writer of Ephesians may have been employing what we call today *sensus plenior* and not typology as Lincoln supposes; but in either case it is hard to imagine a different

---

156. Bratcher and Nida, *Translator's Handbook*, 93.
157. Hoehner, *Ephesians*, 799.
158. Lincoln, *Ephesians*, 382.

conclusion. Moreover, there is no clear-cut difference between the two approaches.

Other pronominal statements used with reference to the Ephesian churches appear in 1 Timothy (1:15; 2:7); 2 Timothy (1:11; 4:6); as well as Titus (1:3, 5).[159]

CONCLUSION

Personal pronouns in the nominative case are employed regularly in the NT to give prominence to the subject, according to Young. He goes on to note that when these pronouns are present, they "usually convey emphasis (e.g., importance, gravity, surprise, anger, contrast, comparison, or identity).[160]

Our survey of the Pauline usage of the independent pronoun (ἐγώ) reveals a variety of functions not unlike the prominent pronominal in Rastafari lexicon. "First, the pronoun sometimes serves as an autobiographical index (Rom 11:1b). Other times it is used to highlight apostolic authority (Rom 11:13), or to underscore an interpretative situation which may be connected somehow to apostolic authority (Rom 11:19)."[161] According to Dodd: " In places Paul's self-references engage the pastoral situation faced, while in other places his self-characterizations may have more to do with generally held social requirements surrounding self discussion. He often uses paradigmatic 'I' expressions as punch lines, summarizing and providing a transition to the next phase of his letters, and at other times his self-exemplification and personal example is at the heart of his argument."[162] Amen.

---

159. They read respectively: πιστὸς ὁ λόγος καὶ πάσης ἀποδοχῆς ἄξιος, ὅτι Χριστὸς Ἰησοῦς ἦλθεν εἰς τὸν κόσμον ἁμαρτωλοὺς σῶσαι, ὧν πρῶτός εἰμι ἐγώ

εἰς ὃ ἐτέθην ἐγὼ κῆρυξ καὶ ἀπόστολος, ἀλήθειαν λέγω οὐ ψεύδομαι, διδάσκαλος ἐθνῶν ἐν πίστει καὶ ἀληθείᾳ εἰς ὃ ἐτέθην ἐγὼ κῆρυξ καὶ ἀπόστολος καὶ διδάσκαλος

Ἐγὼ γὰρ ἤδη σπένδομαι, καὶ ὁ καιρὸς τῆς ἀναλύσεώς μου ἐφέστηκεν

ἐφανέρωσεν δὲ καιροῖς ἰδίοις τὸν λόγον αὐτοῦ ἐν κηρύγματι, ὃ ἐπιστεύθην ἐγὼ κατ' ἐπιταγὴν τοῦ σωτῆρος ἡμῶν θεοῦ

Τούτου χάριν ἀπέλιπόν σε ἐν Κρήτῃ, ἵνα τὰ λείποντα ἐπιδιορθώσῃ καὶ καταστήσῃς κατὰ πόλιν πρεσβυτέρους, ὡς ἐγώ σοι διεταξάμην. For the exegesis of these 'I' passages, see Marshall, *The Pastoral Epistles*, 126–35; 150–3; 397–401; 433–35; 708–9; 805–7.

160. Young, *New Testament Greek*, 72.

161. Palmer, *Pronominal 'I,'* 254.

162. Dodd, *Paradigmatic 'I'*, 171.

6

Romans 8 and the People of God in Messiah[1]

ROMANS 8 BEGINS WITH the significant statement: "Now, therefore, there is no more condemnation for those who are in Messiah Jesus."[2]

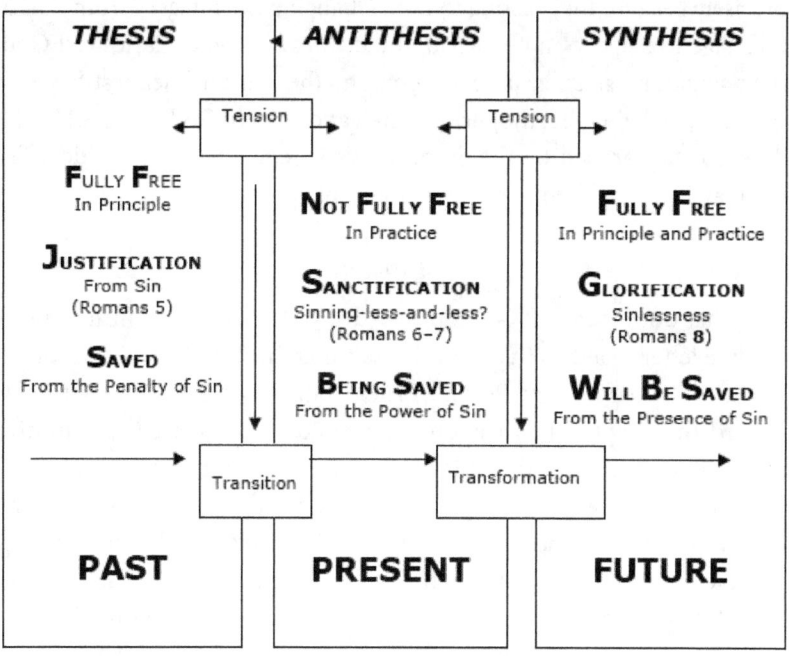

Table 1: Messianic Community in Tension and Transformation

---

1. For the relationship of the chapter with the preceding, see Table 1 above, and for a useful reflection on verse 28, see Appendix B. Although Paul was often in prison, he preferred to see himself as "In Messiah"—i.e., incorporated, instead of incarcerated!

2. My rendition; cf. John 3:16–18.

IDENTITY

Who are those in the Messiah, and what is the significance of the phrase which comes at the end of the verse? We may begin our answer to the first question by pointing out that we have a description of the people of God as early as chapter one of the epistle where those addressed are designated, "To all in Rome who are loved by God and called to be saints" (Rom 1:7; NIV). Later we learn that this same group is the sole beneficiary of the divine blessing of "Rectification," to use the language of Witherington.[3] Further, the concept of initial rectification is linked to its progressive work of sanctification which renders the people of God spiritually responsible for not allowing sin to continue as their master (6:12–14). In chapter 7:1–6, those in Messiah are the very ones who are enabled to bear fruit, precisely because they belong to him. Changing the imagery from that of marriage to sonship in chapter 8, the in-Messiah beneficiaries call God, their single and singular parent, Abba, and the Spirit himself testifies with their inmost being that they are children and heirs of God (Rom 8:16–17). As such they are led by the Spirit, an experience that further identifies them as authentic members of the Messianic in-crowd.

Spirituality

But what does it mean to be Spirit-led? We turn once again to a prior Pauline letter to aid us in our understanding. In a book section entitled, "Is 1Cor. 14 a Museum Piece?" Ernest Tatham catalogs four attitudes toward the chapter: (1) it is obsolete, valid only during the primitive apostolic era; (2) the principles of liberty and "prophecy" have disappeared; (3) all the gifts and guidance in the chapter are relevant to the contemporary churches; and (4) what Tatham calls, the "beachcombers" approach "which walks through this chapter much as a beachcomber would stroll along the seashore searching for shells. He pulls up this one, carefully examines it, shakes his head, and then tosses the defective shell back into the sea. But the next one brings a murmur of delight. He tucks it into the bag. Some are rejected and some are preserved."[4] Concerning this view Tatham remarks, "He who only walks through this chapter, accepting one verse as having present day application, but refuting another as a relic of the first century, will end up with a very small bag of salvage."[5] I concur with this judgment.

---

3. *Paul's Letter to the Romans*, 131.
4. Tatham, *Let the Tide Come In*, 88–89.
5. Ibid., 89.

First Corinthians 14 is the third and final section of Paul's ABA structure that embraces chapters 12 and 13. The unit "begins with a more general word (chapter 12), which is followed by a theological interlude (chap.13), and a very specific response to the matter in hand (chap.14)... . The whole argument aims at the specific corrections in chapter 14."[6] Fee sees the argument dividing into two parts. First the apostle argues his case for absolute clarity in the assembly by carrying out a sustained contrast between tongues and prophecy (vv. 1–25). When this course of action is followed, then both believer (vv. 1–19) and unbeliever (vv. 20–25) stand to benefit. Second, not only is there need for clarity in the assembly, there is also a pressing need for propriety in worship (vv. 26–40). Those two major correctives served particularly to eliminate the abuse of spiritual gifts in the worshiping community, especially the misuse of tongues "which seems to be both singular in its emphasis and disorderly in its expression (cf. 14: 12, 23, 33, 40)."[7] Verses 26–40, though themselves correctional, serve as Paul's concluding remarks of the unit. The opening words of the paragraph, "What then shall we say," give notice of this. What follows offers some insight into the Corinthians' worship experience. When they came together they were well prepared to make abundant contributions, for each had a significant part to play (v. 26). But in their enthusiasm they had forgotten the purpose of their gathering, which is summed up in the key word *oikodome* ("edification"). It was the Spirit's directive or leading (*agō*) that ensured that edification would take place. The term *agō* is used seven times in chapter 14 alone and has the idea of "bring [ing] to the point of destination."[8] When used in this way it involves a subject that is providing direction and an object "deciding" to follow the guidance (Luke 4:9; Acts 6:12). Whenever the two components (direction and decision) are present, the object (person) may actually be said to be led. If the direction alone is present—that is, if the person does not *decide* to follow the direction to its desired goal, the leading can be said to be potential. With the exception of special cases where the supernatural is involved, the direction is usually objective. The decision, of course, is subjective.

We may now turn to Paul's use of the term to test this hypothesis.[49] In Romans 2:4 we read that God's kindness leads to repentance. Of course, the "individual" being addressed in the context has not made any

6. Fee, *First Corinthians*, 571.
7. Ibid.
8. Thayer, *Lexicon*, 10.

positive move based on this direction (God's kindness), so the leading is only potential. Chapter 8:14 of the same book links *agō* with the Spirit. Can we find an objective direction in it? If the verse is read without its context we would have to give a negative reply. But Cranfield[9] has shown that the leading of verse 14 is inextricably linked to the previous verse. Those who are in fact led of the Spirit are the ones who are in the habit of dealing with the "flesh" in response to the pertinent injunctions (cf. 1 Pet. 1:15, 16). The context of Galatians 5:8 makes the same point.[51]

The next significant use of *agō* appears in 1 Cor 12:2. Here Paul, it seems, is anxious to demonstrate that true guidance of the Spirit that he already shared with the believers in Galatia (5:16–17), and which he would later mention in his letter to the Romans (8:13–14). How does leading take place within the context of the worship experience of the mystery religions, and how does the leading take place among the people of God? Paul replies to both of these questions in 1 Corinthians 12–14: the former in Chapter 12 and the latter in chapter 14. Wayne House asks the relevant question: "To what degree the mystery cults affected the thinking and worship of the Corinthian church, and how did that influence Paul's discussion in 1 Cor. 12–14?"[10] First Corinthians 12:2 hints at an answer. In this verse Martin sees "the uncontrolled abandon to spiritual ecstasy. . . . The feature of a trance-like state that characterized the Corinthians' former pagan life . . . [that] was carried over into their worship services."[11] So I take it that the apostle is contrasting genuine guidance of the Spirit with that which is false. A strong feature of the Corinthians' former worship experience was the coercive element that was present in their "leading." This, I think, is brought out by the stronger verb translated "led astray" (*apagō*) in the NIV. It is qualified by *agō*. I believe also that the passive construction of both words should not be overlooked. If we can detect in Paul the use of "divine" passives (cf. 1 Cor 15:3–42), maybe we have in the two terms in combination a "diabolic" passive. In light of Paul's mention of demons leading up to this passage, this suggestion is quite plausible (cf. 10: 19–22).

But, as I am positing, the leading of God's Spirit is different in the sense that it provides direction without coercion and allows us to chose freely, for, as Paul says elsewhere, "where the Spirit of the Lord is, there is freedom" (2 Cor 3:17; NIV). This freedom is analogous to the kind mentioned in 1 Cor 7:39, where the direction of the Spirit is that

---

9. *Romans*, 395.
10. Wayne House, "Tongues," 139.
11. Martin, *The Spirit*, 9.

the widow marries a believer. Having decided to follow this direction she is "led" of the Spirit and consequently exercises her freedom in the Spirit. This leading is both natural and normative, and is in stark contrast to the Corinthians' pagan experience: "The pneumatic character of worship in the mystery religions was always connected with states of ecstasy, whereas Paul never seems to make the connection. To him the possession of the *pneuma* [Spirit] is the normal, abiding condition of the Christian."[12] The kind of leading that is reflected in Romans 8:14, then, as well as Corinthians 14, is the type of lived experience that is the "abiding condition of the Christian," the wo/man is in Messiah.

IN THE SON

We now turn to the important feature highlighted above, the one that appears more pregnant with theological significance than the one embedded in Romans 8:14: Paul's employment of "In Messiah"/ ἐν Χριστῷ (*en Christō*).[13] Many NT scholars now agree that "In Messiah"/ ἐν Χριστῷ (*en Christō*) *is* a significant phrase in Pauline theology, though few if any at all, can articulate its precise theological import. In the earlier part of the last century Deissmann[14] put forward the view that the "In Messiah"/ ἐν Χριστῷ (*en Christō*) *formulation* is to be understood primarily in a mystical sense. For him our being *en Christō* (ἐν Χριστῷ) is analogous to being in air and vice versa. This mystical union, then, is made possible by the vicarious presence of the Spirit of God and the formulation of the union, according him, was also quite intelligible to first century believers in their Hellenistic environment.[15] To be "in Messiah," then, is virtually synonymous with being "in the Spirit."

This is quite in keeping with the notion that the "In Messiah" construction invariably relates to "the glorified Christ, not to the historic Jesus,"[16] especially when the thought is connected to that of John 7:37–39. Davies[17] expands the thesis of Deissmann[18] by giving it a more corporate or ecclesial sense, a sense recognized also by Bulttman[19] and Grundmann.[20]

12. Wayne House, "Tongues," 140.
13. For Bonhoeffer's view on this, see Green, *A Theology of Sociality*, 93–99.
14. Deissmann, *Paul: A Study in Social and Religious History*, 135–142.
15. Ibid., 142.
16. Sanday and Headlam, *Commentary*, 87.
17. Davies, *Paul*.
18. Deissmann, *Paul*, 86.
19. Bultmann, *Theology*, 327.
20. Grundmann, "*Christos*," TDNT, 9: 552.

Wright's analysis forces him to return to the notion of corporate personality (at least a mild form of it)—a notion thoroughly rejected by some. In rejecting the In Adam analogue, Wright asserts, "I suggest, instead, that by far the most likely and satisfactory explanation of the phenomenon is as follows. (a) The usage of ἐν Χριστῷ is incorporative, that is, Paul regularly uses the word to connote, and sometimes even to *denote*, the whole people of whom the Messiah is the representative."[21] Evidence for this, Wright believes, can be found in the OT, for example, in the incorporative idiom of 2 Samuels 19:40–43.

But is it necessary to jettison the Adamic analogue in order to posit the incorporative sense? Recently, Schreiner sought to demonstrate the usefulness of the former in understanding the latter, when he writes, "Those who are in Adam experience all the liabilities of being descended from him. Similarly, those in Christ experience all that blessing that accrue to those who belong to God."[22] Although I think the use of the word "experience" is unfortunate, and that he has failed to account for the death of believers in light of 1 Corinthians 15:22, Schreiner's position appears much more promising than Deissmann's mystical view or Wright's attenuated incorporative explanation. The following comparative chart by Ellis,[23] based on 2 Corinthians 5: 1–10, helps to make the point.

In Adam	In Christ
the old aeon	the new aeon
tent-house	heavenly house
naked	clothed
mortality	life
faith	sight
at home in the body	away from the body
away from the lord	at home with the Lord
in the body	at Christ's judgment seat

For Sanders "In Messiah" is just one of Paul's constructions to denote participation (others include 'Members of Christ's Body' and 'One Spirit'). As such, "Attempts to decide which is the key phrase . . . do not seem decisive or even essential for understanding the centrality of the

---

21. Wright, *The Climax of the Covenant*, 46.
22. Schreiner, *Paul*, 159.
23. Ellis, "2 Corinthians 5," 223.

general theme of participation. The centrality [is this]: *it is the theme, above all, to which Paul appeals both in parenesis [pedagogy] and polemic. Further, the very diversity of the terminology helps to show how the general conception of participation permeated his thought.*"[24]

In one of the earliest letters of Paul the "In Messiah" formulation is used in an overtly ecclesial manner. The church of Thessalonica is said to be in "God the father and the lord Jesus Christ" (1 Thess 1:1; cf. 2 Thess 1:1; Gal 1:22; 1 Cor 1:2.). Here the Greek preposition *en* ("in") qualifies both "God" and "Lord." What is the force of the preposition? Malherbe[25] argues that ἐν (*en*) should be understood in an instrumental sense in this verse. Taken as such the Apostle is saying that the church at Thessalonica was founded by God the father and (through) his son Jesus Christ. But this instrumental sense of the phrase is not at all certain,[26] and it is surprising that Malherbe did not mention the other main alternative suggested by Bruce (that ἐν Χριστῷ, though unusual in its collocation with "God," should perhaps be taken in its usual spherical sense).[27] A better candidate for the instrumental sense is to be found in 2 Thess 3:12 (so AV), but even in that context there is uncertainty, judging from the way how recent translators have handled it (cf. N/RSV).

Another of what I am calling the ecclesial use of "In Messiah" (ἐν Χριστῷ, *en Christō*) appears in 1 Thessalonians 2:14 where the membership of the Thessalonian congregations is commended for being imitators of the Judean churches of God *in Christ Jesus*. Like in 1:1, the Thessalonian believers are God's. But unlike the construction found in that verse, they are "In Messiah" (ἐν Χριστῷ, *en Christō*).

The next occurrence of "In Messiah" (ἐν Χριστῷ, *en Christō*) appears in a context where the founder of the congregation is at pains to explain to his Macedonian converts that they have no advantage at the Parousia over the members who had recently (?) passed on. Evidently, the church was more than a little concerned about this matter. If the coming of the Lord was imminent, as they were apparently taught, what will happen to those who had fallen asleep? The apostle's response is that the deceased—i.e., "The dead in Christ"—will rise to join the living in a great "Enochian Translation" (4:16, 17; cf. Gen 5:24).

24. *Paul*, 456. Italics Sanders'.
25. Malherbe, *Thessalonians*, 101.
26. Wanamaker, *1 and 2 Thessalonians*, 70.
27. *Paul*, 137–38.

The final appearance of the phrase "In Messiah" (ἐν Χριστῷ, *en Christō*) is in 5:18 where the Thessalonians believers are enjoined to express gratitude to God in every circumstance, because such thanksgiving is part and parcel of the divine will which embraces their rejoicing (v.16) and praying (v. 17).

From Galatians 2:4 we learn that one of the benefits of being in Christ is freedom—a freedom apparently that can be lost. This appears to be confirmed by verse 17, which enigmatically juxtaposes "being justified in Christ and being found sinners," although the end of the verse seems to negate that thought. Paul's thought concerning Christ's redemption that results in the Abrahamic blessing for all (cf. v. 28) is less opaque (3:13–14). Both the Abrahamic blessing and the divine sonship mentioned in verse 26 are further benefits found uniquely in Christ.

It is no surprise, then, that we are told that neither rituals of the past nor rituals of the present amount to anything when it comes on to eschatological justification (5:5–6).

The first chapter of 1 Corinthians itemizes additional benefits of being in Christ in terms of grace (v. 4), wisdom, redemption (cf. Rom 3:24) and righteousness, i.e., sanctification (vv. 2, 30).

Yet these "In Messiah" (ἐν Χριστῷ, *en Christō*) benefits do not guarantee an automatic display of genuine spirituality. Consequently, immature believers may think of themselves as "wise in Christ" (4:10), when in fact they are mere "babes" (3:1). Spiritual growth in such a scenario is made possible in part by recognizing one's true spiritual heritage and need for genuine parental guidance (4:15; ἐν Χριστῷ. Cf. 4:17). Verses 18 and 19 of the fifteenth chapter strongly imply that the ἐν Χριστῷ benefits are more than temporal. There is a post-mortem dimension to them as well (v. 22).

Early in the second Corinthian correspondence we learn that the servants of the new covenant experience continual victory through divine causality and the agency of Christ. (2:14). With this sort of divine connectedness in Christ, it is incumbent on new covenant ministers not to peddle the gospel or to be insincere in any way (2:17).[28]

We also learn from this epistle that the people of God under his new covenant are characterized by openness to divine revelation that is matched only by the prophets of old, particularly their exemplar Moses.

---

28. For the transforming power of this gospel over generations, see Royes, *Roots & Wings*.

This openness, like many other new covenant privileges, is also found in Christ (3:14)—all a part of God's new work of creation and reconciliation (5:17, 19; cf. Eph 2:10, 13 in particular is significant against the background of one of the seven wonders of the ancient world—the temple of Artemis).

Moving to the final section of the epistle, Paul even employs the ἐν Χριστῷ formulation to speak of himself in the third person. This is to facilitate his reluctant boasting (cf. Rom 15:17; Philemon 8), to drive home a point (12:2, 19).

It is in Ephesians that we are expressly informed that the repertoire of heavenly benefits is channeled through Christ alone to his people (1:3; cf. Phil 4:19), and that the entire universe will one day find its center in the Son of God (1:10)—the object of faith (cf. Col 1:4), and the locus of divine power and privilege (1:12, 20; 2:5; 3:6). All of this is with the full courtesy of divine benevolence, favor (2:7, 10), and wisdom displayed in the church and her head (3:8–11).

For the writer of this letter, the proper doxological posture is also characteristically Messianic to the core (3:21), because divine forgiveness does not in any way bypass the Anointed One (4:32).

To a concerned Philippians church, Paul writes about the fruitfulness of his work in terms of his evangelistic thrust, while being incarcerated: "I want you to know, brethren, that what has happened to me has really served to advance the gospel, so that it has become known throughout the whole praetorian guard and to all the rest that my imprisonment is for Christ" (1:12, 13).

The Authorized Version brings out better the author's formulaic construction (v.13) in these words, "So that my bonds in Christ are manifest in all the palace, and in all other places."

It is said that boasting is quite in order if the right theme be adopted. Paul, in all likelihood, would add to that the right "location" as well (1: 25–26), because if God's presence furnishes fullness of joy (Ps 16), then all encouragement and peace are in Christ (2:1; 4:7)—and experienced by practicing the mind of Christ (2:5). This paves the way for the offering of the true worship of God (3:3) on earth and beyond (3:14).

So pervasive is the Pauline ἐν Χριστῷ formula that even a first century cultural expression takes on new meaning in its wake (4:21; cf. Rom 16:3, 7, 9, 10). Even in an ostensibly private piece, Paul uses his favorite prepositional phrase. As an emissary of Christ, he makes it his point of duty to refresh others. But he is humble enough to receive from others as well (Philemon 20), notwithstanding the boldness with which he could write (v.8).

In Colossians 1:27, 28 we learn that Christ is the object of the apostle's proclamation, as well as the soil, as it were, in which each believer thrives, strives, grows. The ground of this is the co-crucifixion/co-resurrection reality expounded eloquently in the book of Romans (e.g., 6:8, 11).

Many NT scholars, including Bornkamm,[29] have observed that Paul's "In Messiah" formulations are wide-ranging and carry various semantic nuances.

> Often it is simply equivalent to our "Christian," "as a Christian," words which . . . were nonexistent in primitive Christianity [contra Acts 11; 1 Peter?]. In this case the term describes a way of speaking, thinking, acting, or serving. . . . Frequently the term sums up what has come about for believers through Christ and constitutes salvation. . . . "In Christ" can also have the full meaning of the new basic and all-comprehending reality into which believers are transferred once they have been delivered from the power of corruption.[30]

This is a fitting summary if ever there was one. Bornkamm immediately goes on to express his distaste of any mystical notion surrounding the phrase. This to my mind is understandable, given the lack of proper definition of mysticism in this regard. However, what I find puzzling about Bornkamm's position is his denial that ἐν Χριστῷ is devoid of any profound theological import. If the term, as he confesses, "sums what has come about for believers through Christ and constitutes salvation," how can this be so?

'I' in Messiah

As Bornkamm has pointed, Paul's "In Messiah" formulation was for him a kind of shorthand for the ubiquitous "Christian" today. Observing that the term has three vowels, two of which are "I"s, some have attempted to define a Christian symbolically as a person *in* "Christ" and who *follows* "Christ." The definition as far as it goes encapsulates both the mystical

29. Bornkamm, *Paul*, 154.
30. Ibid., 154–55.

and practical aspects of being Christian, although it has very little scholarly appeal. Anderson,[31] along similar lines, has couched virtually all of the "In Messiah" benefits in individual terms as follows:

- I have been justified (Rom.5:1).
- I have been redeemed and forgiven (Col.1:14)
- I have been spiritually circumcised (Col. 2:11)
- I died with Christ [Gal. 2:20]
- I have been raised up with Christ (Col. 3:1)
- My life is now hidden with Christ in God (Col. 3:3)

Although the complaint can be registered that this kind of individualistic delineation of the apostle's key phrase misses the communal contexts in which ἐν Χριστῷ appears, it does underline the wide ranging bestowals of the one among the many. An important feature of Anderson's outline is its flexibility in including approximate semantic categories alongside ἐν Χριστῷ. A similar flexibility is seen in Deissmann's comments which immediately appear under his "I in Christ" sub-heading. Deissmann writes: "Christ is Spirit; therefore he can live in Paul and Paul in Him. Just as the air of life . . . is 'in' us and fills us, and yet at the same time live in this air and breathe it, so it is also with the Christ-intimacy."[32]

It is from this mystical communion that the foregoing benefits (as well as the ones mention by Deissmann)[33] flow. For Deissmann, neither baptism nor the Lord's Supper, vital they may be in their own right, is effective in bringing about the Christocentric communion. "The decisive factor . . . is God's grace. The Pauline Christian can [then] say with Paul, 'By the grace of God I am what I am.'" Deissmann goes on to say:

> Powerful and original as the spiritual experience of Christ was with Paul, there were not lacking other stimuli, which influenced him, derived most directly, I think, from the Septuagint religion. The Greek Old Testament has, and here we must recognize an important Hellenization of the original, a great number of prominent passages in which the formulae 'in God' or 'in the Lord' are used in a mystical sense. The words of the prophet: 'Yet I [egō]

---

31. Anderson, *In Christ*, 19–277; only a few headings have been selected.
32. Deissmann, *Paul*, 140.
33. Ibid., 138–39.

will rejoice in the Lord [Habakkuk. 3:18]' sounds like the prelude of the Pauline Jubilate: Rejoice in the Lord [Phil 3:1].[34]

The "in God" formulation, according to Deissmann,[35] was a favorite of Paul as well, and is closely aligned with ἐν Χριστῷ. This is borne out by a comparison of the frequent occurrences of "in God" (ἐν θεῷ, *en theō*) in the Psalms (cf. Acts 17:28). Despite the fact that the Pauline 'I' and churches were "In Messiah," they still experienced inter- as well as intra-communal struggle.

No doubt it was out of such struggle that that wonderful paradox was born: "I–yet not I, which repeatedly [e.g.,1 Cor 15:10; Gal 2:20] flashes out of the lines of his letters."[36]

Davies,[37] as we have pointed out before, emphasized the ecclesial character of ἐν Χριστῷ. However, he did not miss the individualistic features in Paul: " [W]hile we admit the social context of the formula ἐν Χριστῷ there can be no question that to be 'in Christ' signified for Paul the most intensely personal relation with Christ. . . . It is no accident that Paul through Luther, could be claimed as the father of modern individualism";[38] and that "Paul speaks of 'I in Christ' and 'Christ in me.'"[39] Davies also speaks to the issue of the aforementioned struggle by pointing out that the 'I' as representative of the believer is simultaneously in Christ and in the flesh,[40] as well as in the Spirit.[41]

CONCLUSION

In sum, the quasi-enigmatic phrase "In Messiah" is used most frequently (so Davies) to describe the nature of Christians and their spiritually symbiotic relationship to the Lord. Deissmann is probably the first scholar to recognize the soteriological import of the phrase, expounding it in first-century mystical terms. If we accept Wikenhauser's[42] reductionis-

34. Ibid., 145–146.
35. Deissmann, *Paul*, 146.
36. Ibid., 154.
37. Davies, *Paul*, 78, 86, 87.
38. Ibid., 87.
39. Ibid., 87 , n.4.
40. Ibid., 112.
41. Ibid., 117.
42. Wikenhauser, *Pauline Mysticism*, 19.

tic definition of mysticism as "the entry of man into Divinity and the entry of the Divinity into man," Deissmann's exposition in this regard may become palatable. For Paul, ἐν Χριστῷ was a multifaceted construction which enabled him to speak to issues vertical and horizontal, while maintaining the distinctive emphases of the Messianic community within its own religiously pluralistic milieu.

In Paul's *magnum opus*[43] many of the motifs that are associated with the in-Messiah (ἐν Χριστῷ) formulation above are again mentioned and given fresh exposition and elaboration. We are not surprised, then, that eternal life and full acquittal have their locus in Messiah/Christ (Rom 6:23; 8:1–2; cf. John 3:16), that the believers are secure in God's love, despite the vicissitudes of life (8:39), and that genuine Christian unity is ἐν Χριστῷ based. We have further explored the identity[44] of the child of God within the Messianic community as one who is liberated by the Spirit (Rom 8:1), and led by the self-same Spirit to express her/his sonship (Rom 8:16), in living a life of holiness (Rom 8:13–14) undergirded by divine prayer (Rom 8:26–27, 34).

---

43. "The expression ἐν Χριστῷ appears five times in Rom., namely, 9:1; 12:5 and 16: 7, 9, 10. In addition, there are other Christological combinations with ἐν. ἐν Χριστῷ Ἰησοῦ: six times (3:24; 6:11; 8:1–2; 15:17; 16:3); ἐν κυρίῳ Ιησου: once (14:14); ἐν κυρίω: seven times (16:22, 8, 11, 12 [bis], 13, 22); and Χριστῷ Ἰησοῦ τῷ κυρίῳ . . . : twice (6:23; 8:29). . . . ἐν Χριστῷ alone occurs over 150 times in the Pauline corpus" (Yorke, *The Church*, 76 n. 40).

44. The Christian, as we have seen above, can be identified as a person *in* Christ who *follows* Christ: a son slain with the Savior (Rom 6:3); servant sanctified by Scripture (Rom 6:17–18); saint struggling against sin and Satan (Rom 1:7; 7:18; 16:20); and soldier slaying along with the Spirit (Rom 8:12–13; 37).

PART THREE

Missiological and Pastoral

7

Romans 10 in Biblical Context

PAUL'S STORY AND THE MOSAIC TRADITION

IT IS BECOMING INCREASINGLY clear that though Paul's letters are occasional pieces they are not devoid of theological content. This theological content, however minimal it may be, carries with it a strong narrative feature that serves as the very foundation of the theological framework. As a result, Paul's letters are not to be read as "only independent snippets of 'truth' or isolated gems of logic" but as "discursive exercises that explicate a narrative about God's saving involvement in the world."[1] If this observation is correct, then one should expect to find in Paul's longest discursive exercise evidence of a narrative substratum holding together its theologically shaped composition within its epistolary superstructure. Both J.M.G. Barclay and N. T. Wright have recently set themselves the task of laying bare Paul's narrative strategy in his letter to the Romans.

Wright's proposal in this regard is that chapters 3–8 contain the basic story line of Israel's redemption from Egypt. This narrative substructure, drawn from the Exodus, also holds the key to our understanding of how the two allegedly disparate juristic (1–4) and participationist (5–8) sections of the letter cohere. Wright begins his exploration of the "New Exodus" motif in Romans by suggesting that Paul's exposition of baptism has in mind the Red Sea crossing, a connection Paul makes in 1 Cor 10:2. The connection in Romans is seen particularly in 6:17–18, where the metaphor of slavery and its radical reversal thereof (New Exodus liberation) is invoked.

Wright then poses the question, "what effect does this reading of chapter 6 have on 6–8 as a whole?" His own answer follows immediately: "If 6 tells the story of the Exodus, or at least the crossing of the Red Sea,

---

1. B. Longenecker, *Narrative Dynamics*, 4.

the next thing we should expect is the arrival at Sinai and the giving of the Torah. This, of course, is exactly the topic of Romans 7:1–8:11."[2]

The narrative sequence, therefore, moves from "Egyptian" slavery to sin (exacerbated by the law) by way of the "Red Sea event of baptism" to a new leading through the "wilderness" (Rom 8:12–17). The new journey will eventually see the eschatological people of God entering into their inheritance.

J.M.G. Barclay[3] recognizing that Paul may be viewed as a storyteller in his own right, explores "the theological uses to which Paul puts his first-person narrative."[4] Barclay makes the observation that Romans offers "a striking 'I' text in 7:7–25 which begins with some quasinarrative elements (7:7–13)." However, he expresses serious doubts concerning the pericope's autobiographical value "except in the most attenuated sense." What Paul's rhetorical 'I' does is to dramatize the discourse of the "paradoxical relationship of law and sin" by probing its personal dimensions.[5]

Barclay is more interested in 1:7–15 and 15:14–33 as revealers of Paul's personal story. Moreover, Paul also "presents himself as an example of the 'remnant saved by grace' (11:1–6)" and finds even in his apostleship to the Gentiles some positive role in Israel's future (11:13–16). Thus Paul's story is presented in Romans as *entangled* with the story of the church and the story of Israel. Foundational to all of this, in Barclay's view, is the molding of Paul's story in the form of a "christomorphic historiography."

I believe that the desire to find narrative features in the Pauline corpus is essentially correct, and both Barclay's and Wright's contributions have the potential of advancing our understanding of Romans through their respective proposals. It now remains for others to develop that which they have sketched in their brief essays, and to further refine their overall thesis through the correction of details here and there.

One suggestion, though, that I think is a bit far fetched is Wright's linking of the Red Sea crossing with baptism in Romans 6. Paul undoubtedly makes a similar connection in 1 Cor 10:2, as Wright pointed out, but in Romans 6 the writer is probably drawing upon traditional

2. Wright, "New Exodus," 24.
3. Barclay, "Paul's Story," 147–156.
4. Ibid 147 n. 34.
5. Ibid., 147.

material. Maybe a better connection between the books of Exodus and Romans is the phrase "signs and wonders" (Rom 15:18–19a; cf. Ex 7:3), which sets "the miraculous demonstrations of the power of the Spirit in the preaching of the gospel and the founding of the Christian communities in the context of the Exodus tradition."[6]

Barclay's proposal is not fundamentally different from Wright's in its insistence to draw inter-textual links with the OT. He is correct in drawing our attention to how Paul positions himself implicitly in the stories he tells, or preferable (so Barclay), how the testimonies he gives press home his point.[7]

More important than Paul's self-presentations in Romans is his manifest desire to root his understanding of the gospel in Scripture.[8] This is done in several ways: as explicit "authoritative warrants," and as indirect markers of thematic and theological concerns, which provide significant clues to his lines of argumentation.[9] In this regard, Hays finds within Paul's programmatic statement in Rom 1:16–17 several Septuagint echoes. For example, Hays observes that the Pauline declaration "I am not ashamed" has been badly handled by expositors on account of their failure to identify its intertextual links with certain lament Psalms such as 43:10 and 24:2, and Is 50:7–8.[10] I would add to Hays's list of "shame" texts Genesis 2:24, where we find the first man standing in God's presence unashamed. Paul's point, then, is this: it is the gospel that powerfully removes the shame of humankind, allowing it once again to stand in the divine presence with confidence.

Elsewhere Paul refers to the work of the gospel in people's lives as a new creation (2 Cor 5:17). Both the old creation (Gen 2:24) and the new stand unashamed as a result of divine mercy. Interestingly, both "shame" texts seem quite out of place in their respective context. As we have seen above, Wright traces Paul's central section (3–8) in Romans to the pentateuchal account of the Exodus. If my proposal is on target, the Pauline allusions to the Pentateuch go beyond that.[11] We also see possible echoes

---

6. Grieb, *Story of Romans*, 138.

7. Barclay, "Paul's Story," seems unaware of Wright's "Exodus."

8. Grieb, *Story of Romans*, 138. Barclay, "Paul's Story," seems unaware of Wright's "Exodus." Hays, *Echoes*, 34.

9. Ibid., 34–35.

10. Cf. Eissfeldt, *Old Testament*, 115.

11. Stowers, *A Rereading of Romans*, 159–66, is adamant that nothing of the sort is

of Gen 3 in Romans. For example, the first appearance of ἐγώ (*egō*, "I") in the LXX is a picture of wretchedness and weakness. There is no hint in the passage that the character Cain is aware of any wickedness or wretchedness, but it does seem that the narrator wants his hearers to see Cain as such. There is then an echo of Cain in Romans 7.[12]

A comparison of Genesis 3–4 and Romans 1–3 is highly suggestive as well. Both Genesis chapters 3 and 4 appear to be couched in the form of a courtroom drama with their incisive interrogatory discourse (3:9, 11, 13; 4:9–10).[13] In Romans 1–3 one senses a certain kind of forensic setting that depicts nothing but guilt, shame and weakness (cf. Rom 5:6; 10:1-4) on the part of the defenseless defendants (Rom1:20c). What is interesting is that only the alienated experience forensic embarrassment. Those who are found in God's will stand unashamed (Gen 2:25; cf. Rom 1:1, 16; 5:1; 8:1; 10:11–13).[14]

Hays[15] has already shown that what was for Isaiah (50:7–8) a hope of future vindication was for Paul a present realization. "Thus, Isaiah's future rebounds through Paul's voice into a new temporal framework defined by God's already efficacious act of eschatological deliverance in Christ."[16]

> If then Gen 2:25 is admitted as one of the faint but compelling echoes of the LXX in Paul, we have yet another testimony of how the law and the prophets prefigure the gospel, for the good news Paul proclaims, at the very least, restores wo/man to paradise where s/he stands in God's presence with confidence (Rom. 5:1-2). For Paul, this astounding reversal of fortunes should never qualify as the world's best-kept secret.[17]

Accordingly, in Romans "I am not ashamed" becomes the ground of "I am a debtor" (1:14), which is later embellished by Isaiah's "The feet

---

found in Rom 1–3.

12. Cf. 'I' on the lips of Cain, presented as the first user of the 'I' of weakness (Gen 4:9); cf. this with his mother's exuberant language at his birth, "now I, a woman, have in turn produced a man." "Man" is the only occurrence of איש to refer to an infant (Lieber, *Etz Hayim*, 24).

13. Sailhamer, *The Pentateuch as Narrative*, 106.

14. The "shame" words in the LXX and the NT passages belong to the same semantic domain.

15. Hays, *Echoes*, 39.

16. Ibid., 39.

17. Ibid.

of one heralding a peaceful report" (52:7 LXX; cf. Rom 10:15), and given careful thought in 15:22.

Earlier, reference was made to the forensic flavoring of Rom 1–3. This is in agreement with Hays' proposal. However, for him these crucial chapters are a recapitalization of the narrative structure of their "textual grand-parent," 2 Samuel 11–12.[18] In fact, the route to 2 Samuel is an indirect one via a penitential piece (Psalm 50:3–6 LXX), with its manifest language of weakness. Undoubtedly, as slender as this connection is, it provides a stronger case for a Septuagintal echo than Gen 3–4. What Hays, however, would concede, I believe, is that some echoes in Paul and the NT are louder than others.

One section of Romans that could be likened to the so-called silent years between Malachi and Matthew, as far as direct quotations are concerned, is 5:1–8:39. This is in contrast to 1:16–4:25; 9:1–11:36 and the parenetic sections of 12:1–15:13. In these passages we have "extensive use of Scripture in Paul's argumentation."[19] But the very presence and plethora of these citations underscore in no uncertain terms how much the writer of Romans was immersed in his sacred literature and how its essential story and worldview shaped his literary activity, and (according to the book of Acts) his pastoral and missionary itinerary. It is not surprising, then, that one can trace in Paul's letters an almost equal amount of OT allusions whose echo (the overall story line) or echoes (sub-plots) cry out for attention.[20] For example, very few would doubt that Paul has in mind Gen 3 in Romans 5 (cf. Enoch 14:22). And we will hear other sounds in chapters 7 and 15 that contribute to the portrait of Paul as a skillful storyteller, who utilized the literary and rhetorical conventions of his day to make his case for "His-story." Perhaps a prime example of Paul's narrative sophistry is the way in which he handles Hab 2:4b as the bedrock on which his introductory thematic statement is erected. This prompts Watts[21] to suggest that one can analyze the distribution of language of 1:6–17 (already colored by the Habakkuk text) throughout the major sections of 1:1–3:20; 3:21–5:21; 6:1–8:39; 9:1–11:36; and 12:1–15:1. In these portions forming the backbone of the epistle, one also finds key terms such as "salvation," "power," "gospel," "believe,"

18. Ibid., 49.
19. Longenecker, *Biblical Exegesis*, xviii.
20. Of course, there is always the lurking danger of "auditory delusions."
21. Watts, "For I am not Ashamed, 18.

"righteousness," "Jew," "Greek," "life," and their cognates,[22] tying them closely to the introductory paragraph. So pervasive is the influence of Habakkuk on Romans, according to Watts,[23] that he also finds a plausible explanation for the unique presence of a doxology at 16:25–27, which, in his view, echoes Hab 3:2–17.

Although Watts does not mention chapter 15 as one of the passages influenced by Habakkuk, it can be argued, I believe, that this missionary paragraph is linked to Rom 1, forming an epistolary frame along with it. And within this context some see a clear prophetic consciousness reflected in Paul's language. Evans,[24] for example, uses 1 Cor 14:37 ("If any thinks, he is a prophet") as his point of departure to discuss propheticism in Romans. Evans's case is mainly built on Paul's citation of Isaiah 52:7 in Romans 10 and its probable allusion to Isaiah 61:1. Crucial to Evan's proposal is the key word εὐαγγελίζεσθαι (*euaggelizesthai*, "evangelize") that appears in the two Isaiah verses. Evans also points out the recognition of recent research that the concept of ἀποστέλλω (*apostellō*, "send," and its OT equivalent) seen in Romans 10:15 is quite close.

When one adds to this the observation that "the very nature of Paul's conversion invites comparison with the prophet (cf. Is 1: 1, 6:1–13; Jer 1:5; Ezek 1:1; 8:4; Obadiah 1; Nah 1:1; Hab 2:2)," and that visionary/revelatory communication (cf. 1 Cor 15:8; Gal 1:15–16; 1 Cor 12: 4–7)[25] is common to both the prophetic and apostolic traditions, the case for seeing a nexus between the two traditions appears stronger. Add to this the fact that the only quotation in 15:14–33, with its strong missionary thrust, is Isaiah 52:15 (cf. Is 52:5, 7 and in Rom 11:15), the prophetic echo in Romans becomes even more distinct.

This prophetic influence can be seen from a list of the quotations found in Romans 10, from the three divisions of the Hebrew Bible (*Law, Prophets, and the Writings*) in the following instances of transcription (Greek), transliteration (italics), and translation (NASB).

---

22. Ibid., 18 n. 74.
23. Ibid., 24.
24. Evans, "Paul and the Prophets," 115–118.
25. Ibid., 118.

ὁ ποιήσας αὐτὰ²⁶ ἄνθρωπος ζήσεται ἐν αὐτοῖς
ho poiēsas anthrōpos zēsetai en autois

> The man who practices the righteousness which is based on law shall live by that righteousness (v. 5, citing Lev 18:5).

μὴ εἴπῃς ἐν τῇ καρδίᾳ σου· τίς ἀναβήσεται εἰς τὸν οὐρανόν;
mē eipēs en tē kardia sou; tis anabēsetai eis to ouranon

> Do not say in your heart, 'Who will ascend into heaven?' (v.6, Deut; 30:12–14?)

ἤ· τίς καταβήσεται εἰς τὴν ἄβυσσον;
ē tis katabēsetai eis tēn abysson

> Or 'Who will descend into the abyss?' (v.7, citing Deut 30:12–14?).

ἐγγύς σου τὸ ῥῆμά ἐστιν ἐν τῷ στόματί σου καὶ ἐν τῇ καρδίᾳ σου
eggus sou to rēma estin en tō stomati sou kai en tē kardia sou

> "The word is near you, in your mouth and in your heart " (v. 8, citing Deut 9:4; 30:12–14).

ὁ πιστεύων ἐπ' αὐτῷ οὐ καταισχυνθήσεται
ho pisteuōn ep autō ou kataischunthēsetai

> "Whoever believes in Him will not be disappointed." (v. 11, citing Is 28:16).

ὡς ὡραῖοι οἱ πόδες τῶν εὐαγγελιζομένων [τὰ] ἀγαθά
hōs hōraioi oi podes tōn euaggelizomenōn ta agatha

> "How beautiful are the feet of those who bring glad tidings of good things!" (v. 15, citing Is 52:7).

κύριε, τίς ἐπίστευσεν τῇ ἀκοῇ ἡμῶν;
kurie tis episteusen tē akoē ēmōn

> "LORD, who has believed our report?" (v.16, citing Is 53:1).

---

26. The pronoun is not in the LXX. The Greek text is that of UBS⁴.

εἰς πᾶσαν τὴν γῆν ἐξῆλθεν ὁ φθόγγος αὐτῶν καὶ εἰς τὰ πέρατα τῆς οἰκουμένης τὰ ῥήματα αὐτῶν
eis pasan tēn gēn exēlthen ho phthoggos autōn kai eis ta perata tēs oikoumenēs ta rēmata autōn

> "Their voice has gone out into all the earth, And their words to the ends of the world." (v.18, citing Ps 19:4).

ἐγὼ παραζηλώσω ὑμᾶς²⁷ ἐπ' οὐκ ἔθνει, ἐπ' ἔθνει ἀσυνέτῳ παροργιῶ ὑμᾶς
egō parazēlōsō humas ep ouk ethei ep ethnei asunetō parorgiō humas

> "I will make you jealous by that which is not a nation, By a nation without understanding will I anger you." (v.19, citing Deut 32:21).

εὑρέθην [ἐν] τοῖς ἐμὲ μὴ ζητοῦσιν, ἐμφανὴς ἐγενόμην τοῖς ἐμὲ μὴ ἐπερωτῶσιν
heuretēn en tois eme mē zētousin emphanēs egenomēn tois eme mē eperōtōsin

> "I was found by those who sought Me not, I became manifest to those who did not ask for Me." (v.20, citing Is 61:1).

Ολην τὴν ἡμέραν ἐξεπέτασα τὰς χεῖράς μου πρὸς λαὸν ἀπειθοῦντα καὶ ἀντιλέγοντα
Olēn tēn hēmeran exepetasa tas cheiras mou pros laon apeithounta kai antilegonta

> "All the day long I have stretched out My hands to a disobedient and obstinate people." (v.21, citing Is 65:2).

That the Hebrew Bible²⁸ was the Bible of Paul is now beyond question, but was it the only key influence on his life and ministry? What about the words and works of Jesus, whom he later acknowledged as Messiah?

---

27. The pronoun is not in the LXX.
28. Both in translation (LXX) and otherwise.

Romans 10 in Biblical Context 153

PAUL'S STORY AND THE MESSIANIC TRADITION

It is our conviction that the Jesus tradition influenced Paul considerably, perhaps even more than the Hebrew Bible and the LXX combined.[29] This is hinted at in Acts 20 where Luke quotes the apostle as saying:[30] "You yourselves know that these hands ministered to my own needs and to the men who were with me. In everything I showed you that by working hard in this manner you must help the weak and remember the words of the Lord Jesus, that He Himself said, 'It is more blessed to give than to receive'"(Acts 20:34–35).

Based on the above citation on the lips of Paul and the fact that his missionary companion eventually penned the Third Gospel, it is inconceivable that the apostle to the Gentiles could have been ignorant of the Jesus tradition which stands behind our canonical Gospels.

Both Luke and Paul show keen interest in Gentile conversions and congregations, and both were companions in gospel ministry (2 Tim 4; Acts 9–28). If the Third Gospel is Lukan, then there is a sense in which the canonical letter to the Romans is the gospel according to Paul. The fact that Paul's Gospel takes the form of a letter demonstrates the conviction of the writer that contextualization (Appendix A) is an imperative of the Christian faith.

Compare the following:

Matthew	Incarnate Royalty (perfect King; 1 Cor 15:25)
Mark	Incarnate Ministry (perfect Servant; Phil 2:5–7)
Luke	Ideal Humanity (perfect Man; Rom 5:12–19)
John	Incarnate Deity (God; Rom 10:13)

If we take Luke's Gospel as our point of departure we may provide a sketch both of the Messianic tradition and its background in the Hebrew Bible that must have been in the historical and theological purview of the apostle to the Gentiles.

Paul would have known, then, that from the perspective of biblical history only three persons have ever borne the stamp of perfect humanity. These are Adam and his wife, Eve, and later on someone whom the New Testament Paul himself calls "the second man," or "the last Adam."

---

29. See, for example, Kim, "Jesus Sayings," *DPL*, 474–92; and Wenham, *Paul*, 71–137.

30. Cf. also Luke's (chapters 1–3 and passim) fulsome incarnation record with Paul's brevity in Gal 4:4–6.

We all know what happened to the original pair of perfect human beings. They lost their immortality. They lost their integrity. And they became in a very real sense sub-human. At first blush this "sub-human" label seems strange and out of place as a description of Adam and Eve after their massive failure. But it is just another way of saying that they became imperfect. It is this imperfect and sub-human image that was passed on to Adam's descendants. Compare, for example, Genesis 5:1 which reaffirms the fact that Adam was made in the divine image and verse 3 of the same chapter which informs us that Adam's son was born in his father's likeness. Later on the Spirit-led hymn writer, reflecting on his own failure, will bemoan the fact that he was born in sin and shaped in iniquity (Paslm 51:5). This was yet another way to speak of the source of our human imperfection, our sub-human, even animal behavior at times.

It is against such a background that we examine the biblical portrait of ideal humanity portrayed by Paul's companion in ministry (Col 4:14; 2 Tim 4:11) in the Third Gospel. Already in the Old Testament we find several glimpses of this ideal humanity in the form of Messianic prophecies. We may begin with Genesis 3 right after the perfect couple became what we are: imperfect. In handing down sentence to the major stakeholders, the Judge, among other things, declared that the Seed of the woman would bruise the serpent's head. If the serpent here represents all that is evil, then the ideal Seed, in contrast , stands for all that is holy and righteous. If Adam stood condemned as the head of an imperfect race, the Seed of the woman is presented as the perfect One to champion the cause of that fallen humanity. It is through this Seed that all the nations of the world will receive the blessing of restored perfection (Genesis 26:4; Galatians 3:16). When we come to Genesis 49:10 we learn that the perfect Seed will be an ideal Sovereign from the tribe of Judah. The books of Exodus through Numbers further portray this ideal figure as the perfect Sacrifice symbolized by the spotless animals to be offered to God in worship.

This thought was later taken up by the prophet (Isaiah 53) and the songwriter (Psalm 22), and finally John the baptizer (John1:29). In the book of Deuteronomy 18:15 we find Moses' prediction of an ideal Spokesman whose full identity is wrapped up in the Son (Matt 17:5; Heb

1:1). In Ezekiel 1:10 we have four symbolic portrayals (faces of a man, a lion, an ox and, an eagle) that were thought by some early Bible students to be types of the four Gospels. In the reckoning of some, the lion of Ezekiel's vision represents Matthew's Gospel, the ox-Mark's Gospel, and the eagle, John's. The man's face will then be the Gospel of Luke. Whether these connections were intended by the Spirit of God is difficult to tell, but they do seem appropriate when it is considered that Matthew has a royal theme, Mark a servant theme and John a heavenly theme.

It is in John's Gospel that it is recorded that Jesus wailed (11:35).[31] Luke, on the other hand, presents Jesus as the ideal man, symbolized in the prophet's vision as the face of a human being. It is the contemplation of this human face, according to the Apostle and friend of Luke, that brings about real and lasting transformation (2 Cor 3:18). We will return to Paul later, after we have surveyed the Third Gospel in relation to its emphasis on Jesus as perfect humanity.

The first perfect man had no parents (Luke 3:38). The second Man only one (Luke 3:23). Her name was Mary. Only Matthew and Luke record for us the circumstances under which the Best of men came into the world through a woman. And only Luke informs that that which was formed in Mary's womb was holy. Both Matthew and Luke give the genealogy of the perfect man, and both trace his line through David (Matt 1:1; Luke 3:31).

Jesus, the ideal human, is great David's greater son. But David himself was conceived in sin (Psalm 51:5). This means David was a sinner from conception; his greatest descendant, Jesus, was holy and perfect from day one. Luke also shows interest in ideal human development when he writes: "and Jesus increased in wisdom and statue, and in favor with God and man" (Luke 2:52). There was nothing lacking in our Lord's intellectual, physical, spiritual or social maturation. He was and is the ideal man. And it was as the ideal man that he began his ministry, a ministry which still remains a model for all Christians today. Let us examine this a little.

Luke portrays the ideal man as one who is interested in the plight of widows in particular (7:11–17; 18:1–5) and women in general (Luke 7:36–50; 8:1–3; 10:38–42; 13:10–17; 21:1–4). But the ideal man is no less interested in the plight of men. In fact, so great was his concern for the depraved men of his day that he ministered for the most part in

---

31. There is one theory that men die sooner than women because they don't cry. If this is correct, Jesus was and exception.

the worst section of Palestine, Galilee. From that locale he chose eleven of his twelve disciples. Only one came from the residential area of the Jerusalem-Judea metropolitan. Judas was his name. There are two other Lukan emphases that we need to look at before examining what Paul has to say about the ideal man. In the Third Gospel one finds quite a number of references to prayer. What is very revealing is that a significant number of these references surrounds the prayer life of the ideal man. I always thought that only imperfect people like you and me need to pray regularly and earnestly. But lo and behold! we find the perfect man praying earnestly in the New Testament (e.g., Heb 5: 6, 7; Rom 8:34; John 17), especially in Luke's Gospel (3:21; 5:16; 6:12; 11:1; 22:32–40; 22: 44–45; 23:44).[32]

The perfect man not only prayed regularly; he always allowed the Spirit of God to control and guide him. Again, this is a bit surprising. I can understand ordinary mortals with all our weaknesses seeking the supernatural help of the divine Spirit. But the ideal man? Yes indeed. And this is precisely how he becomes our ideal role model. In other words real men (from God's point of view) are those who meet temptations head on with the Spirit's help (Luke 4:1) , endure them with the Spirit's help, and at the end of the day, come out victorious (and continue to live) with the Spirit's help (Luke 4:14). Real men, like the Messiah, are Spirit-anointed men (Luke 4:16–18). And of course Luke makes it plain in his second volume that no man today has an excuse not to receive the Spirit, since we are living in the last days (Acts 2:15–17).

With the above in mind, it is no wonder that the apostle Paul refers to our Lord Jesus Christ as the second man! (1Cor 15:47).

Historically, of course, we know that Cain came after Adam. But Paul is not merely referring to history. By calling Christ the second man he is making, I believe, a very important theological point: after Adam, Christ is the only second hundred-percent man! All others in between have fallen far short of the ideal. However, the Pauline good news is this: the more Christlike we become the more human like we will be, until we all attain perfection. (Eph 4:13; 2 Cor 3:18). And, of course, the godlier we will become, since God is Messiah-like in all his ways.[33]

---

32. Where Jesus said repeatedly: *"Father forgive them . . ."*

33. J. I. Packer, *Concise Theology*, 104–33. In the mean time we strive to be like this ideal man, who lived sinlessly, who died for our sins, who was vivified for our sanctification.

> Paul [like his companion, Luke] is also familiar with traditions about the character of Jesus. He refers to his meekness and gentleness (2 Cor. 10:1), his obedience to God (Rom. 5:19), his endurance (2 Thess. 3:5), his grace (2 Cor. 8:9), his love (Rom. 8:35), his utter self-abnegation (Phi. 2:9f.), his righteousness (Rom. 5:18), even his sinlessness (2 Cor. 5:21). [It is pointed out] that these references must be historically sound, for this characterization is not derived from any known Jewish picture of the Messiah; "for no Jewish writings or expectations, not even that of the Servant of Yahweh, could have given Paul the outline of a being of such tenderness, sympathy, love and grace." ….

The kerygma of Paul is essentially the same as that of Jesus, namely, that in the person and mission of Jesus God has visited human beings to bring them the messianic salvation. But there is one great difference. Paul stands on the other side of the cross and resurrection and is able to see something that Jesus had never been able to teach; the eschatological meaning of Jesus' death and resurrection. The death and resurrection of Jesus bear the same essential meaning as Jesus' life, words, and deeds: the presence of the redemptive rule of God, a divine visitation. Paul understands that what was being accomplished in Jesus' life was incomplete apart from the cross and the empty tomb. While the blessings of the Kingdom of God were present in Jesus' words and deeds, the greatest blessing of God's Kingdom was the conquest of death and the gift of life; and this was accomplished only by Jesus' death and resurrection.[34]

PAUL'S STORY IN ROMANS AND THE MESSIANIC TRADITION

Stott shares the following parallels between the Jesus tradition (in italics) in Mathew, Mark, Luke and John and the second half of Romans:

> 'Bless those who persecute you; bless and do not curse' (12:14)
> *'Bless those who curse you'* (Luke 6.28).
>
> 'Do not repay anyone evil for evil'(12:17)
> *'Do not resist an evil person'* (Mt. 5:39)
>
> 'Live at peace with everyone' (12:18; cf. 14:19)
> *'Blessed are the peacemakers'* (Mt. 5:9)
> *'Be at peace with each other'* (Mk. 9:50)

34. Ladd, *Theology*, 452–53.

'If your enemy is hungry, feed him' (12:20)
'Love your enemies, do good to those who have you' (Luke 6:27; cf., verse 35 and Mt. 5:44).

'Give everyone what you owe him: if you owe taxes, pay taxes . . . (13:7).
'Is it right to pay your taxes to Caesar or not? . . . Give to Caesar what is Caesar's and to God what is God's' (Mk 12:14, 17)

'Love one another' (13:8)
'Love one another' (John 13:34f.)

'He who loves his fellow-man has fulfilled he law' (13:8)
'Love the Lord your God. . . . Love your neighbour as yourself. All the Law and the Prophets hang on these two commandments' (Mt. 22:37ff.)

'The commandments . . . are summed up in this one rule: "Love your neighbour as yourself"' (13:9)
'Do to others what you would have them do to you, for this sums up the Law and the Prophets' (Mt. 7:12).

'Understanding the present time' (13:11a)
'How is it that you don't know how to interpret this present time?' (Luke 12:56)

'Wake up from your slumber, because our salvation is nearer now . . .' (13:11b, c)
'Do not let him find you sleeping" (Mk. 13:36); 'Your redemption is drawing near' (Lk 21:28).

There is at least one more text that can be added to Stott's comparative catalog:

"And how can they preach unless they are sent? As it is written, 'How beautiful are the feet of those who bring good news!'" (Rom 10:15; NIV)
"Again Jesus said, 'Peace be with you! As the Father has sent me, I am sending you.'" (John 20:21 ; NIV)

ROMANS 10 AND THE LOGIC OF WORLD EVANGELIZATION

As we examine Romans 10 in the context of the above tradition, we need to point out that the chapter is the second of a triad having to do with the Jewish question in relation to the gospel. The writer from the very beginning affirms the priority of the Jews in matters concerning salvation; but he is writing to a church that is predominantly Gentile in composition, and at the time of dispatch not many Israelites had embraced their Messiah and received his forgiveness. This begs the question: Why are they so few of the chosen people within the Messianic community, when for example, this said community started out with three thousand one hundred and twenty Jewish believers?

Paul's response to this question straddles chapters 9–11. In chapter 9 he discusses the election of Abraham's seed and what that means for a clearer understanding of the divine sovereignty/humanity responsibility nexus. In chapter 11 the same issue is taken up with renewed vigor with a focus on remnant eschatology. Here too the Gentles are addressed regarding their attitude toward the Jewish question. If chapters 9 and 11 emphasize the sovereignty of God, it is chapter 10 that places accent on human responsibility and the ease with which it can be carried out, that is, the responsibility of the Jews to appropriate salvation through faith in Messiah (1–12). In a word, "Anyone who calls on the name of Yeshua will experience liberation" (v. 13). It is this citation from Joel's prophecy which introduces what we are calling Paul's logic of Christian mission:[35]

- *Vocation*—(10:13: For whosoever shall *call* upon the name of the Lord shall be saved.)

- *Persuasion* —(10:14a: How then shall they call on him in whom they have not *believed*?)

- *Information*—(10:14b: And how shall they believe in him of whom they have not *heard*?)

- *Proclamation*—(10:14c: And how shall they hear without a *preacher*?)

- *Commission*—(10:15: And how shall they preach, except they be *sent*? as it is written, How beautiful are the feet of them that preach the gospel of peace, and bring glad tidings of good things!)

---

35. The "logic" becomes clearer by first converting Paul's interrogatives to declaratives.

When the italicized terms are read in reverse, we also see a clear sequence of the first segment of the Great Commission which emphasizes the activity of evangelization—the church being *commissioned* to *proclaim* the *information* of the death, burial and resurrection of God's Anointed (1 Cor. 15: 1–3), so that the Jewish nation may be *persuaded* to *vocalize*[36] its commitment to their Redeemer-God. This strongly suggests that the writer was not only aware of his own personal commission (Acts 9), but, as well, with the kernel of that which was also given to the original apostles recorded in Matthew-Acts.[37]

A careful look at this record may be instructive. It is worthwhile to note from the very outset that this Commission does not appear in only one of the Gospels but in all four, and also in the book of Acts.

In John's account we have the Lord saying to the disciples, "If you forgive anyone his sins, they are forgiven; if you do not forgive them, they are not forgiven" (John 20:23 NIV). Concerning this verse, Reinecker states, "The Church, not the Apostles, is now the authority to declare that . . . sins are forgiven . . . sins are retained."[38] This is true because the two appearances of the word forgiven are in a tense that may indicate prior action. As Ryrie suggests, "Heaven, not the Apostles, initiate all . . . while the Apostles announce these things."[39] It is the duty of all who preach the Gospel to declare forgiven the sins of those who trust the Savior.

Before this happens, though, repentance and forgiveness must be preached in his Name (Luke 24:27). The same word for "preach" in this passage is used in Mark's account of the Commission; it means to proclaim authoritatively and without apology (Mark 16:15). Mark states clearly the content of such proclamation: the good news itself. Matthew records the outdoor version of the Commission and gives added insight as to what the Messianic community should be doing. This account highlights three activities:

1. Making disciples

2. Baptizing these disciples

3. Teaching (Matt 28:16–20)

---

36. "Call" in the NT is seldom used in the sense of call for ministry; e.g., Rom 8:30; 10:13; I Cor 1:9; Mark 2:17; Acts 2:39; Matt 22:3, 9, 14.

37. See Table 2 below; the words that are in square brackets are implied. The book of Romans itself appears to be an exposition of the Great Commission with its two sections, chapters 1–11 and 12–16, focusing on evangelization and edification respectively.

38. Reinecker, *Linguistic Key*, 17.

39. *RSB*, 1368.

Paul seems to have had this emphasis in mind when he wrote to the Romans, setting out the Gospel. In outlining the first eight chapters, one observes that 1–5 deal with the Gospel for *sinners*, how they might be saved from the *penalty* of sin. It deals with *justification* and the matter of *sins*. The portion 6–8, on the other hand, deals with the Gospel for *saints*, how they might be saved from the *power* of sin. Sanctification is the issue here and also sin as a principle. What Matthew and Paul emphasize is that leading a soul to the Messiah is not the end, just the beginning of our obedience to this mandate. In the book of Acts disciples are told that they should be witnesses. A careful reading of this book shows the apostles testifying to two matters:

1. The resurrection of the Messiah (Acts 1:8, 22; 2:32; 5:32)
2. Salvation experience (Acts 22:6–15; 26:12–18)

From this it may be concluded that a potent testimony is one which draws attention to the risen Lord working in one's life.[40]

Text	Matthew 28:16–20	Mark 16:14–18	Luke 24:44–49	John 20:19–23	Acts 1:6–8
Authority	Messiah	[Messiah]	Messiah	Messiah	Messiah
Task	Make Disciples	Proclaim Good News	Proclaim Good News	Declare Forgiveness	Witness
Scope	All Nations	All Creation	All Nations	[The World]	End of Earth
Ability	Messiah	[Holy Spirit]	Holy Spirit	Holy Spirit	Holy Spirit
Message	Messianic Call and Code	Good News	Repentance	[Forgiveness]	[Messiah]

Table 2: The Great Commission

40. It is interesting to note that our English words *witness* and *testimony* are synonymous. The former mostly translates the Greek word *martyr*, from which we get our English, martyr (an exact transliteration of the Greek). Martyrs in ancient church history were persons who surrendered their lives because of their testimony. For accounts of modern day martyrs, see Schirrmacker, *Towards a Theology of Martyrdom*, and for a manual as to how to become one in light of 2 Tim 3:10–13, Stewart, *Purposeful Evangelism*.

If the NT is in the OT concealed and the NT is the OT revealed,[41] then the good news which frames the new covenant and fulfills the old is the heart of the Apostle Paul's theology and ministry. The Apostle Paul gives the basic outline of this Evangel in I Corinthians 15:1–3. It states that Christ died for our sins according to the Scriptures. The Apostle was no doubt referring to the Old Testament writings. They not only predicted Christ's death but also gave, though partially, the meaning of it. Isaiah 53, a passage that Paul no doubt had in mind, states that Christ was wounded for our transgressions, bruised for our iniquities, and was chastised for our peace. The substitutionary aspect of that work is clearly highlighted. Christ was in our place, bruised by Jehovah. Christ's bruising was a result of his bearing our sins as if he had committed them (Isaiah 53:6; I Peter 2:24). God, who will by no means clear the guilty (Exodus 34:6–7) and who pronounces the wages of sin (Romans 6:23), had to maintain his justice by punishing all sinners in Christ.

Paul further states in I Corinthians 15:1–3 that after his burial, Christ was resurrected according to the Scriptures (cf. Ps 16). Many in the Corinthian church has repudiated the doctrine of a resurrection, and to bring them back on course Paul appealed to the Gospel that they had embraced.

His argument is, "But if it is preached that Christ has been raised from the dead, how can some of you say there is no resurrection of the dead? If there is no resurrection of the dead, then not even Christ has been raised" (I Cor 15:12–13). But the Gospel declares triumphantly, "Christ has indeed been raised from the dead" (I Cor 15:20 NIV).

That is the fact, but what is the significance of it? Part of the answer is found in Romans 4:25: "He . . . was raised to life for our justification" (NIV). To justify, in this sense, is to declare righteous all those who recognize and acknowledge their own unrighteousness, (Rom 3:10; Is 64:6).

CONCLUSION

Finally, a word must be said as to why the Moses trajectory sketched above had to be replaced with the Jesus tradition. It all concerns the present plight of God's crown creation. According to Peters: "Sin is written in bold letters upon the pages of the Bible. Only four chapters are exempt from its evil. According to Genesis 1–2, sin was not a part of original

---

41. Geisler, *From God to Us*, 8.

human history. Neither is it found in Revelation 21–22. There is thus a brief pre-sin history (Genesis 1–2) and a post-sin history (Revelation 21–22). The rest of the Bible (Genesis 3–Revelation 20) is a record of human sin and Divine intervention, preparation, accomplishment, and actualization of salvation."[42]

This important observation points out the need for evangelism. Except for the four chapters mentioned above, we see man in his terrible plight struggling against his unseen enemies. Romans 3:23 tells us that man's struggle is futile, since he is constantly falling short of the glory of God. This verse implies that man was made to glorify God, but because of sin he fails to do so. This is further confirmed by I Corinthians 10:31. Redeemed man has been set free from the shackles of sin to bring glory to God. Apart from the statement of Romans 3:23, what else do we learn about man's condition?

According to 2 Corinthians 4:3, man is lost. This means that he is not serving his purpose. What use is a misplaced kitchen knife to a housewife? Man is out of place and, in a sense, he is of no use to God. The Greek word rendered "lost" in the passage also carries the idea of ruin and inevitable doom. Verse 4 of the same passage tells us that he is unable to perceive his purpose for living unless aided by God (Rom 3:11).

Ephesians 2:1 adds that man is dead, or unresponsive to God, yet responding to sin. This suggests that man is unable to serve his purpose, but paradoxically, he is serving the purpose of another since he is also enslaved (Eph 2:2). Man's condition surely seems hopeless! But with God all things are possible. The Apostle Paul states confidently that the Gospel acts powerfully in the lives of those who believe it (Rom 1:16). With this promise and with the plight of man in mind, one can see that evangelism is a must.

Genesis 3 records man's plunge into sin, a sad chapter indeed. Did all this take God by surprise? Not at all, because the omniscience of the Almighty would rule this out. God knows the future as well as the present. According to Revelation 13:8, the Lamb was slain from the foundation of the world. This clearly suggests that God had a plan for man's redemption before he sinned. If this is true, then it would seem that the Old Testament is an outworking of that plan, laying the very foundation for the slaying of the Lamb. In fact, in the very chapter which records man's fall we have what scholars call and recognize as the *protevange-*

---

42. Peters, *A Biblical Theology of Missions*, 15.

lium, the first taste of good news: "And I will put enmity between you and the woman and between your offspring and hers; he will crush your head, and you will strike his heal" (Gen 3:15 NIV).

When man sinned, God had to judge the guilty parties but in his judgment he remembered mercy. In the process of condemning Satan, a promise to man was announced. God's intervention had saved the day. God's intervention was necessary if man was to survive, for if he could not adequately clothe himself physically in the sight of God, what chance did he have of rigging up a garment of righteousness(Gen 3:7–8, 21)?. As one proceeds in the Old Testament, the plan of God to deliver man from his dilemma becomes more evident. Genesis 12:3 tells us that through Abraham the curse upon man was to be reversed (Gen 3:16–19). Later on we learn that the elect line of Abraham had something to share with the world since Jehovah himself designated them his witnesses (Is 43:10). No doubt they were to testify of Jehovah's hatred of sin and also his love for the sinner, among other things.

When we come to the Gospels,[43] we have the final step in the making of the Evangel, the incarnation of God himself (Matt 1:23). Since all four Evangelists carry the account of the death and resurrection of the Incarnate One, and since the final week of his earthly life occupies roughly a fifth of the Gospel material, this then constitutes the most important aspect of the preparation for evangelism, the good news of how all humanity can be reconciled to God through the act of justification. This is Paul's burden in Romans 10, and elsewhere.

---

43. On one of these, see Vassel's " Socio-political Concern." For a recent recommitment to the task of world evangelization, see Newman, *Cape Town Commitment*.

8

Romans 12 and the Gifts of the Spirit within the Context of the Pauline Letters

INTRODUCTION

ROMANS 12 REPRESENTS A crucial turning point in the letter. If the first eight chapters emphasize a Christian creed centered around the Messianic good news, then the ensuing chapters lay strong emphasis on Christian conduct, that is, how the Gospel becomes an integral part of the lived experience of the people of God. In the first three verses of chapter 12, there is then a call to authentic worship and service on the part of believers, coupled with an invitation to come to an experiential and fulsome understanding of the divine will[1] which shaped the lifestyle and guided the ministry of the One who became the last dying sacrifice and the first living one in the new era.

---

1. See Table 3 below as well as Appendix D for models.

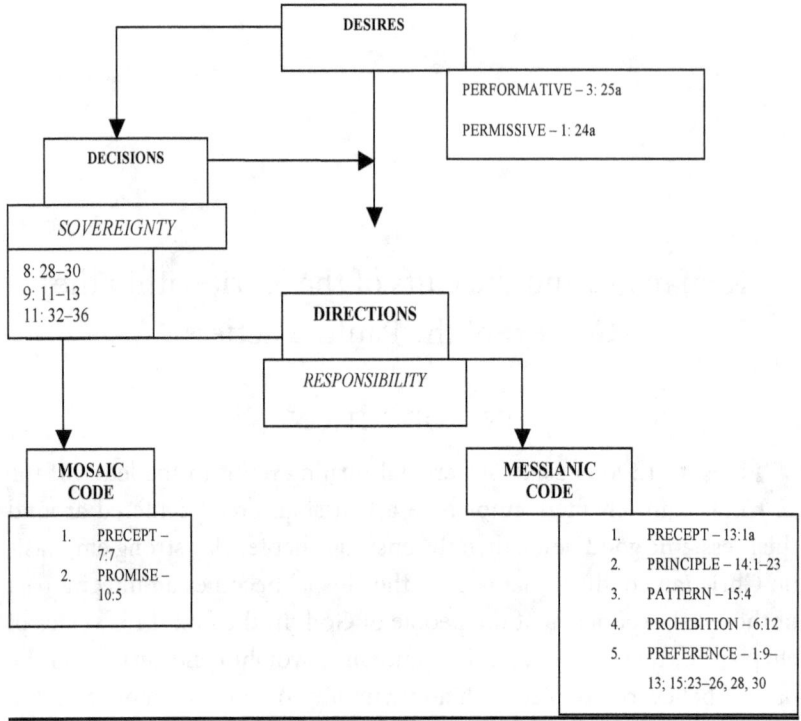

Table 3: GOD'S WILL IN ROMANS

After this, the writer proceeds to guide the way as to how the Messianic community can meaningfully participate in good works and benefit through the employment of spiritual abilities, to the glory of God.

> *For by the grace given me I say to every one of you: Do not think of yourself more highly than you ought, but rather think of yourself with sober judgment, in accordance with the measure of faith God has given you. Just as each of us has one body with many members, and these members do not all have the same function, so in Christ we who are many form one body, and each member belongs to all the others. We have different gifts, according to the grace given us. If a man's gift is prophesying, let him use it in proportion to his faith. If it is serving, let him serve; if it is teaching, let him teach; if it is encouraging, let him encourage; if it is contributing to the needs of others, let him give generously; if it is leadership, let him govern diligently; if it is showing mercy, let him do it cheerfully.* (Romans 12:3–8, NIV)

On account of the similarity between this passage and that of First Corinthians 12 we will treat them together under the following headings.

DEFINITION OF SPIRITUAL GIFTS

In the first six chapters of 1 Corinthians the apostle Paul is evidently dealing with the various reports he had received about the church. But commencing with 7:1, he now begins to respond to questions put to him by the Corinthians themselves.

In answering these queries from the Corinthian correspondence, the apostle employs the same introductory formula throughout the rest of the epistle, "Now concerning." The phrase occurs in chapter 7 twice (vv. 1, 25), where the subject of marriage is discussed. Chapter 8:1 is the next occurrence, and there we find the discussion turning to the subject of meat sacrificed to idols.

The final use of this key phrase is found in 16:12; there it is definitely a personal reference to Apollos. What is not certain is whether or not the believers at Corinth had asked about him in their letter to Paul. But the penultimate reference in 16:1 (collection for God's people) is no doubt in keeping with those that preceded it in terms of letter response. "Now concerning" (*peri de*) also begins chapters 12–14.

The theme of worship (cf. Rom 11:33–12:1) can be traced back to 1 Corinthians 8, and it can hardly be doubted that this theme comes to a head in chapters 12–14. The initial chapter which deals generally with worship and spiritual gifts may be analyzed in this way:

   a. Spiritual gifts and deity 1–3

   b. Spiritual gifts and the Trinity 4–6

   c. Spiritual gifts and diversity 7–11

   d. Spiritual gifts and unity 12–20

   e. Spiritual gifts and ministry 21–31

Spiritual Gifts and Deity

First Corinthians 12:1–3 lay the ground work for all subsequent discussions (including Rom 12) of spiritual gifts and worship. The basic question seems to be: How do these gifts relate to deity? Before any meaningful dialogue can proceed in regards to the nature of *charismata* ("gifts"), one must see the vertical connection. Only then can the horizontal perspective be appreciated. With his characteristic "Now concerning," Paul now begins to answer the question(s) having to do with spiritual gifts. I think it is worthwhile to point out that the term rendered "spiritual gifts" in many translations such as the NIV is of uncertain gender. It can either be taken as masculine (spiritual persons) or neuter. Koenig[2] defends translating *pneumatikōn* as "spiritual gifts," and this seems to be the sense of the word in 9:11 and 14:1. But because the term is patently used in a masculine way elsewhere in the letter, and because the fundamental question being dealt with between the apostle and the church is the issue of spirituality, it is probably best to retain both ideas and translate *pneumatikōn* as "spiritual affairs." This is also in keeping with the general introductory nature of the chapter. Of "spiritual affairs," then, Paul did not want the assembly "to be ignorant."

First, he wants to remind (or inform) the Corinthians that charismatic utterances are related to divinity. This he does by contrasting their former experience as idolaters with their present experience as the people of God (vv. 2–3). Under the Spirit's influence, Jesus is properly recognized as the source and focus of spiritual gifts. But any other deity apart from the "Lord" must surely be a dubious source of spiritual energy in the context of worship.

Spiritual Gifts and the Trinity

The next three verses continue the thought that spiritual gifts have their origin in the living and true God, while preparing the Corinthians for a major emphasis of this chapter, namely, that of the diversity and unity within the body of Christ. The preparation is an exalted one in that the apostle demonstrates in fine style that the unity and diversity of spiritual gifts are to be found in the triune God himself. In an unmistakable poetic parallelism we read:

* DIVERSITIES of gift there are, but the same *Spirit*;
* DIVERSITIES of service there are, but the same *Lord*;
* DIVERSITIES of workings there are, but the same *God*.[3]

The parallelism seeks to bring out the connection between the triune God and spiritual gifts, while pointing out the diversity that is shared by both. Though the literary correspondence must not be understood in its strictest sense,[4] it is certainly not devoid of theological significance.

---

2. Koenig, *Charismata*, 107
3. Fee, *First Corinthians*, 584; italics mine.
4. Carson, *Showing the Spirit*, 33.

Contrary to Barrett, then, the "Trinitarian formula" in these verses is not "artless and unconscious."[5] They display the apostle's literary skill, which is already embedded in the chiastic structure of the unit. Having denied Paul's artistry at this point, it is no surprise that Barrett also questions the unity of the periscope (12–14). But where he fails contextually (and thematically) he makes up for it lexically in pointing out that "different kinds of gifts" (NIV) is better rendered "distributions."[6] That indeed is the emphasis of the term as is seen in the related verb in verse 11.[7]

What is it that is distributed by the triune God? The Greek text says χαρισμάτων (*charismatōn*, "gifts"), διακονιῶν (*diakoniōn*, "services,") and ἐνεργημάτων (*energēmatōn*, "works"). Before we look at the meaning of each of these words in turn, it is worthwhile to note that they are meant to be taken synonymously. However, the warning issued by Carson that they are not absolute synonyms is well taken.[8] All three terms, then, help us to understand the nature of spiritual gifts in a general sense, and the body metaphor that follows (vv. 12–26) also serves to sharpen their meaning in respect of their function.

The first term, "gifts," has its root in a term (*charisma*) which usually bears the idea of unmerited favor (Rom 1:11). In the entire New Testament *charisma* occurs a mere seventeen times and the apostle Paul is responsible for all but one of its uses.[9]

A study of all the references to *charisma* shows that the terms admits of more than one meaning (e.g., "celibacy," "salvation,"). But as a distinctive Pauline term the grace of God is almost invariably behind it, and in its plural form it denotes the abilities for service in the Christian community.[10]

The next word which aids us in understanding the concept of spiritual gifts is "services." The stress of this term is on ministry in a general sense. In the New Testament we find the meaning "waiting at the table" or "providing for physical sustenance" (Luke10:40; cf. Acts 6:1). While Luke also connects it with preaching, Paul covers under this term whatever that edifies (Eph 4:11–12; cf. Rom 12:7). The term

5. Barrett, *First Epistle*, 284.
6. Barrett, *First Corinthians*, 314–15.
7. Carson, *Showing the Spirit*, 32.
8. Ibid., 34.
9. Significantly the only employment outside the Pauline corpus is related to spiritual gifts (1 Pet 4:10; on this see Jobes, *Peter*). Conzelmann, *TDNT*, 9:403, feels Peter follows Paul in this regard. It is used with χαρισμάτων in Rom 1:11.
10. The other Pauline occurrences are found in 2 Cor 1:11; Rom 1:11; 5:15, 16: 6:23; 11:24; 12:6; 1 Tim 4:14; and 2 Tim 1:6.

is used in the context of serving unbelievers as well (2 Cor 5:18–19). In First Corinthians the apostle would have us understand the term in the general sense of "the discharge of a loving service" such as was rendered by Stephanas (1 Cor 16:15), while in other letters he gives to it a more specific sense (Rom 11–13; 2 Cor 4:1).[11] Commenting on the term in this context, Barrett[12] aptly writes, "the word here has nothing to do with 'ministry' in the technical sense; *gifts* [emphasis his] are not occasions for boasting but opportunities of service, to the community and through the community to the Lord."

"Works" is the next word in parallel with "gifts," and it too enriches our understanding of spiritual abilities. It only appears twice in this form in the New Testament and underlines the active force behind the exercise of Church service. Like "gifts," "works" is a distinctive Pauline term. Vine[13] suggests that "works" points to the effect produced by God's energy (to use the English derivative).[14] The three parallel terms we have looked at (including *pneumatikōn*, above) all contribute to the richness of the vocabulary surrounding the concept of spiritual gifts—what Koenig calls "the language of giftedness."[15] It seems, therefore, that one's mental grasp of spiritual gifts will be greatly impoverished without taking into consideration these important terms. But, according to the latter part of verse 6, what is more essential to grasp is that it is God who operates (or energizes) all these gifts among his people.

Spiritual Gifts and Diversity

There are two main emphases in verses 7–11: the Spirit of God, and the gifts of the Spirit. The latter emphasis serves chiefly to bring out the diversity of gifts, whose diversity is already alluded to in the Godhead (vv. 4–6). The Spirit is clearly mentioned previously in the Trinitarian formula. When these two emphases are taken together the message of

---

11. Martin, *Spirit and the Congregation*, 10, writes: "*Kurios* is the title of authority, and has been suggestively placed in a context of the Church at Worship. . . . As Christians invoke this name, they place their lives under the unshared control of the exalted Lord, and by 'confession' they express their willing obedience to his power and direction in their lives."

12. Barrett, *Corinthians*, 284.

13. Vine, *Expository Dictionary*, 2:223.

14. "The thought is that of God's power in action or ways in which the divine power is applied. Thus, a *charisma* which is given for the purpose of service or ministry can be further described as a manifestation of divine power" (Dominy, "Paul," 52.)

15. Koenig, *Charismata*, 54.

the paragraph becomes clear: though there are a variety of spiritual gifts, they all equally manifest[16] the Spirit's presence. It follows then that no one particular gift should be the *sine qua non* of genuine spirituality.

Using verse 7 as a bridge,[17] Paul now displays the Spirit's presence in the Christian community. This he does by employing a scheme of *anaphora* (repetition of the same word at the beginning of successive sentences) to underscore his point of diversity. Various attempts have been made to classify Paul's initial list of gifts in this chapter. Bennett[18] has the following:

A. Gifts of inspiration (the power to *say*)[19]

   1. The gifts of tongues
   2. The gift of interpretation
   3. The gift of prophecy

B. Gifts of demonstration (the power to *do*)

   4. Gifts of healing
   5. The working of miracles
   6. The gift of faith

C. Gifts of revelation (the power to *know*)

   7. Discerning of spirits
   8. Word of knowledge

---

16. Because all the gifts listed in these verses (7–11) are "natural abilities," (so Edwards, *Let Us Reason*), the Spirit's work is only to "manifest" them (v. 7) in the life of the believer. Of course, this conclusion assumes that the construction in question can only be construed as a subjective genitive, but this is not at all certain. 2 Cor 4:2 ("the manifestation of truth") shows that the phrase with the genitive can be used objectively. Dunn, *Jesus and the Spirit*, 212, believes there is a possible double meaning, but Fee, *First Corinthians*, 589, and Montague, *Holy Spirit*, 148, both favor the objective genitive. In any case, to insist that the "manifestation" is given and not a "gift" is hardly justified, because the phrase gathers up the three related terms we have discussed above and becomes, in my view, part of Paul's "language of giftedness." The original "is a general term including *charismata* and *energemata*" (Alford, "Corinthians," 2:578). So also Dunn, *Jesus and the Spirit*, 209.

17. Carson *Showing the Spirit*, 34.

18. Bennett, *Holy Spirit*, 92.

19. The list is expanded below. I have slightly adapted headings A and B for stylistic purposes. Cole, "Spiritual Gifts," places NT gifts under three categories based on *charisma* (gifts of motivation), *diakonia* (gifts of ministry) and *phanerosis* (gifts of manifestation).

Both non-charismatic Edwards[20] and charismatic Bittlinger[21] deny that the Apostle Paul makes a distinction between natural and supernatural gifts. Dunn,[22] on the other hand, is cautious about such a view but errs at the other extreme by seeing all the gifts as supernatural. The acknowledgement of Anderson and others[23] that only some of the gifts are indeed miraculous is, I believe, the correct way to understand Paul's catalog of gifts in these verses.

Healing

The "gifts of healings"[24] mentioned in verse 9 is taken to be miraculous in nature by some scholars. Turner,[25] for example, readily finds historical precedents in the life of the apostles. Because some tend to restrict the healing gift(s) to the apostles, it is instructive to observe that Philip, who was surely not counted among the apostolic band, exercised this gift (Acts 8:4–8).

Also worthy of note is that an individual is seen as the healer, the locus of God's healing of others, as Turner puts it, for while some accept that God heals, they have a problem in acknowledging human intermediaries. Along this line Bittlinger[26] has suggested that the plural, "gifts," may point to each occurrence of healing as a "gift" in its own right. In this way every therapeutic activity is a *charisma*. Edwards[27] would no doubt agree with this, but such therapeutic activity is basically confined to the work of a doctor, evangelist, or counselor, in his view. It is probably best to view the plurals as denoting a diversity of healings which include the miraculous.[28]

---

20. Edwards, *Let Us Reason*, 11.
21. Bittlinger, *Gifts and Graces*, 70.
22. Dunn, *Jesus and the Spirit*, 255.
23. *Statement of Faith*, 10.
24. Literal rendering of the Greek; also vv. 28, 29. The qualitative nature of these gifts is underscored by the absence of the Greek article; Robertson and Davis, *New Short Grammar*, 276.
25. Turner. "Spiritual Gifts," 24.
26. Bittlinger, *Gifts and Graces*, 34.
27. Edwards, *Let Us Reason*, 26.
28. Robertson and Plummer, *A Critical and Exegetical Commentary*, 266.

Gifts of Miracles

Following the gift of healing we have the gift of miracles in verse 10. Both words are in the plural and are linked with the concept of power. They seem to convey the idea of supernatural ability, rather than an "ordinary" gift. In fact, *dynamis* (a miracle) by itself is related to the realm of the miraculous in certain contexts. The deeds of the Lord were called *dynameis* (miracles) in Mark 6:2. Because of their extraordinary character they evoked praise and even astonishment (Matt 13:54). Peter gave testimony of this in Acts 2:22, adding to *dynameis* two other terms, "wonders and signs," to emphasize his point (cf. Paul's testimony to the Corinthians in 2 Cor 12:12).

With this background evidence (cf. Gal 3:5), it is difficult to agree with Edwards[29] that *dynamis* should not be construed as an ability to work miracles. If the many fine English translations (such as the RSV, NASB, and NIV) can be faulted for taking the term as such, what can one say about the renderings of the Spanish (*Milagros*), French (*miracles*), German (*wunder*), and Hebrew (*gebur*) at this point?

But what kind of miracles does this gift include? Robertson and Plummer[30] suggest that it covers works such as the exorcising of demons and, possibly, the judgment of Elymas, the sorcerer, while Barrett[31] and Robertson[32] include miracles of nature as well.

Prophecy

Following close on the heels of the gift of miracles in verse 10 is that of prophecy. For Edwards the meaning of this word is bound up with its etymology, which has the sense of "interpretation." An example of this may be seen in the ministry of Daniel who "did most if not all of his prophecies by interpreting dreams and other messages of God to man." Following the lead of "many translators" Edwards' definition of prophecy is, "making God's message plain."[33]

Henry,[34] on the other hand, sees this gift akin to that of the Old Testament prophets with two components to it, that of "forthtelling" and

29. Edwards, *Let Us Reason*, 8.
30. Robertson and Plummer, *Critical and Exegetical Commentary*, 266.
31. Barrett, *First Corinthians*, 286.
32. Robertson, *Answers*, 102.
33. Edwards, *Let Us Reason*, 7.
34. "The Gift and Gifts of the Holy Spirit," 5.

"foretelling." Anderson and his team[35] only intimate that this is a special leadership gift. What really is the character of this gift? Is it identical with the Old Testament activity? Are we to understand it in a subordinate sense as Henry suggests?[36]

In a penetrating study on the gift of prophecy in the New Testament, Wayne Grudem[37] offers much help in answering these questions. He defines the gift of prophecy as "telling something that God has spontaneously brought to mind." He then compares prophecy in the New Testament with that of the Old. Grudem further demonstrates that the former had considerable less authority than the latter. The Old Testament prophets, he rightly points out, had the responsibility to speak and write words that bore absolute divine authority (Deut 18:18–20; Jer 1:9; Ez 2:7). This responsibility, however, was not given to New Testament prophets but to the apostles.

"There are clear indications that New Testament prophets did not speak with divine authority," Grudem continues. For instances, we find the Apostle Paul "disobeying" prophecy in Acts 21:4, something he could not have done in the Old Testament without culpability (cf. the prophecy of Agabus in Acts 21:10–11, and Paul's injunction in 1 Thess 5:20–21). "There is one other type of evidence that New Testament congregational prophets spoke with less authority than the apostles of Scriptures: The apostles did not solve the problem of who would speak for God when they were gone by encouraging Christians to listen to prophets, but by pointing to Scripture."[38]

There is much to be said for Grudem's position. Its chief credit is that it has a sound exegetical base. However, my main problem with his exposition emerges at the point where he seeks to build his superstructure on the solid foundation he has laid. He infers that since New Testament prophecy is sometimes flawed, we should consider it to be "merely human words, *not* [his emphasis] God's words."[39] Grudem, I think, has successfully shown that such prophecy is not on the same

---

35. *Statement of Faith*, 10.

36. Ibid., 5.

37. Grudem, "Why Christians Can Still Prophesy," 29–31; cf. his *Gift of Prophecy in 1 Corinthians*; and *Gift*. For two fine assessments of Grudem's views., see Gaffin, "A Cessationist View," 23–94, and Thomas, *Understanding Spiritual Gifts*, 133–42.

38. Ibid.

39. Ibid.

level as the canon. But if preaching is to be considered the "Word of God" (cf. 1 Pet 4:11), should not prophecy based on revelation (1 Cor 14:30–31) be accorded a similar status?

This criticism notwithstanding one can hardly doubt the significant contribution of Grudem's thesis. It shows us that Henry's definition of the gift, embracing both a declarative ("forthtelling") and predictive ("foretelling") element, can be maintained. At the same time, it also points up the weakness of Edwards' position on prophecy as mere preaching.

Tongues

Edwards wrote his book primarily to clarify the nature of "tongues" and it is to that gift we turn our attention. I think Edwards is rightly critical of those who would define the gift of tongues as "ecstatic utterances, dark sayings, meaningless phraseology, totally unfitted for communication with other persons."[40]

Edwards asserts that the word "tongue" in Scripture bears the same meaning it has outside of Scripture, that is, it refers to the physical organ or a language. His interest particularly is in the way *glossa* ("tongue/s") is used by Paul in the Corinthian correspondence. In comparing the apostle with some other New Testament writers, Edwards makes the following assertions:[41]

1. "The Corinthians 'tongues' were not miraculously acquired new tongues." This, he says, was only a promise made in Mark 16:17 which finds fulfillment in the book of Acts (2, 10, 19).

2. "The Corinthian tongues were not supernatural." This is so because it is described as something spiritual in chapter 14 and the adjective simply has the idea of that which is fit for the Spirit's use. After all "a spiritual man is not a supernatural man."

3. "The Corinthians tongues were not used as signs as is the case of Mark 16:20. They were a sign to unbelieving Jews only." (14:22).

4. "The Corinthian tongues were not empty speech sounds in the sense of kenophobia" (1 Tim. 6:20; 2 Tim. 2:16).

5. "The Corinthian tongues were not strange sounds as the 1966 Today's English Version read at 12:10."

40. Edward, *op. cit.*, 1.
41. Ibid., 10–13.

6. "The Corinthian tongues were not glossolalia." "Glossolalia," says Edwards, "is a term used by theologians to mean 'tongue speech.' It combines two Greek roots into one word . . . but is not found in 1 Corinthians or anywhere in the New Testament. . . . 'Tongue speech' is making sounds which come from the tongue without the use of the mind."

7. "The Corinthian tongues were not angels' language. Paul, in 13:1, was only advancing a case for the sake of argument."

8. "The Corinthian tongues were not languages that no man could understand." 1 Cor. 14:2 has led many to hold this position, but, according to Edwards, the verb *akouo* is to be understood in this context to mean "obey" or "heed."

By way of evaluation, it may be said that there is nothing intrinsic in the word *glossa* that would preclude it being used in a miraculous sense in Corinth, as Edwards' first proposition asserts. The same thing could be said concerning the second proposition. Only the usage and context of the term can determine whether or not *glossa* is used in a supernatural or miraculous way. If the use of tongues in Acts helps us to understand the term qua languages, it may also inform our understanding of the term as it relates to the supernatural. To say that a spiritual man is not supernatural is beside the point, and fails to see that some men were used supernaturally (e.g., the disciples in Matt. 10).

Proposition three may be correct but one is not quite sure that the sign in verse 22 is only for the Jews. Hodges[42] takes the same line of thought. However, his former colleague[43] feels that such restriction is unnecessary.

If indeed we are to be guided by the usage of *glossa* in the New Testament, then one can readily agree with the fourth and fifth propositions, for kinds of tongues include "those [that are] intelligible to some hearers, though not normally commanded by the speakers, as in Acts 2:6–8 and those which could not be understood by speakers or hearers, unless someone present could exercise the ninth and last gift [i.e. the interpretation of tongues] in this series."[44]

The sixth proposition fails to take into consideration the fact that not all interpreters use the technical term *glossolalia* to refer to non-

---

42. Hodges, "The Purpose of Tongues," 229.
43. Hoehner, "The Purpose of Tongues," 60.
44. Bruce, *Corinthians*, 119.

cognitive utterances. As it stands, the lexical item is neutral and subject to the exegete's understanding of the biblical term itself.

Edwards' last two propositions are quite in keeping with Paul's use of the term *glossa* in my view. However, if Fee's reconstruction of the Corinthian problem is correct, the Corinthians may have thought that their prized gift was indeed angels' language.[45] This, of course, does not affect Edwards' argument at this point.

The apostle now sums up this section on the gifts that manifest the Spirit in verse 11 by once again highlighting the verb "operates" (*energeō*), used of God in verse 6 (here with the Spirit), and the cognate of the word rendered "different kinds" (NIV) in verses 4–6.

Spiritual Gifts and Unity

Verses 12–20, while still maintaining the concept of diversity, now focus on the unity for which all the spiritually gifted should strive as they seek to advance the cause of Christ in their local church setting. Indeed, it is a unity that is already there because the Church constitutes the "body" of Christ, a body created by the baptism of the Spirit. By using the analogy of the body, Paul effectively addresses the divisiveness in the Corinthian assembly. He makes at least two crucial points from his illustration.

First, he insists that every believer is a necessary member of the church (vv. 14–16). Evidently, in the assembly at Corinth the believers were experiencing more than their fair share of envy and jealousy.

> The case is that of a Christian who had one *charisma* and denied access to what others in the community felt were the more important gifts (evidently *glossolalia*). He begins to doubt his own standing as a believer, and regards himself as a cut off from the church. Paul vigorously denies this conclusion and has a pastoral word of encouragement for such an individual.[46]

Second, Paul maintains that every believer needs the help of every other believer (vv. 17–20). Each member of the human body works in conjunction with the rest. The same principles holds true in the body of Christ; therefore the believers at Corinth were courting a serious error in thinking that one particular gift may serve the purpose of the Christian community ("If the whole body were an eye . . . ear?"). It is for this reason that God has "arranged the parts in the body, every one of them, just as he wanted them to be" (NIV). So, "both the resentment of the weak

45. Fee, First *Corinthians*, 630.
46. Martin, *The Spirit and the Congregation*, 25–26.

and the pride of the strong are answered by this apostolic insistence on 'many parts, but one body' (v. 20)."⁴⁷

Spiritual Gifts and Ministry

The final section of the chapter (vv. 21-31) demonstrates the complementary nature of the members of the body in serving one another through the various *charismata*. This accounts for the additional listings of gifts, the pointed questions, and the injunction to seek the greater gifts.

All this means, then, that the definition proffered by Anderson and company is on good ground. Edwards, on the other hand, in formulating his definition of spiritual gift, does not give enough consideration to *charisma* (grace-bestowal). Consequently, "spiritual gifts" are only natural abilities. I do not mean to deny that some gifts may in fact be natural abilities, that is, capacities a person possesses from birth (1 Cor 7:7?).⁴⁸ What I want to underscore is that the usage of *charismata*, "gifts," and its corresponding *domata* in Ephesians 4:8,⁴⁹ is broad enough to include gifts that are miraculous as well.

Only one of the gifts mentioned in 1 Corinthians 12 is explicitly referred to in Romans chapter 12.

We may usefully summarize the Pauline lists of spiritual gifts thus:

GIFTS OF INSPIRATION (POWER TO COMMUNICATE)
(Rom 12:6; 1 Cor 12: 28-29; 14:1-30; Eph 2:20; 4:11)

1. Tongues: supernatural capacity to speak in a foreign language (1 Cor 12:10a)

2. Interpretation: supernatural ability to translate tongues (1 Cor 12:10b)

3. Wisdom: revelational capacity to give prudent advice (1 Cor 12:8)

---

47. Ibid., 27.

48. For this gift in its context, see Excursus 3 below.

49. For excellent discussions on spiritual gifts using Ephesians 4 as a basic frame of reference, see Black, *When He Ascended*, and Roper, "Equipping the Saints." See also, Roberts, *Discovering*, who has "hospitality," (p.18) as a gift. For a review of Black's book, see York, "Holy Spirit Book Worthy to be Read." Cf. Jobes' (*1 Peter*, 281) pertinent comment on 1 Peter 4:10-11a: "The final resource for the preservation of the Christian community is the stewardship of gifts of God's grace they have received for the purpose of servicing others. . . . Peter uses the same word, χάρισμα, (*charisma*, gift), that Paul uses to refer to specific spiritual gifts . . . ."

4. Knowledge: revelational capacity to gain vital information (1 Cor 12:8b)

5. Evangelism: ability to train people in the sharing of the gospel (Eph 4:11)

6. Teaching: ability to clearly impart the contents and claims of Scripture (Eph 4:11b)

7. Exhortation: ability to counsel or encourage (Rom 12:8)

8. Music: ability to communicate in psalms, hymns and spiritual songs (1 Cor 14:26)

GIFTS OF DEMONSTRATION (POWER TO DO)

9. Healings: supernatural and natural abilities to provide holistic therapy (1 Cor 12:9)

10. Miracles: supernatural ability to cast out demons/inflict punishment (1 Cor 12:10)

11. Mercy: ability to bring comfort and cheer to the afflicted (Rom 12:8b)

12. Giving: gift of generosity (Rom 12:8a)

GIFTS OF REVELATION (POWER TO KNOW)

13. Discernment: revelational capacity to sense the demonic (1 Cor 12:10)

14. Knowledge: revelational capacity to gain vital information (1 Cor 12:8b)

15. Wisdom: ability to give prudent advice (1 Cor 12:8a)

GIFTS OF ADMINISTRATION (POWER TO LEAD)

16. Helps: ability to serve unobtrusively (1 Cor 12:28)

17. Apostleship: pioneering ability in church planting (Eph 4:11)

18. Pastor: special ability to nurture and care for God's people (Eph 4:11)

19. Faith: exemplary and extraordinary reliance on God to meet specific needs (Rom 12:9)

20. Leadership: special ability to influence people to do God will (Rom 12:8).

We now pursue the question of the permanence of the miraculous gifts.

THE DURATION OF SPIRITUAL GIFTS[50]

"The continuance of miracles and spiritual gifts in the Christian Church after the close of the Apostolic Age up to the present time is a difficult subject."[51] That notwithstanding, this section attempts to wrestle with the problem to determine whether or not the sign gifts are here today. For some, this is certainly an exercise in futility since a miracle should be expected on a daily basis. A few have suggested that none of the spiritual gifts mentioned in the NT falls in the category of the miraculous.[52] I will proceed on the assumption that the gifts of prophecy, tongues, healing and miracles were indeed miraculous.[53] One group that came out with a position on this issue is the Assemblies of Christian Brethren in Jamaica, whose unofficial Statement of Faith affirms the cessation of the sign-gifts.[54]

In the NT the *sine qua non* of Christian initiation is the reception of the Spirit (Rom. 8:9b). This is richly illustrated in the book of Acts where we find new converts being associated with the Spirit in one way or the other (Acts 2:38; 8:14–25; 19:1–10). In some instances, the reception of the Spirit was accompanied by signs and wonders. In the case of the Galatian churches, for example, the signs are described as *dunameis* ("miracles," REB). "This text shows that what Paul elsewhere calls 'signs and wonders' was also a regular and expected expression of their life

---

50. See also Black, *When He Ascended*, 165–82.
51. Davies, *I Will Pour out My Spirit*, 230; also Packer, *Concise Theology*, 226–228.
52. Arnold Bittlinger, *Gifts and Graces*, 70–71; Edwards, *Let Us Reason*, 7.
53. In this chapter a gift is defined as miraculous if it is dependent on direct divine power/revelation for its operation. Cf. "God's Spirit possesses individuals and empowers them through the endowments of gifts. Some of the gifts are sensational, e.g., healing, working of miracles, tongues (1 Cor 12) while others are ordinary" (George Mulrain, "*Baptism and Belief in Spirits*," 39).
54. This chapter is essentially a revision of chapter 6 of Palmer's, *Spiritual Gifts*. Ryrie, *The Holy Spirit*, 118–19, feels that believers today are indebted to Plymouth Brethren for drawing attention to the presence and power of the Spirit in the Church. According to Packer, *Keep in Step*, 24, they also proclaimed the universality of gifts and full participation among pew members. "Luther recovered the doctrine of justification by faith, Baptists believers' baptism, Wesley assurance of salvation, Brethren NT forms of worship and participation, Pentecostals the baptism and gifts of the Spirit [and] Charismatics the sense of being the body of Christ." (Wright, "Restoration," *Themelios*, 6). "One distinctive feature of Pentecostal worship is the emphasis of expression among members . . . and patience exercised by worshippers" (Smith, *Pentecostalism in Jamaica*, 12–13).

in the Spirit. What we cannot know from this distance, of course, is all that Paul would mean by the phrase 'works miracles among you.' But the phrasing elsewhere in the corpus suggests a variety of supernatural phenomena, including healing."[55]

In the lengthy period following the Apostolic era to the present, there have been many claims and counter-claims with reference to the controversial gifts. This is mainly because the evidence for their continuance is inconclusive. During the Patristic period, Justin Martyr could talk about the "prophetical gifts [which] remain with us, even to the present time." Iranaeus likewise spoke of some who "drive out devils [and] others [who] have foreknowledge of things to come; they see vision, and utter prophetic expressions [and] others still [who] heal the sick." He even claimed the dead were raised up "and remained among us for many years."[56] By way of contrast, their are those, like Chrysostom in the fourth century, who spoke about the obscurity of first Corinthians 12. Such obscurity, asserts Chrysostom, is partially due to the cessation of certain gifts.[57] But what seems clear is that from the time of Montanus until the end of the nineteenth century, the sign gifts were never a part of any major movement.[58] However, "There is enough evidence that some form of 'charismatic' gifts continued sporadically across the centuries of Church history."[59]

Since the beginning of the twentieth century, which is generally regarded as the starting point of the modern Pentecostal movement, the question of the continuation/cessation of the sign-gifts has been vigorously debated.[60] The Pentecostals and Charismatics, on the one hand, maintain that all gifts are in vogue today, while many in the mainline churches, on the other, deny this claim.[61] What are some of the key biblical texts that bear on the issue?

---

55. Fee, *God's Empowering Presence*, 384. "Paul is not simply referring to something which the Galatians had witnessed once for all when they believed the gospel" (Bruce, *Galatians,* 151. This is the force of the participles "supplies" and "works."

56. Roberts and Donaldson, *Ante-Nicene Fathers*, 1:240, 409.

57. Robert Gromacki, *Modern Tongues Movement*, 16–17.

58. Davies, *I Will Pour Out My Spirit*. The followers of Montanus (2nd Cent.) "revealed a tendency to exalt the special charisms in Church at the expense of the regular offices and officers," (Berkhof, *History of Christian Doctrine*, 54).

59. D. A. Carson, *Showing the Spirit*, 166.

60. Gromacki, *Modern Tongues Movement*, 27.

61. Many Dispensationalists and Reformed interpreters hold to this traditional claim, but there is nothing in either system that forces one to accept it. For example, a

There is at least one passage of Scripture that relates significantly to the discussion: 1 Corinthians 13:8–13. The passage appears within an ABA structure which embraces chapters 12 and 14:

A. The need for diversity and unity 12:1–30

    B. The need for charity 12:31–13–13:13

A. The need for charity and unity 14:1–40

The central section (B) may be outlined as follows:

* Love is Pre-eminent (13:1–3)
* Love is Perfect (13:4–7)
* Love is Permanent (13:8–13)

In the "poem,"[62] Paul makes the point that love is of paramount importance, before focusing on some of its qualities that immediately relate to the Corinthian situation (4–7). Finally, the lasting value of this

---

dispensationalist, Philip R. Newell, could write: "Many Christians today, though often quite 'Bible students,' practically forget or ignore *the immediate presence of the Holy Ghost, with his all necessary gifts,* saying, 'These belonged to the early days; but we have the written Word now, and do not need the gifts as the Early Church.' And this self-sufficiency is leading to the same form of truth without power, that the Jews had in Christ's day." (His emphasis) The late Reformed pastor, James M. Boice, *Foundations*, 614, admitted that "healing and miracles could exist but occur infrequently... We dare not put God in a box on this matter, saying that he cannot give the gifts of healing or miracles today. He can.'" Cf. Lowery, "The Theology of Paul's Missionary Epistles," 289.

62. This section is a rhetorical digression with a stylistic focus designed to challenge the "loveless" Corinthians by placarding the beauty of *agape;* (See Witherington, *Conflict and Community*, 264–73). The literary genre is not at all agreed upon by NT scholars. Is it really a poetic piece, some kind of exalted prose, or a paradigm of classical Greek device? (Fee, *First Corinthians*), 626; J. Smith, "The Genre of 1 Corinthians 13," *NovT*, 193–216). Whatever it is there is no denying the apostle's artistry at this point. It appears, then, that much work needs to be done in answering queries like: Is *agape* (v. 4–8, including the elliptical lines) a metonym for Christ? (McCasland, "Some New Testament Metonyms for God," *JBL*, 99–113); or a Pauline personification? (Spencer, *Paul's Literary Style*, 302–3; Bruce, *Paul*, 120). And how do the particles of 12:31–13:1 as well as the tense/aspectual features affect the overall structure and style of the pericope? (Katherine Callow, "The disappearing *de* in 1 Corinthians," 185; Fanning, *Verbal Aspect*, 208–54). According to Eugene Nida, we employ language in thinking (cognitive function), to give injunctions (imperative function), to *make emotive gestures* (expressive function) to maintain inter-personal relationships (integrative function) and to effect a change in someone else's status (performative function); ("Paradoxes in Translating," 8). All of these features (except the last) are more or less present in the pericope. For the integrity of the entire epistle, see Betz and Mitchell, "First Epistle " in *ABD*, 1139–1147.

virtue is underscored by contrasting it with the gifts of prophecy, knowledge and tongues, and comparing it with faith and hope (8–13). The gifts will cease but faith, hope and love, the greatest of the three, will not terminate. The main thrust of this pericope then is not to discuss the issue of the permanence of spiritual gifts but the supremacy of the grace of love. Nevertheless, it does make a worthwhile contribution to the study of the question.

Sensing this, Ryrie, based on his exegesis of verse 8, argues for the cessation of tongues. He writes: "There are positive indications in verse 8 that tongues would cease before prophecies and knowledge. Of prophecies (the oral communication of God's truth . . .) and knowledge (the special understanding of those prophecies) it is written that they shall be done away (*katargeō*). Of tongues it is said that they shall cease (*pauō*). Furthermore, the verb 'done away' indicates that someone (God) shall make them inoperative. The verb 'cease' used in connection with tongues is middle voice, indicating that they would die out of their own accord."[63]

But when will these things be? According to verse 10 "when perfection comes." The term "perfection" is understood in several ways.

Close-of-the-canon View

Vine, for example, believes it is a reference to the completion of the canon.[64] For him there is no evidence of the continuance of sign-gifts after the apostolic times. Since the Holy Scriptures provide the people of God with all that is necessary for guidance, instruction, and edification, there is certainly no need for these spectacular gifts. A problem with this view is that it does not accord well with the context and it gives to "perfection" a meaning that is not attested elsewhere. (Cf. Eph 4:13; Phil 3:15; Col 4:12).

---

63. Ryrie's understanding of the middle voice is now seriously questioned by recent grammarians; see, for example Porter, *Idioms*, 92, and Mounce, *Basics*, 125, who says, "Regardless of one's views on the topic of spiritual gifts, we feel this is an incorrect use of the middle. . . . When one looks at the other eight occurrences of the verb, it is seen that the verb is a middle deponent and not reflexive. The best example is Luke 8:24 'Jesus rebuked the wind and calmed the water and they ceased.' The wind and water certainly did not cease in and of themselves."

64. Vine, *Romans*, 179; contra Anderson et al., *This We Believe*, 14.

Completion-of-the-early-church-period View

According to Dillow, the NT writers viewed the gifts of tongues only in connection with the "infancy" period of the church. This means that the gift would cease once the church reaches maturity.[65] Support for this view is sought in verse 11: "When I become a man I put childish ways behind me" (NIV). When Paul used *nepios* (child) and *aner* (man) he was illustrating the transition of the church "'shaking off' . . . the parental restrictions. . . . and former dependent status" on Judaism. But with the destruction of the temple in AD 70, all this was changed, marking the cessation of tongues.

Dillow approaches the problem from still another angle when he writes: "A careful reading of the ancient prophecies leaves one with the definite impression that the miraculous as a way of life [will be] characteristic of the believer only during the Kingdom when Christ returns. . . . Since they were intimately related with God's Kingdom, and since we are not yet in that Kingdom, the miracles of the first century, including tongues, must be viewed as temporary irruption of the Kingdom and not a norm for this non-Kingdom age."[66]

Dillow's first argument, while having an element of plausibility, breaks down at verse 12 where the "perfect" is somehow related with seeing God "face to face."[67] His second line of reasoning seems convincing in my estimation, but it suffers from a truncated understanding of the Kingdom.[68] As Erickson suggests, the Kingdom is not just a realm in the future, it is also a relationship and divine rule in the present.[69] Therefore, there might be more "irruptions" than Dillow cares to believe.

---

65. Dillow, *Speaking in Tongues*, 108–11; also Thomas, *Understanding Spiritual Gifts*, 110–114, 199–204. "If the full maturity of the church were in view, this would be an acceptable interpretation . . . [but] if some lesser form of maturity is meant . . . this interpretation faces insurmountable difficulties" (Deere, *Surprised By the Power of the Spirit*, 141); and Fee's "It is perhaps an indictment on Western Christianity that we should consider to be 'mature' our rather totally cerebral and domesticated, but bland, brand of faith, with the concomitant absence of the Spirit in terms of his supernatural gifts!" (*God's Empowering Presence*, 207).

66. Dillow, *Speaking in Tongues*, 108–11.

67. Grudem, *Gift of Prophecy*, 231–33. See also Grudem's *Systematic Theology*, 1049–61 in which he responds to his critics.

68. For a more balanced treatment of the concept, see Kreitzer, "Kingdom of God," 26.

69. Erickson, *Christian Theology*, 1164; also McGrath, *Christian Theology*, 469–70; and Ladd, *Theology of the New Testament*, 603–4.

Cessation-of-life View

In wrestling with the same problem, Mare leaves room for another possibility. "It seems more normal to understand *teleion* in v. 10 to mean that 'perfection' is to come about . . . when the Christian dies and is taken to be with the Lord (2. Cor. 5:1–10)."[70] Even if one accepts that 2 Corinthians 5 is dealing with the intermediate state, it does appear incongruous to speak about this period as "perfect." Moreover *teleion* is not used in this connection elsewhere.[71]

Consummation-of-the ages View

Still another suggestion comes from John Macarthur who posits a post-millennial understanding of "perfection."[72] One wonders, though, why the apostle would be concerned at this point with the eternal state when he seems to say in 1 Corinthians 15 that the church age will close at least a thousand years before.[73]

Coming-of-Christ View

A more adequate position is defended by Blomberg and Turner,[74] that *teleion* is a reference to the parousia. Carson also points out that verse 12b "entails a state of affairs where my knowledge is in some way comparable with God's present knowledge of me."[75] While this position may not be without difficulty itself, it does seem to do justice to the context.[76] The

---

70. Mare, "*First Corinthians*," 269. Cf. Winter, "1 Corinthians," 1181.

71. LN, 2:658; Balz and Schneider, *DNT*, 2:342–44; Moulton, *Challenge of the Concordance*, 274–77.

72. MacArthur, *The Charismatics*, 165. MacArthur's second attempt to evaluate the movement (*Charasmatic Chaos*) is reviewed by Cadogan and Palmer, *The Sunday Gleaner* (April 18, 1993, 6d); see also Wayne Gruden's "Does God give Revelation Today?" *Charisma*, 38–44.

73. Turner, Spiritual Gifts Then and Now," *VE*, 7–64, has also shown that part of the language of verse 12 *(prosopan pros prosopon*, "face facing face," is alliterative rhetoric for a Theophany. This virtually assures us that Paul had in mind the Parousia. Cf. *eidon gar theon prosopon pros prosopon*, "for I saw God face to face," (Genesis 32:31–32a LXX) and *eidon ton aggelon Kuriou prosopan pros prosopon*, "I saw the angel of the Lord face to face." (Judges 6:22b–23); Rahlfs, *Septuaginta*, 52, 431. These two citations are conspicuously absent from the indices of quotations, allusions and verbal parallels in Aland, *GNT*, 887–901.

74. C. Blomberg, *First Corinthians*, 262–63; Turner, "Spiritual Gifts," 7–64.

75. D. A. Carson, *Showing the Spirit*, 70.

76. Keener, *The Bible Background Commentary*, 480.

difficulty is felt by all; thus Edgar, a cessationist, confesses: "No Bible verse specifically states that tongues, signs, and wonders will continue. . . . Nor is there a verse that specifically states they will cease."[77]

If the question is approached from a theological angle, one that reflects the New Testament eschatological orientation, there is promise of more progress. For the NT writers, the apostle Paul in particular, "the decisive era in the fulfillment of God's promises has been reached or inaugurated in Christ, so that in some sense the fulfillment is already present. But the consummation has yet to come and significant events in God's program are eagerly expected in the future.[78]

If all this is granted, what good or purpose would sign-gifts serve today? After all, if they only served to authenticate the preaching of the Word as some[79] affirm, why would there be any need for these spectacular endowments today? We may begin to answer this question by pointing out that nowhere in the NT is it stated that the sign-gifts were only intended for such a purpose. In fact, 1 Corinthians 12–14 places these gifts along side non-miraculous endowments which are given to the church for edification.[80] In addition, they may be used in carrying out the task of completely evangelizing the world while at the same time serving to convince each generation of the reality of God.[81] On a more practical level, it could also be pointed out that some of the forces which hinder the process of edification may need the assistance of such sign-gifts of miracles and healing to effect their removal. For example, when Fred Dickason released his first book on angels,[82] he felt pretty certain that Christians could not be demonized (at least in the sense of being possessed). But in that same year he encountered his first case of "possession" and, "since that time," he testifies, "I have encountered more

---

77. Edgar, "Cessation," 374. DeArteaga, *Quenching the Spirit,* provides a very helpful survey of the history of cessationism, but his classifying of cessationists as belonging to a modern day Pharisaic class is too strong.

78. Fanning, "A Theology of Hebrews," 404.

79. E.g., Anderson, op. cit., 14. Virtually all the framers of this document are cessationists, with the exception of Ted Edwards, *Let Us Reason,* and Lance Henry, "The Gift and Gifts of the Holy Spirit," 5, who appears to be a partial cessationist. According to him, apostles and prophets are "foundation gifts and in this restrictive sense they have ceased. But in a subordinate sense they are to be found in the Church today. Henry's position seems to be at variance with that of Dyer, "Where Have all the Prophets Gone?" 6–7.

80. Schatzman, *A Pauline Theology*, 78.

81. Palmer, *Spiritual Gifts*, 8.

82. Dickason, *Angels.*

that 400 cases of demonization."[83] Certainly in situations like these the gifts of miracles and healings are not superfluous.

In conclusion, I think Abraham's counsel recorded in Luke 16:29–31 is still very applicable today. But while miracles are not necessarily needed in an evangelistic setting, a brother or sister[84] with pertinent gifts may be called upon occasionally to minister accordingly; and the sovereign Lord may choose to intervene in an unusual say ("Already") though his full demonstration of power still lies in the future ("Not Yet"). The Kingdom, then, inaugurated in the First Century,[85] may very well be consummated in the Twenty First, with all its gifts and blessing.

SUMMARY

We have sought to define spiritual gifts in terms of their source, purpose, and effect. We also observed that the apostle Paul outlines a sampling of *charismata* which display the presence of the Spirit among the people of God. All Christians are beneficiaries of the Spirit's sovereign distribution. Therefore, the Messianic community should recognize the unity of the "body" and the interdependence of its diverse "members." Such recognition undercuts feelings of superiority and inferiority and promotes a healthy self awareness within the said community, thus paving the way for a genuine demonstration of spirituality and service today. Finally, the exercise of spiritual gifts should always aim toward exalting the cause of Christ (Rom 1:1–4; 1 Cor 12:3), exhibiting Christian character (Rom 12:8–14; 1 Cor 13 :4–7), and the edification of the church of Christ (Rom 16; 1 Cor 14).[86]

---

83. Dickason, *Demon Possession*, 188–91. I personally doubt that a true believer can actually be possessed by demons, but whether the needed deliverance is from "obsession," or "oppression," we should use all of the spiritual resources at our disposal.

84. See, for example, the report of the work of evangelical exorcist, Dr. Donald Stewart, in *The Daily Observer* (May 23, 1995), and a response by a satanist in the same print medium on June 20 [p. 22].

85. Whereas the Corinthians believers of the first century were guilty of "an over-realized" eschatology (Anthony Thiselton, "Realized Eschatology at Corinth," 510–26), many theologians today appear guilty of an "under-realized" expectation. This a non-Christian physicist like Frank J. Tipler, *The Physics of Immortality* , xiii, finds quite strange: "It is . . . surprising to me that theologians have ignored the ultimate future of the cosmos. . . . I have been interacting with theologians and professors of religious studies for some six years now, and I have gotten the impression that, with a few exceptions, they are quite ignorant of eschatology."

86. Adapted from Dunn, "Prophetic 'I'-Sayings," 189–90; here the focus is on the

Excursus 3

Spiritual Gifts and the Naked Truth

In the middle of the first century a church was having its fair share of problem with nudity: some Christian men were evidently refusing to take off their clothes after their wedding! With their knowledge of the Pentateuch in general (assumed, for example, by Paul in chapter 10:1–10), one would think that a text like Genesis 2:25 ("And they were both naked, the husband and his wife, and were not ashamed.") should have had some bearing on matters like that in Christian Corinth. What had more weight was the slogan "It is good for a man not to touch a woman," which gave expression to the philosophy of the day that matter, being evil, did not matter. Based on this, the Corinthian husbands sought to establish their own brand of holiness on holy wedlock, to the frustration of their wives. Unfortunately for these men they did not have the benefit of this piece of wisdom:

> *This is piquant irony: here we are with all our high notions of ourselves as intellectual and spiritual beings, and the most profound form of knowledge for us is the plain business of skin on skin. It is humiliating. When two members of this godlike, cerebral species approach the heights of communion between themselves, what do they do? Think? Speculate? Meditate? No, they take off their clothes. Do they want to get their brains together? No. It is the most appalling of ironies: their search for union takes them quite literally in a direction away from where their brains are.*[87]

The Corinthian men thought they were intellectuals all right (1:18–2:8). They also thought themselves spiritual (3:1; 14:37). But the apostle and planter of The church disagreed. First Corinthians is his corrective to a number of problems they were experiencing, and chapter 7 is Paul's response to some of their family issues. These issues can be conveniently read using the following "charismatic" framework.

Lordship of Christ, love of God, and the laity.

87. *Song of Solomon*, 35, n. 2.

GIFT OF SEX (1–5)

Marriage begins with a societal and spiritual event, at the center of which is a covenant. It is then consummated by a physical and spiritual act: Marriage Heterosexual Union

"Leave"	"Cleave"
Public Covennat	Private Consummation
(Societal Domain)	(Sexual Domain)

The physical act[88] is treated in some circles as if it were a four-letter word. But if you have never thought about this "four-letter word," according to a distinguished Jamaican scholar, it is either you are too young, too old, or too *lie*. Some of the Corinthian men, apparently, fell in the last category. Others, unable to control themselves, were visiting the first century equivalent of brothels; thus the apostle's strong word: "Flee prostitution!" (6:18). This gift of God was never meant to be used in this way. The Corinthian congregation should have known this all along because the proper functions of sex are clearly laid out in their Bible (our OT).

What are these functions? The book of Genesis suggests that sex is for *procreation* and *partnership* (1:28a; 2:24–25). There is also a hint that sex in marriage is for pleas*ure* as well, since the meaning of their "bedroom" (Eden) is *pleasure*. Isaac was one OT husband who knew this well, to judge from his "sporting" (AV) behavior toward Rebecca (26:8; in the context this is foreplay all the way). Apparently before Isaac's conception "sporting" had ceased in Abraham's household for sometime, causing Sarah to cynically remark "shall I have pleasure [same root as "Eden"], my husband being old also?" But it is the chapters of Canticles (4:10–5:1, in particular) and Proverbs 5:15–21, which speak eloquently to this point.

As was said before, the Corinthians should have known all of this. But because of the moral degradation of the society, the apostle added one more function to the above list: *prevention*. This was partly to counter the popular slogan, "it is good for a man not to touch [a euphemism for sex] a woman," and to prepare them for a neglected area of spiritual warfare mentioned in verses 4–5.

---

88. See Harrison, "Sex and its Theology," 248–52.

GIFT OF SINGLENESS (7:6-9)

In these verses Paul is at pains to point out that singleness is an option, despite the fact that it is also an endowment. Verse 7 lists two charismatic gifts that are seldom if any at all mentioned in church circles: the gifts of celibacy and intimacy (or singleness and "togetherness"). The apostle Paul had the former and he wished that every one had this gift, because it is ideally suited for service, a topic to which he will return later in the chapter.

GIFT OF SEPARATION? (10-16)

Marriage is for keeps. On this point Paul did not have to give his inspired opinion as he did above on the matter of singleness (vv. 6, 7), because Christ himself had already given a categorical ruling on this issue (Matt 5:32). But what happens when a couple is not getting along? Certainly they should seek counseling. If this fails, then separation is permissible, but only with a view to reconciliation. When the Lord discussed this same issue with his own disciples they considered it a hard saying (Matt 19:9-10).

GIFT OF SERVICE (17-35)

The importance of this consideration for the writer can been seen in the number of lines assigned to it. Serving God in a Christ-rejecting world was already a difficult proposition for Paul the bachelor/divorcee. For the Corinthians who were married it would have been even more difficult (v 28). It is more or less the same in the twenty first century (in which the engagement-*ring* and the married- *ring* precede the suffer-*ring*! v. 28). That's why the apostle's counsel in this chapter is timeless. What is he saying?

Firstly, every Christian, whatever his/her calling in life, is a *servant* of Christ, and that should take precedent over every other status (vv. 17-24). In light of this, getting married (or re-married) takes on a new meaning. Why? Because the time for kingdom-service is at a premium (v 29). So how then should married people order their priorities?

Romans 12 and the Gifts of the Spirit 191

I remember when I just got married my philosophy of service looked something like this:

- God first
- Ministry next
- Family third

Then later it was like this:

- God
- Family
- Ministry

This to my mind was an improvement on the above. However, neither philosophy has the careful Pauline nuance found in verses 29–35. What Paul argues in these verses is that family and ministry must exist in flexible tension. That is, 1 and 2 above may swap places depending on the need of the hour (v. 29a), mutual consent (v. 5a), and the will of God for that particular circumstance (v 19b). But *El Numero Uno* remains preeminent. It is in this light that we understand what might seem to be a strange injunction: ". . . from now on those who have wives should be as though they had none" (v. 29b; NASB). Of course, the balance is restored in verses 32–35, which point out that married people have a serious handicap in the Lord's service when compared with singles. Knowing this Paul became a "eunuch" to give himself fully to kingdom business (Matt 19:12b).

GIFT OF SELECTION (VV. 36–39)

Verse 36 introduces a first century situation that would be analogous to a long engagement today in which the guy is experiencing the heat of verse 9. Should this brother bring forward the wedding date to cool down the situation? Or should it be allowed to remain, while taking the risk of having the divine anger burn against him on account of fornication? Self-control in this scenario (or should we say inferno?) is strongly recommended (v.37). But we must not miss Paul's point in regard to the matter of choice: the date of the wedding is not fixed (like the law of the Medes and Persians). It is flexible (v 38).

All well and good for the wedding date; but what about a lifetime mate? Isn't s/he "fixed" in the sense that God has one person for everyone? The answer is an emphatic No! If that were the case, the Saducean question of Matt 22:28 would be nonsensical in that cultural setting, and the poor woman in the story would have been in breach of the will of God six times over—a clear case of serial polygamy! Of course, each of her husbands would have been innocent of such a charge since he only married the *one* person that God had for him (but not so David, or worst, his son Solomon, who were both guilty of simultaneous polygamy). No, God does not have one person for everybody, as is popularly taught. But what 1 Corinthians 7:28 teaches is that marriage is a choice and verse 39 implies further that the person you want to marry has a choice as well. That's the naked truth. And there is a caveat: Do not take the devil for a father-in-law (v. 39b).

CONCLUSION

Once upon a time Truth and Error ended up on the same beach. Truth had arrived first, not knowing that her erroneous enemy was soon to follow. When Error arrived Truth was already in the water taking a swim. Instead of doing the same (and to avoid risking a debate with Truth about the flawed agenda of post-modernism and whether or not there are absolute ethical principles), Error simply stole the clothes of Truth and ran away. That's why today Error can often be found in the garb of truth—and that's why we still talk about the naked Truth.

Now for our summary: First Corinthians 7 declares that marriage:
- Must be *a permanent affair (v 39a)*
- Will be *a problematic affair (v 28b)*
- May be *a procreative affair (v 14b)*
- Can be *a pleasurable affair (v 3)*

That's the naked truth.

9

Pronominal "I" in Romans 15

WE WILL NOW EXAMINE chapter 15 in light of the literary framework of the entire letter as well as its affinities to chapter 7. The overall structure of Romans may be set out as follows:

A 1–5 Gospel for Sinners: Liberation in terms of Justification (International)

B 6–8 Gospel for Saints: Liberation from Sin's Power (Doctrinal)

A′ 9–11 Gospel for Sinners: Liberation from Sins' Penalty (National)

B′ 12–16 Gospel for Saints: Liberation in terms of Sanctification (Practical)

BOTH CHAPTERS 7 AND 15 fall under the 'B' scheme, and in both chapters 7:9–24 and 15:14–33 Paul uses a sustained "I" throughout to develop his argument. Both passages end with a petition/praise section. Also, the occurrence of the construction αὐτὸς ἐγώ (*autos ego*, I myself) in 7:25 (B) and 15:14 (B′) appears more than coincidental. Myers[1] observes as well that in chapters 1–4 (our A section) the third person is primarily employed, but in 6–8 (B above) the first and second persons predominate.

Another observation relevant to our investigation has to do with the initial chapter of the letter as it pertains to chapters 7 and 15. Here a number of scholars have identified 1:16 as programmatically significant to the rest of the epistle.[2] The verse has as its main focus the gospel of

---

1. "*Chiastic Inversion,*" 30 n.1. This chapter is an adaptation of Palmer, *Pronominal 'I,'* 190–219.

2. E.g., Jewett, *Romans*, 135. Hunter, *Romans*, sees three significant I-statements in Rom 1:14–16, which delineate, respectively, the writers earnestness, readiness and boldness.

God, "the single theme in Romans,"³ about which the writer has reason to be proud. The following verse states that only within the gospel is a quality of divine righteousness available. The gospel is then expounded in relation to Gentiles (chapter 1) and Jews (chapter 2), with reference to justification (chapters 1–5) and its implications in terms of sanctification and service (chapters 6–16).

We further observe that Paul's lexical choice of the verb ἐπαισχύνομαι (*espaischunomai*, ashamed) is strongly suggestive of the weakness language he is going to develop later in relation to himself paradigmatically, and in reference to the cross both soteriologically (chapter 7) and missiologically (chapter 15). It was to the dominant Greco-Roman culture that the cross (and the evangel emanating from it) was considered foolishness—something of which to be ashamed. If ἐπαισχύνομαι is a stand in for the affirmative "I confess," as Harrisville⁴ suggests, "I am not ashamed" may hint at a sub-theme that will later on (in a more elaborate fashion) provide a suitable backdrop for the power inherent in the evangel. It might not be too much, then, to seek to establish the following nexus between chapters 7 (The "I" struggles: language of shame and weakness, followed by language of victory-7:25–8:1–4) and chapter 15 (The "I" serves: the language of shame is abandoned for language of boldness and dependence, within the framework of the *Dei voluntas* [will of God]-15:14).

If our observation is correct, then the link between the two "I" chapters becomes clearer and the writer's gospel resume´ can now be read in that light. Accordingly, the language of struggle in chapter 7 and service in chapter 15 is skillfully employed to illustrate the transforming power of the gospel explicated in the letter.⁵ In outlining the gospel in such a way, the apostle hopes to solicit the aid of the Christians at Rome in order to help fulfill the divine mandate to evangelize Gentile audiences.⁶

---

3. Ibid.

4. *Romans*, 24.

5. There may be a faint echo here of the commissioning of the prophet Isaiah. First there is a display of weakness in response to a theophany (Isa 6:5), then a response to serve (v. 8).

6. For "It is today widely acknowledged that Paul was the first Christian theologian precisely because he was the first Christian missionary" (Bosch, *Transforming Mission*, 124).

In developing his thesis that Paul's apostolic self-awareness controls the book's soteriological focus, Chae[7] proposes the following schema:

1:1–7 Personal Prospect of the approach to Romans
 = 15:14–21 Personal retrospect of the approach to Romans
   Theme: Paul's apostleship to the Gentiles in harmony with OT

1:8–15 Earlier plans to visit Rome
 = 15: 22–33 Future plan to visit Rome
   Theme: A strong desire for the apostolic visit

1:16–17 Thematic introduction to the main body of Romans
 = 15: 7–13 Thematic conclusion of the main body of Romans
   Theme: The inclusion of the Gentiles in God's salvation

Chae's scheme is well in keeping with Bosch's[8] observation concerning the general missionary character of the Pauline corpus. What may be added to Chae's proposal is that the apostolic self-awareness that he sees so evident throughout the letter includes emphatic expressions of inadequacy observed in earlier epistles and skillfully interwoven in the fabric of chapter 7. Seen in this way, the I-statements of these pivotal chapters come together to form an integral part of the overall literary strategy of the letter.

Therefore, while it is conceded that the main body of Paul's discourse in this letter comes to an end at 15:1–13 with its two benedictions in verses 5 and 13, significant conceptual links with the central section remain (cf. 1:5 and 12:3 and the connection between 11:13–14, 25 and 15:27–28). We know, for instance, that Paul's "finally" must not be read like a twenty-first century climatic marker, but like a summarizing device before going on to another matter (cf. Phil 3:1).

More significantly, what he appears to be doing in 15:14–33 is to provide a needed complement to important matters raised in the first chapter. These matters, though hinted at first, could not be fully discussed until they are properly grounded in the gospel outlined in the previous chapters.

The first I-statement of Rom 15:14–33 follows closely on the heels of the writer's final attempt to urge the Roman Christians to maintain a harmonious relationship with one another as the people of God. But pri-

---

7. *Paul*, 24.
8. Chae seems unaware of Bosch's influential work.

or to writing the letter, Paul had never been to the capital as a Christian emissary; so on what basis and on whose authority does he write such a letter? It is possibly a question like this that prompted the thought expressed in verse 14: "I myself am convinced, my brothers, that you yourselves are full of goodness, complete in knowledge and competent to instruct one another" (NIV).

In these words we encounter an occurrence of ἐγώ (*egō*, I) which is part and parcel of a diplomatic construction.[9] Like in 7:25, ἐγώ is conjoined to αὐτός (*autos*, myself), adding to its inherent emphatic presence. But unlike chapter 7 on a whole, its use in this passage is along much more positive lines. Whereas in chapter 7 ἐγώ is employed in such a way as to leave the writer in an embarrassing position, 15:14 redeems his usage in a contrasting and exaggerated manner that charges of insincerity and flattery may be leveled. Cranfield[10] prefers to posit that the apostle is expressing courtesy when he writes of the Romans being characterized by "goodness."[11]

The emphatic καὶ αὐτὸς ἐγώ (*kai autos egō*, and I myself) is matched by καὶ αὐτοί (*kai autoi*, and [you] yourselves), the construction that directly introduces Paul's commendation. Black[12] speculates that the writer's personal emphasis suggests that he did not expect the Roman church to believe "he could have such high regard for the virtues" predicated of them. Black's speculation appears to move on firmer ground when he asserts further that there is "no doubt [Paul's] hearers believed he had been influenced against them." Of course, there is no shred of evidence of this. The reason for Paul's evidence lies elsewhere.

First, Paul's friends and acquaintances may have informed him of the steady growth of the Christians at Rome. The informants are possibly among those mentioned in 16:3–15, whom the writer had met previously and who, at the time of writing, were now back in the capital. It is also conceivable that the hyperbolic language of verse 14 may very well belong originally to those informants, whom Paul felt free to cite either in modified form or verbatim. If this be the case, all charges of insincerity, and the like, will prove baseless. Whatever the true situation behind Paul's expres-

9. Grieb, *Romans*, 136.
10. *Romans*, 752.
11. Bruce, *Romans*, 246, draws a comparison between the Roman believers at this point and that which is observed of the recipients of the letter to the Hebrews (5:12).
12. *Romans*, 202.

sion at this point, there can be little doubt Paul believed in his own characterization of the addressees, if for no other reason than that the gospel they had come to embrace and promulgate had the kind of transforming power to produce the very virtues he highlights in verse 14.[13] Moreover, it is becoming increasingly recognized that this type of expression is expected of conventional confidence formulae during that era.[14]

Olson[15] views the entire paragraph under consideration (15: 4–33) as highlighting apostolic self-confidence (possibly extending to chapter 16 as well). According to his reading of the passage, verses 14–16 constitute an apology for writing "very boldly." Beginning with verse 17, Paul turns from his written ministry to that which he does in person. The "I will be bold" of verse 18 echoes the "very bold" of verse 15; "to speak" and "words and deeds" echo "wrote." The confidence of verse 17 concerns all that Paul does ἐν Χριστῷ Ἰησοῦ τὰ πρὸς τὸν θεόν (*en Christō Iēsou ta pros to Theon*, by Messiah Jesus in respect of matters pertaining to God).

For O' Brien,[16] 15:14–21 offers a synopsis of Paul's missionary career from its very inception up to the time of writing. And, as we shall see later, this overview of his personal missionary engagement is merely a progress report, since he expects the addressees to become a part of his drive to take the gospel west of the capital. Seen in this light we can begin to understand the integral character of verses 14–21 in relation to that which precedes. These verses, in the language of O' Brien, are "the theological corollary of [Paul's] Gospel exposition which has been featured in the body of Romans."[17]

What role, then, does the Pauline "I" play in this context, and how does it differ from what we have examined elsewhere? Paul, by way of a triple emphasis[18] with ἐγώ being an important part of his rhetoric,[19] personally and sincerely commends the Roman congregation. The com-

---

13. Schreiner, *Romans*, 765.
14. Rapa, "Meaning," 221.
15. "Pauline Expressions," 585.
16. *Gospel and Mission*, 47.
17. Ibid.
18. The presence of αὐτός, as well as the position of the cluster of which it is part, are two emphatic features.
19. Olson, "Pauline Expressions," 282, n. 1.

mendation, according to Olson,[20] appears to draw upon ancient diplomatic use of the confidence formula in which a writer makes some sort of an apology to help "to soften the tone of what is written, or to avoid the appearance of temerity."

Verse 15 continues Paul's diplomatic piece with language that betrays his self-consciousness in writing rather daringly on certain topics. How has he written daringly or boldly? Sanday and Headlam,[21] perhaps too neatly, see the "boldness" expressed not so much in sentiment but in manner, and the prepositional phrase ἀπὸ μέρους (*apo merous*)[22] possibly referring to 6:12-23; 8:9; 11:17-33; 12:3; 13:3-10; 14 and 15:1. Later commentators, however, have given up what may be called this piecemeal approach to understanding the phrase. Following Barth, we conclude that what "we read in 15:14-21[23] is written with reference to the whole epistle," while at the same time admitting that some portions are more daring than others (e.g., 14:1–15:13).

The "I" language of the previous verse is continued in verse 15, but in an unemphatic fashion. This is hardly surprising. In verse 14 Paul goes out of his way to lavish praise on his addressees. But in the next verse such emphasis is not expected in the writer's apology. The net effect of this is that the unobtrusive "I" in "I have written" (NIV; ἔγραψα, *egrapsa*) helps to throw in sharp relief the ἐγώ laden statement of verse 14. If we take ἀπὸ μέρους "as a polite self-deprecatory reference,"[24] the contrast is even more impressive.

The second part of verse 15 (on account of God's kindness to me) reveals a fundamental reason Paul wrote in general, and more specifically, why he wrote with boldness: it is by virtue of his special calling as an apostle. The verse also seems to reflect a purpose for writing,[25] with what is almost certainly a litotes ("as if to remind you of them again" NIV). Thus Manson could write: "[Paul] has his own God-given status (cf. Gal

---

20. Ibid., 585.

21. *Romans*, 404.

22. "On some points" (NRSV), or as we have rendered the phrase above, "certain topics."

23. The many suggestions seeking to give full clarity to verse 15 testify to the truthfulness of Barth's (*Romans*, 175) admission to the effect that we are ignorant in regard to what Paul particularly had in mind.

24. Dunn, *Romans*, 2:859.

25. REB translates the phrase with a telic clause.

1:15), in virtue of which he makes bold to write them his little memorandum about essential Christianity (a deliberate understatement if ever there was one)."[26] This "God-given status," that is, Paul's apostleship, has been thoroughly examined in the context of chapter 15 in recent times by Chae,[27] who, in my judgment, has made a worthwhile contribution to the discussion concerning the purpose of the Roman correspondence.

Chae traces the history of the debate concerning Paul's apostleship to F. C. Baur's summary of the significance of determining a purpose for the epistle as a basis of proper interpretation—an area in which, according to Chae, there is much confusion. Chae himself proposes that the purpose of Paul's letter to the Romans is best understood in light of his apostolic self-awareness in reference to the Gentiles. Crucial to Chae's thesis is 15:14-21. This seems to accord well with the boldness-motif discussed above, as well as with verse 17 of the initial chapter (cf. 11:13; 15:15-16; Gal 1:15-16).

In fact, as Chae highlights, the purpose clauses in the passage (e.g., v.16) should go a far way in helping to determine Paul's intention in writing. It is Chae's conclusion, then, that the clauses of 15:14-33 inform us of Paul's stated purpose to address the predominantly Gentile congregation out of his strong awareness of being the apostle to that particular grouping of humankind. Chae admits that the passage on which he builds so much of his argument is late in the letter. But when it is realized that 1:1-17 is thematically linked to 15:14-21, and that the intervening section (it may be safely assumed) was written with the same apostolic consciousness, it is justifiable to support Chae's thesis. It is difficult to draw another conclusion, if one's attention is mainly on 15:14-21.

What other scholars are saying though is that the epistle on a whole seems to reveal more than one purpose. The one with which verses 15-16 are somehow bound up is Paul's messianic ministry to the Gentile world of his day—a ministry that is deeply reminiscent of the Levitical priesthood. However, Jewett[28] urges instead a Hellenistic backdrop to the kind of language selected by Paul. The linguistic association is that of an ambassador. The lexical choice may very well betray the writer's *double entendre* resulting in the mixed audience of Gentiles and Jews being impressed with the rhetoric.

26. *Studies*, 952.
27. *Paul*, 18-37.
28. *Romans*, 906-7.

The personal reference (ἔχω/*echō*, I have) in verse 17 is more of a conventional type.[29] It is neither emphatic as in verse 14 nor a circumlocution as in verse 16. In verse 17 Paul returns to the theme of confidence begun in verse 14. But unlike that verse the expression of confidence is self directed, though properly qualified by "in Christ Jesus." "Such expression of self confidence comes from Paul's awareness of the ministry that he has carried out among the Gentiles so far."[30] But, as Fitzmyer also pointed out, the apostle's "pride and boast" is ultimately grounded in the Messiah (and v.18 will confirm this), in contrast to that to which the "Jew" (whose boast is in Torah) "referred" in chapter 2:17, 23.[31]

But what does Paul really mean when he declares in verse 18, "For I will not dare to speak of any of those things which Christ has not accomplished through me, in word and deed, to make the Gentiles obedient?"

For Yagi[32] the verse is one more instance, like Galatians 2:19–20, that demonstrates the "double structure" of the Pauline "I". According to Yagi the co-crucifixion of Paul effected a change of "subject," resulting in Christ becoming the apostle's ultimate Subject. "For Paul [then] the ultimate subject and the ego are both one and two at the same time . . . We can say Christ *acted as Paul* [his italics] because Christ can work in history only through those who are aware of the reality of Christ. In this way the ultimate subject and the ego of Paul are one."[33] Yagi's understanding of the association of Christ and Paul in Romans 15:18 is quite close to Rastafarian theology, notwithstanding his later qualification of the "paradoxical identity of the divine and human."[34]

The "I" of verse 18 governs the thought of verses 19 and 20 as well, all part and parcel of the apostle's careful explanation of his philosophy of missionary engagement and showcasing of the kind of success he had had that was the result of Christ working through him. As he was accustomed to do, Paul invokes scriptural support for what he has just

---

29. The verse harks back to the richly described ministry outlined in vv. 15 and 16, thus the inferential particle at the beginning.

30. Fitzmyer, *Romans*, 713.

31. Ibid., 712.

32. ""I" in the Words of Jesus," 118–119.

33. Ibid.

34. Yagi writes from a Buddhist perspective. For Rasta theology, see Palmer, *Messianic 'I,'* 17–80.

outlined.³⁵ The text cited is from Isaiah 52:15b. O' Brien³⁶ expresses the thought that the citation of this particular text by Paul reveals that he "believed . . . he was carrying on the work of the servant of Yahweh."³⁷ If O' Brien is correct, then Paul's "I" statement in these verses takes on a different complexion, though Paul, as O' Brien is careful to point out, is not identifying himself with the Servant of Yahweh.³⁸

PAUL'S MISSIONARY ITINERARY AND THE WILL OF GOD

In the closing verses of chapter 15, the apostle Paul shares his evangelistic plans with the Roman believers, after having delineated his missionary achievements by the hand of the Almighty. Associations with chapter 1 are patent in verses 22–29 in that "Paul elaborates the reasons for his impending visit to Rome that was announced in 1:11–13."³⁹ And in both sections Paul's "I" statements are prominently displayed and strategically connected to the divine will in its twofold expression.⁴⁰

Here (according to Josephus) it appears that the apostle still held to the doctrine of the Pharisees, who "when they determine that all things are done by fate, they do not take away the freedom from men of acting as they think fit; since their notion is that it hath pleased God to make a temperament, whereby what he wills is done, but so that the will of men can act virtuously or viciously."⁴¹

---

35. For example, Rom 1:17; 3: 4, 10–18; 4:7–8; 8:36; 9:9; 10:18–21; 11: 9; etc.

36. *Gospel and Mission*, 46.

37. Chirichigno and Archer, *OT quotations*, correctly note that both the LXX and the NT render the Hebrew verbs as prophetic perfects, but fail to point out the περὶ αὐτοῦ (not explicit in the Hebrew) Paul has exploited.

38. Dunn, *Romans*, 869, however, comes close to making this identification: "[T]he passage cited . . . effectively ties together Paul's conviction of his call to fulfill the Servant's commission to the Gentiles."

39. Jewett, *Romans*, 921.

40. It would appear that this two-fold expression is a Jewish understanding extrapolated from Deut 29:29b (contra Lieber, *Etz Hayim*, 1168), which alludes to secret and shared aspects of the *Dei voluntas*/the will of God; cf. R. Akiba's (Danby, *The Mishnah*, 452), "Everything is foreseen [secret?], yet freedom of choice is given [shared?]." Murray, *Romans*, 223, calls the former decretive and the latter perceptive.

41. Whiston, *Josephus*, 477. What Bultmann, *Essays*, 281, calls "The old Jewish formula, which is indeed found elsewhere in the world, 'what God wills,' 'if God wills,' turns up again and again in Paul, even in the expressions ἐν τῷ θελήματι θεοῦ, διὰ θελήματος θεοῦ (Rom 1.10; 15.32), thus 'according to the will of God,' 'if it is the will of God I will come to you' and the like. . . . Paul can make precisely the same pro-

"This," (NIV) then, divides Paul's evangelistic report from his itinerary delineated in verses 23–32. The "I" statement of verse 22 merely summarizes the report, while at the same time providing a rationale for the delayed visit to the capital.

Schreiner, however, has suggested that the verb "hindered" (ἐνεκοπτόμην, *enekoptomēn*)[42] is theologically pregnant. According to him, Paul was "hindered by God, since other work was appointed for him in the east." This is intriguing. One wonders, though, why would the writer elect to use a divine passive at this juncture that deliberately masks the reasons for his failure to visit Rome, while at the same time providing an explicit explanation for such failure in the preceding verses. As early as the first chapter, Paul had made his intention known to visit the Roman Christians (v.11), as well as his frequent attempts to do so. No reason was given why those attempts were unsuccessful.[43] Neither has Schreiner given justification for seeing a divine passive in verse 22.

But the possibility remains that he may be correct given the fact that a similar construction is found in chapter 1:13, and that in none of Paul's other epistles is the impression ever given that he was in the habit of offering lame excuses for his own inaction. There is in fact evidence elsewhere that Paul was prevented by God himself from carrying out some evangelistic enterprise (Acts 16:6).

Additionally, one may further posit a kind of theological *inclusio* at 15:22 and 15:32, with both verses having links to the will of God (*Dei voluntas*) that provides the backdrop for the intervening verses. In 15:17–22, the divine will is implicitly mentioned. In 15: 23–32 it is explicit. The former embraces the writer's missionary past, and the latter, his plan. This structure provides another piece of evidence of the careful crafting of the letter in its employment of a literary device to serve a theological end. Since the "I" statements within the *inclusio* are best understood in that context, we will now examine the concept of the divine will within the framework of Paul's worldview (*Weltanschauung*), and we may appropriately begin with the following observation on the

---

nouncement of κύριος, too, as is made of God. And so God and Christ can alternate in synonymous *parellelismus membrorum* (1 Cor 7.17)."

42. Schreiner, *Romans*, 774; he translates this verb as, "I was *often* [my emphasis] hindered," to bring out the (possibly) iterative force.

43. This has prompted speculations from some commentators. For example, Bruce, *Romans*, 72, has proffered the suggestion that "the imperial edict of AD 49 expelling Jews from Rome" may have been one such hindrance.

passage: "[Paul] writes very personally (maintaining and 'I-You' directness throughout), affectionately ('my brothers', 15:14), and candidly. He opens his heart to them about the past, present and future ministry.... In these ways he gives us insight into the outworking of God's providence[44] in his life and work."[45]

It would appear that Paul was ever conscious of this divine providence in his ministry. Evidence of this may be gleaned from the book of Acts, but the main lines of evidence can be clearly observed in our primary sources: the epistles. For example, in Romans 1:10 Paul shares with his audience his earnest prayers to God to carry out his wish to pay them a visit. Such prayers, he indicates, were fully submitted τῷ θελήματι τοῦ θεοῦ (tō thelēmati tou theou, God's secret will?). In the following chapter, Paul again uses θέλημα (thelēma, will), but this time in an absolute sense. What seems clear from the context is that the reference is to what we have called above God's "shared" will (cf. Deut 29:29c), or the law (Rom 2:18).

The next explicit reference to the divine will comes in 12:2 in connection with Paul's exhortation to the church to offer itself to God in a total act of worship and service. The description of this aspect of God's will as perfect (cf. Ps 19:7), as well as the presence of "approve" in the text all seem to point in the direction of the *shared* purpose of God.[46] Murray shares this conclusion: "It is the will of God as it pertains to our responsible activity in progressive sanctification. The decretive [secret] will of God is not the norm according to which our life is to be patterned."[47]

Concerning 15:32, Murray also opts for what he calls the "decretive will," which is "realized through providence (cf. Matt. 18:14; John 13; Rom. 1:10; Gal. 1:14; Eph. 1:5, 11; 1Pet. 3:17; 2 Pet. 1:211; Rev. 4:11)."[48] This belief in the divine will, both in its secret and shared dimensions, appears to have been widespread amongst Jews and Christians of Paul's day, as the foregoing citations testify. Other examples are as follows: "Upon the whole, a man that will peruse this history, may principally

44. If providence is defined as the unfolding of the divine will, it is interesting to note that Stott, *Romans*, 377, dubs 15:14–16:27, "The Providence of God in the Ministry of Paul." On the complexity and intricacy of theology, missiology, and history in Paul, see, Bosch, *Transforming Mission*, 123–132.

45. Stott, *Romans*, 377.

46. Of course, there are also clear allusions to the *Dei voluntas* in chapters 9–11, specifically to its inscrutable features.

47. *Romans*, 115.

48. Murray, Roman, 223.

learn from it, that all events succeed well, even to an incredible degree, and the reward of felicity is proposed by God; but then it is to those who follow his will, and do not venture to break his excellent laws."[49] "Will" in this citation is almost certainly a reference to the revealed version, though not necessarily written.[50]

But the phenomenon is not limited to Judeo-Christian circles. For instance, after expressing gratitude to Serapis for rescuing him at sea, Apion, a Roman soldier, urges his father to respond to him, and adds these words: "ἐλπίζω ταχὺ Προκόπσαι τῶν θεῶν θελόντων/*elpizō tachy proskopsai tōn theōn thelontōn*/ I'm hoping to make quick progress by the will of the gods."[51] What is not readily evident from a text like this is the bifurcation of the divine will into secret (decretive) and shared (prescriptive) polarities.

This, however, cannot be said of the following excerpt: "Of the things that are, God has put some under our control, and others not under our control."[52] Presumably, the phrase "others not under our control" is indeed the very matter which a Jew or a Christian, like the apostle Paul, may subsume under "the secret things" of the Lord (Deut 29:29). Both for the writer of Deut 29:29 and Epictetus (1:11–12; cf. 2:444), writing centuries apart, human responsibility must be treated with the utmost seriousness. Thus the latter could also write: "We must make the best of what is under our control, as God wills," and the former: "But those things which are revealed belong to us and to our children forever, that we may do all the words of this law."[53]

Focusing on the will of God in this way allows us to see yet another mode in which the first person "I" functions in some Pauline contexts. As a stranger to the Roman congregation (albeit, an important one being the apostle to the Gentiles), Paul was not only anxious to impress its members with his knowledge of the gospel and its wide-ranging ramifications (thus the close reasoning of 1:16–11:36), but also to provide

---

49. *Ant.* 1:14.

50. Cf. respectively, the medieval and Jamaican "*Homo proponit, Deus disponit . . . Man plan . . . Gad wipe out*" (Chevannes, *Betwixt and Between*, 145).

51. Deissmann, *Light,* 168. Cf. the following by Socrates (?): "I have been seeking, according to my ability, to find a place; whether I have sought it in a right way or not, and whether I have succeeded or not, I shall truly know in a little while, *If God will,* when *I myself* arrive in the other world." (Demas, *Plato Selections,* 164; my italics).

52. Epictetus, *Discourses,* 2:445.

53. Palmer, *Messianic 'I,'* 134.

paradigmatic structures within the letter for their benefit. The exemplary employment of "I" statements appears to be an integral part of this literary strategy.

So how is this carried out in chapter 15? One way to answer this question is to observe that as early as the initial chapter the "I" is portrayed as being in submission to the divine will (1:10). Of course, given the religious climate of the first century, this concept was not necessarily a new one to the Roman believers, as was hinted at above. However, ecumenical knowledge that humans depend on their deities would not prevent a teacher of Paul's ilk from providing paradigmatic instances as to what it means to acknowledge the providential moments of the God and father of the Lord Jesus Christ, the one who synergizes all of life's experiences into something beneficial for his people (Rom 8:28). Under the secret will of God, then, the "I" submits, waits, and prays (Rom 15:30), and may even experience a measure of frustration (Rom 1:13). Therefore, "One can readily sense ... [Paul's] relief when he writes Romans 15: at last he can take up again the work he was really called to do!"[54] On the other hand, we also observe in 15:22–33 a freedom to choose, to plan, to self-actualize.

As an apostle of Christ, then, in whose liberty he stands and serves (Gal 5:1; cf.1 Cor 7:22), the *imago Christi* (Messianic image) was the foundation of Paul's *missio Dei* (mission divine). Therefore, it was quite natural for him to express this liberty in outlining his missionary itinerary in terms that underscore at one and the same time the parameters of his freedom as well as its latitude; thus the following string of "I" statements in vv. 24–32.[55]

The first statement (v. 24) beginning with "I go" (πορεύωμαι, *poreuōmai*), like the one in verse 25, is a present tense construction which vividly presents the writer's resolve to execute the very plans that are laid out in the letter. The second "I" statement (I hope) in verse 24, supportive of the first, expresses some measure of uncertainty concerning another aspect of the plan, that is, the willingness or readiness of the Roman believers to "fund his vision for the Spanish mission."[56] Whether

---

54. Knox, "Romans 15:14–23," 7.

55. πορεύωμαι ... ἐλπίζω ... ἐμπλησθῶ ... πορεύομαι ... ἀπελεύσομαι ... οἶδα ... ἐλεύσομαι ... παρακαλῶ ... ῥυσθῶ ... συναναπαύσωμαι.

56. Grieb, *Romans*, 140. According to Haacker, *Theology*, 19, a possible obstacle to Paul's receiving the travel money was the serious tensions "within or between the local

the apostle was able to receive this kind of support or whether he managed to reach Spain, no one is able to tell for sure.

However, Clement, writing at the end of the first century and roughly thirty five years after Romans, says that Paul "After preaching both in the east and west, he gained the illustrious reputation due to his faith, having taught righteousness to the whole world, and come to the extreme limit of the west."[57] Holmes[58] appears confident that the phrase "the extreme limit of the west" (τὸ τέρμα τῆς δύσεως, *to terma tēs duseōs*) refers to "the Straits of Gibraltar." But neither Paul's language at this point nor any extra-biblical material gives us any certain knowledge on the matter of his subsequent work in Spain.

The final "I" statement in verse 24 was "probably a familiar polite locution in current use,"[59] and may be periphrastically rendered as in NRSV, "once I have enjoyed your company for a little while."[60] According to Edwards, this "I" statement "At the very least, . . . is a tender admission of [Paul's] need for spiritual nurture from Rome." And in writing in this manner "He pays the Romans a great compliment in conveying that he stands in need of their company."[61] Although Edwards might be reading too much into a difficult expression, his observation of Paul's dependence on the Christian community for κοινωνία (*koinōnia*, fellowship) is certainly true, as the language of Rom 1:12 suggests.

But before reaching the capital of the empire, the apostle's itinerary will take him to the mother church in Jerusalem for another kind of ministry (vv. 26–28a). After this, Paul says, he will make his way to Spain via Rome. Here especially "we must keep in mind that Paul's activity as a missionary is the primary 'practice' into which all his letter-writing[62] is embedded and which it is meant to serve."[63] Rome, then, would become one of these strategic centers not because it needed a church there, but

---

groups of believers. . . . The support by only one faction of Christianity in Rome would not have served the purposes which Paul had in mind." Cf. Rom 14:1–15:6.

57. Holmes, *Apostolic Fathers*, 35.

58. Ibid.

59. Black, *Romans*, 204.

60. Ἀπὸ Μέρους here "denotes a relative short period of time" (Vorster, "New Testament," 148).

61. *Romans*, 348.

62. This includes, of course, his paradigmatic "I" statements, whether in the service of his soteriology (chapter 7) or missiology (chapter 15).

63. Haacker, *Theology*, 20.

because of its centrality within the empire and proximity to Spain, Paul's ultimate port of call.

But did not the apostle declare his intention to evangelize Rome (1:15)? And would not this declaration a breach of the very principle he outlined in 15:20–21? Three things may be said in response. The fact that a church was already established in the city would not necessarily prevent the apostle to the Gentiles from having some fruit of his own (new converts; 1:13), bearing in mind that these new converts could be easily incorporated into one of the local assemblies (e.g., chapter 16), and that Rome after all was for Paul a transition point (v. 28), not a place to start a rival congregation. Second, if 1:15 is rendered, "[F]or my part *I was prepared* [my emphasis] to preach the gospel to you in Rome as well,"[64] then the tension between chapters 1 and 15 is removed. Third, even if the traditional rendering of 1:15 is retained, we have to bear in mind that Paul's preaching of the gospel is seldom limited to the winning of unbelievers to the faith.[65]

Verse 29, with its triple pronominal emphasis ("I know . . . when I come[66] . . . I shall come"), expresses an unparalleled confidence (in so far as this letter unfolds), and promises unprecedented blessing in the pregnant phrase, "in the fullness of Messianic blessing."

The final paragraph within the chapter is introduced by the Pauline plea, "I urge you sisters and brothers" (v. 30). This introductory clause is followed by its complement which contains an embryonic Trinitarian reference (through our Lord Jesus Christ . . . and by the love of the Spirit). Both "by our Lord Jesus Christ" and "by the love of the Spirit" provide the basis of the request, with "God" being the authoritative source from whom the answer is urgently anticipated, and to whom the strong petition is made. The verse also appears to be some kind of variation on the pronominal theme in that the thought expressed is both theological and exemplary, since the request for personal prayer in the NT is relatively rare and is bound to constitute a paradigmatic point. Also, the strength of the infinitive (to strive together) also seems to re-enforce the point, in so far as it subtly suggests the apostle's dependence on God.

---

64. Käsemann, *Romans*, 14.

65. See also items B and B′ (the overall structure of the epistle) above.

66. ἐρχόμενος; actually a nominative participle used with a "greater vividness in description" (Fanning, *Verbal Aspect*, 409).

The content of the kind of prayer Paul has in mind, that is, the way that he expects the Romans to intercede on his behalf is delineated in verses 31 and 32. The first of these two verses echoes 7:24 with its mention of the verb ῥύομαι (*ruomai*, I may be delivered). In fact verses 14–32, particularly the "I" statements, somewhat mirror 7:14–25 with its fair share of "I" locutions, many of which are of the emphatic variety.

Verse 32 contains the final "I" statement in the chapter. Apart from completing the apostle's prayer request begun in the previous purpose clause, the verse also underscores the critical reality of the divine will that was discussed above. Here the reference seems certain to be what we have called above God's secret will that appears at times to be fixed and at other times flexible, especially in regard to prayer. Henceforth, all of Paul's plans to reach Rome are entirely in the hand of God,[67]—even his anticipation of mutual refreshment expressed in his, "so that by God's will I may come to you with joy and be refreshed in your company" (v. 32; NRSV).

Although 15:14–33 does not have a preponderance of first person pronouns, it is significant on account of the fact that Paul very likely intended the passage to be read and heard as paradigmatic clauses, especially when placed alongside their textual echoes of 1:8–13. All the verbs in question point to the "appropriateness of making plans" since "God neither commanded Paul to go to Rome, nor forbade such a journey."[68] The paradigmatic structure at this level is clearly that of the "historical" type, that is, one based upon the apostle's own experience and not that of the "created" kind, to use one of Aristotle's categories.[69] And if Kümmel's[70] listing of Pauline fictives (e.g., Rom 3:5, 7) is anything to go by, we are on safe ground in positing a historical backdrop for the "I" locutions of this passage.

---

67. "*Les mots par la volenté de Dieu, nous rappellent combien c'est une chose nécessaire pour nous de vaquer à des priers, parce que c'est Dieu seul qui dirige toutes nos voies par sa providence*" (Calvin, *Épitre aux Romains*, 348)/ "The phrase *through the will of God* reminds us of the necessity of devoting ourselves to prayer, since God alone directs all our paths by his providence" (Calvin, *Romans*, 318).

68. Friesen, *Decision Making*, 235.

69. "There are two kinds of examples ('paradigms,' παραδειγμάτων); namely, one which consists in relating things that have happened before, another in inventing them oneself." In this passage, Aristotle only elaborated on the latter category (Aristotle, *Art of Rhetoric*, 273).

70. Kümmel, *Romans 7*, 121.

All this highlights a theme which is a neglected one in NT scholarship. Thus Schreiner writes regarding the apostle's career and primary aim: "He was a missionary who wrote letters to churches in order to sustain his converts in their new found faith. He saw himself as a missionary commissioned by God to extend the saving message of the gospel to all nations."[71]

Paul also expected his converts, and even those who were not his converts (e.g., the Romans and Colossians), to be actively engaged in the missionary enterprise. In this regard the "I" statements of chapters 1 and 15 are to be read as paradigmatic.

SUMMARY

It seems that Paul in Romans employs his "I" statements in two distinctive ways.[72] In chapter 7, the personal pronoun is for the most part employed to underscore his language of weakness, whereas elsewhere he uses specific terms for the same concept. 7:14–25 in particular demonstrates that the apostle is well able to vary his mode of communication in order to impress upon his addressees important theological themes. The theme of chapters 6–8 appears to be that of salvation as it relates to the believing community, and chapter 7, then, explores the relation of the "I" to this. It is within this literary context that Paul's weakness language shines through.

Chapter 15, on the other hand, employs the identical pronoun in a less emphatic way. In fact, though the "I" expressions of this chapter are not marked (with verse 14 the notable exception), emphasis is achieved differently, that is, through the use of epistolary and rhetorical features from the Greco-Roman milieu. All this seems to bring into sharp focus the paradigmatic character of 15:14–32—a passage that gains further prominence from its correspondence with elements of chapter 1.

---

71. Schreiner, *Romans*, 38.

72. Outside of chapters 7 and 15 the pronoun sometimes serves as an autobiographical pointer, whether by way of ethnic solidarity (Rom 11:1b) or overwhelming national concern (Rom 9:3: ηὐχόμην γὰρ ἀνάθεμα εἶναι αὐτὸς ἐγὼ ἀπὸ τοῦ Χριστοῦ ὑπὲρ τῶν ἀδελφῶν μου τῶν συγγενῶν μου κατὰ σάρκα). Other times it is used to draw attention to apostolic authority (Rom 11:13), and the like (Rom 11:19).

10

Romans 16 and "Archbishop Priscilla"

Female Pastors in the Early Church?

INTRODUCTION

Women in the Church
Have their special role
Equal in salvation
But not to have control

Preaching is forbidden
And so is pastoral rule
But apart from those restrictions
Everything is cool

This doesn't mean we are inferior,
Less intelligent, gifted or weak
It simply means what it says
We are not to rule or speak

We are called to function
Each, in a peculiar way
To Minister with our spiritual gift
For which we are the perfect fit

Therefore, we implore you sister
There is much scope to serve
For needs are always many
And hands are always few
Just waiting dear sister
For God to hear from you[1]

---

1. A summary of the traditional position in verse by my friend Dr. Billy Hall. Mine is inverse.

W E[2] MAY BEGIN WITH the founding of the church in Acts 2.[3] When the Spirit came at Pentecost in fulfillment of the Founder's promise (Acts 1:5; cf. 11:15–17),[4] one hundred and twenty believers were awaiting his arrival in an upper room—both sisters and brothers (Acts 1:12–14). These were not only the embryonic members of the soon-to-be-formed body of Christ; they were in a real sense the first leaders of that entity. At the very least this was true of the men. All were intimately related to the ascended Lord and were uniquely equipped to teach the 3000 people who became believers (Acts 2:42). It is difficult to imagine only the men teaching the new converts in the several house churches in and around Jerusalem.[5] In support of the above, Peter's citation of Joel 2 regarding God's Spirit being poured out on all flesh is saying, among other things, that leadership among the people of God will no longer be confined to male prophets, priests, kings but upon potential prophetesses (this started in the OT)[6] and priestesses as well (Acts 2:16–18; cf. Rev. 1:6). So we are not surprised to find within the first century a wife and husband team engaged in the exposition of Sacred Scripture: "He [Apollos] began to speak boldly in the synagogue. When Priscilla

2. Now a word about my presuppositions and exegetical parameters: for me the text of Scripture is fully authoritative, being as it is, the very Word of God preserved (Thompson, *Roots*, 15–16; Lee, "A Child of God," 69–81). A necessary corollary to this is that it bears binding relevance to my faith commitments, lifestyle, and ministry. Exegetically, the best approach to derive maximum benefit from God's Word is a synergistic and eclectic one that includes dependence on the Spirit who inspired it, and the application of sound hermeneutical principles (Howe, *Women in Church Leadership*; Hungenberger, "Women in Church Office," 341–60. As Leon, "Literature Review," has pointed out, the fundamental reason for differences of opinion concerning the question discussed in this chapter has to do with varying hermeneutical perspectives.

3. Based on our Lord's prediction in Matt 16:18–19, I take it that the "church" was not yet in existence. If the universal church is the body of Christ made of Jews and Gentiles, there was no such entity in the OT. Instead of defining a local church as "where two or three are gathered," we should perhaps see it as a group of professing believers that meet regularly to do God's will along the lines of Acts 2:42.

4. The baptism of the Spirit mentioned in these verses may be defined as the act of God whereby he places believers into the body of Christ. This is certainly the thought of 1 Cor 12:13 (Cf. Dunn, *Baptism*).

5. Liefeld, *Interest*, 31. "The inference, therefore, that the church had at this stage its own meeting-house is anything but secure. It is quite possible to take κατ' οἶκον ['from house to house'; v. 46] in a distributive sense—*in their various houses*" (Barrett, *Acts*, 170; his italics).

6. Jewish tradition recognizes seven prophetesses: Sarah, Miriam, Deborah, Hannah, Abigail, Huldah and Esther! (Scherman, *Tanach*, 2038).

and Aquila heard him, they invited him to their home and explained to him the way of God more adequately" (Acts 18:26; NIV). Romans,[7] the book following Acts, further informs us that this wife and husband team had a church in their house (Rom 16:3–5).[8] Bearing in mind Acts 18:26 that Priscilla and Aquila were not merely hosting the people of God on a weekend but they were actually providing leadership to the nascent church particularly in the area of the exposition of OT Scripture, it is difficult to escape the conclusion that Priscilla did indeed carry out a pastoral role (cf. Acts 2:42; 2 Tim 3:16–17). First Cor 16:19 makes a similar point: "The churches in the province of Asia send you greetings. Aquila and Priscilla greet you warmly in the Lord, *and so does the church that meets at their house*" (my italics). In this context the mention of children in 1 Timothy 3:4[9] makes better sense, since the house is the church on Sundays (cf. 1 Cor 16:2).

THE CHURCH OF EPHESUS AND THE LEADERSHIP QUESTION

Ephesians 4

The church of Ephesus is perhaps the most fortunate in the New Testament in that it is somehow associated with seven inspired epistles: Ephesians, 1 Timothy, 2 Timothy, 1 John, 2 John, 3 John, and the last in Revelation 2.[10] What is the relevance of all this? At least three of these letters make a contribution to our understanding of what church leadership was like in the first century. In Ephesians 4, for example, we are informed that when Christ ascended he gave gifts to "people" (v. 8; NRSV). The term translated "men" in King James as well as the NIV is a generic one and has reference to both genders. The linguistic phenomenon of using a masculine plural term to include both sexes is common to the two main languages of the Bible. For instance, most of the references

---

7. Grieb *The Story of Romans*, 144: "Nothing in Romans suggests that Paul had any difficulty with women exercising leading functions or any reason to doubt their reliability as teachers and preachers."

8. "Greet also the church that meets at their house" (v. 5). Note the order "Priscilla and Aquila" in Rom 16:3 and Acts 18:27 (NIV). The expected word order for a union of this nature is found in 1 Cor 16: 19 (Aquila and Priscilla; cf. Joseph and Mary).

9. "One that ruleth well his [or 'her'] own house, having . . . children in subjection with all gravity" (KJV). We will return to this passage later.

10. Hultgren *The Pastoral Epistles*, 150.

to "children of Israel" in the Old Testament are literally "sons of Israel." The same is true of passages like Rom 8:14, Gal 3:7, 26; 4: 6; 1 Thess 5:5 and Hebrews 12:8. Therefore, all the gifted individuals mentioned in Ephesians 4:11 are to be understood as male and female *leaders* who function according to the "grace . . . [and] the measure of the gift of Christ" (v.7).[11] It is clear from the context that these sisters and brothers alluded to in verse 11 are exercising leadership, or better, are expected to carry out leadership functions, because verses 12 and 13 in particular lead to such a conclusion: *"to prepare God's people for works of service, so that the body of Christ may be built up* until we all reach unity in the faith and in the knowledge of the Son of God and become mature, attaining to the whole measure of the fullness of Christ" (NIV; italics added). If, as we are positing, the gifts of Ephesians 4:11 are special leadership endowments, how do they differ from other lists, and how do believers with similar endowments function within or without the body? In order to formulate an answer, some important distinctions must be made. If, for example, the gift of evangelism enables a sister or brother to effectively witness to unbelievers, it is still the privilege of every believer to witness. But the sister or brother with this gift has the additional responsibility of training or equipping members of the body to do evangelism. The same line of reasoning applies to the gifts of teaching, church planting (apostles),[12] shepherding, and prophesying.[13] To adapt a truism from education: these gifted individuals not only give a fish to be eaten for a day, they equip others to do fishing so that they may eat for a lifetime. This is an essential part of Christian leadership within the local church, since "Equipping the saints is the purpose, task and responsibility of the Church leaders."[14] Thus we hear from one first century leader to another

11. For availability of these gifts today, see Palmer, *Pauline Charismata*, and Black, *When He Ascended*.

12. The term ἀποστόλους carries the same sense as 'missionaries' in a broader sense (Dodd, *Romans*, 238).

13. Interestingly, the people who occupied the prophetic office in the OT were all called of God, but this did not preclude the establishment of a school of the prophets ('sons of the prophets'; e.g., 2 Kings 4:1 [KJV])!

14. Roper, "Equipping the Saints," 55. Arnold, *Power and Magic*, 159; cited in O' Brien, *Ephesians*, 301, agrees. Says he: Christ "provides both charisma [gift] and office in an inseparable unity;" so too Lincoln, *Ephesians*, 249: "What does the exalted Christ give to the church? He gives people, these particular people who proclaim the word and lead." He also points out that Eph 4:11 could be translated "the apostles, the prophets, the evangelists, the pastors and teachers . . . ," thus emphasizing the leadership character of each of the gifts by way of the definite article.

first century leader (ministering in Ephesus): "And the things you have heard me say in the presence of many witnesses entrust to reliable men[15] who will also be qualified to teach others" (2 Tim 2:2; NIV). Bearing in mind the nature of our study, we will now focus our attention on only two of the gifts mentioned in Ephesians 4:11, that of the apostle and that of the pastor/teacher. If we are correct in coming to the conclusion that all the gifts in this verse are special leadership gifts and that none of them is limited to a particular gender within the body of Christ, then the further conclusion seems reasonable: Christ has also given to his church female apostles and pastors "to prepare God's people for works of service, so that the body of Christ may be built up" (v. 12). To have it any other way is to short circuit the divinely intended process of edification, and so impoverish the body. We have already seen from Acts 18 and Romans 16 that Priscilla was carrying out a pastoral[16] role in her house-church, along with her husband.

In the same chapter of Romans (v. 7) we have another prominent sister (Junia) being classed among the apostles: "Greet Andronicus and Junia, my relatives who were in prison with me; they are prominent among the apostles, and they were in Christ before I was" (NRSV). The verse presents two pertinent exegetical problems. The first has to do with the gender of Junia. The NIV ("Greet Andronicus and Junias") construes the original as masculine (contra the NRSV above), and at least one commentator believes "It is impossible to know for sure if the second of the names is the feminine. . . ."[17] Notwithstanding this level of skepticism, the evidence for taking the original term as feminine is getting stronger by the hour, because whereas Junia was a common first century name,[18] Junias is still unattested.[19]

---

15. The same word (ἀνθρώποις) as in Eph 4:7, and the sense is the same: "people" including sisters.

16. 'Pastors' in Eph 4:11 appears only once in the NT. The term is virtually synonymous with 'elders' (Acts 20:17, 28; 14:23; 1Tim 4: 14; 5:17, 19), 'overseers' or 'bishops' (Phil 1:1; 1 Tim 3:1) (O' Brien *Ephesians*, 299). The term is also linked with 'teachers' in Eph 4:11 by the same article "describing overlapping functions. . . . All pastors teach (since teaching is an essential part of pastoral ministry), but not all teachers are pastors. The latter exercise their leadership role by feeding God's flock with his word." (O' Brien, *Ephesians*, 300; cf. Wallace, *Greek Grammar*, 284; Hoehner, *Ephesians*, 544).

17. Kroll, *The Book of Romans*, 239.

18. It "occurs more than 250 times in Greek and Latin inscriptions" (Metzger, *Textual Commentary*, 475).

19. Osborne *Romans*, 406–407; Schreiner, *Paul*, 400; Lampe, "The Roman Christians of Romans 16," 222–224.

The next problem surrounds the phrase "prominent among the apostles" ("who are of note among the apostles" KJV). Does it mean that Andronicus and Junia were well known by those within the apostolic circle, or that they themselves were outstanding apostles? Our answer in part depends on our definition of apostles. In the New Testament, at least two classes of apostles are delineated: those that belonged to the original band (Acts 1:12–26; cf. 1 Cor 15:9) and those who possess the gift (1 Cor 12: 29a). Based on the criteria of Acts 1, Barnabas has to be placed in this latter grouping (Acts 14:14). And if we understand "prominent among the apostles"[20] in an inclusive way (like Johnson and others),[21] Junia[22] is also similarly positioned—and, of course, the other female apostles of Ephesians 4:11. The other key term of Ephesians 4:11 is that of the pastor/teacher, one of "the main offices" emphasized by the writer.[23] Black[24] rightly points out that the one definite article governing both "pastors and teachers" strongly suggests that one office is view. This is done, presumably, to underscore the main function of the church leader, which is that of teaching (cf. Acts 20:27–30). If we treat the two terms separately or together, there is just nothing within the context that says that any of these gifts is limited to a certain segment of the priesthood (cf. Rev 1:5b–6). If the inspired writer had wanted to, he would have most certainly made it clear that only brothers, and not sisters, can occupy the office of the pastor.

First Timothy 3

"This is the most discussed passage in the world today. Interpretations range from seeing Paul as a liberator and champion of women's rights

---

20. Declares Belleville ("Re-examination," 231): "Church tradition from the Old Latin and Vulgate versions and early Greek and Latin fathers onwards affirms and lauds a female apostle. Yet modern scholarship has not been comfortable with the attribution. . . . [A]n examination of primary usage in the computer databases of Hellenistic Greek literary works, papyri, inscriptions, and artifacts confirms . . . [Junia] and shows . . . ['chief among'] plus the plural dative bears without exception the inclusive sense 'notable among.'"

21. Johnson, *Reading Romans*, 233–234; For example, Browning, *Oxford Dictionary of the Bible*, 213; Bauckham, *Gospel Women*, 109–202.

22. Witherington, *Paul's Letter to the Romans*, 399, conjectures that Junia may have been "among those mentioned in 1 Cor. 15:7 as apostles to whom Christ appeared" and therefore an apostle in the primary sense.

23. Black, *Pastoral Ministry and Church Growth*, 128.

24. Ibid., 130.

to dismissing Paul as wrong and irrelevant in today's culture. George Bernard Shaw even called Paul, the "eternal enemy of women."[25]

Regarding the qualifications of 1 Tim 3 we need to bear in mind that it is natural for the language to be couched in such a way as to give the impression that only males can become church leaders, because of the nature of the common form of communication of the day. Therefore, similar to the point made above regarding terms such as "pastors" and "apostles," a word like "brothers" actually means "sisters and brothers," unless of course the context indicates otherwise (e.g., 1Cor 10:1; Rom 12:1).[26] The same is true of the key pronoun of 1 Timothy 3:1. The Authorized Version, both in its "ancient" (17th cent.) and modern (20th; i.e., the New King James) forms, renders this indefinite pronoun (*tis*) as "man." Of course, such a translation can be understood in a generic sense, but, especially in this passage, it can be misleading. Other English Versions, therefore, have "anyone" (NIV) or "whoever" (NRSV)[27] instead. A partial survey of the usage of this pronoun in the Pauline literature may be useful (the occurrences cited below are in italics and are taken from KJV): "For scarcely for a righteous man will *one* die: yet peradventure for a good man *some* [one] would even dare to die" (Rom 5:7). "But ye are not in the flesh, but in the Spirit, if so be that the Spirit of God dwell in you. Now if any *man* have not the Spirit of Christ, he is none of his" (Rom 8:9). "Lest *any* [one] should say that I had baptized in mine own name" (1 Cor 1:15). "For while *one* saith, I am of Paul; and another, I *am* of Apollos; are ye not carnal?" (1Cor 3:4). "Now if *any man* build upon this foundation gold, silver, precious stones, wood, hay, stubble" (1 Cor 3:12). "If *any man* defile the temple of God, him shall God destroy; for the temple of God is holy, which temple ye are. Let no man deceive himself. If *any man* among you seemeth to be wise in this world, let him become a fool, that he may be wise" (1 Cor 3:17, 18). "Moreover it is required in stewards, that a *man* be found faithful" (1 Cor 4:2). "But now I have written unto you not to keep company, if *any man* that is called brother/[sister][28] be a fornicator, or covetous, or an idolater, or a railer,

---

25. Mounce, *The Pastoral Epistles*, 103.

26. See, for example, Paul's OT citation in which he fleshes out "daughters" 2 Cor 6:18.

27. LN, 814–815.

28. The word "brother" in the original is preceded by *tis* and clearly refers to either gender within the context. Sisters are not exempt from the strong censure. There are

or a drunkard, or an extortioner; with such an one no not to eat" (1 Cor 5:11). "Dare *any* of you, having a matter against another, go to law before the unjust, and not before the saints?" (1 Cor 6:1). "And if any *man* think that he knoweth any thing, he knoweth nothing yet as he ought to know. But if any *man* love God, the same is known of him" (1 Cor 8:2, 3). "But we know that the law *is* good, if a *man* use it lawfully" (1 Tim 1:8).

Whenever this pronoun is employed it is invariably a reference to "someone" without any regard to gender, unless it governs a noun that is gender specific.[29] An example from 1 Timothy may be cited: "If any *woman* who is a believer has widows in her family, she should help them and not let the church be burdened with them, so that the church can help those widows who are really in need" (5:16).[30]

The point of this survey is to lay emphasis on the apostle's opening statement of 1 Timothy 3:1: "Here is a trustworthy saying: If *anyone* sets his [or "her"] heart on being an overseer, [s/]he desires a noble task." Writing today in our gender inclusive culture, Paul, I believe, would have written just such sentence. But what about chapter 2 of First Timothy which appears to strictly prohibit a woman from teaching or having authority over the man? As is pointed out,[31] this prohibition against women (better, "wives" in my view) addresses a situation of heresy at the time, underscoring the need to remind ourselves of the occasional nature of the letter.[32] In other words, if both wife and husband are co-pastors (Aquila and Priscilla or Junia and her husband), there is no need for one or the other to "usurp authority,"[33] which, apparently, some of the

---

approximately 383 occurrences of this pronoun in the Greek New Testament, many of which are employed as interrogatives. The same inclusive idea is true of *pas* in 1 John 3:2: "Everyone [*pas*] who has this hope in him purifies himself, just as he is pure." Clearly, the "everyone" in this context does not exclude the sisters, notwithstanding the masculine gender of *pas*. The feminine, interestingly, is *pasa- pasa* (making room for my 'stammering').

29. LN, 814–815. And even in some cases such as 1 Cor 5:11 (see above) it is generic.

30. Here, interestingly, the KJV has "man or woman!"

31. Fee *1 & 2 Timothy, Titus*, 72–79: "The little evidence we do have implies that heads of households from the earliest converts were normally appointed to such positions (Acts 14: 23; 1 Cor. 1:16 and 16: 15–16)" (p. 79).

32. For example, only the Ephesian-Laodecian churches are given instructions concerning love of spouses and children (Eph 5: 25; Col 3:19; Tit 2:4); only the Corinthians are rebuked for their abuse of tongues.

33. For a study of this term, see Baldwin, "A Difficult Word," 65–80.

Ephesian wives were doing. The principle is applicable to both genders, just as 1 Timothy 5:6 would apply as well to a widower.[34]

> 1 Timothy 2:8–15 is the paragraph in the New Testament which provides the injunctions . . . most cited as conclusive by those who oppose preaching, teaching, and leadership ministries for women in the church.[35] It is inappropriate, however, to isolate verses 11–12 from the immediate context of 1 Timothy 2:8–15. If any paragraph is perceived as culturally bound (as 2:8–10 often is) or especially difficult in terms of Pauline Theology (as 2:15 often is), it must realized that these same issues must be confronted in understanding 2:11–14.[36]

2 John

The final Ephesian[37] (house) church we will look at is the one addressed in the epistle of 2 John. "John addresses this short letter to 'the chosen lady' (and her children), whom some take to be a woman who allowed a church to meet in her house and others take to be a personification of a particular church."[38] The perspective that is deemed to be the correct one here is that the letter is addressed to "a woman who allowed a church to meet in her house."[39] In the wider context of epistolary literature, every letter written to an individual (such as Timothy or Titus or Philemon) presupposes a literal person. The main difficulty here is that the person is a woman. So it would appear that many Bible students prefer to 'allegorize' her. Such an allegorical or metaphorical approach also eliminates the question as to what role does this woman play in the church she houses. If Paul, when addressing a First Timothy or his

---

34. Again, when the Ephesian believers first heard that the ascended Lord gave gifts to humankind (Eph 4:11–12) in terms of apostles, pastors and teachers, they in all likelihood would have understood that these offices were not limited to men, simply because the plurals are gender inclusive like the "all" of Rom 3:23.

35. See especially, Piper and Grudem, *Recovering Biblical Manhood & Womanhood*.

36. Scholer, "1 Timothy 2: 9–15," 7; see also Tee, *Free to Speak?*, 1–42, 105–122.

37. Smalley, *1, 2, 3 John*, xxxiii; Westcott, *Epistles of St. John* xxxii. Says Irenaeus: "Now the church at Ephesus was founded by Paul, but John stayed there until the time of Trajan" (Cited in Eusebius, *EH*, 243).

38. Elwell and Yarbrough *Encountering the New Testament*, 369.

39. Based uon the hermeneutical 'canon': If the plain sense makes sense, seek no other sense, lest you end up with nonsense. Grassmick, *Principles and Practice*, 12, calls this principle the 'Plain meaning'.

'brother,' Second Timothy (or Titus or Philemon) is writing to a church leader (and by extension her/his church), why is it that the apostle John is writing only to a "congregation"[40] and not to a church leader, as he does to Gaius (3 John)? It is Spencer[41] who has provided the most compelling argument at this juncture for taking the "The elect lady" as a duly elected church official. She points out that the term translated "lady"[42] is the feminine of "lord" or "master," and, like its grammatically masculine counterpart, "lady" (especially in this context) represents an authority figure. "Consequently, the children are 'hers,' just as the children of 1 John are 'his' (John's) . . . Moreover, in the last verse John indicates that there was another such woman who also was an overseer over a church community."[43] Admittedly, 2 John provides the weakest argument for female leadership in the early church, but, if accepted, it becomes a part of the cumulative evidence presented earlier.

CONCLUSION

We have presented a case for seeing within the pages of the New Testament a phenomenon that is seldom examined—that veiled within the language of grammatically plural nouns, such as apostles and pastors, is the stark reality of female church leaders. The case is strongest, we believe, in Ephesians 4 and meets its stiffest challenge in First Timothy 2. But once the two letters are interpreted within their own occasional contexts, the tension between the two is greatly minimized.

Finally, all the pertinent passages are so difficult to grasp given the limitation of our tools *inter alia,* that it hardly behooves the writer to insist on how inescapably orthodox his position will become.[44]

---

40. Westermann *Handbook,* 159.

41. Spencer, *Beyond the Curse,* 109–111.

42. κυρία (*Kyria,* vv. 1, 5). "From ancient times opinion has been divided as to whether this letter was addressed to an anonymous noble lady, though she might have actually been called 'Electa' (from the Gk. *Ekleka,* 'chosen'), as Clement of Alexandra supposed, or even 'Kyria' (a direct transliteration from the Gk. *Kyria,* 'lady'), or whether it was addressed to a Christian community metaphorically identified as 'the chosen lady and her children.' Some commentators (. . . Ryrie) favor a person as the designee, while other commentators (. . . Bruce, Marshall, Stott) favor a local church" (Barker, "2 John," 361).

43. Spencer, *Beyond the Curse,* 110.

44. Taking time out from writing my book, 'The Three Most Humble Christians in the World Today,' to do this chapter was not really difficult at all, since I am having a

Excursus 4

The Importance of Sound Doctrine

by Dieumeme Noelliste

PROFESSOR OF THEOLOGICAL ETHICS
DENVER SEMINARY

Doctrine is certainly not a popular term these days. To many, the mere mention of the word evokes the idea of narrow-mindedness, adherence to strange and peculiar beliefs which encourage sectarianism, and a ghettoized approach to life. Seen in this light doctrine is thought to be divisive and thus harmful to Christian unity. Since unity is held as an ideal of superior value, it is deemed justifiable to dispense with doctrine whenever it clashes with the pursuit of unity.

There are others who go even further. One does not need to establish the "guilt" of doctrine in order to set it aside. The prevailing mindset, the concern of the present age has declared its irrelevance. While at one time it was alright to pursue right doctrine, today this is no longer the case. The concern is no longer with right belief, but with right doing. Orthopraxis has superseded orthodoxy. What matters first and foremost is the quality of one's action, not the soundness of one's belief.

It must be acknowledged that the unsympathetic attitude being displayed toward doctrine is not devoid of basis. The history of the church is replete with evidence which shows the devastating effects an unhealthy preoccupation with doctrine can have. It also shows the inadequacy and indeed the bankruptcy of an approach to Christian life which is content in affirming the sufficiency of the doctrinal. Such an approach truncates genuine Christian faith, robs it of its transforming ferment, and compromises its practical relevance. "Faith without works is dead" (James 2:17).

---

hard time finding the other two. For a comprehensive and balanced treatment of the Old and New Testament material, see Hurley, *Man & Woman*; and for the importance and limitation of orthodoxy, see, respectively, Noelliste (Excursus 4) and Roper, "Jesus Son of the Most High God" (Mark 5)," 199–201.

Now it should be evident to all reasonable people that a thing should not be discarded simply because of the wrong and misguided use that has been made of it. This is a simplistic approach which mistakenly tries to solve one wrong by another wrong! To acknowledge that a thing is insufficient is not to say that it is useless or unnecessary. If doctrine has been abused in the past and is being abused in the present, the responsible stance to adopt is not to disdain it but to approach it in a healthy and sound way.

Doctrine may have been mistakenly pursued at the exclusion of praxis in the past, but the way to remedy this is not to declare the ousting of doctrine and the enthronement of praxis, but to affirm the coregency of orthodoxy and orthopraxis. The pursuit of right belief and involvement in right doing are not antithetical enterprises. They are complimentary and mutually enriching endeavors. Christian faith can dispense with neither. Its authenticity depends on both.

Why then should right belief and sound doctrine be pursued in an age of theological pluralism and epistemological relativism? The New Testament, and particularly the writings of Paul, takes the view that sound teaching is essential to Christian faith and practice. Four summary statements, all deduced from, and corroborated by the Biblical data, set forth the case of essentiality of sound doctrine.

First: Sound doctrine is essential to the preservation of the truth of the Gospel

One cannot claim to take the New Testament seriously and fail to realize that there is a doctrinal standard which is connected with the gospel; there is a standard which needs to be preserved if the faith itself is not to become distorted and perverted. There seems to be a doctrinal core, a theological minimum and basic essentials that must be understood, adhered to, defended and preserved for posterity. These essentials are non-negotiable. But for the moment they are tampered with, and the integrity of the gospel itself is compromised.

In Galatians, Paul could not be more emphatic about the necessity to keep intact the basic content of the faith: "Even if we or an angel from heaven should preach a gospel other than the one we preach to you, let him be eternally condemned" (1:6). And a "gospel" which is emptied of the basic elements of the faith is no gospel at all. These elements constitute a sacred trust, a deposit that must be safely kept and then passed to others. "What you have heard from me, keep as a pattern of sound teaching. . . . Guard the good deposit that was entrusted to you" (2 Timothy 1:13, 14).

The need to reassure, that is, to "safe keep" the faith is as urgent today as when it was first expressed by Paul. The list of counterfeit Christianities which now crowd the religious marketplace is a long one! The counterfeiters of today are not less cunning than their counterparts of yesteryear. They have learnt well the art of couching their doctrinal perversions in attractive and nice sounding language.

Sometimes the counterfeiters' message so resembles the gospel that often even astute Christians are persuaded of their "veracity." In times like these, the preservation of the pure faith must be pursued vigorously. We must critically sift through today's rubble, rescue the precious gem, and safeguard it for posterity.

SECOND: SOUND DOCTRINE IS ESSENTIAL TO THE INTEGRITY AND MISSION OF THE CHURCH

The church is called to be many things these days. It is called a haven for the weary, a friend of the outcasts, a defender of the oppressed, a servant of the world, a place of fellowship and nurture, and it should be all of these things. But there is another aspect of the church's life that is often overlooked, and yet it is essential to its integrity. The church is called to be a place of truth—truth understood ethically, but also theologically.

In I Timothy 3:15, Paul defines the church as "the household of God, the pillar and foundation of the truth." That he has theological truth in view is clear in the very next verse, where he offers a succinct but all-encompassing exposition of the doctrine of Christ. In one stroke of the pen, the apostle affirms Christ's incarnation, resurrection and exaltation. He gives credence to Christ's humanity and divinity. This, for him, is the great mystery of godliness—"the truth" of which the church is the guardian.

If the church is anything at all, it must be a place where the truth about Christ and the redemption he accomplished is found and expounded. To the extent that the church distances itself from this cardinal truth, it compromises the integrity of its being and mission. Ronald Ward expresses it well in his commentary on this passage: "The church is not a twittering little bird to sing the Redeemer's praise. It is not a gentle breeze to waft the message over the countryside; it is not a kindly cloud to rain refreshing mercy on the earth beneath. . . . It is the *pillar and bulwark of the truth*. . . . [It] is the means to the continued presentation of the truth to the world. . . . The world must be told the gospel and the church is the means chosen by God for this purpose."[45]

Third: Sound doctrine is an essential qualification of the Minister of Christ

In our time this is minimized. If people are asked to identify the qualifications considered essential for the work of ministry, few would place adherence to sound doctrine high on the list—if they mention it at all. Things like intellectual acumen, professional competence, moral uprightness would outlast commitment to sound doctrine. Many see a virtue in doctrinal "wishywashiness." It is seen as evidence of broadmindedness. But the New Testament does not see it that way.

Those who aspire to ministerial leadership must adhere to the deep truths of the faith with a clear conscience, "and must be able to teach them to others" (1 Timothy 3:2, 9). The minister is required to watch his lifestyle as well as his doctrine closely (4:16). Adherence to sound teaching marks him out as a good minister" (1 Timothy 4:6), but lack of interest in sound and wholesome teaching and opposition to it is a mark of professional incompetence (1 Timothy 1:7), and an indication of moral and spiritual defects (1 Timothy 6;3).

One may have a good heart, one may be gifted with extraordinary abilities and skills; but with all of these, one is not quite ready to take care of the flock of God until one has a solid grasp of the fundamentals of the faith. A good minister of Christ is one who is brought up "in the truths of the faith" (1 Timothy 4:6).

Fourth: Sound doctrine is essential for the protection of the people of God

One of the things that those who downplay the importance of sound doctrine fail to realize is that at issue here is not simply a question of theological correctness, but the very well-being of people. Sound doctrine is not merely academic. It is a down-to-earth matter, with far-reaching implications for life here and now. Paul's counsel to Timothy is that by watching both life and doctrine, "you will save both yourself and your hearers" (1 Timothy 4:16).

45. *Commentary*, 62–63.

Sound doctrine is a much needed protection for the people of God. It protects them aginst distraction. It makes us less vulnerable to new teachings (Eph. 4:14–16) and participate in worthless and irrelevant discussions. Knowing where we stand makes us secure and stable. It makes us more tolerant and less contentious, for it gives us the ability to distinguish between what really matters and what does not—between the essential and the incidental. In a sense, sound doctrine promotes unity!

Further, sound doctrine protects against *deception*. The reality of deception is readily acknowledged by the New Testament writers. But they know no better antidote against it than the teaching of the truth. Knowing that believers at Ephesus would be targets of deception, Paul drew the attention of their leaders to the fact that he has acquainted them with the truth of God's will and that they have to draw on this resource to protect the church of God against the impending danger (Acts 20:25–28)

Deception is no benign matter. It is deadly. Those who entrust themselves to deceiving gurus and false messiahs do not only shipwreck their faith but they endanger their very lives spiritually and physically. Throughout history, millions have met a tragic end in this way. So, when the people of God are protected against deception, they are protected against *destruction*.

If there is any truth at all to what has been said, it follows that we cannot, we dare not, dispense with sound doctrine. At stake is the future of the faith. At stake is the integrity of the church. At stake is the fitness of the minister as a servant of Christ. At stake is the very life of the people of God entrusted to our care. Sound doctrine should not be discarded. It is critically essential.

Appendix A

Contextualizing Theology in the Caribbean

David Ho Sang, DPhil (Oxon)

INTRODUCTION

REGARDLESS OF HIS THEOLOGICAL persuasion, denomination affiliation, geographical location, or area of expertise, the Bible College administrator or instructor in the Caribbean could hardly have failed to have encountered the term "contextualization." Having come in vogue merely seven years ago, this topic is certainly foremost in recent missiological as well as theological discussions. A study of this issue is not merely an instructive exercise because of its contemporaneity, but a vital necessity since it addresses itself not only to methodology but to the very heart of the Gospel itself. (Without wishing to be presumptuous or facetious, the persons most equipped to deal with this issue are committed, capable, trained, Spirit-filled national church leaders, pastors, and theologians, some of whom are present at this conference).[1]

The purpose of this paper is fourfold. Firstly, it is intended to orient those who are unfamiliar with the concept and the main issues involved in this discussion. Thus, such factors as the importance, difficulties, emphases, critical issues, risks, criteria, guidelines, categories, and Biblical examples of contextualization will be highlighted. Secondly, this paper attempts to begin to lay a basis for further work in this area by Caribbean Evangelicals. The present dearth of literature on this subject produced by Caribbean Evangelicals is unfortunate but understandable, since this issue is not only a relatively new concept but there are relatively few

---

1. See excerpt of a personal letter form Aharon Sapsezian to F. Ross Kinsler in: F. Ross Kinsler, "Mission and Context: The Current Debate about Contextualization," *Evangelical Missions Quarterly* 14 (January 1978): 24.

Evangelicals with the commitments, capability, training and/or time to carefully address themselves to this issue. The vital question may not be "Is it necessary?" but more pragmatically "Is it contextualization a top priority issue in the Caribbean Church?" And if so "Who is qualified to undertake this responsibility?"

Thirdly, this paper attempts to suggest beginning strategy for dealing with this issue in the Caribbean. Finally, to concretize the discussion several theological and practical issues which relate to the concept of contextualization will be suggested for further exploration. Thus, because of its orientational and foundational nature the emphasis of this paper will be on breadth rather than depth, a survey of the lay of the land rather than intense prospecting at a particular site.

The limitations and adverse conditions under which this paper labours are many, but hopefully not sever enough to make it completely worthless. As already mentioned, the dearth (or absence) of literature written on this subject by Evangelicals, together with inadequate library holdings (which characterize the majority of Bible College libraries in the Caribbean) make careful, thorough research somewhat frustrating. The significant works, if available, are either written from a liberal perspective or from a North American missionary standpoint. In the latter case, even though articles have been written by Third World theologians, the orientation is primarily North American since the majority of these nationals have received their theological education there.

Practically, because of pastoral responsibilities in a local church as well as teaching obligations in a Bible College the writer has not found sufficient time to do full justice to this profound subject. In addition the author's youth, relative inexperience, and lack of exposure also pose a credibility question. Finally, because of the author's lack of first hand knowledge of the rest of the Caribbean the paper may more appropriately be entitled: "Contextualizing Theology in Jamaica," although there will be several points of contact because of our similar social, cultural, economic, political, and religious heritage.

Before embarking on this study it must be made clear hat this paper is not intended for the average Caribbean lay person but for the theologian, Bible College administrator and/or instructor, church leader, pastor, and/or the thinking layperson.

HISTORY OF THE WORD

The historical origin of the word "contextualization" as it is currently used in theological and missiological circles, may be traced to the publication in October 1972 of Ministry in Context: The Third Mandate Programme of the Theological Education Fund 1970–1977[2] which centred around this concept. In some ways the focus on "contextualization" as a way towards reform in theological education is understandable, for even in the call for "advance" in the First Mandate (1958–1964) a supplementary statement that the Theological Education Fund should seek "to develop and strengthen indigenous theological education" revealed a growing skepticism as to whether the use of Western standards as the frame of reference would necessarily strengthen indigenous theological education.[3] The call for "Rethink" in the Second Mandate (1965–1969) revealed a more explicit concern reflected in their definition of excellence to be sought in theological education, the aim being defined in terms of using ". . . resources so as to help teachers and students to a deeper understanding of the Gospel in the context of the particular cultural and religious setting of the church . . ."[4] Thus, non-evangelicals have been advocates of contextualization earlier and more prominently than Evangelicals.

On a whole, Evangelicals have been either reluctant, tardy, or superficial in addressing themselves to the contextualization discussion. The International Congress on World Evangelization held at Lausanne in July 1974 was one of the first places where this subject received some attention.[5] However, these treatments tended to reflect Evangelical shallowness as Harvie Conn astutely observes. His critique on Kato's presentation is that "Abstracting the message of the Gospel from its form Kato's argument concentrates largely on the expressions of the culture in worship—liturgy, dress, ecclesiastical services. It seems to take little

---

2. Theological Education Fund, Ministry in Context: The Third Mandate Programme of the Theological Education Fund 1970–1977 (Bromley, Kent: Theological Education Fund, 1972).

3. Shoki Coe, "In Search of Renewal in Theological Education," *Theological Education* 9 (Summer 1973), 235.

4. Theological Education Fund, Ministry in Context, 12–13.

5. See Byang H. Kato, "The Gospel, Cultural Context and Religious Syncretism," and M. Bradshaw and P. Savage, "The Gospel, Contextualization and Syncretism Report," in *Let the Earth Hear His Voice*, ed. J. D. Douglas (Minneapolis: World Wide Publications, 1975), 1216–28.

cognizance of the shift from indigenization to contextualization, and especially to the heart of the contextualization debate—the Gospel in interaction with the culture."[6]

The elative immaturity exhibited by Evangelicals in this area may be due to such factors as the isolation of missions from theology and theological reflection, North American cultural pragmatism, and the fear of liberal constructions. However, committed Evangelicals from the Third World have recognized not only the weakness in this area but also the necessity for engaging in the task of contextualization. For example, Emilio Antonio Nunez of Guatemala admits that "a serious effort in contextualization is only beginning among us. . . . We are far behind in the training of leaders capable of carrying out contextualization: leaders rooted deeply in the Word of God and fully identified with their own culture, leaders who know well the *text* and the *context* . . ."[7] As far as this writer knows there has not yet been a definitive Evangelical response from the Caribbean addressing itself to this issue.

DEFINITION

What really does the word "contextualization" mean and imply? Depending on the circles in which one moves, this term may mean different things to different people. For example, the Theological Education Fund Report describes contextualization as including all that is implied in indigenization but also takes into account the processes of secularity, technology, and struggle for human justice, which characterize the historical movement of nations in the Third World."[8] While agreeing that this term expresses a deeper concept than indigenization, Kato understands the term to mean "making concepts or ideals relevant in a given situation. In reference to Christian practices, it is an effort to express the never changing Word of God in ever changing modes for relevance."[9] In a study group on contextualization at Lausanne in 1974 (the discussion

---

6. Harvie M. Conn, "Contextualization: Where Do We Begin?" in Evangelicals and Liberation, ed. Carl E. Amerding (Nutley, New Jersey: Presbyterian & Reformed Publishing Co., 1977), 97.

7. Emilio Antonio Nunez, "Contextualization—Latin American Theology," *Latin American Pulse* 40 (February 1976), 6.

8. Theological Education Fund, *Ministry in Context*, 20.

9. Kato, "The Gospel," 1217.

framed in the missiological context of the evangelization of the world), the following four definitions emerged:

1. The identification of the Gospel form, its cultural clothing
2. The communication of the Gospel in pertinent, meaningful cultural forms both external (e.g. Liturgical garments) and thought forms (eg., Time-space dimensions)
3. The communication that spoke to the issues and needs of the person and his society.
4. The meaningful and honest response made by that person in cultural and societal context under the guidance of the Holy Spirit.[10]

In the opinion of the author, apart from being vague and incomprehensible to the average reader, the first definition (in theory as well as practice) represents a capitulation to humanistic patterns of ethnology-sociology heavily overlaid on a smattering of Scripture. On the other hand, contextualization cannot merely be reduced to "a simple category of the effective communication of the content of the Gospel to the cultural context."[11] Knapp's definition of the word is perhaps the most satisfactory one encountered thus far. He defines contextualization as follows: "Contextualization in the dynamic process through which the church continually challenges and/or incorporates—transforms elements of the cultural and social milieu of which it is an integral part in its daily struggle to be obedient to the Lord Jesus Christ in its life and mission in the world."[12]

RELATIONSHIP TO INDIGENIZATION

In defending the use of the word "contextualization" Shoki Coe, general director of the Theological Education Fund and probably the first to give it is original meaning claims that "We try to convey all that is implied in the familiar term *indigenization*, yet seek to press beyond for a more dynamic concept which is open to change and which is also future—oriented."[13] In essence, the liberal spokesmen for contextualization are

10. Bradshaw and Savage, "The Gospel", 1226.
11. Conn, "Where do We Begin?" 104.
12. Stephen Knapp, "Contextualizing and its Implications for U. S. Evangelical Churches and Missions," (Abington, Pa.: Partnership in Mission, 1976) 15.
13. Shoki Coe, "Contextualizing Theology," in *Mission Trends No. 3: Third World*

saying that there is need to explore not only the anthropological and religious dimensions of culture (which indigenization emphasizes) but also the social and economic dimensions of each situation in order to discover the full, significance of the Gospel in that situation. Norman Ericson's explanation of the distinction between indigenization and contextualization is somewhat simplistic but helpful. He claims that: "The difference seems to be a matter of chronology and degree. Indigenization was an early effort in (newly?) evangelized nations to utilize the nationals and to incorporate certain native cultural forms which were virtually consistent with Western Christianity. But contextualization is a later breakthrough aiming to adopt the new culture *in toto*."[14]

On the other hand, other Evangelicals such as James Oliver Buswell III see the distinction between the two terms as merely semantical.[15] It seems most appropriate at this point to stress the fact that the word "contextualization" has different connotations to different people.

ASPECTS OF CONTEXTUALIZATION

Practically and simplistically, as a general rule of thumb, when the non-evangelical theologian uses the term "contextualization" he is primarily dealing with the content of the Gospel, whereas when the Evangelical theologian uses this term he is probably applying it to the methodology of presenting the Gospel. Thus, the non-evangelical's use of the word, "indigenization is virtually synonymous to the Evangelical's use of the word "contextualization". For example, Kato speaks of contextualization in terms of such things as liturgy, dress, language, church service, and any other form of expression of the Gospel truth[16] while the non-evangelical would identify this as indigenization. It is quite understandable that the Evangelical should place the emphasis on methodology, for it is inherently assumed that the content of the Gospel message remains unchanged. This issue will be dealt with later in the paper when the essence of the Gospel is considered.

Theologies, eds. Gerald H. Anderson and Thomas F. Stransky (New York: Paulist Press, 1976; Grand Rapids: Eerdmans, 1976), 21.

14. Norman R. Ericson, "Reply" in *Theology and Mission*, ed. David J. Hesselgrave (Grand Rapids: Baker Book House, 1978), 121.

15. James O. Buswell III, "Contextualization: Theory, Tradition and Method," in *Theology and Mission*, ed. David J. Hesselgrave (Grand Rapids: Baker Book House, 1978), 93–94.

16. Kato, "The Gospel," 1217–18.

THE FOCI OF CONTEXTUALIZATION

In the contextualization discussion at least three emphases are evident.

1. Focus on the indigenous theologian. This emphasis is illustrated by Von Allmen who claims that "no true" indigenization of contextualization' can take place (merely) because foreigners, the 'missionaries,' suggest it; on the contrary, true indigenization takes place only because the 'indigenous' church has itself become truly missionary, with or without the blessing of the missionaries.'"[17]This tends to be the focus of Caribbean theologians in the established churches.

2. Focus on the missionary communicator. This emphasis highlights the problems of cross-cultural communication which face the missionary. This approach is illustrated by Nicholls who explains contextualization as "the translation of the unchanging content of the Gospel of the Kingdom into verbal form meaningful to peoples in their separate cultures and within their particular existential situations."[18]

3. Focus on the target population. This perspective is the obverse side of the previous focus, emphasizing not the missionary communicator but the target population which is receiving the Gospel dressed in unfamiliar cultural context. A careful examination will indicate that since communication involves both the communication and the recipients, the latter two foci are inseparable. These two foci would probably be in the minds of Caribbean Evangelical theologians who are well acquainted with the term "contextualization">

THE NECESSITY OF CONTEXTUALIZATION

Regardless of one's understanding of this term, the overwhelming majority of theologians and missiologists see contextualization as a vital necessity.[19] As noted by Ericson, "Contextualization has been at all

---

17. Daniel von Allmen, "The Birth of Theology," *International Review of Mission* 64 (January 1975): 39.

18. Bruce Nicholls, "Theological Education and Evangelization Report," in *Let the Earth Hear His Voice*, ed. J. D. Douglas (Minneapolis: World Wide Publications, 1975), 647.

19. E. G. See Theological Education Funds, *Ministry in Context*, p. 19 and Kato, "The Gospel," 1217.

points a concomitant of the divine communication to man . . . singularly expressed in the incarnation."[20]

OBJECTIONS TO CONTEXTUALIZATION

Although the majority of informed Evangelicals see contextualization (as they understand it) as an imperative, some are bound to raise either theological or practical objections. In the first category of objections some may claim that since the Gospel is timeless, universal, and unchanging, there is absolutely no need for this exercise. However, it may be argued that although the essence of the Gospel remains the same the modes of expression are not inspired or sacrosanct. In a similar vein, the objection that "what was good for Paul and Silas is good enough for me" betrays not only an elevation of tradition to the level of Scripture (a charge which Protestants often level against Roman Catholics), but also an irrational, insecure desire to preserve the comfortable status quo at all costs even if this cannot be defended on Scriptural grounds. Some so-called practical objections would be that this exercise is either a complete waste of valuable time and resources or that it does not edify the church. However, if we are guilty of presenting an emasculated, distorted, or tradition-bound Gospel which is heavily laden with alien superficial trappings and/or presented in an archaic, anachronistic manner it is incumbent on us to be engaged in the processes of decontextualization and recontextualization.

EXPLANATIONS FOR FAILURE TO CONTEXTUALIZE

Reasons for failure to contextualize are legion. Ericson suggests the following six reasons why Evangelicals have often failed to contextualize:

1. The characteristic emphasis on the unity of Scripture
2. The single-minded way in which Evangelicals view and use the canonical literature
3. Contextual studies of the New Testament have been minimal
4. The effort to abstract and absolutize the teachings of the Bible

---

20. Norman R. Ericson, "Implications from the New Testament for Contextualization," in *Theology and Mission*, ed. David J. Hesselgrave (Grand Rapids: Baker Book House, 197), 85.

5. Simplistic implementation of Evangelism
6. Lack of emphasis upon Hermeneutic[21]

Principalizing E. W. Fashold-Luke's[22] reasons for the failure of West African Churches to produce relevant and meaningful theologies for their peoples, the additional reasons may be appended:

7. Third World Churches are churches without theologies and theological concern
8. Little or no attempt has been made to train theologians
9. The few trained theologians have received their training in Western cultural situations
10. Western missionaries came from theological backgrounds where aspects of discontinuity between Christianity and every culture were stressed to the exclusion of the aspects of continuity with local cultures.

Finally, Buswell suggests that one reason for the failure to relinquish the church to indigenous cultural forms and leadership is

11. Strong feelings of insecurity which assail the missionary in an unfamiliar cultural context which leads him to structure things in familiar cultural forms.[23]

DIFFICULTIES IN CONTEXTUALIZATION

It would be foolhardy o enthusiastically plunge into the process of contextualization without first noting the obstacles which stand in the way. The following six are suggested by the author: [NL 1-6]

1. The missionary himself is/was too involved in the process
2. The underestimation of the ability of the nationals by the missionaries or the nationals themselves
3. The people for whom it is intended are no longer there

---

21. Norman R. Ericson, "Implications from the New Testament for Contextualization," in *Theology and Mission*, ed. David J. Hesselgrave (Grand Rapids: Baker Book House, 197), 71–73.

22. E. W. Fashole-Luke, "The Quest for African Christian Theologies," in *Mission Trends* No. 3, eds. Gerald H. Anderson and Thomas f. Stransky (New York: Paulist Press, 1976; Grand Rapids: Eerdmans, 1976), 137–38.

23. Buswell, "Contextualization," 101–2.

4. The non-homogenous and diverse nature of the native population

5. The native theologians have received a Western oriented education which leave them open to the danger of being either unable to principalize of unprepared to cope

6. The delicate and difficult task of identifying the negotiables from the non-negotiables, the valid from the invalid

THE ESSENCE OF THE GOSPEL

In the process of contextualization the question arises as to whether there is an unchanging, unalterable frame of reference. For the Evangelical, there is an essential core which is independent of any culture. This core of truth which cannot be tampered with, is that the transcendent, immanent God has spoken definitely through Jesus Christ who has effected eternal salvation through His life, death and resurrection (cf. 1 Corinthians 15: 3–11). This body of truth called the Gospel must be declared with a view to appropriation, if one is to be faithful in communicating the Gospel. How then is the content of the Gospel related to theology and contextualization?

THEOLOGY AND CONTEXTUALIZATION

On careful reflection, it is apparent that the scope of contextualization is bounded by the parameters of one's theology. The writer has identified at least four different approaches to theology.

1. The 'Accommodational Approach' considers prevailing customs and religious practices in the country and attempts to adopt or adapt those which are appropriate and consistent with the Gospel. This is by no means an easy task for the process of evaluation in indeed a delicate one requiring people who are committed to their God and His Word, willing to investigate carefully the religious, sociological, anthropological and ethnological factors. This approach could lead to valid of invalid accommodations. Foe example, Don Richardson's principle of redemptive analogy described in *Peace Child*[24] appears to be a valid one, but an attempt to teach the doc-

---

24. Don Richardson, *Peace Child* (Glendale, California: Gospel Light Publications, 1974), passim.

trine of the Trinity using the Korean mythology of creation[25] appears invalid.

2. The 'Situational Approach' exemplified by liberation theologians as well as a good number of Caribbean theologians in the established churches attempts to formulate theology after reflecting on one's experience in life. Although the attempt to make one's faith relevant is commendable, this approach is fraught with at least two major dangers—(1) the danger of starting from the sinful human situation rather than the Word of God and (2) the danger of political analyses taking precedence over Biblical theology.

3. The 'Perpendicular Approach' exemplified by many Evangelicals and perhaps by the majority of Evangelicals in the Caribbean emphasizes the priority of a personal relationship with Jesus Christ and the vital necessity of proclaiming the Gospel message. While this emphasis is commendable, it often leads to rejection, disparagement, disregard, or insensitivity of certain cultures (whether they be ones own or not). Furthermore, this betrays a lack of awareness of the cultural aspects of Christianity. In this approach, contextualization is either unknown, ignored, minimized, or even resisted.

4. The fourth approach which the writer would like to term the Biblical Approach attempts to incorporate all the positive aspects of the other three approaches.

From somewhat of a difference perspective Robert Moore identifies and explains three different types of theologies which have evolved over the course o history—(1) The Theology of Absorption (2) The Theology of Imposition and (3) The Theology of Imitation and suggests that the task of Caribbean theology is in one sense a Theology of Exploration.[26] As noted by Charles H. Kraft, "theologizing is meant to be relevant," and it is most unfortunate when an unsuitable theological system is adopted by or imposed upon those of another culture or subculture. This misfortune often takes place when (1) a given approach to theology is regarded

---

25. See Sung Bum Yun, "Tang-Gun Mythology in Vestigium Trinitatis," *Christian Thought* (October 1963): 16.

26. Robert Moore, "The Historical Basis of Theological Reflection," in *Troubling of the Waters*, ed. Idris Hamid (San Fernando, Trinidad: Rahaman Printery, 1973), 39–42.

as highly prestigious and/or (2) proponents of that theological system claim that their system is not only correct but also supracultural and/of (3) the proponents have the power to impose their system on others.[27]

As logical and ideal as it may sound, the task of identifying the supracultural content of Christianity from its forms and expressions in a culture (whether it be ours or not) is by no means an easy one. Furthermore, identification is only the first step, the next step being the attempt to disengage the supra cultural from the cultural. In explaining the present state of affairs, Buswell, a North American admits that Political power and technological progress were fused with Christian piety into an inevitably ethnocentric, if benevolent, ethos. All 'uncivilized' societies were appraised by the power—progress—piety ethos as inferior *on all counts*.[28]

Unfortunately, this missionary mentality, which showed flagrant disregard for the receiving culture which was not theirs, is still with us today, yea even among nationals.

As to North America's role in the contextualization discussion it is ironical that although it has been the most prolific in producing literature on contextualization it is perhaps culturally the least suited for this task because of its specialization, isolationism, superiority complex, and ignorance or other peoples.

THE NATURE OF THE QUEST

Although there is only one Gospel the nature of the quest for contextualizing theology is to translate the one faith of Jesus Christ to suit the tongue, style, genius, character and culture of the particular society.

Several critical issues emerge in this quest for contextualization. The first, which concerns its scope recognizes that contextualization is not merely concerned with the communication of the Gospel (i.e. Methodology), but with the nature of the Gospel itself. This fact is recognized not only by non-evangelicals but by a growing number of Evangelicals. For example, F. Ross Kinsler notes the record number of missionaries being sent by the United States to Third World countries

---

27. Charles M. Kraft, "The Contextualization of Theology," *Evangelical Missions Quarterly* 14 (January 1978): 35.

28. Buswell, "Contextualization", 104.

and finds this difficult to reconcile with their over consumption of material wealth.[29]

A second major issue concerns the procedure in contextualization. As already mentioned the 'Situational Approach' looks at the Biblical text from the standpoint of its *Sitz Im Leben*. However, the dangers inherent in this approach are that human experiences may become normative rather than the Word of God and the message may become relativistic, existential, and situational. A much safer approach is to look at one's situation from the standpoint of the text realizing that any theology which is truly Biblical must take shape within the cultures and problems of the people of God in every place. Because the term 'Biblical Theology' may be nebulous, confusing, ambiguous, and/or abused, the writer suggests the term 'Contextualizing Theology' as an alternative in this situation.

A third crucial issue focuses upon the question of syncretism. The following are some of the definitions used or given at the International Congress on World Evangelization at Lausanne in 1974:

1. A fruit cocktail of religions (John Scott)[30]

2. Any form of religion in which elements from more than one original religious tradition are combined (Eric Sharpe)[31]

3. The sort of accommodation to the cultural values of a people that results in a mixture of Biblical truth and ethnic religion (Bruce Nicholls)[32]

4. Occurs when critical and basic elements of the Gospel are lost in the process of contextualization are replaced by religious elements from the receiving culture (M. Bradshaw and P. Savage)[33]

From these definitions, it is quite clear that this term carries pejorative implications with Evangelicals. Kato's reasons for growing syncretistic tendencies in Africa are instructive in showing its sources and causes. They are as follows: (1) the prevailing wind of religious relativism in the older churches (2) the crying need for universal solidarity in the world (3) political awareness which carries with it a search for ideologi-

29. Ross Kinsler, "Mission and Context," 26.
30. Kato, "The Gospel," 1218.
31. Ibid.
32. Nicholls, "Theological Education," 647.
33. Bradshaw and Savage, "The Gospel," 1227.

cal identity (4) emotional concerns for ancestors who died before the advent of Christianity (5) cultural revolution which calls for a return to socio-religio-cultural way of life (6) inadequate Biblical teaching (7) the African's love to get along well with everybody (8) liberal Christianity (9) the study of comparative religions without the effort to assert the uniqueness of Christianity and (10) the genuine desire to make Christianity truly African has not been matched with the power of discernment not to tamper with the Word of God.[34]

Thus there is always the risk of syncretism when experimentation is done (on words, concepts, and customs) to express Christian meaning. However, Kraft asserts that the greatest risk of syncretism comes "from those who try like the Pharisees and Judaizers to preserve the foreign expressions of God's message."[35]

Finally, a fourth important issue (which may be classified as a risk) involves the overly-zealous Evangelical enamoured by the concept of contextualizing theology. This may lead to a superficial analysis of Biblical data, religious systems, sociology, anthropology and ethnology which may in turn lead to "a capitulation to humanistic patterns overlaid on the Scriptures."[36]

CRITERIA FOR CONTEXTUALIZATION

The following five criteria, put in question form are suggested by the writer in evaluating contextualization, the first three criteria dealing with the theological aspect and the last two dealing with the methodological aspect.

1. Has the Biblical message penetrated and adopted the cultural forms and stood in judgment upon them?
2. Have the insights from Scripture as well as religion, sociology, anthropology, and ethnology been carefully applied?
3. Has the core of the Gospel been retained?
4. Has the meaning been accurately conveyed?
5. Has the communication (whether verbal or behavioural) been effective?

34. Kato, "The Gospel," 1218–18.
35. Kraft, "Contextualization," 36.
36. Conn, "Where Do We Begin?" 100–1.

CONTROLS FOR CONTEXTUALIZATION

What guarantee does one have that an attempt at contextualization will be valid? While this "validity guarantee" is not totally assured, the following three controls have been suggested by Ericson:

1. The commandments of the Lord (1 Corinthians 7:10; cf. 7:25)
2. The counsel of the Holy Spirit given to the faithful, mature Christian (1 Cor 7:25; cf. 7:40)
3. The corrective force of the divine Word.[37]

CATEGORIES OF CONTEXTUALIZATION

At this point it may be obvious to some that the concept of contextualization may be broken down into different kinds, and as Buswell notes, many of them have already had a respectable history, both in missiology and in field applications.[38] In addition to Buswell's three categories: Contextualization of (1) The Witness (2) The Church and its Leadership and (3) the Word[39], the writer would suggest a fourth category: The Contextualization of Theology.

(1) Contextualization of Theology. While it is vigorously held that there is an essential core in the Gospel and that some present formulations such as the doctrines of the Person and Work of Christ, ma, and sin illustrate the supracultural nature of the Christian faith, other present formulations in the Caribbean (which may be explicit or implicit) such as inspiration, divine sovereignty, salvation history, salvation, eschatology, and political systems need to be carefully examined. Admittedly we are at a considerable disadvantage, for the nationals most qualified for this task—pastors and theologians—have been indoctrinated into Western thought patterns. Added to this, is the extreme theological conservatism characteristic of Evangelicals throughout the worlds as well as the great diversity within Evangelicalism in the Caribbean which is a reflection of the diversity within Western Evangelicalism.

On the questions of inspiration, do we need to indiscriminately adopt the position of the extreme rightist John R. Rice, the right winger Harold Lindsell, the middle-of-the-roader Kenneth Kantzer, or the left

37. Ericson, "Implications," 84–85.
38. Buswell, "Contextualization", 89.
39. Ibid., 90–99.

winger Paul Jewett? Now one is not showing disrespect, discounting the usefulness of this type of research or questioning the commitment, scholarship, and contribution of these men, but do we have to be "mimic-men" merely parroting the beliefs of our Western big brother? This must certainly not be taken as a rejection of tradition or our rich Evangelical heritage but a call to know why we believe what we believe.

With respect to divine sovereignty, it must not be tacitly assumed that political power and economic wealth is automatically or necessarily an indication of divine approbation, or that these peoples are the exclusive agents through whom salvation history is being accomplished. On the salvation issue, the exclusively pietistic and vertical understanding of salvation which creates a sharp dichotomy between the vertical and horizontal dimensions must be identified as unbiblical. It is most encouraging to see that North American Evangelicals are again awakening to the social implications of the Gospel, but what better place is there to experience this reality than in a Third World setting such as the Caribbean?

Vitally related to salvation in its totality is the predominantly other-worldly and futuristic emphasis. While it is true that the blessed hope is something to be anticipated with great excitement, it does not absolve Christians of their present domestic, ecclesiastical and civil responsibilities during their sojourn here on earth.

Finally, in the area of politics (which interests most, if not all West Indians) it must not be assumed that God sanctions either the capitalistic or socialistic form of government.

Contextualization of the Word.

This category of contextualization deals with translation and ethnotheology, an area in which the Wycliffe Bible translators have been outstanding. The question arises as to the need for a translation of the Bible into the local dialect of the country. One decided advantage is that Creole patois is used by the majority of nationals "to convey emotive experience, to hand down local customs, for proverbs and wise sayings on intimate occasions and even in religious ceremonies."[40] Thus the verbal patois may be most effective in communicating Biblical truth. However, the disadvantages of the written patois outweigh the advantages. Not only is this a massive undertaking for able, available national linguists but the fact that the local dialect is not standardized and the primary people for whom it is intended either cannot read it of have passed away, militates against such an undertaking. Besides not only is English (or French) well understood by the majority of the populace, but the local dialect it very close to it.

Contextualization of the Witness.

In Buswell's scheme this deals with making the Gospel message intelligible in the idiom of the language and culture of the receivers. The writer sees this kind of contextualization as inextricably bound up with the next category, one emphasizing the presentation of the Gospel in terms of a traditional culture, the other emphasizing the response. Hence, a discussion on both these categories will follow.

Contextualization of the Church and its Leadership.

As already mentioned, this deals with the issue of indigenization. As this runs the whole gamut of church life, only a few areas which are relevant to the Caribbean church setting will be mentioned. For example, in the areas of both evangelistic and expository preaching are we indiscriminately and unthinkingly adopting the methodology and style of the North American evangelist or British expositor without any regard for any possible difference in contexts? Do we always need to proclaim the Gospel or edify the saints only in the King's English regardless of the audience? Is there any place for using local customs, practices, and folklore to illustrate spiritual truth?[40]

On the question of church liturgy are we guilty of perpetuating irrelevant and anachronistic forms of worship totally uncharacteristic of our people? Are we in need of a radically new theology of worship as Knolly Clarke suggests?[41] With respect of music, do we consciously or unconsciously believe that our music is inferior to the North American or British brand? Is there any place for Calypso or Reggae music in the church? In a related area is there room for expression of worship in art form of dance (cf. II Samuel 6:16)? In our celebration of the Eucharist have we lost the joyfulness and spontaneity of this occasion because of unemotional (and well-meaning) missionaries have squelched our emotions, telling us how unreliable and unspiritual it is to openly display our emotions?

---

40. Knolly Clarke, "Liturgy and Culture in the Caribbean," in *Troubling of the Waters*, ed. Idris Hamid (San Fernando, Trinidad: Rahaman Printery, 1973) 154.

41. Ibid., 146.

On the subject of dress, is the jacket and tie the only acceptable mode of dress that God approves of in the church? Or is the cooler, more comfortable, and less expensive bush jacket just as acceptable to God? Is the wearing of pants suits to church by women really unbiblical?

In relation to theological education, is our Bible College curriculum and system of training men for the ministry relevant and appropriate to the Caribbean? Finally, on practical issues such as Sunday cricket and common-law relationships is our position based on mere traditional formulations or on a sound Biblical and theological base?

A word of advice. While the method is important for the effective communication of God's truth it must be borne in mind that the message and method are inseparable and that the message takes precedence. Therefore we need to be careful about majoring on the minors.

THE NEW TESTAMENT AND CONTEXTUALIZATION

It is most important to note that the dynamic of the New Testament literature "rather than being an abstraction of principles, ideas or dogmatics . . . is a treasury of the experiences of the early church."[42] Thus, it is not surprising that examples of contextualization may be found within the New Testament itself. For example, when the theological question arose as to the place of circumcision in the salvation of the Gentiles, the decision of the Jerusalem Council did not forbid Jewish Christians from continuing to practice circumcision or compel Gentile Christians to observe this custom.[43] Hence the principle of contextualization, used by the New Testament is a valid one.

STRATEGY FOR CONTEXTUALIZATION

Now that the necessity for contextualization has been established, the nature of the quest stated; the criteria outlined, and the controls suggested, what ought to be the course of action. The writer suggest that a vigorous but not overly-enthusiastic pursuit be made of the interpretation of the Bible in context by competent, well-equipped, Spirit-filled Biblical scholars, preferably nationals. This pursuit is by no means an

---

42. Ericson, "Implications," 71.

43. Ericson's examples of contextualization from I Corinthians 5: 1–8; Colossians 3: 18–4:1 and Matthew 18: 15–17; Corinthians 5: 3–5; Philippians 4: 2–3 are somewhat questionable.

easy task for anyone as the basic hermeneutical issue of determining the descriptive (what the Bible reports) from the prescriptive (what the Bible teaches) is continually at stake.

In addition to expertise and commitment to the Bible, a knowledge of other religions (in the context), sociology, anthropology, and ethnology will prove most beneficial in the contextualization process. In pursuing this process of contextualization the two extremes ought to be avoided. Undue conservatism leads to inertia and hence to a faith encumbered with strange cultural trappings, local or foreign. Undue ardor leads to carelessness and hence to mistakes such as adulteration of the Gospel by syncretism of secularism. However, the writer sees no option but to begin or continue the pursuit both in the major areas of theology as well as methodology.

The process of contextualization is twofold, for "authentic contextualization must be open constantly to the painful, process of de-contextualization, for the sake of de-contextualization, for the sake of re-contextualization."[44]

Although obvious to some it must be stated that "theology" as abstracted statement is not theology, for the purpose of theology is not merely a right conceptual understanding but right praxis.

PROBLEMS OF CONTEXTUALIZATION IN THE CARIBBEAN

Although many of the general problems of contextualization were encountered implicitly or explicitly in the sections: Objections to Contextualization, Explanation for Failure to Contextualize and Difficulties in Contextualization, the writer has identified eight major problems facing the Caribbean churches with respect to contextualization. They are as follows: (1) Gross ignorance regarding the concept of contextualization (2) Sheer apathy (3) A simplistic brand of Christianity which disregards culture (4) An other-worldly, futuristic oriented Christianity which renounces everything the world (5) Heavy financial support from North America and hence the operation of the inverse Goldeb Rule (i.e. He who has the gold makes the rules) (6) Lack of qualified, committed, Spirit-filled men familiar with the context (7) The tendency toward 'A Theology of Imitation' as a result of the copy-cat mentality among the Christians of the Caribbean (8) The non-homo-

---

44. Coe, "Contextualizing Theology," 24.

geneity or diversity of peoples even on the same island due to religious, racial, education, social or economic factors.

However, despite these major obstacles, if contextualization is seen as an imperative inherent in the Gospel, there is no alternative but to go on. In conclusion, it must be remembered that the purpose of contextualization is not the producing of new theologies but theologizing in such a way that reflection leads to praxis.

Appendix B

All Things Work Together...

By Gay Ward-Foster

After the completion of a course in dietetics/nutrition at CAST in 1987, I began to pray earnestly for God's provision of a suitable job. There was only one place that I did not want to be placed and that was at the Bustamante Hospital for Children, and I told God so. I had been there for six weeks of work experience and due to personal discomfort at the sight of children suffering, I had decided that if I was going to work in a hospital setting I would prefer to be in an adult institution. When the Ministry of Health called, they offered me a position at the *Bustamante Hospital for Children!* After some struggle I reluctantly accepted the job offer. However, I was not comfortable and I began to pray and apply for a transfer to another institution.

I remember praying and reflecting on the situation one evening at home. I decided that I was simply going to accept wherever I was placed and fulfill my duties to the best of my abilities. The next morning, I received a note from a friend of mine telling me to apply for a vacancy that had opened up in Kingston. I wondered why at the moment that I had decided to stop murmuring and fighting to get out, God seemed to be opening an exit. Within two months the necessary arrangements had been made and I began my new job.

I had often wondered whether or not experiences such as those outlined above occur by pure chance. Is life just a series of unrelated events, some good and enjoyable, others disappointing and distressing? Or is there some sovereign and universal principle that we need to acknowledge that will help us make sense of the perplexing circumstances that we (especially as Christians) often face? The Apostle Paul affirmed the principle enshrined in the latter of the two questions: "and we know that all things work together for good to them that love God, to them who are called according to his purpose" (Romans 8:28).

ROMANS 8:28: A BASIS FOR PEACEFUL EXISTENCE

Knowing that God in His sovereignty and goodness watches over us and that in all our experiences, He works for our good, should relieve us of our anxiety. In God we can be truly free from worry.

ROMANS 8:28: A BASIS FOR PRODUCTIVE MINISTRY

We often gullibly believe that the 'grass is greener on the other side.' If only God had placed me there, I would be able to do so much more. If only this . . . , if only that . . .' As servants of God, I challenge us to do away with this type of thinking, and to bloom wherever God, in His sovereignty, has placed us. Irrespective of our circumstances, if we are truly able to acknowledge and affirm daily the principles of this verse, our ministries will be productive.

ROMANS 8:28: A BASIS FOR A POSITIVE OUTLOOK

To walk around expecting the worst and being very pessimistic about life is to fail to acknowledge the hand of God at work on our behalf. A positive attitude to life is based on the knowledge that God is intimately concerned with the details of my life. If we despair of life, can we really expect those to whom we witness to accept our message that we are the children of a God who works all things to our benefit?

ROMANS 8:28 A BASIS FOR PRAYERFUL DEPENDENCE

D. L. Moody once said: "trust in yourself and you are doomed to disappointment; trust in you friends and they will die and leave you; trust in money and you may have it taken from you; trust in reputation and some slanderous tongue may destroy it. But trust in God and you will never be confounded in time and eternity". Paul acknowledged our own weak attempts at prayer and that along with this reality, the Holy Spirit intercedes for us in accordance with the full will of God. A life of prayerful dependence on God reminds us who is in control: a sovereign, good and loving God.

If, like Paul, we know that in all things God works for our good, let's make this principle the basis for peaceful existence, productive ministry, a positive outlook on life and a prayerful dependence on God who does all things well.

Appendix C

Dialectic of Sanctification

THESIS: Romans 6 *FREE*	ANTITHESIS: Romans 7 *NOT FREE*	SYNTHESIS: Romans 8 ***GENUINELY FREE*** ***NOT YET TOTALLY FREE***
	→ → ***TENSION***	"Because the creature itself also shall be delivered from the bondage of corruption into the *glorious liberty* of the children of 'God.'" (v. 21)
	→	→ ***TRANSITION***
"Any one who has died is *free* from sin" (v. 7) →	"I am unspiritual *sold as a slave* to son" (v. 14b)	***TRANSFORMATION***

248

APPENDIX D

Dei Voluntas
(Eph 5:17; Jer 10:23

DIVINE DESIRES

DECISIONS	DIRECTIONS
A. God goes by these (Duet 29:29a)	A. God's people live by these (Duet 29:29b)
B. Inscrutable (Rom 11: 30f) ..	B. (Eph. 5:17) Responsible to know & do (Eph 5:18)
C. *Permissive & Performative* (Acts 2:23)	C. *Perfect* (Rom 12:2; Psa 19:7)
D. We should submit to them (Jam. 4:13; Rom 8:28)	D. We need divine enablement to carry them out (Eph. 5:18)
E. Miscellaneous Scriptural Evidence	E. Various Scriptural Expressions
1. Prov 19:21 2. Isa 14:24ff 3. Dan 4:34ff 4. Rom 9:6 ff 5. Eph 1:5 ff 6. Prov 16:1ff 7. Lam 3:37	1. Precepts - 1 Thes 5:17 2. Principles - Gen 4:4 3. Pattern - Rom 15:4, 4. Perfections- Eph 5:1 5. Prudence - Eph 5:15 6. Prayer - James 1:15 7. Preference - Ps. 37:5; Rom. 1:9–13, 15:22ff

|Mesographic Code|

|Mosaic Code| |Messianic Code|
|2 3 4 | |1 2 3 4|

"Where there is no *revelation of God's will* the people perish." (Prov. 29:18a. My translation; Dvp)

Appendix E

Sabbath, Sunday, and the Third-Millennium Saint

> A very strange situation exists among Christians today. All Christians worship the same God; they all have the very same Jesus as Saviour. All Christians accept essentially the same Bible. Yet they have two days of worship! On one hand there is a large group of sincere Christians, who tell us, "Sunday is the Christian day of worship!" Another equally sincere group replies, "No, Saturday, the seventh day, is the day on which Christians should worship!" How can we decide the question? The only way to know religious truth is to go to God's word. It does not matter what a church may teach or what a preacher may preach; the only really important question is: "What does God say in the Bible?

The paragraph above forms the introduction to a pamphlet entitled, "How Sunday Keeping Started."

The purpose of the pamphlet is to demonstrate that the day of worship was never divinely changed from Saturday to Sunday.[1] The author of the pamphlet first discusses eight occurrences of the phrase "first day of the week" and convincingly shows that none of these texts authorizes such a change. The references are Matthew 28:1; Mark 16:1,2; Mark 16:9; Luke 24:1; John 20:1; and 1 Corinthians 16:1,2.

The writer then argues that the term "Lords day" found in Revelation 1:10 is not a reference to the first day of the week. Based on Matthew 12:8, s/he concludes that the "Lord's day" is Saturday. "How then did Sunday observance come into the Church?" s/he asks. Taking a cue from Daniel 7:25, the writer answers the own question: "It came about as a direct result of Satan's attempts to counterfeit God's work." Later on the Roman

---

1. Another tract, entitled "The Mark of the Beast," goes a step further by identifying Sunday observance as the mark of the beast.

Catholic Church is clearly identified as the group which "took the lead among Christians in attempting to change the weekly day to Sunday."

I am in agreement with the pamphlet on a couple of matters. First, I thoroughly endorse the statement which affirms that the only thing that matters on the question of the Sabbath is what God says in His Word. I also agree that there is no text in the Bible that mentions any change of the Sabbath from Saturday to Sunday. However, to insist that Christians keep the Sabbath today is entirely a different matter. While it is true that the idea of the Sabbath is as old as creation (Gen 2:2-3), it is to be carefully noted that the command to keep the Sabbath was given only to the Israelites (Ex 31:12-17). In Psalm 147:19-20 the Psalmist celebrates the fact that God's law was received by his people alone. He concludes by saying, "He hath not dealt so with any nation; as for his judgements they have not known them." In other words, the Egyptians, Babylonians, and other nearby peoples did not have the written word of God. Therefore, those surrounding nations were not required to worship on a Saturday. The same is true today. If, however, an outsider wanted to enter into covenant relationship with the God of the Israelites, that person would have had to accept the Mosaic stipulations as well.

When we come to the New Testament we find the Lord Jesus Christ keeping the Sabbath as an obedient Jew. The Apostle Paul also visited the synagogues on the Sabbath. Was he merely keeping the Sabbath as a good Christian? Before this question is answered, let us examine two passages from his writings.

COLOSSIANS 2:13-15

In this portion the apostle carefully points out some of the accomplishments of Christ on the cross.

These include:

1. Remission of sins (v. 13)

2. Cancellation of the law (v.14)

3. Spoliation of demons (v. 15)

Based on these achievements the apostle warns: "Allow no one, therefore, to take you to task [or criticize you] about what you eat or drink or over the observance of a festival, new moon, or Sabbath" (v. 16, REB).[2]

2. In the following verse the Apostle points out, with some literary flourish, that the

In light of the above, the following question should be pondered: why is the Sabbath imperative conspicuously absent from the New Testament? I am quite sure that sabbatarians have an answer to this query, but I find it difficult to see how they can avoid its implication for the believer today.³

ROMANS 14:5–7

Although the Apostle Paul recognized that the Old Testament law was not binding on believers in his day (Rom 6:14, cf. Heb 7:12), he nevertheless allowed for the observance of any day a Christian may have wished to set apart. Thus he writes, "One man considers one day more sacred than another; another man should be fully convinced in his own mind. He who regards one day special does so to the Lord" (Rom 14:5–6a; REB).

So, is Sunday the Christian Sabbath? Certainly not. However, since Christians have been delivered from the Mosaic Law (Rom 7:1–6), they now serve God "in newness of spirit, and not in the oldness of the letter." This allows freedom to worship on any appropriate day. Knowing this, the early Christians settled into a pattern of Sunday worship. It would appear that it was these same believers who dubbed the first day of the week "the Lord's day" (Rev 1:10), most likely because of its association with the resurrection of Christ (Matt 28), his subsequent Sunday appearances (John 20:19, 26), and the advent of the Spirit on the first day of the week.⁴ This may be confirmed by other early Christian writings.⁵

Why then did the Apostle Paul visit the synagogues on the Sabbath? Without a doubt, he was carrying out the very principle he wrote about

---

Sabbath (along with rites mentioned in v. 16) is a shadow (*skia*), the substance (*soma*) of which is Christ.

3. Especially in the light of the fact that in Col 2 the nearest (though not exclusive) antecedent of "which" (AV; v. 17) or "these" (NIV) is the Sabbath.

4. This can be inferred from the "7 weeks since Passover that had been fulfilled." (F. F. Bruce, *The Acts of the Apostles*. London: Tyndale, 1951, 81).

5. For example, in *the Didache*, xiv. 1, the term rendered "Lord's" (*Kuriake*) in Revelation 1:10 is used for Sunday. "After having assembled and confessed your transgressions break the bread [and] give thanks on The Dominical day (*kuriaken*) of the Lord." G.P Gould (ed.), *The Apostolic Fathers* vol. 1 (Cambridge, M.A: Harvard, 1912), 330. "The phrase [the Lord's day] is clearly and consistently used of Sunday from the second half of the second century on,"G. K. Beale, *The Book of Revelation* (Grand Rapids: Eerdmans, 1999), 203. Even the SDA scholar, S. Bacchiocchi, (*From Sabbath to Sunday* [Rome: PGU, 1977], 123–30) rejects the Lord's day=Sabbath view. Unfortunately, though, he opts for the equally untenable eschatological day of the Lord.

in 1 Corinthians 9:19–21. He wanted to evangelize his fellow Jews. Of particular interest here is the Apostle's testimony regarding his relationship with the Old Testament law on the one hand and its New Testament counterpart on the other. "To Jews I behave like a Jew, to win the Jews, that is, to win those under the law. I behave as if under the law, though not myself subject to the law (v. 20, REB)."

Those who are under the law according to this verse are the Jewish people. The Apostle Paul himself was a Jew. Yet, writing as a Christian missionary, he categorically declares that "I . . . myself [am] not subject to the law" Amazing! But does this mean that the Apostle to the Gentiles was lawless? God forbid! The cowboy from the Wild West could have shouted "hallelujah"! I'm no longer under the law; I'm an outlaw," but he would not have had any support from Paul's letters. Some first-century believers may have thought along those lines but this kind of thinking was seriously challenged (cf. Rom 6:14–23; Gal 4:21–5:1).

There was a time when a certain Saul of Tarsus took pride in being under the Mosaic Law (Phil 3:5–10). But the Christ event made a gigantic difference in his life, so much so that his new ground of boasting was in the Messianic code (1 Cor 9:21; ". . . under law to Christ") and the Messianic cross, which forms its basis (Gal 6:14). So must the twenty-first century saint keep the Sabbath? S/he may if s/he wishes. But if s/he mandates this for everybody s/he would, I believe, be guilty of "putting a yoke upon the neck of the disciples which neither our fathers nor we are able to bear."

Appendix F

Should Christians Be Involved in Jamaican Politics?

By Erica Campbell

THE LEADERSHIP ROLE WHICH the Reverend Herro Blair played in the newly formed third party in Jamaica, the National Democratic Movement, brought a series of old questions back into public debate as Jamaicans prepared for the 1997 general elections. While the controversy over the separation of church and state—which has dominated public discourse in the United States for the last three decades—has never been a serious Caribbean problem, the present political climate is causing Jamaican Christians to raise new questions about their role in the political process. How Christians should regard the state, what kind of allegiance they should have to government or a political party in Jamaica, whether politics is necessarily evil or a necessary evil in Jamaican society, and what the role of the Church should be in Jamaican society are old questions that are always topical and scarcely void of controversy; they mirror the varied perceptions people have of politics and what they regard as the proper role of the Church in the political process.

In this essay, we argue that politics is not necessarily evil and, in fact, is good; government is intended to ensure fairness in society, protect citizens, encourage good and punish evil-not just impose taxes on the poor and facilitate the rich. As a consequence, the relationship between the church and the state should be one of ethical collaboration. Active Christian participation in the political process to promote "the good" can be considered a duty to one's God and country. Like earlier Jamaica Christian political activists (Sam Sharpe, George Williams Gordon, Paul Bogle, Alexander Bedward and Marcus Garvey), Christians should view their involvement in the political struggle as a God-given duty to society. As the 1981 House of Delegates to the North Carolina Council of Churches affirms, "Vigorous involvement in political causes and political activities are a vital aspect of Christian witness in the modern world" (House of Delegates 1).

JAMAICA'S POLITICAL-RELIGIOUS TRADITION

Some Christians who adopt an ascetic notion of Christianity see their relationship to political systems as one of withdrawal; they stay a conspicuous, if not comfortable, distance from the political process. In other sectors of the Jamaica society, Christians are expected to make an impact on the political system but only from a distance. Others, who embrace what H. Richard Niebuhr calls a Christ-against-culture attitude, regard the church's role in society as one of critique; a watchdog which, more often than not, utters only prophetic condemnation of the existing political systems. Still others believe the church should transform culture but must not get too deeply involved in politics. For example, some Christians have credited the church with playing a crucial role in the dismantling of apartheid in South Africa and leading the fight for civil rights and desegregation in the United States, but they claim it must not corrupt itself in the present political culture of Jamaica. The Church is regarded primarily as the messenger of individual spiritual salvation with a secondary, though not unimportant role as the moral conscience of the nation. Christians are expected to speak out on issues such as crime, dishonesty, injustice, bigotry and corruption but they must not get too political.

This, however, is not the most enduring political religious tradition of Jamaica. Since the early 1980s, Baptist missionaries (e.g. William Knibb) and Afro-Jamaican religious leaders and lay preachers (Sam Sharpe and Paul Bogle) played a vital role in Jamaica's political struggle for liberation, equality, independence and social change. Jamaican Christians were so heavily involved in the Sam Sharpe Christmas rebellion of 1831-which was originally planned as a peaceful nonviolent direct action against slavery-that it is dubbed "the Baptist War." Christians led a yuletide rebellion against oppression which forced the British Government to hasten emancipation by several years. Christians were again at the forefront of the struggle against oppression in the Moran Bay Rebellion of 1865; a political action precipitated by the total absence of justice for Blacks, the landlessness of the poor masses willing to engage in agriculture, and embarrassingly poor wages given to workers in St. Thomas-in-the-East (the eastern parish of Jamaica).

Baptist, Nativist Baptist and other Afro-Jamaican religious traditions which flourished in the post-emancipation era gave leadership to prophetic political activity through the fiery and brave Baptist preacher Paul Bogle and his very articulate and courageous Assemblyman George William Gordon-who shifted his allegiance from the high church (Church of England) to Native Baptist (Heuman 5). Bogle, Gordon (who was in Kingston and did not take part in the rebellion) and about 400 others, mostly innocent Native Baptist Christians, paid the ultimate price for their prophetic progressive political thought and action in the Jamaica of Governor Edward Eyre-a bloodthirsty, heartless, brute beast who was appointed Lt. Governor of Jamaica on the basis of his two year stint as office assistant (a glorified messenger boy) in the office of the Governor of Trinidad and Tobago, the colour of his skin and the fact that he was British. On the eve of the rebellion, Eyre was acting Governor while Sir Charles Darling was on leave in Britain.

In the 1880s and 1890s, the Christian leader Alexander Bedward was dubbed strange and crazy for his unfamiliar prophetic and apocalyptic voice in defense of the oppressed. Jamaican Christians were members of the first Teachers Union formed in 1895. They were also members of the "Club Movement" which followed the teachers' example of organized labour during the first two decades of the 1900s, a movement which led to the rise of unionism and the legalizing of organized labour in Jamaica in 1919 (Phillips 110). Marcus Garvey and other Christians in the UNIA formed and influenced the formation of political parties in Jamaica. Other Christians have served their constituencies, supervised general elections, acted as trusted advisors to politicians, made peace between warring political factions, especially in the battle zones of Kingston's inner city, and held offices in local government.

Many pulpits have been used as a political platform for the spread of Jamaican nationalism (so well epitomized in Norman Washington Manley, Afro-Jamaicanism, patriotism, justice and peace. For this reason, the church is regarded as an active participant in and a force to reckon with in Jamaican social and political life. Professor Nettleford noted in 1978 that since Independence, the clergy in the "established churches" have also attempted to make Eurocentric Christian orthodoxy and liturgy culturally, socially and politically relevant to society. While some preachers resisted "the revolutionary rhetoric of socialism and change of the 1970s, many of the young clergy from a variety of denominations are to be found actively on the side of what would be called progressive politics, supporting social change and consciously seeking ways and means of projecting God with a human face."[1]

Politicians themselves have often recognized the love affair between the Jamaica Church and the state.

Political leaders have repeatedly declared Jamaica to be "Christian country." Political creeds are given Christian sources of origin or inspiration when they are to be promulgated and "sold" to the general mass of people.[2] As Nettleford observes, "The Chairman of the Jamaica Council of Churches could in 1989 make public claim for the church to run future general elections in collaboration with the bipartisan national Electoral Commission."[3]

CHRISTIANS AND JAMAICAN POLITICS OF THE 1990S

In spite of recent skepticism about Christian participation in Jamaican politics, the country has a strong democratic tradition in which both Christians and non-Christians are active. Since the late 1940s Jamaicans have exercised their franchise and voted in the Westminster system of government in which two parties vie for the leadership of the country. The 1997 general elections witnessed a three party contest with the incumbent Peoples' National Party, their usual rival since the 1940s, the Jamaica Labour Party, and he National Democratic Movement all wooing the Jamaican voter. It may seem on the surface that the democratic system is ideal and, by virtue of its competitive nature, would produce candidates of high quality. These, in turn, would make the system strong, vibrant and fair to all Jamaicans. But increasingly, people are viewing Jamaican politics in a very negative light.

In the past two years, there has been much talk in the media about the uncommitted and alienated voters who have become disenchanted by the greed and corruption they see in the government. Man party supporters are now disgusted at the politicians and what they regard as the glaring inadequacies and moral degradation of the Jamaican political

---

1. Nettleford, *Caribbean Cultural Identity*, 21.
2. Ibid., 19.
3. *Jamaica in Early Independence*, 6.

culture, its inability to alleviate the severe hardship among the masses of the people (the new sufferers), or to solve the crime problem which has reached epidemic proportion throughout the country. Other voters are alienated by what Jamaican call "ginalism" and "politricks" (a form of political dishonesty and outright dirty party politics) and "patron-clientelism."

Politics in Jamaica is very intense and in some cases very violent. Paradoxically, this violent has its roots in the political divisions of the 1940s—at a time when Jamaican nationalism was showcasing some of its most articulate leaders and issuing a clarion call for unity of purpose. As Peter Phillips noted,

After 1940 . . . the Bustamante-led Bustamante Industrial Trade union, broke ranks with the Trades Union Council to provide a mass base for Bustamante's Labour Party, which functioned in opposition to the Peoples' National Party led by Norman Manley which had emerged as the bearer of the nationalist demand for self-government.[4]

This split was later followed by the expelling of the communist element from the Peoples' National Party, which them broke ranks with the Trades Union Council and set up "its own affiliate union, the National Workers Union." Although these "breakups" in unionism seem quite tame and not related to the political violence in modern Jamaica, Phillips intimates that "The division of the labour movement, along contending lines of party affiliation contributed to the growing violence and "tribalism" associated with interunion rivalry. . . ."[5]

From the late 1940s on, the spirit of rivalry and animosity gradually became part and parcel of Jamaican electioneering and party politics.

Today, party allegiances are very entrenched and often passed on from generation to generation; one crosses party lines at great risk. In the interest of good family relation, some of our Jamaican friends were forced to forego the excitement of exercising their franchise for the first time in the 1980 elections because their parents dared then to "remain under their roof" while voting for a party other than the one Mom and Dad supported. This commitment to partisan politics is so strong that it destroys relationships when it gives way to very heated arguments that often erupt in violent confrontation among neighbours and in families of opposing political allegiances. The 1980 general elections province

4. Phillips, "Race," 110.
5. Ibid., 111.

more than amply evidence of the extent to which party loyalties can yield deadly results; over 800 people died in political violence throughout Jamaica. The statistics seem more characteristic of a civil war than a "democratic" election. Carl Stone says:

> This great intensity of feelings, emotional loyalties and aggressive and combative sentiments of support . . . has to be understood as a response to the need for power on the part of the majority classes. . . . The bottom 40% of income earners make up 95% of the . . . hard-core membership . . . Because of the poor and socially disadvantaged are in the majority, it is their cultural style and emotional and social needs that shape the style of the political party's internal life. For them, the party is their road to power and social opportunity and is therefore deserving of total commitment and great sacrifices in defending its interests.[6]

Although the poor underclass constitutes the majority of the membership of the political parties, they are not the movers and shakers in the decision-making machinery of a given, party. The middle class professional leadership actually makes final decisions at the party level. One wonders, therefore, why loyalty to a particular political party is considered so important in the quest fro empowerment and social and economic opportunity in Jamaica. Unfortunately, "patron-clientelism" is really "The dominant feature of the organization of mass support for competitive political parties in the Third World. The core of this system is the exchange of economic and social favours to a poor and socially fragmented population in return for party support."[7]

These favours are given out of scarce and limited resources, access to which is best gained from the seat of political power, the government.

Ensuring that one's political party wins the general and, to a lesser extent, the local election, is often regarded as a matter of life and death. This explains the violence and even the formation of garrison constituencies which, through force and subtle coercive means, are formed to ensure a party that the votes in that constituency are secure. The link between clientelism and garrison constituencies is more entrenched in the ghettos where the poor, dispossessed and disempowered are found in large numbers. In that environment, might is right. The gun is the coveted means of settling even the most trivial dispute. Gangsters, thugs,

6. Carl Stone, *Class*, 1985.
7. Stone, *Democracy*, 91–92.

drug dealers and political hoodlums who control the streets and decide who lives and who dies, make a mockery of law and order of civilized society and political ethics. This is politics at its worst; it makes the uglier side of Jamaican life the source of rules by which the political game is played out in the streets and at the ballot box.

The politician' role in the creation of garrisons through clientelism, and the violence and "bogus" voting that their supporters engage in, lead people to believe that the political system is not only corrupt, bankrupt, and beyond repair, but bad for one's health. "People will murder you if you are not careful while campaigning in some constituencies" said a woman. This reality definitely influences one's respect for politicians and determines the level at which Christians can be politically active in Jamaica without losing their integrity and their lives. If the country's resources are being used to benefit the party faithful, or more precisely to keep them subjugated and committed to the party, then the respect which is supposedly due the political leaders in unwarranted. Understandably, many people feel they have a just cause to withhold honour from those to whom honour is not due and, like talk show host Wilmot Perkins, develop a cynicism about the country's possibilities for progress and an utter mistrust of politicians. The question is, however, what is the best solution to the problem and how far will cynicism go without sparking a bloody revolution similar to the one in Grenada?

Some Jamaicans, including a few Christians, are of the opinion that politics has become so corrupt in Jamaica that only a revolution can bring about radical change to the system; they believe it is needed to break the cycle of violence, patron-clientelism and poverty. But Jamaicans who are frustrated with the political system would only add insult to injury by contemplating a violent revolution as a solution to the country's problems. The recent history of Granada can serve as a warning. Many Grenadians, including the clergy, who were disgusted at the political corruption in the Grenada United Labour party, welcomed the violent overthrow of the corrupt Gairy government in 1979. Thousands of Maurice Bishop supporters, many of them Christians, celebrated in the streets throughout the island at the news that the People's Revolutionary Government (PRG) had ousted the recalcitrant Prime Minister Eric Matthew Gairy and his cabinet from office. Finally, we thought, Grenada is back on the road to responsible government in a civil society.

But the mayhem that followed in the wake of the counter-revolutionary disaster of 1983 and its aftermath, taught us that "he who lives by the sword, perishes by the sword." A large number of civilians, many of hem Christians, were executed by Bernard Coard's military henchmen while others jumped to their death of the cliff at Fort George. Two university educated Christian friends of Samuel Murrell, one a chemist and the other a biologist, who helped to make the explosives that blew up Gairy's barracks in St. Georges in 1979 were themselves later treated brutally by their own PRG hoodlums. One was executed in the Fort George "slaughter" by Bernard Coard's Militia on October 19, on the eve of the American invasion, and the other was kept in a miserable confinement without trial for many years—poorly fed and severely tortured. When Murrell visited him in his cell in the PRG's maximum security prison in January 1981 (allowed only in his capacity as clergy) he had lost the use of several fingers and his face was barely recognizable; although his spirits were very high. It is a miracle that he survived to complete his MD in New York where he now practises medicine.

In the Grenada of Bernard Coard and his wife (1979–1983), there was no place for sharp critical and independent minds or freedom of expression. Religion, which Karl Marx regarded as the opiate of the people (dope or ganja), was tolerated as a means to a political end. The political system which the PRG brought into being was tightly controlled be radical Leninist Marxist bureaucrats who sought to manipulate the moderates in the party (Prime Minister Maurice Bishop, Unison Whiteman, Kendrick Radiix, Jacqueline Creft, George Louison and others) and eliminate all opposition and voices of dissent. The fact that these moderates in the PRG were all friends and acquaintances of Samuel Murrell when he worked at the Bank of Nova Scotia in St. Georges made their death even more tragic and painful to him.

This is a problem that Jamaica does not need, and we are confident will not experience; as bad as things may seem, politics in Jamaica is not as depraved and future is not as bleak as it was in Gairy's Grenada. Jamaicans cherish their freedom of speech, freedom of the press and freedom of religion. Prime Minister Patterson of Jamaica has no known Mongoose Gang or henchmen slaughtering people who oppose his party; he does not stash Jamaican tax dollars away in a personal Swiss Bank account; he has not taken over the prosperous hotels in Jamaica as Gairy did; and his cabined spends its time seeking solutions to Jamaica's vexing problems rather than counting unidentified flying objects (a Gairy fixation). Jamaica also leads Grenada and many other eastern Caribbean countries in industrial development, education, health care, sports and science and technology. Indeed, there is much hope, both in the private and public sectors, for Jamaica to overcome its restructuring problems as a precursor to economic stability and the eradication of poverty and violent crime in the nation.

Becoming a part of a violent opposition to constituted authority is one thing, but once political authority is undermined the maintenance of law and order becomes much more difficult than it is under a corrupt political system. Because of the way in which society is structured locally and internationally, government is not as expendable as some critics think. Government is there to ensure national security, peace among neighbours, just dealings between patrons and proprietors and employers and employees, the defense of the vulnerable and health and well-being of al citizens. Political leaders who engage in that do not encourage and support families and communities. It needs to address the country's penchant for imports rather than developing its ability to be self-sufficient. Christians should resist the divestment of key areas of Jamaica's economy to foreign entrepreneurs, which further aggravates the pain and suffering of the poor. The church should criticize the non-intervention of the government in the exploitative employer-employee relationship in the work place. But Christian prophets must not allow a particular ideological leaning to prejudice their critique of an issue of grave concern to the nation. Moral and biblical principles should be a guiding rod for Christian political activity. God's concern for the poor must play a central role in determining our attitude toward government policies and their implementation. This is by no means an easy task and must be done with integrity and accurate knowledge' for governments make decisions based on a variety of considerations which must be carefully analyzed. This is why dialogue between church and state is important and research for the acquisition of accurate information on an issue must be done before "prophetic utterances" are made from the pulpit. The Christian who gets involved in political affairs at this level must be an informed citizen and an educator who helps others understand the difficulties involved in governing a developing country with limited resources but expensive taste buds.

Bevis Byfield says there is a feeling that, "by and large, societies as they are now organized, have, in the main, contributed little to the transformation of the lives of the people who live within those societies. What we need is a reordering of the structuring of those societies so that emancipation and redemption of people can be realized." Byfield uses four terms to describe a "Trickle down" theory of economics, which assumes that if the rich get richer, then the poor will get richer as a result. He says it is:

1. Paternalistic—the rich make decisions about what is good for the poor.

2. Manipulative—the poor have to conform to the wishes of the rich.

3. Inadequate—it comes out of a system fraught with injustice.

4. Oppressive—it leads to unholy alliances between financiers in rich nations and tiny oligarchies in the poor nations, both of which have an interest in keeping the poor from challenging the system which keeps them poor.[8]

This may be fine analysis of the situation but in order to tackle the problems, one may have to become involved in decision-making at the highest level of government, and this means active political and/or economic involvement. The need to do what one ought to and can do to change the system is ever present. Christians should seek to move the society from what is to what ought to be. But how can this be accomplished? Political and economic life is very complex and the problems are deep rooted and endemic. It takes persons of courage, knowledge, insight and strength of character to make a real difference in the fight to effect social, economic and political change in the country. It is much easier to identify the country's problems than to be actively involved in solving them. Christians and non-Christians alike who recognize Jamaica's political crisis and know what the solution is, need to be proactive in society rather than reactive.

The question of the extent to which the church should be involved in political activities of course, cannot be conclusively settled in this short paper. There are so many dangers and unanswered questions surrounding this issue that the church is damned if it is politically active and it is doubly damned if it is not. While the role of the church in

---

8. Byfield, "Theology from Below," 4, 9.

society as a champion of social justice, peacemaking and moral values is absolutely essential, ,partisan politics can stifle the church's message might be undermined and "emasculated temporarily" if it promotes one rising populist branch of politics over an established order, thought never ignored. The church's prophetic voice must always be hard in a society where "government continues to be seen as dispenser of largesse in the form of jobs, contracts, as well as social services outside [sic] and in times of crisis."[9] and when political leaders step outside the bounds of their constituted authority.

In her response to Bishop Neville DeSouza's "Christian Action for Social Change" *(in Social Change: Christian and Social Science Perspectives)*, Maxine Henry-Wilson chided the Bishop for limiting the role of the Church to social change that does not include political action. This she sees as a failure or reluctance to meet the entire challenge." She argues quite strongly that:

> Social change is one facet of a network of activities of actions. Fundamental to any hope of or strategy for social change, must be an assessment of the power structures in the society and the concomitant designing of methods and approaches to deal with these structures. Any failure to come to terms with power and power relations in the society is quixotic and can only lead to some questioning of the real commitment to change. It has been stated that the church must take its place . . . . on the side of the poor. But history and reality shows us that the poor has no economic and/or political control . . . . It is impossible to correct social maladies in any lasting and profound way without redressing existing economic and political relations.[10]

CHRISTIAN SCRIPTURE AND POLITICAL ACTION: ROMANS 13:1–7

No discussion on the Christian's relationship to the state could be complete without an examination of biblical teachings which form the source of Christian thought and action; the controversy over Christian involvement in Jamaican politics is not without biblical warrant and theological reflections. In fact, since the fourth century, people have viewed Romans 13:1–7 as the official biblical teaching on the Christian's duty to the state.

9. Nettleford, *Jamaica*, 6.
10. Wilson, "Comments," 33–34.

Appendix F   265

According to ethicist John Howard Yoder, since the post-Constantine era this text has served as a sort of capsule constitution to guide the Christian statesman and stateswoman. Consequently, the periscope has stirred up enormous controversy in the history of biblical interpretation.

In modern times, Nazis, fascists, dictators and other political ideologues have used the biblical text to their advantage. Some Americans have cited Romans 13 in support of government and the draft into the U.S. military. Fundamentalists Christians have quoted this text to pronounce anathema on those who refused to cooperate with America's questionable military aggression against foreign nations like Vietnam and Grenada, and also to denounce the international anti-Apartheid movement. Some extremist interpretations led ethicist Reinhold Niebuhr to argue that the text allows an unqualified endorsement of government and a vehicle for too uncritical a devotion to political systems, ideologies and leaders. But Romans 13:1–7 supports neither revolution nor legitimation of government. The text does not address directly the question of the Christian's active participation in a political movement or political life and offers inadequate principles for the Christian's relationship to the state in general.

Many scholars even question whether the periscope was originally a part of Paul's letter to the Romans since it is self-contained and seems to interrupt the context of what precedes and follows the text.[11] Some argue that nowhere else does Paul discuss the state or the Christian's relation to it. The text also seems to assume the indefinite continuance of the present order which, according to Romans 13:11, is at the point of disappearing.[12] Those objections can, of course, be answered with several observations. The Roman Christians' situation may have required that this topic be addressed. Paul's epistles show a keen interest in dealing with specific local problems. Nowhere in the passage is it states that human government is going to continue indefinitely. Paul's recognition in 13:11 that the perfect kingdom is yet to come points to the fact that human government falls short of God's ideal. Far from contradicting Paul, the thoughts expressed in Romans 13: 1–7 simply make Christians aware that they must do their part to make the present order as good s it can be. Finally, the apostle's style has never been one to commend him to literary critics. "Smooth

11. Murrell, "Wrestling with the Bible," 13, 21.
12. Ibid., 13, 21, Bruce, 99.

transitions are not so characteristic of Paul's style that there is any need for surprise at an abrupt change of subject."[13]

British theologian F. F. Bruce, who agrees that the pericope is self-contained, does not believe that the flow of Paul's argument is interrupted. He notes that the paragraph which precedes Romans 13:1–7 encourages Christians to have a good attitude to non-Christians, even those who try to hurt them. The pericope contains the injunction: "If possible, so far as it depends upon you, live peaceably with all persons" (Romans (12:18); this may include "living peaceably with the representatives of the State" (Bruce 101).[14] J. Moiser also sees a connection between the preceding verses and Romans 13: 1–7:

> Taking together these two pericopes . . . can be justified, not primarily on lexical grounds . . . but on grounds of content" blessing persecutors (12:14), refraining from revenge (12:19), and subjecting oneself to authority (13:1) clearly form a unity . . . . A possible solution to addressing difficulties which come out of the confused writing, is to interpret the text as a juxtaposition of two separate, but related ideas. Christians need to renounce thoughts of revenge both against each other (12:1–20) and against the state (12:21—13:7). In this way, 12:14 functions as a superscript to the section 12:15–13:7.[15]

Paul wrote this letter to deal with political and theological problems in the Roman church. By mid first century, early Christians in Palestine were meeting in small cells on the fringes of the synagogues. In time, a conflict developed between the Christians and the Jews in Rome, a conflict so great that the Roman authorities had to intervene. To preserve the Pax Romana, Claudius gave an edict to expel the key figures in the dispute. No distinction was made between Jews and Christians; both fell under the Jewish rubric. Eventually, those who were expelled from the city returned to Rome in new settings. Despite the passing of time, some animosity towards the State existed among those who had witnessed the expulsion.[16] Consequently, Paul wrote establishing a theological basis for this appeal for unity within the church and offered practical advice

13. Bruce, *Mind*, 99.
14. Ibid., 101.
15. Moiser, "Rethinking Romans 12–15," 576.
16. Crafton, "Paul's Rhetorical Vision," 323; Moiser, "Rethinking Romans 12–15," 577.

on Christian conduct in society. Of special concern to him is the need for the church to maintain good relations with the state so that the gospel is not hindered in any way. As Jeffery Crafton puts it, "Paul creates a rhetorical vision in which he and the Roman Christians are actors in a larger divine purpose . . . Paul's intention is to involve the readers in his world, as much as possible, through theological argument, through emotional and ethical appeal and through demonstration of the ways in which he and the Romans are already participants in this world."[17]

Unlike the "Palestinian Zealots who recognized no king but God and would pay taxes to no one but God, Paul may have wanted to dissuade Jewish Christians in the capital from taking part in revolutionary movements."[18] In this context he urges Christians to submit to civil authority and render unto Caesar the things that are Caesar's and unto God the things that belong to God. In the interest of the future survival of the church, Paul argues that governmental authorities are "derived from God" (appointed by God) and that the person in authority is the "servant of God" to promote the good in society and punish the evil (13:1–4); it is not the person in the office, per se, but the office itself that has God's approval. While God may recognize the need for government in Germany, Uganda and Iraq, for example, Hitler, Amin and Hussein were not sent by God.

APPLYING SCRIPTURE TO JAMAICA'S POLITICAL SITUATION

However one interprets the notion that God ordained government, Paul's use of the term "submission" poses a serious problem to many Jamaican Christians, especially those who have to endure injustice, manipulation and exploitation from unscrupulous persons in positions of power. Many wonder how God could require submission to those who, by their behaviour and conduct, are not in line with God's right and just will. Of course, one can argue that in Romans 13:1–7 Paul is presenting his version of an ideal state which does not exist in actual reality. But Paul was addressing a real situation in Rome and his readers knew that their state was less than ideal. He tells them that God ordained the principle of governing and that Christians were to submit to governmental law since

---

17. Crafton, "Paul's Rhetorical Vision," 319–320.
18. Morris, *Romans*, 458.

it promotes good and punishes evil "for there is no authority except that which God has established." One should respect governmental authority out of conscience as well as out of fear of punishment. Paul is suggesting that Christians should not act on the basis of what is comfortable and safe but according to what promotes the gospel. We should not render evil and certainly not 'fight fire with fire." Passive resistance, moral and spiritual infiltration, and obedience to Christ and legal authority are the essence of Paul's teaching in Romans.

This line of argument, of course, seems to put Jamaican Christians in a position of do-nothing pacifism. It implies a passive, conformist disposition even in the midst of blatant, reckless and 'deviant behaviour" on the part of government. Submission, however, is not synonymous with blind allegiance. The idea that the state is ordained by God and it is God's servant shows that absolute authority lies, not with government, but in God Himself' absolute power in human hands corrupt absolutely. To Christians, absolute submission to government rather than the divine is idolatrous. It goes against the clear call in Romans 12 for nonconformity to the world's philosophy and conformity to God's expectations and ideal. Submission to human leadership is therefore conditional rather than absolute; governments are to be obeyed only when they promote the good and do not arrogate to themselves absolute authority over people's lives under God. "Caesar [then] is to be respected to the extent to which he protects the poor and vulnerable against abuses by the rich and powerful, renders justice to all citizens of the state irrespective of pigmentation, class or creed and maintains the public trust."[19]

Therefore, what should Jamaican Christians do if their government ceases to promote the good but becomes recalcitrant in encouraging garrison politics that furthers oppression and exploitation of the poor? This is a matter for individual conscience as well as corporate ecclesiastical polity. By virtue of one's relationship to God, the Christian whose heart and ears are open to the cries of the oppressed has the moral obligation to speak out against acts of injustice and exploitation in the wider society. As theologian Leon Morris says, "The Christian is to recognize that order is important in any state. But if the state exceeds its lawful function, if it plainly directs subjects to actions that are wrong, then that is another matter."[20] Although Morris cites Jesus as saying "render to

19. Murrell, "Wrestling," 19.
20. Morris, *Romans*, 462.

Caesar only the things that are Caesar's for we are to render to God what is God's" (Mark 12:7), he does not say how a Christian should respond to an immoral government.[21]

Bruce, however, said emphatically, "The state not only may, but must be resisted when it demands the allegiance due to God alone."[22] Christians may use the political process to oust corrupt politicians from office and withdraw their support from bloodthirsty dictators. However, bloody revolution (as in Grenada) and tribalism (as in Rwanda) should be avoided at all cost and the Christian should not take up arms (as in the American Frontier and Northern Ireland), except, perhaps, in special situations of self-defense. The Christian should adopt a stance of peaceful and passive resistance where possible but certainly not passive acceptance. In their struggle against bigotry, oppression and terror, Mahatma Gandhi, Rosa Parks, Martin Luther King Jr., Nelson Mandela and many others have demonstrated that nonviolent direct action can be more powerful and effective in forcing progressive social and political change than the barrel of a gun used in Grenada, Cuba, Northern Ireland and Nazi Germany.

From Romans 13:1–7 one can deduce that political involvement at the level of civic duty is implied and advocacy for justice is understood. But what about a Christian actually walking in the corridors of power and becoming a governmental authority? Does Paul or biblical teaching support that idea? There seems to be not prohibition in this case. Paul certainly speaks to the Christian citizen but he gives not instructions to the Christian politician. The apostle does not prohibit a Christian functioning as a political leader, and it does seem quite in order for Christians to make direct input into the progress and development of the nation. Since government was established by God and its official are His servants to do good (Rom 13:4) politics in and of itself, though it has a peculiar character in Jamaica, is not evil. God intends that governments act justly and behave in a way that will be beneficial to the governed. How much more equipped is the Christian to act as the servant of God in the capacity of ward of he State! Leading a nation with justice and equality for all is, perhaps, the highest form of service one could render to God and country.

21. Ibid.
22. Bruce, 101.

Martin Luther, the sixteenth century reformer, often taught his young parish trainees (ministers in training) to allow whatever Scriptures demand. Judeo-Christian Scriptures present no obstacle to Christians entering politics; and where there are not prohibitions, determining how one should contribute to the political process is an individual choice. This can be done in many ways: by simply being a good citizen, supporting fair governmental programs, playing a prophetic role in society—praising the good and condemning the unjust and unscrupulous policies and practices of political leaders—or by fulfilling a political ambition of actually becoming a politician; or sharing in the leadership of a party as Reverend Herro Blair did in the NDM.

In Jamaica's democratic society, citizens uphold the ideal, thought not quite a reality, that politics is a process which allows them to determine how they could live together in peace and harmony. Jamaicans believe also that political decisions which affect people's lives should be moral, as much as that is possible. Christians, by virtue of their presence and participation in the political process, can encourage moral rectitude, justice, peace, equality and reconciliation among people and between peoples and their God. Jamaican Christians could therefore learn much from the important planks in the statement adopted by the House of Delegates of the North Carolina Council of Churches in 1981:

1. While Christians should participate in politics with zeal, they should carefully avoid prideful self-righteousness and dogmatic certitude.

2. Concern for those whom Jesus called "the least of these" must be a dominant factor for Christians in determining political judgments and action.

3. A strong interest in genuine equality and a wide sharing of material and social goods should inform Christian thinking and acting in the political sphere.

4. Government can and does serve many good purposes; it is the agency through which the whole society can act to promote the general welfare and serve the common good.

5. Christians should support public policies which strengthen families especially those with children (House of Delegates 1–5).

CONCLUSION

Many qualified Jamaicans who could make a positive contribution to he national's political future shy away from doing so because of political violence and malfeasance. But the politician does not have an exclusive hold on corruption; it is a societal problem. Even the church, and especially the clergy, is occasionally rocked by scandal of national proportion. If, However, the indifference to politics continues, Christians will exclude themselves from many spheres of endeavours with serious consequences. In order for the political system to work fairly and justly for all Jamaicans, decent, moral, and courageous people will have to enter politics.

This discussion about the Christian's involvement in politics is likely to continue for a long time with no clear solution. What is evident, however, is the fact that there are many levels at which Christians relate to and can get involved in government. The two best known are attitude to authority, dealt with directly in Romans 13:1–7, and speaking out on the issues of the day or standing up for justice and the proper use of authority. Entering politics must remain a live option for the Christian, based on the high view of the state presented in Paul's letter to the Romans as well as the need for moral leadership in Caribbean politics.

Appendix G

Reflections on Theological Education

By Rev'd Anthony Chung

EVERY EDUCATIONAL ENDEAVOR HAS some distinctive and undergirding philosophy upon which it is based. It is this distinctive that sets it apart from the others. Such is the case with theological education. We in theological education feel that there is something in our field that sets us apart from the rest. What are the distinctives? Or, to put it another way: What is it that makes "theological education," theological education? After pursuing theological education for over four years, I have given thought to this question as it relates to what theological education *must* do.

Firstly, theological education must make the student intellectually proficient. By this I mean that our minds and thinking capacities must be expanded and widened as we pursue theological education. As theological students we must be able to examine the issues critically and see what is really at stake; what is central and what is peripheral. Intellectual proficiency means being able to present well thought-out and well reasoned positions on the pertinent issues. The Bible is clear that we are called to use our minds. In a culture that is high on subjectivism, in general, and experience, in particular, those of us in theological education must be the ones who will step back from personal involvement and present truthful, objective, and well reasoned arguments on the issues involved.

At another level, intellectual proficiency is what is needed to respond to heresies within the Church and attacks from without. In many of our churches emotionalism has been equated with true spirituality and reasoning with spiritual coldness. Additionally, experience has

Appendix G

become the measure of most, if not all, things. Against this, we who pursue theological education must be the ones to correct heresies and provide the Biblical position. This can only be used correctly if we are intellectually proficient. From outside the church come the attacks from the self-appointed philosophers of the day. Materialism, relativism, individualism, skepticism, and secular humanism have all been presented at the best way to go in this time. Where are the Christian thinkers of our day who are going to respond and chart a new course? Where will they come from? They must come from among us, from we who are involved in theological education. However, we can only accomplish this task if we are intellectually proficient.

Secondly, theological education must make us ministerially competent. Ministerial competence speaks of effectively serving the needs of those in our churches and our communities. It means being able to listen to them and to answer their existential questions. Ministerial competence means more than just saying "Don't Worry"or"Jesus is the Answer." Ministerial competence means finding out what is the question. Yes, Jesus is the answer, but what is the question? *How* is Jesus the answer in their particular situation? Theological education must prepare us to answer that question. That which is gained in the classroom and in the library must be transferred to the churches, the classrooms and the counseling rooms in which we will serve.

When we leave this institution we must be able to help the mother who has just seen her son gunned down and does not understand why. We must be able to say something to the woman in the ghetto who has six children for six different men and none is providing support. These things are all involved in ministerial competence for they all have to do with serving others. Our theological education must take us beyond the sheltered walls of the classroom and the library. If our theological education does not do that, then it needs to be re-thought. Our theological education must involve a theology of ministry.

Finally, theological education must make us spiritually eminent. Whereas intellectual proficiency has to do with our heads and ministerial competence has to do with our hands, spiritual eminence has to do with our hearts. Or, to change the analogy, whereas intellect relates to what we know and think, and ministry to what we do, spirituality has to do with who we are. There are many instances of people who developed full heads and empty hearts, or, to put it another way, hot heads and cold hearts. However, we are called to have cool heads and warm hearts. Spiritual eminence means that our theological education must draw us closer to God. It means that our relationship with God must deepen as our knowledge about Him increases. Spiritual eminence means that our knowledge about God must be translated into knowledge of God.

It is spiritual eminence that provides the love and power that is so vital for an effective ministry. It is spiritual eminence that will protect us from pride and arrogance, two of the theological students' most present temptations. If our theological education does not result in spiritual eminence, "education" is may be, but "theological education" it most certainly is not.

Bibliography

Adamo, David Tuesday. "Christ as the Anthropological Model." *CJRS* 10 (1989) 23–25.
Adamson, J. B. *The Epistle of James*. Grand Rapids: Eerdmans, 1976.
Adewuya, Ayodiji. *Transformed by Grace: Paul's View of Holiness in Romans 6–8*. Eugene, Oregon: Wipf and Stock, 2004.
Aland, Kurt, et al., eds. *The Greek New Testament*. New York: United Bible Societies, 1983.
Alford, Henry. *The Greek New Testament*. London: Hodder & Stoughton, 1861.
Allen, E. Anthony. *Caring for the Whole Person*. Monrovia: MARC, 1995.
———. "The Healing of Christ," in *Ministry Perspectives from the Caribbean: Essays in Honor of Horace O. Russell*, edited by Eron Henry. New York: CDBCAI, 2010.
Allen, Everard. "Speaking in Tongues." *JBR* (April–June 1986) 4.
Alter, Robert. *The World of Biblical Literature*. London: SPCK, 1992.
Ama, Imani Tafari. "A Rastafari Woman's View of Christian Mission in Jamaica." *JMM* (2004) 97–102.
Anderson, A. A. *The Book of Psalms*. Grand Rapids: Eerdmans, 1972.
Anderson, Keith, et al. *This We Believe: Statement of Faith*. Kingston: EWC, 1988.
Anderson, Neil. *Who I am in Christ*. Ventura, CA: Regal, 2001.
Arichea, Daniel C. "Taking Theology Seriously in the Translation Task." In *Discover the Bible*, edited by Roger Omanson, 234–45. Stuttgart: UBS, 2001.
Aristotle. *The Art of Rhetoric*. Translated by J. H. Freese. LCL. Cambridge, MA: Harvard University Press, 1926.
Armstrong, Karen. *A History of God*. New York: Ballantine, 1993.
Arnold, C. E. *Ephesians Power and Magic: The Concept of Power in Ephesians in Light of its Historical Setting*. Cambridge: Cambridge University Press, 1995.
Aune, David. *Westminster Dictionary of New Testament and Early Christian Literature and Rhetoric*. Louisville: Westminster John Knox, 2003.
Averitt, Richard C. *Hard Passages Commentary*. Richmond, IN: Biblical Research, 1977.
———. *Second Year Greek Grammar*. East Point, GA: Scripture Semantics, 1988.
Baaij, Pieter K. *Paulus over Paulus: Exegetische Studie van Romeinen 7*. Kampen: KOK, 1993.
Bacchiocchi, Samuele. *Women in the Church: A Biblical Study on the Role of Women in the Church*. Berrien Springs, MI: Biblical Perspectives, 1988.
Baldwin, H. Scott. "An Important Word: αὐθεντέω in 1 Timothy 2:12." In *Women in the Church: A Fresh Analysis of I Timothy 2:9–15*, edited by Andreas Kostenberger and T. R. Schreiner, 39–42. Grand Rapids: Baker, 1995.
Balla, Peter. *Challenges to New Testament Theology*. Tübingen: J. C. B. Mohr (Paul Siebeck), 1997.
Barclay, John M. G. "Paul's Story: Theology as Testimony". In *Narrative Dynamics in Paul*. Edited by B. Longenecker. Louisville: Westminster John Knox Press, 2002.

Barclay, William. *The Letters to Timothy, Titus and Philemon*. Edinburgh: St. Andrew Press, 1975.

Barker, Glenn. "2 John." In *The Expositor's Bible Commentary*, edited by Frank E. Gaebelien. Grand Rapids: Zondervan, 1991.

Barnes, Roland S. "Miraculous Gifts of the Spirit: Have They Ceased?" *JPP* 7 (January 1984) 18–33.

Barrett, C. K. *A Commentary on the First Epistle to the Corinthians*. New York: Harper & Row, 1968.

———. *Acts 1–14*. ICC. Edinburgh: T & T Clark, 1994.

———. *A Commentary on the Epistle to the Romans*. New York: Harper & Row, 1957.

Bauckham, Richard. *Gospel Women: Studies in the Named Women of the Gospels*. Grand Rapids: Eerdmans, 2002.

Bauer, W., et al. *A Greek-English Lexicon of the New Testament and Other Early Christian Literature*. Chicago: Chicago University Press, 1957.

———. *A Greek-English Lexicon of the New Testament and Other Early Christian Literature*. Chicago: Chicago University Press, 1979.

———. *A Greek-English Lexicon of the New Testament and Other Early Christian Literature*. Chicago: Chicago University Press, 2000.

Baur, F. C. *Paul the Apostle of Jesus Christ*. London: Williams and Norgate, 1876.

Baxter, Sidlow. *Does God Still Guide?* London: Marshall, Morgan & Scott, 1968.

Beck, James. *The Healing Words of Jesus*. Grand Rapids: Baker, 1993.

Beck, J. R., and B. Demarest. *The Human Being in Theology and Psychology: A Biblical Anthropology for the Twenty-First Century*. Grand Rapids: Kregel, 2006.

Beekman, John, and J. Callow. *Translating the Word of God*. Grand Rapids: Zondervan, 1974.

Belleville, Linda. "A Re-examination of Romans 16:7 in Light of Primary Source Materials." *NTS* 51 (2005) 231–249.

Bennett, Dennis. *The Holy Spirit and You*. Eastbourne, Sussex: KingswayPublications, 1971.

Berkhof, L. *The History of Christian Doctrine*. Grand Rapids: Baker, 1975.

Betz, Hans-Dieter. *Galatians: A Commentary on Paul's Letter to the Churches in Galatia*. Hermeneia, Philadelphia: Fortress, 1979.

Betz, H. D., and Margaret M. Mitchell. "First Epistle to the Corinthians." In *ABD* 1139–1147. New York: Doubleday, 1992.

Bittlinger, Arnold. *Gifts and Graces*. Grand Rapids: Eerdmans, 1968.

Black, Dameon. "Pastoral Ministry and Church Growth in Light of the Ephesian Paradigm for Growth: A Study of Ephesians 4:11–16 with Application to the Associated Gospel Assemblies." CGST Thesis, 2002.

Black, David. *Paul: Apostle of Weakness*. New York: Peter Lang, 1984.

Black, D. A., ed. *Linguistics and New Testament Interpretation*. Nashville: Broadman, 1992.

Black, Matthew. *Romans*. London: Marshall, Morgan & Scott, 1973.

Black, Napoleon. *Role of Women*. Kingston: Unpublished. N. D.

———. *When He Ascended: Rediscovering the Gifts of the Holy Spirit and Their Importance to the Church of the Twenty First Century*. Kingston: Yanique, 2006.

Blass, F., et al. *A Greek Grammar of the New Testament and Other Early Christian Literature*. Chicago: Chicago University Press, 1961.

Boers, H. *The Justification of the Gentiles: Paul's Letters to the Galatians and Romans*. Peabody, Massachusetts: Hendrickson, 1994.
Boice, James. M. "Galatians." In *Expositor's Bible Commentary*, vol. 10, edited by F. Gaebelein. Grand Rapids: Zondervan, 1976.
———. *Foundations of the Christian Faith*. Downers Grove, IL: Inter-Varsity Press, 1986.
Boring, Eugene M., et al. *Hellenistic Commentary to the New Testament*. Nashville: Abingdon, 1995.
Bornkamm, G. *Paul*, translated by D. Stalker. New York: Harper & Row, 1969.
Bosch, David J. *Transforming Mission: Paradigm Shifts in Theology of Mission*. Maryknoll, New York: Orbis, 1991.
Bradshaw, M., and Savage, P. "The Gospel, Contextualization, and Syncretism Report." In *Let the Earth Hear His Voice*, edited by J. D. Douglas, 224-28. Minneapolis: World Wide Publications, 1975.
Bratcher, Robert G., and Eugene A. Nida. *A Translator's Handbook on Paul's Letter to the Ephesians*. Stuttgart: United Bible Societies, 1982
Bray, Gerald. *Ancient Christian Texts: 1-2 Corinthians*. Downers Grove: IVP Academic, 2006.
Brown, Colin. *That You May Believe*. Grand Rapids: Eerdmans, 1985.
Browning, W. R. F., ed. *Oxford Dictionary of the Bible*. New York: Oxford: Oxford University Press, 1997.
Brunner, Emil. *The Christian Doctrine of Creation and Redemption*. London: Lutterworth, 1952.
———. *Man in Revolt*. Philadelphia: Westminster, 1947.
Bruce, F. F. *The Acts of the Apostles: The Greek Text with Introduction and Commentary*. London: Tyndale Press, 1951.
———. *1 & 2 Corinthians*. London: Marshall Morgan & Scott, 1971.
———. *Commentary on Galatians*. Grand Rapids: Eerdmans, 1982.
———. *Paul: Apostle of the Heart Set Free*. Grand Rapids: Eerdmans, 1977.
———. *In retrospect: Remembrance of Things Past*. London: Pickering and Inglis.1980.
———. Bruce, F. F. *Romans*. Grand Rapids: Eerdmans, 1985.
———. *A Mind for What Matters*. Grand Rapids: Eerdmans, 1990.
Bruner, Fredrick Dale. *A Theology of the Holy Spirit*. Grand Rapids: Eerdmans, 1970.
Bullinger, E. W. *Figures of Speech Used in the Bible Explained and Illustrated*. Grand Rapids: Eerdmans, 1968.
Bultmann, Rudolf. *Essays Philosophical and Theological*, Translated by C. James, and G. Greig. New York: Macmillan, 1955.
———. *Theology of the New Testament*, translated by Kendrick Grobel. New York: Scriber's, 1968.
———. "καύχημα κτλ." In *TDNT* 3: 645-654.
Burdick, Donald W. *Tongues: To Speak or Not to Speak*. Chicago: Moody, 1968.
Burgess, Stanley M., and Gary B. McGee, eds. *Dictionary of Pentecostal and Charismatic Movements*. Grand Rapids: Zondervan, 1988.
Burton, E. D. *Syntax of the Moods and Tenses in New Testament Greek*. Grand Rapids: Kregel, 1976.
Buswell, James O. III. "Contextualization: Theory, Tradition and Method." In *Theology and Mission*, edited by David J. Hesselgrave, 87-111. Grand Rapids: Baker Book House, 1978.

Byfield, Bevis. "Theology from Below." In *Social Change: Christianity and Social Science Perspectives*, edited by Judith Soares. Kingston: UWI, 1978.
Caird, G. B. *New Testament Theology*. Oxford: Clarendon, 1994.
Cairns, Earl E. *Christianity Through the Centuries*. Grand Rapids: Zondervan, 1981.
Callow, Katherine "The disappearing *de* in 1 Corinthians." In *Linguistics and New Testament Interpretation*, edited by D. A. Black. Nashville: Broadman, 1992.
Calvin, Jean. *Épitre aux Romains*. Strasbourg Aix-en-provence: Éditions Kerygma, 1978.
Calvin, John. *The Epistles of Paul the Apostle to the Romans and Thessalonians*, translated by Ross Mackenzie. Grand Rapids: Eerdmans, 1960.
Campbell, C. R. *Verbal Aspect: The Indicative Mood and Narrative*. Berlin: Peter Lang, 2007.
Campbell, Douglas. *The Deliverance of God: An Apocalyptic Re-reading of Justification in Paul*. Grand Rapids: Eerdmans, 2009.
Campbell, R. Alastair. *The Story We Live By: A Readers Guide to the New Testament*. Oxford: The Bible Reading Fellowship, 2004.
Caragounis, Chris C. *The Development of Greek and the New Testament*. Tübingen: J. C. B Mohr (Paul Siebeck), 2004.
Carson, D. A. *Divine Sovereignty and Human Responsibility: Biblical Perspectives in Tension*. London: Marshall, Morgan and Scott, 1981.
———. *Exegetical Fallacies*. Grand Rapids: Baker, 1984.
———. *Showing the Spirit: A Theological Exposition of 1 Corithians 12–14*. Grand Rapids: Baker, 1987
———. "Reflection on Christian Assurance." *WTJ* 54 (1992) 1–29.
———. *For the Love of God*. Wheaton, Ill: Crossway, 1998.
———. "Why Trust a Cross? Reflections on Romans 3: 21–26." *ERT* 28 (2004) 345–362.
———. *Christ and Culture Revisited*. Grand Rapids: Zondervan, 2008.
Carson, D. A., and D. J. Moo. *An Introduction to the New Testament*. Grand Rapids: Zondervan, 2005.
Carlson, David E. *Counseling and Self-Esteem*. Waco: Word, 1995.
Carter, John D. "Psychology Sin and the DSM: Convergence and Divergence." *JPT* 22 (1994) 377–385.
Carter, John, D., and Bruce Narramore. *The Integration of Psychology and Theology*. Grand Rapids: Zondervan, 1979.
Chae, Daniel Jong-Sang. *Paul as Apostle to the Gentiles: His Apostolic Self-Awareness and its Influence on the Soteriological Argument in Romans*. Carlisle: Paternoster, 1997.
Chevannes, Barry. *Betwixt and Between: Explorations in an African-Caribbean Mindscape*. Kingston: Ian Randle, 2006.
Childs, Brevard. *Isaiah*. Louisville: Westminster (John Knox), 2001.
Chirichigno, G., and G. Archer, eds. *Old Testament Quotations in the New*. Eugene, Oregon: Wipf & Stock, 2005.
Chisholm, Clinton A. *A Matter of Principle*. Spanish Town, Jamaica: Autos Books, 1997.
———. "The Resurrection of Jesus Christ." *Binah* 1 (1996) 8–12.
———. "Female Head Covering." *JBR* (August, 1985) 4.
Chisholm, Robert B. *From Exegesis to Exposition*. Grand Rapids: Eerdmans, 1998.
Clarke, David. K. "Interpreting the Biblical Words for Self." *JPT* 18 (1990) 309–317.
Clarke, Knolly. "Liturgy and Culture in the Caribbean." In *Troubling of the Waters*, edited by Idris Hamid, 147–57. San Fernando, Trinidad: Rahaman Printer, 1973.

Clarke, Peter. "New Religious Movements." In *Dictionary of Biblical Interpretation*, edited by R. J. Coggins, and J. L. Houlden, 493-4. London: SCM, 1994.

Coad, F. R. *A History of the Brethren Movement*. Exeter: Paternoster, 1968.

Coe, Shoki. "Contextualizing Theology." In *Mission Trends*, edited by Gerald H. Anderson and Thomas F. Stransky, 19-24. New York: Paulist Press, 1976.

Coke, Yvonne. *Eternal Father Bless our Land: Father Hugh Sherlock*. Kingston: LMH Publishing, 2000.

Cole, Donovan D. "Spiritual Gifts." Paper presented to the Christian Education Department of CGST. Mimeographed, 1987.

Colson, Charles. *How Now Shall We Live?* Wheaton: Tyndale, 1991.

Collins. Gary. *Man in Transition: The Psychology of Human Development*. Carol Stream: Creation House, 1991.

Conn, Harvie M. "Contextualization: A New Dimension for Cross-Cultural Hermeneutic." *EMQ* 14 (January 1978) 39-46.

———. "Contextualization: Where Do We Begin?" In *Evangelicals and Liberation*, edited by Carl E. Amerding, 90-119. Nutley, New Jersey: Presbyterian and Reformed Publishing Co., 1977.

Connor, Kevin. *The Epistle to the Romans*. Portland, OR: City Christian Publishing, 1998.

Conrad, William E., ed. *The Mission of an Evangelist: Amsterdam 2000*. Minneapolis: World Wide Publications, 2001.

Conzelmann, Hans. *1 Corinthians*. Hermeneia, Philadelphia: Fortress, 1975.

Cosgrove, Mark P. *The Essence of Human Nature*. Grand Rapids: Zondervan, 1977.

Cousar, C. B. *Philippians and Philemon: A Commentary*. Louisville: Westminster (John Knox), 2009.

Crafton, J. "Paul's Rhetorical Vision and the Purpose of Romans: Towards a New Understanding." *NovT* 33 (1990) 317-39.

———. *The Agony of the Apostle*. Sheffield: Sheffield University Press, 1991.

Craigie, Peter. *Psalms 1-50* . WBC. Waco: Word, 1983.

Cranfield, C. E. B. "The Message of James." *SJT* 18 (1965)182-193, 338-345.

———. *A Critical and Exegetical Commentary on the Epistle to the Romans*. ICC. Edinburgh: T & T Clark, 1979.

———. *Romans: A Shorter Commentary*. Grand Rapids: Eerdsman, 1985

Cullmann, Oscar. *Christ and Time*, translated by Floyd V. Filson. Philadelphia: Westminster, 1964.

Culver, Robert. "Let Your Women Keep Silent." In *Women in Ministry: Four Views*, edited by Bonnidell Clouse and Robert Clouse. 25-54. Grand Rapids: Zondervan, 1989.

Custance, Arthur. *The Three Sons of Noah*. http://www.custance.org/library/vol.1.index.html.

Dana, H. E., and J. R. Mantey. *Manual Grammar of the Greek New Testament*. Toronto: Macmillan, 1955.

Danby, Herbert. *The Mishnah*. Oxford: Oxford University Press, 1933.

Darnisch, Lorreta. *Paul and Third World Women Theologians*. Collegeville, Minnesota: Liturgical Press, 1999.

Daughters, Kenneth Alan. "How to Win over Sin: An exposition of Romans 6." The EJ 1 (1991) 113-128.

Davies, R. E. *I Will Pour out My Sprit*. Kent: Monarch, 1992.

Davies, W. D. and D. C. Allison Jr. *A Critical and Exegetical Commentary on the Gospel According to St. Matthew*, vol. 1, ICC. Edinburgh: T. & T. Clark, 1988.

Davies, W. D. *Paul and Rabbinic Judaism*. London: SPCK, 1962.

Dawkins, Richard. *The God Delusion*. Boston: Houghton Mifflin, 2006.

D' Angelo, Rose. "Rehab." In *Women in Scripture*, edited by Carol Meyers. Grand Rapids: Eerdmans, 2000.

DeArtega, W. *Quenching the Spirit: Examining Centuries of Opposition to the Moving of the Spirit*. Lake Mercy, FL: Creation House, 1992.

Deere, Jack. *Surprised By the Power of the Spirit*. Grand Rapids: Zondervan, 1993.

Deissmann, G. Adolph. *Paul: A Study in Social and Religious History*, translated by W. E. Wilson. New York: Harper and Brothers, 1927.

Deissmann, G. Adolph. *Light from the Ancient East*. London: Hodder and Stoughton, 1910.

Demas, Raphael, ed. *Plato Selections*. New York: Charles Scribner's & Sons, 1927.

Dennis, Carlton. *Proverbs and People: A Comparative Study of Afro-Caribbean and Biblical Proverbs*. Ann Arbor, MI: UMI, 1995.

Denny, James. "Romans." In EGT, edited by W.R. Nicoll. London: Hodder and Stoughton, 1912.

Dibelius, M. *The Epistle of James*. Philadelphia: Fortress, 1976.

Dick, Devon. *The Cross and the Machete: Native Baptists in Jamaica-Identity, Ministry and Legacy*. Kingston: Ian Randle, 2010.

Dickason, Fred. *Angels: Elect and Evil*. Chicago: Moody, 1975.

———. *Demon Possession and the Christian*. Westchester.ILL: Crossway, 1987.

Dillow, Joseph. *Speaking in Tongues*. Grand Rapids: Zondervan, 1975.

DiMarco, Angelico-Salvatore. "Rhetoric and Hermeneutic—On a Rhetorical Pattern: Chiasmus and Circularity." In *Rhetoric and New Testament Essays from the 1992 Heidelberg Conference*, edited by Stanley E. Porter, and Thomas H. Olbricht. Sheffield: Sheffield Academic Press, 1993.

Dodd, Brian. *Paul's Paradigmatic 'I': Personal Examples as Literary Strategy*. Sheffield: Sheffield Academic Press, 1999.

Dodd, C. H. *The Epistle of Paul to the Romans*. London: Harper and Brothers, 1932.

Dominy, B. "Paul and Spiritual Gifts." *Southwestern Journal of Theology* 26 (Fall 1983) 49–68.

Donaldson, T.L. "Jewish Christianity, Israel's Stumbling, and the *Sunderweg* Reading of Paul". *JSNT* 29 (2006) 27–54.

Douglas, J. D., ed. *The New International Dictionary of the Christian Church*. 2d ed. Grand Rapids: Zondervan, 1978.

Drane, John W. "Christian Responses to the New Age Spirituality." *ERT* (1997) 332–340.

Dunn, James D.G. *Baptism in the Holy Spirit*. London: SCM, 1970.

———. *Jesus and the Spirit*. Philadelphia: Westminster, 1975.

———. "Prophetic 'I'-Sayings and the Jesus Tradition: The Importance of Testing Prophetic Utterances within Early Christianity." *NTS* 24 (1978) 175–98.

———. *Romans 1–8*. WBC. Waco: Word, 1988.

———. *The Epistles to the Colossians and to Philemon*. Carlisle: Paternoster, 1996.

———. *The Theology of the Apostle Paul*. Grand Rapids: Eerdmans, 2006.

Dyer, Kevin. "Where Have all the Prophets Gone?" *Interest* (September 1982) 6–7.

Earle, K. Eleanor. *Seasons of Life*. Kingston: KEN, 2000.

Earle, Ralph. *Word Meanings in the New Testament*. Grand Rapids: Baker, 1982.
Easy, Oswald N. *The Priesthood of the Believer*. Kingston: Christian Press, 1987.
Edgar, Thomas R. "Cessation of the Sign Gifts." *BibSac* 145 (October–December, 1988) 371–86.
Edmonds, Ennis. "The Ecological Crisis: Is Christianity Responsible?" *BINAH* 2 (1997) 63–76.
Edwards, Clyde. "Statement of Faith." *AA* 5 (June, 1987) 2.
Edwards, James R. *Romans*. Peabody: Hendrickson, 1992.
Edwards, Ted. "Gifts: Miraculous and manifested." Paper presented at special meeting of Bible teachers, Christian Missions, Kingston. Mimeographed, 1985.
———. *Let Us Reason*. Kingston: Hallmark, 1978.
Eissfeldt, Otto. *The Old Testament: An Introduction*, translated by P. R. Ackroyd. New York: Harper & Row, 1965.
Ehrman, Bart. *A Brief Introduction to the New Testament*. New York: OUP, 2008.
EWC. Proposed Statement of Faith. Kingston, Jamaica. Mimeographed, 1986.
Ellis, E. Earle. "How the New Uses the Old." In *New Testament Interpretation: Essays on Principles and Methods*, edited by I. H. Marshall. 199–219. Exeter: Paternoster, 1977.
Ellis, E. E. "2 Corinthians 5: 1-10 in Pauline Eschatology". *NTS* 6 (1960) 211–24.
Ellington, John. "Wit and Humour in Bible Translation." *BT* 42 (1991) 301–13.
Elwell, Walter, and Robert Yarbrough. *Encountering the New Testament*. Grand Rapids: Baker, 1998.
Elwell, Walter A., ed. "Image of God." In *Evangelical Dictionary of Biblical Theology*, by David L. Turner. Grand Rapids: Baker, 1997.
———. *Handbook of Evangelical Theologians*. Grand Rapids: Baker, 1993.
———. *Evangelical Dictionary of Theology*. Grand Rapids: Baker, 1984.
Epictetus. *The Discourses I-II*, translated by W.A. Oldfather. LCL. Cambridge, MA: Harvard University Press, 1926.
Erickson, Millard. *Christian Theology*. Grand Rapids: Baker, 1985.
Ericson, Norman R. "Implications from the New Testament for Contextualization." In *Theology and Mission*, edited by David J. Hesselgrave, 71–85. Grand Rapids: Baker Book House, 1978.
Ervin, Howard M. *Conversion-Initiation and the Baptism of the Holy Spirit.* Peabody, MA: Hendrickson. 1984.
Eusebius. *Ecclesiastical History*. Vol. 1, translated by K. Lake. Cambridge, MA: Harvard University Press, 1926.
Evans, C. A. "Paul and the Prophets." In *Romans & the People of God*, edited by S. V. Soderlund and N. T. Wright. Grand Rapids: Eerdmans, 1999.
Evans, Tony. *Our God is Awesome: Encountering the Greatness of our God*. Chicago: Moody, 1994.
Fanning, Buist M. *Verbal Aspect in New Testament Greek*. Oxford: Clarendon, 1990.
———. "The Theology of James." In *A Biblical Theology of the New Testament*, edited by Roy B. Zuck. Chicago: Moody, 1994.
Fashole-Luke, E. W. "The Quest for African Christian Theologies." In *Mission Trends No. 3: Third World Theologies*, edited by Gerald H. Anderson, and Thomas F. Stransky, 133–50. New York: Paulist Press, 1976.
Fee, Gordon D. *God's EmpoweringPresence*. Peabody: Hendrickson, 1994.
———. *1 & 2 Timothy, Titus*. Peabody, MA: Hendrickson, 1988.

———. "*First Corinthians: The New International Commentary on the New Testament*. Grand Rapids: Eerdmans, 1987.

———. *New Testament Exegesis: A Handbook for Student and Pastors*. Philadelphia: Westminster, 1983.

Fee, Gordon D., and Douglas Stuart. *How to Read the Bible for All it's Worth*. Grand Rapids: Zondervan, 1982.

Ferreira, Jo-Anne. "Understanding Caribbean Culture," CETA Consultation, Trinidad (cassette), 2003.

Findlay, C. G. "St. Paul's First Epistle to the Corinthians." In *The Expositor's Greek Testament*, vol. 2, edited by W. Robert Nicoll. Grand Rapids: Zondervan, 1976.

Fitzmyer. Joseph A. *Romans*. New York: Doubleday, 1993.

Foh, Susan. "The Head of the Woman is the Man." In *Women in Ministry: Four Views*, edited by Bonnidell Clouse and Robert Clouse. 69–105. Grand Rapids: Zondervan, 1989.

Friesen, Gary. *Decision Making and the Will of God: A Biblical Alternative to the Traditional View*. Portland: Multnomah, 1980.

Fung, R. Y. K. *The Epistle to the Galatians*. Grand Rapids: Eerdmans, 1988.

Fung, R. Y. K. "Ministry in the New Testament." In *The Church in the Bible and the World*, edited by D. A. Carson, 158–77. Exeter: Paternoster, 1987.

Gabelein, F. ed. *The Expositor's Bible Commentary*, Vol. 1. Grand Rapids: Zondervan, 1979.

Gaffin, Richard B. *Perspectives on Pentecost*. Phillipsburg, NJ: Presbyterian and Reformed, 1979.

———. "A Cessationist View." In *Are Miraculous Gifts for Today?* Edited by W. Grudem, 23–64. Grand Rapids: Zondervan, 1996.

Gamble, Harry. *A Textual History of the Letter to the Romans*. Grand Rapids: Eerdmans, 1977.

Gangel, Kenneth. "Christian Higher Education at the End of the 20th Century-Part 2: Integrating Faith and Learning." *Bib Sac* 135 (1978) 99–110.

———. "Moral Entropy, Creation, and the Battle for the Mind." *Bib Sac* 137 (1980) 56–169.

Gayle, Clement. "Varieties of Spirituality in the Church." *CJRS* (July 1984) 14–21.

Garland, David. *1 Corinthians*. Grand Rapids: Baker, 2003.

Gasque, Ward W., and P. Ellis. *In God's Community*. Wheaton, IL: Harold Shaw, 1979.

Gaston, L. "Paul and Torah". In *Anti-Semitism and the Foundation of Christianity*, edited by A. T. Davies. New York: Paulist, 1979.

Gathercole, S. J. "Justified by Faith, Justified by Blood: The Evidence of Romans 3:21-4:25." In *Justification and Variegated Nomism: The Paradoxes of Paul*, edited by D. A. Carson, et al. Tübingen: Mohr Siebeck, 2004.

Gee, Donald. *Concerning Spiritual Gifts*. Springfield, MO: The Gospel Publishing House, n.d.

Geisler, Norman. *From God to Us*. Chicago: Moody, 1974.

———. *Creating God in the Image of Man?* Minneapolis: Bethany, 1997.

———. *Miracles and Modern Thought*. Grand Rapids: Zondervan, 1982.

Gladston, Jerry and Charles Plott. "Unholy Wedlock?: The Perils and Promises of Applying Psychology to the Bible." *JPC* 10 (1991) 54–64.

Gordon, Grace. "Deeper Life Ministries: Beginnings of the Charismatic Movement in Jamaica." *CEC* 1 (July 1984) 3–4.

Gorringe, Timothy. *Furthering Humanity: A Theology of Culture*. Hampshire, UK: Ashgate.

Grassmick, John D. *Principles and Practice of Greek Exegesis*. Dallas: DTS, 1974.

Green, Clifford. *Bonhoeffer: A Theology of Sociality*. Grand Rapids: Eerdmans, 1999.

Green, David Samuel. *New Horizon in Male-Female Relationships*. Eugene, Oregon: Wipf & Stock, 2010.

Green, M. *Evangelism in the Early Church*. London: Hodder and Stoughton, 1970.

Greenlee, J. *Introduction to New Testament Textual Criticism*. Grand Rapids: Eerdmans, 1964.

Gregory, Howard. *"En Route to a Pastoral Counseling Model for the Caribbean: A Survey of the Methodology of Caribbean Theology."* CJRS 11(1990) 3-39.

Grieb, A. Katherine. *The Story of Romans: A Narrative Defense of God's Righteousness*. Louisville/London: Westminster John Know Press, 2002.

Gromacki, Robert. *The Modern Tongues Movement*. Philadelphia: Presbyterian and Reformed, 1967.

Grosheide, F. W. *Commentary on the First Epistle to the Corinthians*. NICNT. Grand Rapids: Eerdmans, 1953.

Grudem, Wayne. *The Gift of Prophecy in 1 Corinthians*. Washington: University Press of America, 1982.

———. *The Gift of Prophecy in the New Testament and Today*. Westchester, Illinois: Crossway, 1988.

———. *1 Peter*. Grand Rapids: Eerdmans, 1988.

———. "Why Christians Can Still Prophesy." *CT* 32 (September 1988) 24-35.

———. *Systematic Theology*. Grand Rapids: Zondervan, 1994.

Gundry, Robert H. *Soma in Biblical Theology*. Grand Rapids: Zondervan, 1987.

Gundry, Stanley. *New Testament Survey*. Grand Rapids: Zondervan, 1970.

Guthrie, Donald. *The Pastoral Epistles*. Grand Rapids: Zondervan, 1957.

———. *New Testament Introduction*. Downers Grove, IL: IVP, 1970.

Hagner, D. "C. H. Dodd." In *Dictionary of Major Biblical Interpreters*, edited by D.K. McKim. Nottingham: IVP, 2007.

Haacker, Klaus. *Theology of Paul's Letter to the Romans*. Cambridge: CUP, 2003.

Hall, Billy. "Looking Back over 68 years." *AA* (January 1989) 21.

Hamilton, Don. "The Imperative of Holy Living." *Quest* 3 (1996) 7-10.

Harris, Murray. *The Second Epistle to the Corinthians*. NIGTC. Grand Rapids: Eerdmans, 2005.

———. *Colossians and Philemon*. Grand Rapids: Eerdmans, 1991.

———. "2 Corinthians." In *EBC*, edited by Frank E. Gaebelien. Grand Rapids: Zondervan, 1976.

Harris, Sam. *Letter to a Christian Nation*. New York: Alfred A. Knopf, 2006.

Harrison, Everett. "Galatians." In *The Wycliffe Bible Commentary*, edited by C. Pfeiffer. Chicago: Moody, 1962.

———. *Introduction to the New Testament*. Grand Rapids: Eerdmans, 1990.

Harrison, R. K. *Old Testament Times*. Grand Rapids: Eerdmans, 1970.

———. "Sex and its Theology," 248-52. Leviticus. Leicester: IVP, 1980.

Harrisville, Roy A. *Romans*. Minneapolis: Augsburg, 1980.

Hays, Richard B. *The Echoes of Scripture in the Letters of Paul*. New Haven: Yale University Press, 1989.

Hayter, Mary. "On Human Sexuality and the Image of God." In *Christian Theology Reader*, edited by Alister E. McGrath, 483–85. Oxford: Blackwell, 2006.

Heil, John. *Ephesians*. Leiden: Brill, 2007.

Heim, Knut. "The Perfect King of Psalm 72: An Intertextual Inquiry." In *The Lord's Anointed: Interpretation of OT Messianic Texts*, edited by Philip Satterthwaite, et al. Carlisle: Paternoster, 1995.

Hemphill, Kenneth S. *Spiritual Gifts: Empowering the New Testament Church*. Nashville: Broadman, 1988.

Henry, Lancelot. "The Gift and Gifts of the Holy Spirit." Paper delivered at the EWC (Summer 1985) 4- 5.

Hendrickson, W. *Romans*. NTC. Grand Rapids: Baker, 1981.

Hiebert, D. Edmond. "The Unifying Theme of the Epistle of James." *Bib Sac* 135 (1978) 221–231.

———. *The Epistle of James*. Chicago: Moody, 1979.

Hingley, C. J. H. "Evangelicals and Spirituality." *Themelios* 15 (1990) 86–91.

Hoch, C. B. "The Role of Women in the Church: A survey of Current Approaches." *GTJ* 8 (Fall 1988) 241–45.

Hodges, Zane, and Arthur Farstad. *The Greek New Testament According To the Majority Text*. Nashville: Thomas Nelson, 1982.

Hodges, Zane C. "The Purpose of Tongues." *BibSac* 120 (July–September 1963) 229–30.

Hoehner, H. "The Purpose of Tongues in 1 Corinthians," In *Walvoord: A Tribute*, edited by Donald K Campbell. Chicago: Moody, 1982.

———. *Ephesians*. Grand Rapids: Baker, 2002.

Hoekema, Anthony A., et al., *Five Views on Sanctification*. Grand Rapids: Zondervan, 1987.

Hogg, C. F., and W. E. Vine. *The Epistles to the Thessalonians*. Grand Rapids: Kregel, 1914.

Holmes, Michael, ed. *The Apostolic Fathers*. Grand Rapids: Baker, 1999.

Horrell, David G. "Familiar Friend or Alien Stranger? On Translating the Bible." *ET* 116 (2005) 402–408.

Horsley, Richard A. *Archaeology, History and Society in Galilee: The Social Context of Jesus and the Rabbis*. Valley Forge, PA: Trinity Press International, 1996.

———. "1 Corinthians: A Case Study of Paul's Assembly as an Alternative Society." In *Christianity at Corinth: The Quest for the Pauline Church*, edited by E. Edwards and D. Horrell. Louisville: Westminsister (John Knox).

Horton, Stanley, et al. *Five Views on Sanctification*. Grand Rapids: Zondervan, 1987.

House, H. Wayne. "Should a Woman Prophesy or Preach Before Men?" *BibSac* 145 (April-June 1988) 141–161.

———. "Tongues and the Mystery Religions of Corinth." *BibSac* 140 (April-June 1983) 134–50.

Howard, J. Keir. "Neither Male nor Female: An Examination of the Status of Women." *EQ* 55 (May 1983) 31–42.

Howe, Margaret. *Women in Church Leadership*. Grand Rapids: Zondervan, 1982.

Howell, Don N. "Romans 15: 9b-12: Gentiles as Cumulative Focus of Salvation History." In *Interpreting the New Testament Text: Introduction to the Art and Science of Exegesis*, edited by D. Bock and B. Fanning. Wheaton: Crossway Books, 2006.

Hugenberger, G.P. "Women in Church Office: Hermeneutics or Exegesis? A Survey of Approaches to 1 Timothy 2: 8–15." *JETS* 35 (1992) 341–60.

Hughes, P. E. *Second Epistle to the Corinthians*. Grand Rapids: Eerdmans, 1962.
Hultgren, Arland J. "The Pastoral Epistles." In *The Cambridge Companion of St. Paul.* Cambridge: CUP, 2003.
Hurley, James. *Man & Woman in Biblical Perspective*. Leicester: IVP, 1981.
Ironside, Harry A *Romans*. New Jersey: Loizeaux, 1928.
——. *A Historical Sketch of the Brethren Movement*. New Jersey: Loizeaux, 1985.
Jenkins, C. Ryan. "Faith and Works in Paul and James." *BibSac* 159 (2002) 62–78.
Jewett, Paul K. *Man as Male and Female*. Grand Rapids: Eerdmans, 1975.
Jewett, Robert. *Romans*. Hermeneia. Minneapolis: Fortress, 2007.
Jobes, Karen H. *"1 Peter."* BECNT. Grand Rapids: Baker, 2005.
Johnson, Anthony. *Great Jamaicans*. Kingston: TEEJAY, 2001
Johnson Eric L. "A Place for the Bible in Psychological Science." *JPT* 20 (1992) 346–355.
Johnson, Luke Timothy. *Reading Romans: A Literary and Theological Commentary*. Macon, GA: Smith & Helwys, 2001.
——. "The Letter of James." In *The New Interpreter's Bible*, vol. 12. Nashville: Abingdon. 1998.
——. "James, Letter of." *Dictionary of Biblical Interpretation*, edited by John H. Hayes. Nashville: Abingdon, 1999.
Johnstone, Patrick. *Operation World*. Grand Rapids: Zondervan, 1993.
Jong, Paul C. *Our Lord Who Becomes the Righteousness of God (II): The Righteousness of God That Is Revealed in Romans*. Seoul, Korea: Hephzibah Publishing House, 2002.
Kaiser, Walter C., Jr. *Towards and Old Testament Theology*. Grand Rapids: Zondervan, 1978.
——. *Towards an Exegetical Theology*. Grand Rapids: Zondervan, 1981.
Kaiser, Walter Jr. *The Promise-Plan of God: A Biblical Theology of the Old and New Testaments*. Grand Rapids: Zondervan, 2008.
——. and Moisés Silva, *An Introduction to Biblical Hermeneutics: The Search for Meaning*. Grand Rapids: Zondervan, 1994.
Käsemann, E. *Commentary on Romans*. Translated by G. W. Bromiley. London: SCM, 1980.
Kato, Byang H. "The Gospel, Cultural Context and Religious Syncretism." In *Let the Earth Hear His Voice*, edited by J. D. Douglas, 1216–23. Minneapolis: World Wide Publications, 1975.
Keener, Craig, S. *The Bible Background Commentary*. Downers Grove, ILL: IVP, 1993.
Kerr, G. Lloyd. *Song of Solomon*. Downers Grove, ILL: IVP, 1989.
Kim, Seyoon. "Jesus, Sayings." In *DPL*, edited by G. W. Hawthorne, et al. Downers Grove: IVP, 1993.
Kinsler, F. Ross. "Mission and Contest: The Current Debate about Contextualiztion." *Evangelical Missions Quarterly* 14 (January 1978) 23–29.
Kinukawa, Hisako. "Sexuality and Households," in *Mark: Text @ Context*, edited by Nicole Wilkinson Duran et al. Minneapolis: Fortress, 2011.
Kitchen, K. A. *On the Reliability of the OT*. Grand Rapids: Zondervan, 2006.
Klesios, Michael. "The State of the Planet." *National Geographic* (September 2002) 43–50.
Klooster, F.H. "Aspects of the Soteriology of Karl Barth." *BETS* 2 (1959) 6–14.
Knapp, Stephen. "Contextualization and its Implications for U. S. Evangelical Churches and Missions." Abington, PA: Partnership in Mission, 1976.

Knox, John. "Romans 15:14–23 and Paul's Conception of His Apostolic Mission." *JBL* 83 (1964) 1–11.

Koenig, John. *Charismata: Gods Gifts for God's People.* Philadelphia: Westminster, 1978.

Kraft, Charles H. "The Contextualization of Theology." *EMQ* 14 (January 1978) 31–36.

Krentz, Edgar. "1 Thessalonians: Rhetorical Flourishes and Formal Constraints." In *the Thessalonian Debate: Methodological Discord or Methodological Synthesis?* edited by Karl P. Donfried, and Johannes Beutler. Grand Rapids: Eerdmans, 2000.

Kreitzer, L. J. "Kingdom of God," In *DPL*, edited by G. F. Hawthorne, et al. Leicester:IVP, 1993.

Kroll, Woodrow. *The Book of Romans: Righteousness in Christ.* Chattanooga, Tennessee: AMG Publishers, 2002.

Kümmel, Werner Georg. *Introduction to the New Testament.* Nashville: Abingdon, 1966.

———. *The Theology of the New Testament*, translated by John E. Steely. London: SCM, 1974.

———. *Romans 7 und das Bild of Menschen im Neuen Testament.* Munich: Kaiser, 1974.

Ladd, George Eldon. *A Theology of the New Testament.* Grand Rapids: Eerdsman, 1993.

Lampe, P. "The Roman Christians of Romans 16." In *The Romans Debate,* edited by K. P. Donfried. Peabody: Hendrickson, 1991.

Lawrence, William D. "The Traitor in the Gates: The Christian's Conflict with the Flesh. In *Essay in Honor of J. Dwight Pentecost,* edited by Stanley D Toussaint and Charles H. Dwyer. Chicago. Moody, 1986.

Laws, Sophie. "James." In *ABD,* edited by David Noel Freedman. New York: Doubleday, 1992.

Lee, Carol. "A Child of God Looks at the Doctrine of Verbal Plenary Preservation." In *The Burning Spear* 11 (2005) 69–81.

Leon, Oswald. "Literature Review: Role of Women and the Pastorate." Guided Research, Jamaica Theological Seminary, 2005.

Lieber, David, ed. *Etz Hayim: Torah and Commentary.* New York: JPS, 2004.

Liefeld, Walter L. *New Testament Exposition.* Grand Rapids: Zondervan, 1989.

———. "Viewpoint: House Churches." *Interest* (July-August 1990), 3.

Liddell, H. G, and R. Scott. *An Intermediate Greek-English Lexicon.* Oxford: Clarendon, 1997.

Lincoln, Andrew. *Ephesians.* Waco: Word, 1990

Linton, Faith. *The Gene Denham Story: From Jamaica to Africa.* Kingston: SCFSU, 2001.

———. *What the Preacher Forgot to Tell Me: Identity and Gospel in Jamaica.* Ontario: Bay Ridge, 2009.

Lofthouse, W. F. "I and We in the Pauline Letters." *ET* 64 (1952) 242 -245.

Long, D. B. *Tongues Today?* Toronto: EPI, 1977.

Longenecker, Bruce, ed. *Narrative Dynamics in Paul: A Critical Assessment.* Louisville: Westminster John Knox, 2002.

Longenecker, Richard N "The 'Faith of Abraham: Theme in Paul, James, and Hebrews" *JETS* 23 (1977) 203–212.

———. *New Testament Social Ethics.* Grand Rapids: Eerdmans, 1984.

———. *Galatians.* Dallas: Word, 1990.

———. *Biblical Exegesis in the Apostolic Period.* Vancouver: Regent College, 1999.

———. *Paul, Apostle of Liberty: The Origin and Nature of Paul's Christianity.* Vancouver: Regent College, 2003.

Longenecker, Richard, and M. Tenney, eds. *New Dimensions in New Testament Study*. Grand Rapids: Zondervan, 1974.

Loh, I-Jin, and Eugene Nida. *Handbook on Paul's Letter to the Philippians*. New York: UBS, 1995.

Louw, Johannes, and Eugene Nida, ed. *Greek-English Lexicon of the New Testament Based on Semantic Domains*. New York: UBS, 1989.

Lowe, Bruce. "Oh Διά! How is Romans 4:25 to be Understood?" *JTS* 57 (2006) 149–157.

Lowery, David K. "1 Corinthians." In *The Bible knowledge Commentary*, edited by John F. Walvoord and Roy B. Zuck. Wheaton, IL: Victor, 1983.

———. "The Theology of Paul's Missionary Epistles." In *A Biblical Theology of The New Testament*, edited by Roy B. Zuck. Chicago: Moody, 1994.

Lund, N. W. *Chiasmus in the New Testament*. Peabody, MA: Hendrickson, 1970.

Lust, J, E., et al. *GELS*. Stuttgart: Deutsche Bibelgesellschaft, 1992.

Luther, Martin. *Commentary on the Book of Roman*, translated by J. Theodore Mueller. London: Oliphants, 1954.

Lyons, George. *Pauline Autobiography: Toward a New Approach*. Atlanta: Scholars Press, 1985.

Malherbe, A. J. *The Letters to the Thessalonians*. New York: Doubleday, 2001.

Marley, Bob. *Songs of Freedom*. Bath, UK: Wise Publications, 1993.

Marshall, I. Howard. *The Pastoral Epistles*. ICC. London: T & T Clark, 2004.

———. *New Testament Theology*. Downers Grove: IVP, 2004.

Marshall, John W. "Paul's Ethical Appeal in Philippians." In *Rhetoric and the New Testament*, edited by Stanley E Porter, and Thomas H Olbricht. Sheffield: SAP, 1993.

Martin, Ralph P. *New Testament Foundations*. Grand Rapids: Eerdmans, 1978.

———. *The Spirit and the Congregation*. Grand Rapids: Eerdmans, 1984.

———. *James*. WBC. Waco: Word, 1988.

———. *Phillipians*. TNTC. Grand Rapids: Eerdmans, 1988.

———. "Approaches to New Testament Exegesis." In *New Testament Interpretation: Essays on Principles and Methods*, edited by I. H. Marshall. Eugene, OR: Wipf & Stock, 2006.

Marty, Martin. *Reinhold Niebuhr Revisited*. Grand Rapids: Eerdmans, 2009.

Manson, T. W. *Studies in the Gospels and Epistles*. Manchester: Manchester University Press, 1962.

Mayhue, Richard. *Divine Healing Today*. Chicago: Moody, 1983.

McAllister, Godfrey. *You've Got All That it Takes to Succeed*. Kingston: G & M Associates, 1990.

McArthur, John, Jr. *The Charismatics*. Chicago: Moody, 1978.

McCartney, Dan G. *James*. Grand Rapids: Baker, 2009.

McCasland, S. V. "Some New Testament Metonyms for God." *JBL* 68 (June 1949) 99–113.

McDonald, William. *Christ Loved the Church*. Oak Park, IL: Emmaus, 1971.

McGrath, Alister. *The Christian Theology Reader*. Oxford: Blackwell, 1995.

———. "A Particularist View." In *Four Views on Salvation in a Pluralistic World*, edited by D. L. Okholm and T.R. Phillips. Grand Rapids: Zondervan, 1996.

———. *Iustitia Dei: A History of the Christian Doctrine of Justification*. Cambridge: CUP, 1998.

———. *Christian Theology: An Introduction*. Oxford: Blackwell, 2010.

McLemore, C.W. "Defense Mechanisms." In *Baker Encyclopedia of Psychology*, edited by David Benner. Grand Rapids: Baker, 1985.
Meeks, Wayne. *The Writings of St. Paul*. New York: Norton & Company, 1972.
Meier, Paul D., et al. *Introduction to Psychology and Counseling*. Grand Rapids :Baker, 1982.
Merrill, Eugene. "Isaiah 40–55 as Anti-Babylonian Polemic." *GTJ* 8 (1987) 3–18.
Metzger, Bruce M. "The Formulas Introducing Quotations of Scripture in the New Testament and the Mishnah." *JBL* 70 (1951) 297–307.
———. *A Textual Commentary on the Greek New Testament*. Stuttgart: Deutsche Bibelgesellschaft, 1994.
———. *Reminiscences of an Octogenarian*. Peabody, Massachusetts: Hendrickson, 1997.
Middendorf, Michael Paul. *The "I" in the Storm: A Study of Romans 7*. St. Louis: CAP, 1997.
Mitchell, John. "Does God Heal Today?" *BibSac* 122 (January-March 1965) 41–53.
Moffatt, J. *Commentary on 1 Corinthians*. London: Hodder and Stoughton, 1943.
Moiser, J. "Rethinking Romans 12–15." *NTS* 36 (1990) 571–82.
Moltmann, Jürgen. *Weiter Raum: Eine Lebensgeschichte*. Gütersloh: Gütersloher Verlagshaus, 2006.
———. *A Broad Place: An Autobiography*, translated by Margaret Kohl. Minneapolis: Fortress, 2008.
Montague, George. *The Holy Spirit*. New York: Paulist Press, 1976.
Moo. Douglas J. "Israel and Paul in Romans 7:7–12." *NTS* 32 (1986) 122–135.
———. *James*. Grand Rapids: Eerdmans, 1985.
———. *Romans*. Chicago: Moody, 1991.
———. *The Epistle to the Romans*. Grand Rapids: Eerdmans, 1996.
———. *2 Peter, Jude*. Grand Rapids: Zondervan, 1996.
———. *The Letter of James*. Grand Rapids: Eerdmans, 2000.
Moore, Robert. "The Historical Basis of Theological Reflection." In *Troubling of the Waters*, edited by Idris Hamid, 37–45. San Fernando, Trinidad: Rahaman Printery, 1973.
Morris, Leon. *1 Corinthians*. Downers Grove, IL: IVP Academic, 1958.
———. "Commentary on James". *EBC*, vol. 12. Grand Rapids: Zondervan, 1984.
———. *1 Corinthians*. Grand Rapids: Eerdmans, 1985.
———. *Romans*. Grand Rapids: Eerdmans, 1988.
Moule, C. F. D. *An Idiom Book of New Testament Greek*. CUP, 1959.
Moulton, Harold K. *The Challenge of the Concordance: Some New Testament Words Studied in Depth*. London: Samuel Bagster & Sons, 1977.
Moulton, James Hope. *A Grammar of New Testament Greek, volume 1: Prolegomena*. Edinburgh: T & T Clark, 1908.
Moulton, J. H., and George Milligan. *The Vocabulary of the Greek Testament*. Grand Rapids: Eerdmans, 1930.
Mounce, William. *The Pastoral Epistles*. Nashville: Nelson, 2000.
Mounce, H. K .*Basics of Biblical Greek*. Grand Rapids: Zondervan, 1991.
Motyer, Alex. *The Message of James*. Leicester: IVP, 1985.
Muck, Terry. "Spiritual Gifts." *CT* 31 (October 1987) 14–15.
Mulrain, George. "Christ Amidst Crisis." *Caribbean Journal of Religious Studies* 6 (1985) 35–52.
———. "Baptism and Belief in Spirits." *CJRS* 7 (April 1986) 39.

Muilenburg, J. *"Ezekiel."* In *Peake's Commentary on the Bible*, edited by Matthew Black & H. H. Rowley. Surrey: Nelson, 1962.

Murrell, Sam. "Wrestling with the Bible." *CJET* 8 (1987) 35–52.

Murray, John. *The Epistle to the Romans*. Grand Rapids: Eerdmans, 1968.

Mutabaruka. *The First Poems / The Next Poems*. Kingston: Paul Issa, 2005.

Mutabaruka. 'Christianity: 2000 Years of Illusion on the African Mind.' (Cassette). A lecture given at UWI (Mona), Black History month, 2000.

Myers, Charles. "Chiastic Inversion in the Argument of Romans 3–8." *NovT* 35 (1993) 30–47.

Narramore, Bruce. *You Are Someone Special*. Grand Rapids: Zondervan, 1972.

———. "Parent Leadership Styles and Biblical Anthropology." *BibSac* 135 (1978) 345–57

Narramore, Clyde. *The Psychology of Counseling*. Grand Rapids: Zondervan, 1960.

Needham, David. *Birthright*. Portland, OR: Multnomah, 1979.

Neill, Stephen. *The Interpretation of the New Testament: 1861–1961*. London: London University Press, 1966.

Nelson, Melvin R. "The Psychology of Spiritual Conflict." *JPT* 4 (1976) 34–41.

Ness, Alex W. *The Holy Spirit*, vol. 1. Ontario: CCP, 1979.

Nestle, D. E. *Novum Testamentum Graece et Germanice*. Stuttgart: Württembergische Bibelanstalt, 1908.

Nestle, Eberhard, ed. *Novum Testamentum Graece*. Stuttgart: Deutsche Bibelstiftung, 1979.

Nettleford, Rex. *Jamaica in Early Independence: Essays on the Early Years*. Kingston: Heinemann, 1989.

———. *Caribbean Cultural Identity: The Case of Jamaica*. Kingston, Institute of Jamaica, 1978.

Newbigin, L. *Foolishness to the Greeks: Gospel and Western Culture*. Grand Rapids: Eerdmans, 1986.

Newell, William R. *Romans Verse by Verse*. Chicago: Moody, 1938.

Nicholls, Bruce J. "Theological Education and Evangelization." In *Let the Earth Hear His Voice*, edited by J. D. Douglas, 634–48. Minneapolis: World Wide Publications, 1975.

Niebuhr, H. R. *Christianity and Culture*. New York: Harper & Row, 1951.

Noll, Stephen F. "Elim" In *NIDOTTE*, edited by Willem A. Van Gemeren. Grand Rapids: Zondervan, 1997.

Noelliste, Dieumeme. "Faith Transforming Context: In Search of a Theology for a Viable Caribbean." *BINAH* 2 (1997) 45–62.

———. "The Church and Human Emancipation: A Critical Comparison of Liberation Theology and the Latin American Theological Fraternity," PhD diss. Northwestern University, 1987.

Nygren, Anders. *Commentary on Romans*. London: SCM, 1949.

O' Brien, Peter. *Colossians and Philemon*. Grand Rapids: Eerdmans, 1989.

———. *The Epistle to the Philippians*. NIGTC. Grand Rapids: Eerdmans, 1991.

———. *Gospel and Mission in the Writings of Paul: An Exegetical and Theological Analysis*. Grand Rapids: Baker, 1995.

———. *Ephesians*. Grand Rapids: Eerdmans, 1999.

Oliver, Anthony. "Righteousness of God and Man in the Prophets." *BINAH* 2 (1997) 29–44.

Olson, Stanley N. "Pauline Expressions of Confidence in His Addressees." *CBQ* 47 (1985) 282–283.

Osborne, Grant. *Romans*. Downers Grove, IL: IVP, 2004.

Oesterley, W. E. "James." In *EGT*. London: Hodder and Stoughton, 1912.

Owen, Samuel. "Evangelism: Theology, Methods and Message." *AJET* 13 (1994) 86–116.

Packer, J. I. *Keep in Step with the Spirit*. Old Tappan, New Jersey: Revell, 1984.

———. *Concise Theology*. Wheaton, ILL: Tyndale, 1993.

Palmer, D. "The Role of Men." *Christian Publication Newsletter* (April- May 1980) 2.

———. *Spiritual Gifts: An Appraisal of Positions of Christian Brethren in Jamaica*. Ann Arbor, MI: UMI, 1989.

———. "Pauline *Charismata* and the 21st Century." *BINAH* 1(1996) 13–23.

———. "Romans 5 and the Archbishop of Canterbury." *CJET* 5 (2001) 58–70.

———. *Pronominal 'I,' Rastafari and the Lexicon of the New Testament, with Special Reference to Paul's Epistle to the Romans*. Ann Arbor, MI: UMI, 2007.

———. *New Testament Theology in Context*. Kingston, Jahmeckyah: DeoVolente, 2008.

———. *Messianic 'I' and Rastafari in NT Dialogue: BioNarratives, the Apocalypse, and Paul's Letter to the Romans*. Plymouth, UK: UPA, 2010.

Perkins, Anna Kasafi. *Justice as Equality: Michael Manley's Vision of Justice*. New York: Peter Lang, 2010.

Peters, G. H. *A Biblical Theology of Missions*. Chicago: Moody, 1977.

Petersen, Norman R. *Rediscovering Paul: Philemon and the Sociology of Paul's Narrative World*. Philadelphia: Fortress, 1985.

Phillips, John. *Exploring Romans*. Grand Rapids: Kregel, 2002.

Phillips, J. B. *Ring of Truth: A Translator's Testimony*. London: Hodder and Stoughton, 1967.

Phillips, Peter. "Race, Class, Nationalism: Perspective on Twentieth-Century Social Movements in Jamaica." *SES 37* (1988) 3.

Philo. *The Works of Philo*. Peabody, MA: Hendrickson, 1993.

Pierre-Pierre, Maxime. "Theological Education Engaging Culture: Models and Approaches." *CETA Consultation*, Trinidad, 2003.

Piper, John, and Wayne Grudem, eds. *Recovering Biblical Manhood & Womanhood*. Wheaton: Crossway Books, 1991.

Plank, Karl A. *Paul and the Irony of Affliction*. Atlanta: Scholars Press, 1987.

Polkinghorne, G. J. "The Bible in the Church." *CBR* 31 (February 1980) 143–44.

Porter, Stanley E., *Verbal Aspect in the Greek of the New Testament, with Reference to Tense and Mood*. New York: Peter Lang. 1989.

———. *Idioms of the Greek New Testament*. Sheffield: JSOT, 1992.

Pytches, David. "Signs and Wonders Today." *IRM* 85 (April 1986) 137–141.

Quebedeaux, Richard. *The New Charismatics*. New York: Doubleday, 1976.

Rahlfs, Alfred, ed. *Septuaginta*. Stuttgart: Deutsche Bibelgesellshaft, 1979.

Ramachandra, Vinoth. *Gods That Fail: Modern Idolatry and Christian Mission*. Carlisle: Paternoster, 1996.

Ramirez, Eduardo M. "Contextualization in the Local Church." *EMQ* 14 (January 1978) 49–58.

Rapa, Keith. *The Meaning of "Works of the Law" in Galatians and Romans*. New York: Peter Lang, 2001.

Ratzlaff, Dale. *Sabbath in Christ*. Glendale, AZ: Life Assurance Ministries, 2003.

Rea, John. *The Layman's Commentary on the Holy Spirit*. New Jersey: Logo International, 1974.
Reicke, B. I. *The Epistles of James, Peter and Jude*. New York: Doubleday, 1964.
Reumann, John. "Christology of James". In *Who Do Men Say that I Am? Essays on Christology in Honor of Jack Dean Kingsbury*, edited by Mark Allan Powell, David R. Bauer. Louisville: Westminster John Knox, 1999.
Richards, Jo-Ann Faith. *Godincidences: Adventuring with an Awesomely Sovereign, Sovreignly Awesome God*. Bloomington, Indiana: Authorhouse, 2010.
Richardson, W. "Liturgical Order and Glossolalia in 1 Corithians 14:26c- 33a." *NTS* 32 (January 1986) 144–53.
Roberts, A. and J. Donaldson, eds. *The Ante-Nicene Fathers*, vol. 1. Grand Rapids: Eerdmans, 1950.
Roberts, Donald. *Disvovering, Developing & Demonstrating the Gifts of the Spirit within You*. Kingston, JA: DAR, 2004.
Robertson, A T. *A Grammar of the Greek New Testament in the Light of Historical Research*. Nashville: Broadman, 1934.
Robertson, A T., and A Plummer. *A Critical and Exegetical Commentary on the First Epistle of St Paul to the Corinthians*. ICC. Edinburgh: T and T Clark, 1914.
Robertson, A. T., and W. Hersey Davis. *A New Short Grammar of the Greek New Testament*. Grand Rapids: Baker, 1977.
Robertson, Pat. *Answers*. Nashville: Thomas Nelson, 1984.
Robinson, James, et al., eds. *The Sayings Gospel Q in Greek and English, with Parallels from the Gospels of Mark and Thomas*. Minneapolis: Fortress, 2002.
Robinson, John A. T. *Redating the New Testament*. London: SCM, 1976.
———. *Wrestling with Romans*. Philadelphia: Westminster, 1979.
Roetzel, C. *The World That Shaped the New Testament*. Atlanta: John Knox, 2002.
Roper, Garnett. "Equipping the Saints for Ministry." In *The David Jelleyman Lectures*. Kingston: JBU, 1999.
———. "'Signs of the Times: Pastoral Challenges." Paper presented at the Ministerial Conference, JBU, Kingston, 2003.
———. "Jesus Son of the Most High God." In *Messianic 'I' and Rastafari in NT Dialogue*. Plymouth, UK: UPA, 2010.
Ropes, J. H. *A Critical and Exegetical Commentary on the Epistle of St. James*. ICC. Edinburgh: T & T Clark, 1916.
Rose, Terrence B. "Emerging Social Problems in Jamaica and Their Pastoral Implications." *CJRS* 6 (1985) 29–45.
Rowdon, H. H. *The Origin of the Brethren*. London: Pickering and Inglis, 1967.
Royes, Charles. *Roots & Wings: A Legacy of Wealth*. Kingston: CJR, 2010.
Ruef, John. *Paul's First Letter to Corinth*. Philadelphia: Westminister, 1977.
Russell, W. B. "An Alternative Suggestion for the Purpose of Romans". *BibSac* 145 (1988) 174–184.
Ryrie, Charles C. *The Holy Spirit*. Chicago: Moody, 1965.
———. *The Place of Women in the Bible*. Chicago: Moody, 1968.
Sailhamer, John. *The Pentateuch as Narrative*. Grand Rapids: Zondervan, 1992.
Sanday, W., and A.C. Headlam. *A Critical and Exegetical Commentary on the Epistle to the Romans*. ICC. Edinburgh: T & T Clark, 1902.
Sanders, E P. *Paul and Palestinian Judaism: A Comparison of Patterns of Religion*. London: SCM, 1977.

Saucy, Robert L. "Sinners Who Are Forgiven or Saints Who Sin?" BibSac 152 (1995) 400–12

Sawyer, Deborah F. "Feminist Interpretation." In *DBI*, edited by R. J. Coggins, and J. L. Houden. London: SCM, 1990.

Schalatter, A. *The Righteousness of God*. Peabody, MA: Hendrickson, 1995.

Schatzmann, Siegfried. *A Pauline Theology of Charismata*. Peabody: MA: Hendrickson, 1987.

Scherman, Rabbi Nosson, ed. *Tanach*. Brooklyn: Mesorah, 1998.

Schirrmacker, Thomas. *Towards a Theology of Martyrdom: The Persecution of Christians Concerns Us All*. Bonn: Verlag für Kultur und Wissenschaft, 2008.

Scholer, David M. "1 Timothy 2: 9–15 and the Place of Women in the Church's Ministry." In *Women, Authority and the Bible*, edited by Alvera Mickelsen. Downer's Grove: IVP, 1985.

Schmoller, Alfred. *Handkonkordanz zum Griechischen Neuen Testament*. Stuttgart: Deutsche Bibelgesellschaft, 1982.

Schreiner, Thomas R. *Romans*. Grand Rapids: Baker, 1998.

———. *Paul: Apostle of God's Glory in Christ*. Downer Grove, ILL: IVP, 2001.

Schweizer, Eduard. *A Theological Introduction to the New Testament*. Translated by O. R. Dean, Jr. London: SPCK, 1992.

Seifrid, M.A. "Romans." In *Commentary on the New Testament's Use of the Old Testament*, edited by G.K.Beale and D.A. Carson. Grand Rapids: Baker, 2007.

Selassie, Haile. "Building an Enduring Tower." In *One Race, One Gospel, One Task*, edited by C. F. H. Henry and W. S. Mooneyham. Minneapolis: WWP, 1967.

Silva, Moises. *Biblical Words and Their Meaning: An Introduction to Lexical Semantics*. Grand Rapids: Zondervan, 1983.

———. *God, Language and Scripture*. Grand Rapids: Zondervan, 1990.

———. *Philippians*. Grand Rapids: Baker, 2005.

Shulum, Joseph. *A Commentary on the Jewish Roots*. Baltimore, MD: Lederer, 1997.

Smalley, Stephen. *1, 2, 3 John*. Waco: Word, 1991.

Smith, Ashley. *Pentecostalism in Jamaica*. Mandeville: Eureka Press, 1993.

———. "Religion and Contemporary Development." *Caribbean Journal of Religious Studies* 7 (1986) 18–30.

Smith, Charles. *Tongues in Biblical Perspective*. Winona Lake, IN: BMH, 1973.

Smith, J. "The Genre of 1 Corinthians 13 in the Light of Classical rhetoric." *NovT* 33 (July 1991) 193–216.

Snyman, A. H. "Persuasion in Philippians 4:1–20." In *Rhetoric and the New Testament*, edited by Stanley E. Porter and Thomas H. Olbricht. Sheffield: Sheffield Academic Press, 1993.

Southard, Samuel. *Theology and Therapy*. Waco: Word, 1989.

Speiser, E A. "The Creation Epic." In *The Ancient Near East: An Anthology of Texts and Pictures*, vol. 1, edited by J B Pritchard. New Jersey: PUP, 1958.

Spencer, Aida Bensancon. *Paul's Literary Style: A Stylistic and Historical Comparison of 2 Corinthians 11: 16–12:13, Romans 8: 9–39, and Philippians 3:2–4:13*. Lanham: UPA, 1984.

Spencer, Aida B. *Beyond the Curse: Women Called to Ministry*. Peabody, Massachusetts: Hendrickson, 1989.

Springer, James. "West Indian Value System and the Churches Validating Role." In *Troubling of the Waters*, edited by Idris Hamid, 125–38. San Fernando, Trinidad: Rahaman Printery, 1973.

Sproul, R.C. "Works or Faith?" *MSJ* 16 (2005) 1987.

Stavrianos, L S, ed. *Readings in World History*. Boston: Allyn and Bacon, 1962.

Stearns, M. B. "Protestant Theology since 1700." *Bib Sac* 105 (July-September 1948) 320–340.

Stevenson, Leslie. *Seven Theories of Human Nature*. Oxford: OUP, 1974.

Stewart, Donald K. *Purposeful Evangelism and Missions: Missing Dimensions*. Parker, CO: Outskirts Press, 2010.

Stone, Carl. *Democracy and Clientelism in Jamaica*. New Brunswick: Transaction Books, 1980.

———. *Class, State, and Democracy in Jamaica*. Kingston: Institute of Jamaica, 1985.

Stott, John R. W. *The Message of Romans*. Leicester: IVP, 1994.

———. *Involvement: Social and Sexual Relationships in the Modern World*. New Jersey: Revell, 1985.

Stowers, S. K. *A Rereading of Romans: Justice, Jews and the Gentiles*. New Haven, CT: YUP, 1994.

Stott, J. R. W. *The Epistles of St. John*. Grand Rapids: Eerdmans, 1964.

Sue, David, et al. *Understanding Abnormal Behaviour*. Toronto: Haughton Mifflin Company, 1994.

Tamez, Elsa. *The Scandalous Message of James*. New York: Crossroad Publishing, 2002.

Tatford, F. A. *The Islands of the Sea*. Bath, Avon: Echoes of Service, 1986.

Tatham, *Let the Tide Come In*. Carol Stream, ILL: Creation House, 1976.

Taylor, Burchell. *The Church Taking Sides: A Contextual Reading of the Letters to the Seven Churches in the Book of Revelation*. Kingston, JA: BBC, 1995.

———. "Messianic Ideology and Caribbean Theology of Liberation." In *Chanting Down Babylon: The Rastafari Reader*, edited by Nathaniel Samuel Murrell, et al. Philadelphia: TUP, 1998.

Taylor, F. D. *Should I Speak in Tongues?* Toronto: Everyday Publications, 1977.

Tee, Tombari Kpobe. *Free to Speak? The Truth about Silence of Women in the Church in a World of Cultural Diversity*. Kingston: Pelican, 2002.

Thayer, J. H. *Greek-English lexicon of New Testament*. Grand Rapids: Zondervan, 1962.

Theissen, Gerd. *Psychological Aspects of Pauline Theology*. Edinburgh: T & T Clark, 1987.

———. *The Social Setting of Pauline Christianity: Essays on Corinth*. Philadelphia: Fortress, 1988.

Theological Education Fund. *Ministry in Context: The Third Mandate Programme of the Theological Education Fund 1970–1977*. Bromley, England: Theological Education Fund, 1972.

Thiselton, Anthony C. "Realized Eschatology at Corinth." *NTS* 24 (July 1978) 510–26.

Thomas, Donovan. *Confronting Suicide*. Kingston: CLI, 2010.

Thomas, D Winton, ed. *Documents from Old Testament Times*. New York: Harper & Row, 1958.

Thomas, Oral. *Biblical Resistance Hermeneutics within a Caribbean Context*. London: Equinox, 2010.

Thomas, Robert L. *Understanding Spiritual Gifts*. Grand Rapids: Kregel, 1998.

Thompson, Glen. *The Roots of Deception*. Kingston: SRI, 2003.

Thrall, Margaret. *The First and Second Letters of Paul to the Corinthians.* Cambridge: CUP, 1965.
———. *The Second Epistle to the Corinthians 1-7.* ICC. Edinburgh: T & T Clark, 1994.
Tillich, Paul. *Theology of Culture.* London: Oxford, 1959.
Tinkle, Donald, "Evolution, Theory of." In *EB*, edited by Phillip Goetz. Chicago: Encyclopedia Britannica, Inc., 1987.
Tipler, Frank. *The Physics of Immortality.* New York: Doubleday, 1994.
Turnau, Theodore A. "Reflecting Theologically on Popular Culture as Meaningful: The Role of Sin, Grace, and General Revelation." *CTJ* 37 (2002) 270–296.
Turner, M. M. B. "Spiritual Gifts Then and Now." *VE* 15 (1985) 7–64.
Turner, Nigel. *Christian Words.* Edinburgh: T & T Clark, 1980.
Van Unnik, W. C. "The Origin of the Recently Discovered *APOCRYPHON JACOBI.*" In *Sparsa Collecta: The Collected Essays of W. C. Van Unnik.* Leiden: Brill, 1983.
Vanhoozer, Kevin J. "The World Well Staged? Theology, Culture, and Hermeneutics." In *God and Culture,* edited by D. A. Carson & John D. Woodbridge. Grand Rapids: Eerdmans, 1993.
Vassel Sam. "Socio-political Concern of the Gospel of Luke." MA thesis, Wheaton Graduate School, 1982.
———. "Personal Purity." *The ERT* 12 (1988) 359–68.
Vermes, Geza. *Jesus the Jew.* Philadelphia: Fortress, 1981.
———. *The Complete Dead Sea Scrolls in English.* London: Penguin, 1997.
Vincent, M. R. *Epistles to the Philippians and to Philemon.* Edinburgh: T&T Clark, 1897.
Vine, W. E. *Expository Dictionary of New Testament Words.* 4 vols. London: Oliphants, 1940.
———. *1 Corinthians.* London: Oliphants, 1970.
———. *The Epistle to the Romans*: London: Marshall, Morgan & Scott, 1948.
Vorster, W. S. "New Testament Sample Studies." In *Lexicography and Translation,* edited by J. P. Louw. Cape Town: Bible Society of South Africa, 1985.
Wacker, Grant. "American Pentecostals: Who They Are." *CT* 31 (October 1987) 16–21.
Wagner, C. Peter. *Signs and Wonders Today.* Altamonte Springs, FL: Creation House, 1987.
Walker, W. O. "1 Corinthians 11:2–6." *JBL* 95 (March 1975) 94–110.
Wallace, Daniel B. *Greek Grammar Beyond the Basics.* Grand Rapids: Zondervan, 1996.
Waltke, Bruce K., and M. O' Connor. *An Introduction to Biblical Hebrew Syntax.* Winona Lake, Indiana: Eisenbrauns, 1990.
Waltke, Bruce K. *Genesis: Commentary.* Grand Rapids: Zondervan, 2001.
Walton, John. *Genesis.* Grand Rapids: Zondervan, 2001.
Walvoord, John F. "The Holy Spirit and Spiritual Gifts." *BibSac* 143 (April–June 1986) 109–122.
Wanamaker, Charles A. *Commentary on 1 and 2 Thessalonians.* Grand Rapids: Eerdmans, 1990.
Ward, Ronald. *Commentary on 1 & 2 Thessalonians* Waco, TX: Word Books, 1975.
Warner-Lewis, Maureen. *Central Africa in the Caribbean: Transcending Time, Transforming Culture.* Bridgetown: UWI, 2003.
Watson, Duane F. "James 2 and Greco-Roman Argumentation." *NTS* 39 (1993) 94–121.
Watson, W. G. E. *Classical Hebrew Poetry: A Guide to its Techniques.* Sheffield: JSOT. 1986.

Watts, Rikki E. "For I am not Ashamed of the Gospel: Romans 1: 16–17 and Habakkuk 2:4." In *Romans & the People of God*, edited by Sven K. Soderlund and N.T Wright. Grand Rapids: Eerdmans, 1999.

Watty, William, "The De-Colonization of Theology." In *Troubling of the Waters*, edited by Idris Hamis, 49–79. San Fernando, Trinidad: Rahaman Printery, 1973.

Wayne-House, H. "Tongues and the Mystery Religions of Corinth." *BibSac* 140 (1983) 134–50.

Weiss, Karl-Erich. "Die Rastari-Bewegung auf Jamaika." M. Phil. Thesis, Westfasslische Wilhelms-Universitat, Munster, 1986.

Wenham, Gordon. *Genesis 1–15*. Waco: Word, 1987.

Wenham, David. "The Christian Life, a Life of Tension? A Consideration of the Nature of Christian Experience in Paul." In *Pauline Studies: Essays Presented to Professor F.F. Bruce on his 70th birthday, edited by* Donald A. Hagner and Murray Harris. Grand Rapid: Eerdmans, 1980.

———. *Paul: Follower of Christ or Founder of Christianity?* Grand Rapids: Eerdmans, 1995.

Westcott, B. F. *The Epistles of St. John*. London: Macmillan, 1883.

———. *The New Testament in the Original Greek*. New York: Macmillan, 1941.

Westcott, B. F., and F. J. A. Hort. *The Greek New Testament*. Peabody, Massachusetts: Hendrickson, 2007.

Westermann, Claus. *Handbook to the New Testament*. Minneapolis: Augsburg, 1969.

Whiston, William, ed. *The Works of Josephus*. Peabody, MA: Hendrickson, 1987.

Wikenhauser, A. *Pauline Mysticism*. Freiburg: Harder, 1960.

Williams, D. H. "Justification by Faith; A Patristic Doctrine." *JEH* 57 (2006) 649–667.

Williams, A R. "Death on the Nile: A Royal Cemetery Reveals New Clues to Murder, Revenge, and Intrigue in Ancient Egypt." In NG (October 2002) 7–10.

Wilson, Maxine. "Comments." In *Social Change: Christian and Social Science Perspectives*, edited by Judith Soares. Kingston: UWI, 1978.

Wimber, John. *Power Healing*. San Francisco: Harper and Row, 1987.

Witherington, Ben. *Conflict & Community: A Socio-Rhetorical Commentary on 1 and 2 Corinthians*. Grand Rapids: Eerdmans, 1995.

———. *Grace in Galatia: A Commentary on Paul's Letter to the Galatians*. Edinburgh: T & T Clark, 1998.

———. *Paul's Letter to the Romans: A Socio-Rhetorical Commentary*. Grand Rapids: Eerdmans, 2004.

Winer, George Benedict. *A Grammar of the Idiom of the New Testament*. London: Warren F. Draper, 1872.

Winter, B. "1 Corinthians." In *The New Bible Commentary*. Leicester: IVP, 1994.

Wood, Lawrence W. *Pentecostal Grace*. Wilmore, KY: Asbury, 1980.

Wright, N. C. "Restoration and the House Church Movement." *Themelios* 16 (Jan-Feb. 1991) 3–7.

Wright, N. T. *Colossians and Philemon*. Grand Rapids: Eerdmans, 1988.

———. *The New Testament and the People of God*. London: SPCK, 1992.

———. "New Exodus, New Inheritance: The Narrative Structure of Romans 3–8." In *Romans & the People of God*, edited by Sven K. Soderlund and N.T Wright. Grand Rapids: Eerdmans, 1999.

———. "Romans." In *The NIB*, vol. 10. Nashville: Abingdon, 2002.

Wuellner, Wilhelm. 1991. "Paul's Rhetoric of Argumentation in Romans." In *The Romans Debate, edited* by Karl P. Donfried. Peabody, MA: Hendrickson, 1991.

Yagi, S. "'I' in the Words of Jesus." In *The Myth of Christian Uniqueness: Toward a Pluralistic Theology of Religions*, edited by John Hick and Paul Knitter. New York: Orbis, 1987.

Yorke, Gosnell L. O. R. *The Church as the Body of Christ in the Pauline Corpus: A Reexamination.* Washington: UPA, 1991.

———. "Holy Spirit Book, Worthy to be Read." http://www.jamaica-gleaner.com/gleaner/20080503/(spirit)/(spirit)1.html.

Young, Richard A. *Intermediate New Testament Greek: A Linguistic and Exegetical Approach.* Nashville: Broadman & Holman, 1994.

Zemek, George J. "Aiming the Mind: A Key to Godly Living." *GTJ* 5 (1984) 205–27.

Zerwick, Max. *Analysis Philologica Novi Testamenti Graeci.* Romae: PIB, 1984.

Zerwick, M., and M. Grosvenor. *A Grammatical Analysis of the Greek New Testament.* Rome: PBI, 1979.

Scripture Index

Genesis, 17, 23, 25, 26, 29, 33, 43, 47, 49, 50, 52, 53, 67, 68, 93, 147, 148, 154, 162, 163, 164,185, 188, 189, 296, 297
Exodus, 145, 146, 147, 154, 162, 297
Leviticus, 66
Numbers, 33, 113, 154, 260
Joshua, 33
Judges, 15, 185
Ruth, 14
2 Samuel, 134, 149
2 Kings, 213
2 Chronicles, 53
Esther, 211
Job, 245, 265
Psalms, 47, 83, 140, 147, 179, 277, 281
Proverbs, 59, 189, 240, 282
Song of Songs, 188 n. 87
Isaiah, 31, 54, 148, 150, 154, 162, 192, 201, 280, 290
Jeremiah, 27, 28
Ezekiel, 89, 155, 290
Daniel, 173, 231, 251, 277, 280, 296
Joel, 159, 211
Amos, 41
Obadiah, 150
Jonah, xiv
Nahum, 41
Malachi, 149
Matthew, 61, 127, 149, 155, 160, 161, 242, 251, 261, 278, 282, 290
Mark, 29, 30, 33, 35, 58, 67, 74, 104, 112, 155, 157, 160, 172, 175, 184, 220, 251, 270, 293
Luke, 35, 87, 95, 131, 153, 155, 156, 157, 158, 160, 161, 169, 183, 187, 233, 251, 283, 287, 296

John, iv, 9, 11, 14, 15, 17–20, 32, 33, 34, 53, 54, 71, 73, 82, 91–93, 95, 127, 129, 133, 141, 153–158, 160–161, 185, 203, 212, 217–219, 237, 239, 251, 253, 266, 277–278, 280, 281–283, 285–287, 289–298
Acts, 4–9, 14–16, 18–19, 23, 30, 31–33, 35, 54, 62, 64, 67, 71, 73, 87, 90, 100, 131, 138, 140, 149, 153, 1566, 160, 161, 163, 169, 172, 174–176, 180, 202–03, 211–12, 214–15, 217, 224, 250, 253, 265, 260, 278–79
Romans, vii, 16, 19, 20, 34, 39, 41, 43, 44, 47, 49, 51, 55, 57, 59, 62, 81–82, 85–86, 88, 93–96, 100, 129, 131–33, 146, 148–50, 162–66, 178, 193, 200, 203, 205, 214, 246, 248–49, 253, 265–70, 272, 277–78, 280, 284, 286, 290–92, 296–97
1 Corinthians, 280, 293
2 Corinthians, 111, 115–17, 126, 134, 163, 185, 279, 283, 285, 294, 297
Galatians, 86, 98, 102–05, 126, 132, 136, 154, 181, 200, 221, 278–79, 284–85, 288, 292, 297
Ephesians, 8, 121, 124–28, 137, 178, 212–15, 219, 277–79, 285–86, 288, 291
Philippians, 7–8, 57, 102, 117–21, 137, 242, 281, 289, 291, 294, 296
Colossians, 7, 16, 100, 121–23, 125–26, 138, 209, 242, 252, 282, 285, 291, 297
1 Thessalonians, 12, 126, 135, 288
2 Thessalonians, 135, 296,

1 Timothy, 128, 212, 216–18, 223, 277, 286, 294
2 Timothy, 8, 128, 212, 217, 222, 283
Titus, 17, 128, 217–19, 278, 283
Philemon,101, 117, 121,122, 123, 126, 137, 138, 218, 219, 278, 281, 282, 285, 291, 292, 296, 297
Hebrews, 32, 33, 41, 48, 57, 90, 114, 186, 196, 213, 288
James, 58–71, 86–87, 89, 182, 212, 216, 220, 230, 250, 277–79, 281–83, 286
I Peter, 169, n. 9
2 Peter, 85, 290
1 John, 19–20, 32, 34, 91–92, 212, 215, 217, 219, 251, 287
2 John, 212, 218–19, 278
3 John, 212, 218–19, 294
Jude, xv, 58, 290, 292
Revelation, 27, 35, 44, 60, 70, 91, 93, 109, 127, 136, 163, 171, 174, 178–80, 185, 212, 250, 251, 253, 295, 296

Subject Index

A

Abba, 130
Ability, 29, 51, 83, 161, 172–173, 178–179, 204, 224, 233, 263
Abraham, 42–44, 46, 48–53, 55, 66–68, 70–71, 104, 114, 164
Adam, 15, 17, 81, 82, 92, 95, 126, 134, 153, 154, 156
Acts, 4–9, 14–16, 18–19, 23, 30, 31–33, 35, 54, 62, 64, 67, 71, 73, 87, 90, 100, 131, 138, 140, 149, 153, 156, 160–61, 163, 169, 172, 174–76, 180, 202–03, 211–12, 214–15, 217, 224, 250, 253, 265, 260, 278–79
Administration, gifts of, 179
African, 34, 233, 238
Allegorical approach, 218
Allusions, 147, 149, 185, 203
Amos, 41
Anaphora, 171
Anarthrous, 25
Ancient Near East, 22
Angels, 16, 25, 83, 175, 177, 186
Anointed, 115, 137, 156, 160
Antagonists, 109, 115, 119
Antithesis, 108, 249
Apostle, 4–10, 13–15, 17, 19–20, 34, 39–41, 43–48, 50, 52, 55, 67, 74, 77, 80, 85, 95–99, 101, 103–05, 107, 108, 110–116, 118, 120, 122–23, 131–32, 135, 153, 155–56, 162–63, 166–69, 171, 174–75, 177, 185–90, 194, 196, 198–99, 201, 204–07, 209, 214–15, 219, 222, 245, 252–54, 270
Aquila, 212, 217

Aramaic, 10
Archbishop, 34, 72, 73–81, 83, 85, 87, 89, 91, 93, 110, 111, 113, 115, 117, 119, 121, 123
Argumentation, 147, 149
Artemis, 137
Aspect, 6, 11–12, 42, 49, 51, 70, 82, 162, 164, 182, 203, 205, 207, 222, 238, 256
Author, 43, 65, 68, 74, 101, 126, 229, 233, 251
Authority, 101, 111, 114, 119, 128, 160–61, 169, 174, 196, 209, 217, 219, 263, 265, 267–70, 272
Authorized Version, 137, 216
Autobiographical, 95, 97, 100, 128, 146, 209

B

Babel, 30
Baddaraashan, 109
Baptism, 19, 139, 145, 146, 177, 180, 211
Baptizer, 154
Believe, 7, 20, 44, 53–55, 66, 74, 76, 78, 86, 90, 93, 95–96, 104, 106, 112, 122, 125, 127, 132, 146, 149, 150, 156, 159, 163, 172, 183–84, 196, 217, 240, 241, 246, 254, 256, 261, 267, 271, 319
Blood, 6, 24, 25, 34
Boast, 43, 105, 118, 119, 200
Body, 6, 15–19, 24–25, 51, 75, 79, 86, 98, 101, 105, 108, 134, 166, 168, 169, 177, 178, 180, 187, 195, 197, 211, 213, 214, 234
Boldness, 7, 138, 193, 194, 198, 199

Brethren, 5, 106, 107, 137, 180
British Isles, 33
Buddhist perspective, 200
Bustamante Hospital for Children, 245

C

Camus, 74
Canaan, 31, 49
Canon, 14, 49, 127, 174, 183, 218
Carnival, 34
Celibacy, 108, 169, 190
Cessationism, 174, 185–186
Charisma, 169, 170–172, 177–178, 185, 213
Charity, 111, 182
Chiasmus, 58
Christ, 13–19, 21, 41, 46, 54, 57, 62, 73–75, 77–79, 81–82, 84, 87, 91–93, 97–99, 102–07, 110, 113–15, 118–21, 123–27, 133–41, 148, 156, 162, 166, 168, 177, 180, 182, 184–87, 190, 200, 202, 205, 207, 211–16, 222–24, 229, 234–36, 239, 252–54, 256, 269
Christianity, 20, 22, 33, 35, 41, 54, 56, 78, 82, 103, 106, 138, 184, 199, 206, 230, 233, 235–36, 238, 243, 256
Christians, 05, 07, 19, 35, 39–41, 54, 56, 59, 76–78, 84–85, 87, 90, 92, 95, 101, 104, 140, 155, 169, 173, 174, 181, 186–87, 194–96, 202–03, 214, 219, 222, 240, 242, 243, 245, 251–53, 255–58, 261–64, 266–72
Christlikeness, 07, 18
Christological, 58, 103, 141
Church, iv, vii, xi, xiii, xiv, xvii, 4–8, 16, 18–19, 31, 35, 39, 55, 62, 73, 76–79, 83–85, 92, 100, 106–07, 111, 124–25, 127, 132, 135, 137, 141, 146, 159–62, 166–67, 169–70, 177, 179–88, 190, 196, 203, 206–07, 210–20, 222–27, 229–33, 239, 241–42, 251–52, 255–58, 263–65, 267, 268, 272–74

Circumcised, 139
Circumcision, 48–50, 104–05, 118, 242
Civilisation, 23, 29, 34
Clement of Alexandra, 219
Colossians, 7, 16, 100, 121–23, 125–26, 138, 209, 242, 252, 282, 285, 291, 297
Commission, 159–61, 201, 258
Communication, 31, 79, 150, 175, 183, 209, 216, 229, 231–32, 236, 238, 242
Communion, 139, 188
Community, 16, 18, 32, 34–35, 60, 64, 71, 73, 76–77, 83, 86, 93, 105–06, 110, 115–117, 122, 129, 131, 141, 159–60, 166, 169–171, 177–78, 182, 187, 206, 209, 219
Condition, 22, 28–29, 43, 74, 76–78, 80, 90, 127, 133, 163
Confidence, 42, 45, 51–52, 60, 62, 105, 118, 120, 147–148, 197–98, 200, 207
Context, 11–12, 22, 35, 40, 43, 46, 52, 62–63, 66, 68, 74, 82, 88, 91, 93, 95–96, 101, 104, 107, 110, 117, 130–32, 135, 140, 145–47, 149–151, 153, 155, 157, 159, 161, 163, 165–66, 168–69, 176, 178, 183, 185, 189, 194, 197, 199, 202–03, 209, 212–13, 215–19, 225–29, 231, 233, 237, 242–43, 266, 268
Contextualization, 153, 225–244, 279, 281, 283, 287, 288, 292
Corinthians, 92, 105–09, 111, 113, 118, 132, 136, 162, 166, 175–77, 182, 188, 189
Corinthians (First), 280, 293
Corinthians (Second), 111, 115–17, 126, 134, 163, 185, 279, 283, 285, 294, 297
Corruption, 84, 138, 249, 256, 258, 261, 272
Courtroom drama, 32, 148
Creation, 17, 23–26, 35, 51, 76, 83, 90–92, 104–05, 137, 147, 161–162, 252, 261
Credited, 44–48, 52–53, 68, 256

Culture, 17, 21–23, 25, 27, 29–35, 75, 79, 106, 194, 216–17, 227–28, 230, 233–37, 241, 243, 256, 259, 273

D

Dancehall, 34
Daniel, 173, 231, 251, 277, 280, 296
David , 46, 48, 53, 55, 155, 192
Death, 15, 22, 29, 41, 54, 56, 78, 95, 98, 134, 157, 160, 162, 164, 234, 260, 262
Deception, 17, 65, 87, 93, 224
Defence mechanisms, 87
De rigeur, 115
Dei voluntas, 194, 201–203, 250
Deliverance, 32, 39, 57, 63, 99, 148, 187
Demons, 16, 132, 173, 179, 187, 252
Depravity, 17–18, 81, 84–86, 90, 92–93
Destiny, 82, 90, 92–93
Devil, 17, 101, 114, 182
Dialectic of sanctification, viii, 248
Dignity, 17, 21, 81–82, 84, 92–94
Disciples, 15, 53, 156, 160–61, 176, 190, 254
Discourse, 11, 94, 146, 148, 195, 255
Dispensationalists, 61, 181
Diversity, 135, 167–68, 170–72, 177, 182, 239, 244
Divine desires, 250
Divine passives, 132
Doctrine, 14–15, 26, 39, 41, 54, 56, 73, 75, 83, 103, 162, 180–81, 201, 220–24
Dodd, 52, 72, 102, 104–05, 108, 111–113, 115, 117, 120, 122, 128, 213
Doxology, 121, 150
Drama, 24, 32, 148

E

Eagle, 155
Early Church, 182–83, 210, 219, 242
Ecclesiology, 39
Echoes, 42, 52, 58, 122, 147–50, 197, 208

Eden, 189
Edification, 05, 19, 39, 131, 160, 183, 186–87, 214
Education, 21, 34, 58, 75–77, 227–29, 231, 234, 237, 242, 244, 263, 273–75
Egō eimi, 94 n.1
Egyptians, 29, 252
El, 30, 191
El Numero Uno, 191
Elders, 06, 07, 18, 214
Elohim, 25, 83
Emancipation, 35, 256–57, 264
Encouragement, 51, 113, 120, 137, 177
Enuma Elish, 23, 24
Ephesians, 8, 121, 124–28, 137, 178, 212–15, 219, 277–79, 285–86, 288, 291
Epictetus, 204
Epistle, 39–40, 50–52, 55, 58–59, 61–62, 72–73, 100, 102, 104, 106, 112–117, 123, 125, 130, 136–37, 149, 166, 168, 182, 193, 198–99, 207, 218
Equipping the Saints, 178, 213
Eschatology, 39–40, 159, 187, 239
Espeut, Peter, 81
Esther, 211
Ethics, 29, 220, 261
Ethos, 118–120, 236
Euphrates, 49
Evangelization, 39, 160, 164, 227–28, 231, 237
Eve, 17, 82, 126, 153–54, 257, 262
Evolution, 23, 83
Example, 03, 07, 10–11, 18–19, 23, 29, 33, 35, 46, 52–53, 61, 66, 69, 75–76, 83, 85, 88–89, 91, 93, 102, 111, 119, 122, 128, 134, 146–50, 153–54, 159, 172–73, 180–81, 183, 186–88, 201–03, 212–13, 215–17, 228, 230, 234, 236, 241–42, 253, 256–57, 268
Exodus, 145–147, 154, 162, 297
Exordium, 103, 122
Ezekiel, 89, 155, 290

F

Face facing face, 185
Faith, 13, 15–17, 20, 35, 40, 43–45, 47–57, 59–71, 73, 75–80, 91, 93, 102–103, 105, 121, 126, 134, 137, 153, 159, 166, 171, 173, 179–80, 182, 184, 206–07, 209, 211, 213, 220–224, 235– 236, 239, 243
Fellowship, 83, 120, 206, 222
Female leaders, 213
Femininity, 84
Flesh, 42, 53, 81, 97, 99, 103, 118–120, 132, 140, 211, 216
Flexibility, 10, 139
Fool, 116, 216
Forgiveness, 15, 18, 47, 48, 113, 137, 159–61
Foundation, 23, 29, 60, 78, 145, 163, 174, 186, 205, 216, 222
Freedom, 70, 132–133, 136, 201, 205, 253, 262
Freudian theory, 89

G

Genesis, 17, 23, 25, 26, 29, 33, 43, 47, 49–50, 52–53, 67–68, 93, 147–148, 154, 162–64, 185, 188–89, 296, 297
Genre, 59, 182
Gentiles, 15, 48, 54, 118, 146, 153, 194–195, 199–201, 204, 207, 211, 242, 254
gezerah sawah, 43
Gifts, 15–16, 29, 41, 50, 124–25, 130–31, 165–75, 177–91, 212–15, 218
Gifts of motivation, 171
Glorification, 91
Glorified, 91, 133, 257
Glossolalia, 175–77
God, 13–23, 26–28, 30–35, 39, 41, 43–52, 54–58, 60–62, 64, 67–69, 71–78, 80–84, 90–91, 98–99, 101, 103–07, 109, 111–12, 115, 118–19, 121, 124, 126–27, 129, 130–37, 139–41, 146, 153–60, 162–70, 172–74, 177, 179, 182–87, 189–92, 194–95, 197–99, 201–05, 207–13, 216–17, 220, 222–24, 228, 234–35, 237, 238, 240, 242, 245–47, 249–55, 258, 268–71, 275
Goddess, 30, 34
Gospel, 10, 31, 33, 41–42, 44, 53–54, 57, 75–79, 84–85, 94, 103–04, 110, 115, 119, 121, 127, 136–37, 147–49, 153–56, 159–65, 178, 181, 193–95, 197, 201, 204, 207, 209, 215, 221–23, 225, 227–32, 234–41, 243–44, 268–69
Grace, 19, 44, 46, 50, 57, 78, 80, 84–86, 90, 95, 100, 103, 105, 124–26, 139, 146, 157, 166, 169, 178, 183, 213
Greco-Roman World, 31, 117
Greek, 9–10, 12, 16, 42–43, 45, 48, 51, 65–67, 100, 110, 113, 121–22, 128, 135, 139, 150–51, 161, 163, 168, 172, 175, 182, 214–15, 217
Guilt, 32, 74–76, 87, 148, 220

H

Ham, 32
Happiness, 39
Healing, 30, 75, 87, 171–172, 180–82, 186
Heart, 24–25, 29–30, 35, 44, 61, 64, 73, 75–76, 113–14, 116, 128, 151, 162, 203, 207, 217, 223, 225, 227, 269
Heathen 32, 41, 50
Hebrew, 10, 13–14, 29, 41, 50, 68, 90, 150–53, 173, 201
Hebrews, 32–33, 41, 57, 90, 114, 186, 196, 213
Heilsgeschichte, 22, 91
Hellenistic, 22, 33, 43, 106, 133, 199, 215
Hermeneutical, 211, 218, 243
Hermeneutical canon, 218

Subject Index   303

Heterosexual union, 189
History, 07, 09, 13, 22–23, 26, 28, 30–31, 33–35, 39, 53, 72, 78, 86, 91, 99–100, 103, 121, 133, 153, 156, 161, 163, 181, 186, 199–200, 203, 220, 224, 235, 239–40, 261, 265–66
Holiness, 18, 30, 75, 90, 141, 188
Holy, 05–06, 10, 14, 16, 18, 27, 30, 54, 57, 74, 79–80, 90, 108, 124, 154–55, 161, 170–171, 173, 178, 180–81, 183, 186, 188, 216, 229, 239, 246
Holy (Ghost), 5, 10, 181
Home, 4, 35, 65, 73, 99, 110–11, 134, 137, 147, 212, 245
Homily, 34, 54
Homo faber, 21, 23
Homo religious, 23
Homo sapiens, 21
Horses, 33
Humanity, 15, 17, 21, 29, 32–35, 41, 62, 76, 80–82, 84, 89, 93, 153–55, 159, 164, 222
Humiliation, 118
Humor, 53

I

"I", 10–13, 19–22, 25–27, 29, 31, 33–34, 42, 51, 53, 56, 58, 60, 69, 72–75, 78–79, 84–85, 87, 90, 92–128, 130, 132, 134–35, 137, 140, 146–50, 152–53, 156, 158, 161, 184, 186–87, 171–72, 175, 178, 180–81, 184–87, 189, 191, 193–209, 211, 213–14, 216–17, 219, 245–46, 249, 252–54, 273
Identity, 15, 65, 90, 94, 104, 113, 128, 154, 200, 238, 258
Idolatry, 26–27, 30–32
Imago Christi, 72–73, 75, 77, 79, 81, 83–85, 87, 89, 91–93, 205
Imago Dei, 26, 74, 80, 82–84, 92
I-Thou, 104
Immortality, 83, 125, 154, 187
Imperative, 91–92, 153, 182, 232, 244, 253

Inclusio, 61, 202
Indicative, 92
Indigenization, 227–231, 241
Information, 89, 122, 159–160, 178–79, 263
Inheritance, 146
Integrity, 71, 100, 154, 182, 221–22, 224, 261, 263
Intimacy, 139, 190
Inter-textual, 147
Invective, 116
Iraqi, 55, 71
Isaac, 53, 68, 71, 189
Isaiah, 31, 54, 148, 150, 154, 162, 192, 201, 280, 290
Israeli, 55
Itinerary, 113, 149, 202, 205, 206

J

Jacob, 27, 58
Jamaica, 180, 226, 255–63, 265, 270
Jamaica Theological Seminary, xii, 55
James, 39, 58–71, 86–87, 89, 182, 220, 230, 232, 236, 250
Jeremiah, 27–28
Jerusalem, 27–28, 156, 206, 211, 242
Jesus, 11, 13–15, 19, 22, 53–54, 56–58, 67, 74–78, 87, 91, 105, 107, 109, 117–18, 125, 127, 129, 133, 135, 152–53, 155–58, 162, 167, 170–71, 183, 197, 200, 205, 207, 220, 229, 234–36, 251–52, 269, 271, 274
Jews, 31, 48–49, 54, 86, 159, 175–176, 182, 194, 199, 202–03, 211, 254, 267
Job, 245, 265
Joel, 159, 211
John, iv, 9, 11, 14–15, 17–20, 32–34, 53–54, 71, 73, 82, 91–93, 95, 127, 129, 133, 141, 153–58, 160–61, 185, 203, 212, 217–19, 237, 239, 251, 253, 266, 277–78, 280–83, 285–87, 289–98
Joseph, 58, 212

Subject Index

Josephus, 201
Joshua, 33
Jonah, xiv
Journey, 100, 146, 208
Joy, 103, 122, 137, 208
Judaism, 22, 49–50, 54, 109, 184
Jude, xv, 58, 290, 292
Judgement, 19, 30, 67, 69
Judges, 15, 185
Junia, 214–15, 217
Justification, 32, 39–43, 45–49, 51, 53–59, 61, 63, 65–67, 69, 71, 73, 98, 103, 136, 161, 162, 164, 180, 193, 194, 202

K

Kenophobia, 175
Kingdom, 74–75, 83, 91–92, 157, 184, 187, 190–91, 231, 266
Kingston, 245, 257
Koine, 9–10, 13
Lady, 218–19
Language, 9–13, 31–32, 53, 75, 82, 83, 85, 109, 117, 130, 148–50, 170, 175, 177–78, 182, 185, 194, 196–99, 206, 209, 216, 219, 222, 230, 241
Law,
   Mesographic, 43, 250
   Messianic, 98, 250
   Mosaic, 43, 49, 97–98, 250, 253–54
   of *theo*-dynamics, 21
Leaders, 18, 54, 89, 211, 213, 216, 219, 224–25, 228, 256, 258–59, 261, 263, 265–66, 271
Levitical priesthood, 199
Lee, Jean, 66
Liberation, 41–42, 71, 91, 145, 159, 193, 228, 235, 256
Life, 13, 18, 21, 23–24, 27, 29, 31, 34–35, 40–41, 44, 47, 51, 54, 56–57, 61, 64, 66, 68, 70, 72–74, 76, 78–80, 82, 84–88, 91–93, 97–98, 100, 103, 118, 121, 124, 127, 132, 134, 139, 141, 150, 152, 156–157, 161–162, 164, 170, 172, 180, 184, 190, 203, 220, 222–24, 229, 234–35, 238, 241, 245–47, 254, 257, 260–61, 264, 266
Literary strategy, 54, 102, 111, 119, 195, 205
Litotes, 198
Logos, 120
Lord, 19, 24–25, 27–30, 54–55, 58, 68–69, 74, 78, 83, 98–99, 105, 109–11, 117, 124–27, 132, 134–35, 139–40, 151, 153, 156, 158–61, 168–70, 172, 185, 187, 190, 204–05, 207, 211–12, 218–19, 229, 239, 252–53
Lord's Day, 19, 251, 253
Lord's Supper, 19, 139
Love, 20, 27, 30, 43, 57, 59–60, 71–72, 78–79, 105, 110, 113, 124–25, 141, 157–58, 164, 182–83, 187, 207, 217, 238, 246, 258, 275
Luke, 35, 87, 95, 131, 153, 155–58, 160–61, 169, 183, 187, 233, 251, 283, 287, 296
LXX, 09, 47, 50, 54, 83, 148–49, 151–53, 185, 201

M

Magnum opus, 20, 72
Malachi, 149
Manifestation, 63, 93, 170–71
Mark, 29–30, 33, 35, 58, 67, 74, 104, 112, 155, 157, 160, 172, 175, 184, 220, 251, 270, 293
Marley, 70
Marriage, 109, 190–92
Martyrs, 161
Masculinity, 84
Matthew, 61, 127, 149, 155, 160–61, 242, 251, 261, 278, 282, 290
Message, 35, 41, 57, 62–63, 71, 73, 78, 80, 126, 161, 170, 173, 209, 222, 227, 230, 235, 237–38, 241–42, 246, 265

Messiah, 15, 19, 50, 54, 126, 129–131, 133–41, 152, 156–57, 159, 161, 197, 200
Metaphorical approach, 218
Milagros, 173
Ministry, 15, 18, 39, 84, 103, 105, 107, 109, 111, 115–17, 122, 152–55, 160, 162, 165, 167, 169–71, 173, 178, 191, 197, 199–200, 203, 206, 211, 214–15, 223, 246–48, 231, 242, 245, 247, 274–75
Mishnah, 71, 201
Missio Dei, 205
Missionary, 11, 13, 15, 17, 19, 40–41, 100, 118, 149–150, 153, 182, 194–95, 197, 200–02, 205–06, 209, 226, 231, 233, 236, 254
Moltmann, 94
Mortality, 134
Music, 179, 241
Mutabaruka, 62
Mystery, 39, 78, 132, 133, 222
Mysticism, 138, 140, 141
Moon, 26, 252

N

Naked, 69, 134, 188, 192
Name, 18, 30, 45, 53, 72, 79, 94, 101, 123, 155, 156, 159–160, 169, 214, 216
Narrative, 83, 145–146, 148, 149
Nature, 11, 15, 20, 34, 42, 50, 51, 52, 63, 70, 75, 77, 78, 81–85, 87, 90, 93, 94, 96–98, 102, 106, 111, 118, 140, 150, 167, 169, 172, 173, 175, 178, 212, 216, 217, 226, 234, 236, 239, 242, 258
Newness, 91, 253
New Testament, 10, 12, 14, 18, 22, 39–40, 42–43, 45, 48–49, 54, 56, 58–59, 63, 65–66, 72, 78, 84, 93–94, 100, 121–22, 128, 153, 156, 169–170, 173–76, 182, 184, 186, 206, 212, 215, 217–21, 223–24, 232–33, 242, 252–54

Noah, 33
Nomos, 49, 98
Numbers, 33, 113, 154, 260

O

Obadiah, 150
Obedience, 49, 54, 60, 120, 157, 161, 169, 269
Obscenity, 33
Old Testament, 14, 23, 43, 44, 47, 49–50, 54–55, 66, 139, 147, 154, 162–63, 173–74, 213, 253–54
Onesimus, 122–23
Orthodoxy, 65, 220–21, 257
Orthopraxy, 71
OT citation, 50, 52, 150, 153, 159, 201, 204, 211, 216

P

Palace, 74, 137
Paradigmatic "I" 206
Parallelism, 54, 119, 122, 168
Pasa- pasa, 217
Pastoral, 13, 39, 53, 117, 128, 143, 149, 177, 210, 212, 214–16, 226
Patriarch, 46, 48–49, 52–53, 66–67, 69–71
Perfection, 41, 85, 93, 154, 156, 183–185
Paul, 4–20, 30, 35, 39–41, 43–45, 47–53, 55, 57–59, 61–63, 65, 67–69, 71, 73, 75, 77, 85–86, 95–123, 125–27, 129, 132–35, 137–41, 145–50, 152–53, 155–57, 161–63, 166–67, 169–71, 174–75, 177–78, 180–82, 184–88, 190–91, 193–204, 206–09, 212, 214–18, 221–22, 224, 232, 240, 245–47, 252–57, 266–70
Pauline corpus, 95, 97, 99, 101, 103, 105, 107, 109, 111, 113, 115, 117, 119, 121, 123, 125, 127, 141, 146, 169, 195
Pax Romana, 31, 267

Subject Index

Pearson, David, 55
Pentateuch, 147–148, 188
Pentecostal, 86, 180, 181
People, 10, 14–15, 18, 21, 23, 28, 31, 40, 51, 54, 57, 71–78, 80, 85–87, 90, 109, 118, 129–37, 139, 141, 146, 152, 156, 159, 165–67, 170, 178–79, 183, 187, 190–91, 195, 205, 211–14, 221, 223, 228, 230, 233–34, 237, 240–41, 250, 252, 254–55, 258–62, 264–65, 271, 272, 274
Performative, 165, 182, 250
Persecution, 100
Person, 15, 21, 44, 46–47, 53, 65, 69, 74, 75, 77–78, 85–87, 91, 93, 95–96, 99, 106, 113, 120–21, 131, 137–38, 141, 146, 157, 178, 192–93, 197, 204, 208, 218–19, 226, 229, 239, 252, 268
Persuasion, 120, 123, 159, 225
Peter, 53, 81, 85, 138, 162, 169, 172, 178, 259
Philemon, 101, 117, 121–23, 126, 137–38, 218–19, 278, 281–82, 285, 291–92, 296–97
Philippians, 57, 102, 117–21, 137, 242
Philosophical, 279, 299
Piquant irony, 188
Poetry, 41
Political, 13, 33, 73, 184, 246, 255, 277, 280, 284–87, 288
Polygamy, 192, 212
Power, 16, 18, 30, 32, 41–42, 51, 61, 63, 65, 73, 75–76, 85, 95, 106, 108, 125, 136–38, 147, 149, 161, 169, 170–72, 178–80, 182, 184, 187, 193–94, 197, 213, 236, 238, 240, 260, 265, 268–70, 275
Prayer, 26–27, 55, 81, 107, 161, 176, 227–28, 246
Preachers, 97, 212, 232, 276, 278
Preference, 165, 250
Preposition, 42, 87, 155
Presuppositions, 211, 231
Priscilla, 7, 210, 230–32, 235, 237, 241, 242,

Procreation, 189, 209
Productive Ministry, 247, 267
Prohibition, 186, 217, 237, 290
Projection, 1, 108
Promise, 70–73, 96, 183–84, 186, 211
Prophets, 47–48, 66, 90, 156, 168, 170, 178, 193–94, 206, 211
Proposition, 176, 196, 210
Proverbs (Book of), 59, 189, 240, 282
Providence, 203, 228, 223
Prudence, 250, 270
Psalms, 47, 83, 140, 147, 179, 277, 281
Psychology, 19, 23, 101–02, 107–08, 113, 200, 298, 300–02
Punish, 255, 275, 288

R

Rahab, 70, 86, 89, 90
Rastafari, 35, 91, 114, 126, 148, 297, 312–13, 315
Rationalisation, 87, 107
Reason, 33, 54, 60, 70, 90, 105, 117, 121–22, 140, 191–92, 273
Rebellion, 11, 37, 103, 256, 276, 277
Reconciliation, 59, 141, 157, 210, 271, 291
Redemption, 34, 37, 55, 65, 156, 165, 178, 185, 242, 264, 284, 299
Red Sea, 145, 165–166
Religion, 54, 61, 74, 91, 159, 257, 258, 262, 313, 314, 382
Religious studies, 18, 187, 207, 310, 314
Remission, 60, 253, 272
Resourcefulness, 121, 141
Responsibility, 26, 28, 37, 112, 120, 122, 128, 141, 179, 194, 186, 224, 233, 253
Restoration, 111, 114, 133, 200, 279, 317
Retribution, 47, 67
Revival, 25, 53, 73, 93
Rhetorical digression, 182, 202
Rhetorical skills, 116, 122, 138
Righteousness, 28, 32, 41, 43–49, 52–55, 67–68, 95, 136, 150–51, 157,

162, 164, 194, 206, 271, 285, 287–88, 291, 294
Romans, vii, 16, 19–20, 34, 39, 41, 43–44, 47, 49, 51, 55, 57, 59, 62, 81–82, 85–86, 88, 93–96, 100, 129, 131–33, 146, 148–50, 162–66, 178, 193, 200, 203, 205, 214, 246, 248–49, 253, 265–70, 272, 277–78, 280, 284, 286, 290–92, 296–97
Romerbreif, 73
Rome, 4, 6, 31, 39, 41, 73, 106, 130, 194–96, 201–02, 206–07, 253, 267–68, 277
Ruth, 14

S

Sabbath, 5, 252–54, 292
Sadducean question, 192
Saint, 6, 41, 85, 90, 105, 130, 141, 161, 178, 193, 213, 217, 241, 251, 254, 288, 293
Salvation, 14, 16–19, 56–57, 63, 73, 75, 86–87, 91–92, 95, 138, 149, 157–59, 161, 163, 169, 180, 195, 209–10, 234, 239–40, 242, 256, 286, 289
Sanctification, 18, 32, 41, 63, 93, 98, 130, 136, 156, 161, 193–94, 203, 248, 286
Satan, 21, 33, 90, 101–02, 141, 164, 187, 251
Scope, 48, 50, 161, 234, 236, 266
Scripture, 6, 13–14, 16, 22, 29, 41, 43–44, 47–48, 52, 54, 57, 66, 68, 70, 82–83, 89, 92, 127, 141, 147, 149, 162, 174–75, 179, 182–83, 211–12, 229, 232, 238, 271, 277, 282, 285, 293
Scrolls, 96, 296
Seed, 29, 49–50, 114, 154, 159
Selassie, 15, 94,
Septuagint, xviii, xix, 45, 52, 139, 147, 149, 185, 292
Sermon, 35, 59, 68, 75, 80

Serpent, 65, 154
Sex, 85, 189
Sin, 17–18, 20–21, 32, 35, 41–42, 47, 54, 57, 63, 74–75, 77, 84–86, 90, 95–99, 102–03, 109, 111, 123, 130, 141, 146, 152, 154, 156, 160–61, 164, 193, 239, 249
sine qua non, 170, 180
Shalom, 55, 118
Shem, 32–33
Shepherd, 100, 213
Slave, 119
Slavery, 18, 94, 145–46, 256
Socrates, 204
Son, 14–15, 20, 46, 74, 103, 133, 137, 154, 213, 220, 293
Song of Songs, 188 n. 87
Songs, 70, 289
Sonship, 16, 130, 136, 141
Soteriology, 206
Sovereignty, 165
Sōzō, 62
Spain, 32, 206–07
Spirit, 14–16, 18–20, 40, 57, 74, 79–80, 86, 92–93, 104–05, 109, 130, 132–34, 139–41, 147, 154–56, 161, 165, 167–71, 173, 175, 177–81, 183–87, 189, 191, 207, 211, 216, 225, 229, 239, 242–43, 246, 253, 278–80, 282–83, 286, 289–93, 296, 298
Spiritual, 99, 136, 167–68, 170–72, 174, 177–78, 183, 185–86, 275, 281–82, 284, 286, 290–92, 295–96
Spirituality, 130, 282, 284, 286
Storyteller, 146, 149
Strategy, 8, 54, 79, 102, 111, 115, 119, 145, 195, 205, 226, 265
Suicide, 3, 295
Sumerians, 23, 29, 33
Sunday, viii, 185, 242, 251–53
Syntax, 43, 50, 279, 294

T

Task, 62, 161, 277, 294

Teaching, 16, 160, 179
Teleion, 184–85
Temple, xx, 47
Tenderness, 157
Tension, ix, 16, 30, 40, 92–93, 96–100, 123, 129, 191, 205, 207, 219, 249, 280, 297
Testimony, 31, 46, 80, 85–86, 106, 110, 148, 161, 172–73, 254, 277, 292
Theology, v, vii, viii, xi, xii, xiii, xiv, xv, xvii, xviii, xix, xx, 3, 13, 20–23, 25, 27, 29, 31, 33, 35, 41, 45, 49, 53–54, 58, 61–63, 65, 71–73, 81–83, 89, 91, 93, 103, 105–06, 108, 110, 133, 156–57, 161–63, 180, 181–84, 186, 189, 200, 203, 205–06, 218, 225–26, 228–41, 243, 264, 274, 277–83, 285, 287–89, 291–92, 294, 296–98
Theophany, 185, 194
Therapy, 34, 75–77, 93, 170, 294
Third-millennium, viii, 251
Timothy, 6–8, 13, 100–01, 111–12, 117, 121, 128, 212, 215–19, 222–23, 277–78, 283, 286–87, 294
Titus, 17, 128, 217–19, 278, 283
Tolle, lege, 73
Tongues, 34, 131–33, 170–71, 173, 175–76, 178, 180–85, 217, 277, 279, 282–83, 285–86, 288, 294–95, 297
Transformation, ix, 19, 35, 91–92, 129, 155, 249, 264
Translating, 48, 97, 104, 167, 182, 278, 286
Trinity, 15, 74, 167–68, 235, 286
Typler, 187 n. 85

U

Unity, 14–15, 124, 141, 167–68, 177, 182, 187, 213, 220, 224, 232, 259, 267
Unspiritual, 96–97, 241, 249

V

Victory, 74–75, 93, 99, 136, 194
Vindication, 148
Vocation, 04, 60, 93, 159

W

Watty, W., 53, 297
Weakness, 156
Wealth, 10, 30, 34, 61,75–77, 81, 106, 237, 240, 293
Weltanschauung, 202
Western Christianity, 184, 230
Wife, 68, 74, 95, 109, 124, 127, 153, 163, 188, 211, 212, 217, 262
Will of God, 191–92, 194, 201–05, 208, 246, 284
Woman, xiv, 28, 69–70, 84–85, 90, 108, 127, 148, 154–55, 164, 188–89,192, 217–20, 261, 266, 274, 277, 284, 286–87, 292
Word of knowledge, 171
Word of wisdom, 178
Works, 19, 25, 43–44, 46–47, 49–50, 56–57, 60, 62, 63–73, 92, 152, 166, 168, 170, 173, 177, 180, 181, 213–15, 220, 226, 246, 247
Worship, 19, 32, 47, 60, 80, 83, 131–33, 137, 154, 165, 167–68, 180, 203, 227, 241, 251–53
Wrath, 28, 33, 46
Wunder, 173

Y

YHWH, 84
Yorke, Gosnell, 62 n.103

Z

Zeal, 271

www.ingramcontent.com/pod-product-compliance
Lightning Source LLC
Chambersburg PA
CBHW061427300426
44114CB00014B/1576